CIMA

TUDY TEXT

MANAGEMENT

PAPER F2

Advanced Financial Reporting

Our text is designed to help you study **effectively** and **efficiently**.

In this edition we:

- **Highlight** the **most important elements** in the syllabus and the **key skills** you will need

- **Signpost** how each chapter links to the syllabus and the learning outcomes

- Use **overview and summary diagrams** to develop understanding of interrelations between topics

- **Provide** lots of **exam alerts** explaining how what you're learning may be tested

- **Include examples** and **questions** to help you apply what you've learnt

- **Emphasise key points** in **section summaries**

- **Test your knowledge** of what you've studied in **quick quizzes**

- **Examine your understanding** in our **practice question bank**

SUITABLE FOR CIMA 2015 SYLLABUS EXAMS IN 2019
PUBLISHED NOVEMBER 2018

BPP LEARNING MEDIA

Fourth edition 2018

ISBN 9781 5097 2315 7
eISBN 9781 5097 2318 8

British Library Cataloguing-in-Publication Data
A catalogue record for this book is available from the British Library

Published by

BPP Learning Media Ltd
BPP House, Aldine Place,
London W12 8AA

www.bpp.com/learningmedia

Printed in the United Kingdom

Your learning materials, published by BPP Learning Media Ltd, are printed on paper sourced from sustainable, managed forests.

Contents

BPP
LEARNING MEDIA

How our Study Text can help you pass

Streamlined studying	• We show you the best ways to study efficiently
	• Our Text has been designed to ensure you can easily and quickly navigate through it
	• The different features in our Text emphasise important knowledge and techniques
Exam expertise	• **Studying F2** on page xii introduces the key themes of the syllabus and summarises how to pass
	• We help you see the complete picture of the syllabus, so that you can answer questions that range across the whole syllabus
	• Our Text covers the syllabus content – no more, no less
Regular review	• We frequently summarise the key knowledge you need
	• We test what you've learnt by providing questions and quizzes throughout our Text

Our other products

BPP Learning Media also offers these products for the Objective Test exams and the integrated case study (ICS) exams:

i-Pass	Providing computer-based testing in a variety of formats, ideal for self-assessment
Exam Practice Kit	Providing helpful guidance on how to pass the objective test and more question practice
Passcards	Summarising what you should know in visual, easy to remember, form
Integrated Case Study Kit	Providing help with exam skills and question practice for the integrated case study exam

You can purchase these products by visiting learningmedia.bpp.com

Online Learning with BPP

BPP's online learning study modes provide flexibility and convenience, allowing you to study effectively, at a pace that suits you, where and when you choose.

Online Classroom Live	Through live interactive online sessions it provides you with the traditional structure and support of classroom learning, but with the convenience of attending classes wherever you are
Online Classroom	Through pre-recorded online lectures it provides you with the classroom experience via the web with the tutor guidance & support you'd expect from a face to face classroom

You can find out more by visiting www.bpp.com/courses/accountancy/cima

Features in our Study Text

Chapter Overview Diagrams illustrate the connections between the topic areas you are about to cover

KEY TERM

Key Terms are the core vocabulary you need to learn

Exam Alerts show you how subjects are likely to be tested

LEARN

Formulae To Learn are formulae you must remember in the exam

EXAM

Exam Formulae are formulae you will be given in the exam

Examples show how theory is put into practice

Questions give you the practice you need to test your understanding of what you've learnt

Website References link to material that will enhance your understanding of what you're studying

Streamlined studying

What you should do	In order to
Read the Chapter Introduction and look at the Chapter Overview Diagram	See why topics need to be studied and map your way through the chapter
Go quickly through the explanations	Gain the depth of knowledge and understanding that you'll need
Highlight the Key Terms and Formulae To Learn	Make sure you know the basics that you can't do without in the exam
Work through the Examples	See how what you've learnt applies in practice
Prepare Answers to the Questions	See if you can apply what you've learnt in practice
Review the Chapter Summary Diagrams	Remind you of, and reinforce, what you've learnt
Answer the Quick Quiz	Find out if there are any gaps in your knowledge
Answer the Question(s) in the Practice Question Bank	Practise what you've learnt in depth

Should I take notes?

Brief notes may help you remember what you're learning. You should use the notes format that's most helpful to you (lists, diagrams, mindmaps).

Syllabus and learning outcomes

Paper F2 Advanced Financial Reporting

The syllabus comprises:

Topic and Study Weighting

A	Sources of long-term finance	15%
B	Financial reporting	60%
C	Analysis of financial performance and position	25%

Syllabus Learning Outcomes

Lead Outcome		Component Outcome		Chapter
A	**Sources of long-term finance**			
1	Discuss types and sources of long-term finance for an incorporated entity.	(a)	Discuss the characteristics of different types of long-term debt and equity finance	1
		(b)	Discuss the markets for and methods of raising long-term finance.	1
2	Calculate a weighted average cost of capital (WACC) for an incorporated entity.	(a)	Calculate the cost of equity for an incorporated entity using the dividend valuation model	2
		(b)	Calculate the post-tax cost of debt for an incorporated entity	2
		(c)	Calculate the weighted average cost of capital (WACC) for an incorporated entity	2
B	**Financial reporting**			
1	Produce consolidated primary financial statements, incorporating accounting transactions and adjustments, in accordance with relevant international accounting standards, in an ethical manner.	(a)	Produce primary financial statements for a group of entities in accordance with relevant international accounting standards	9, 10, 11, 12, 13, 14, 15
		(b)	Discuss the need for and nature of disclosure of interests in other entities	10
		(c)	Discuss the provisions of relevant international accounting standards in respect of the recognition and measurement of revenue, leases, financial instruments, provisions, share-based payments and deferred taxation	3, 4, 5, 6, 7, 8
		(d)	Produce the accounting entries, in accordance with relevant international accounting standards	3, 4, 5, 6, 7, 8
		(e)	Discuss the ethical selection and adoption of relevant accounting policies and accounting estimates	18

Lead Outcome		Component Outcome		Chapter
2	Demonstrate the impact on the preparation of the consolidated financial statements of certain complex group scenarios.	(a)	Demonstrate the impact on the group financial statements of:	11
			(i) Acquiring additional shareholdings in the period	
			(ii) Disposing of all or part of a shareholding in the period	
		(b)	Demonstrate the impact on the group financial statements of consolidating a foreign subsidiary	11
		(c)	Demonstrate the impact on the group financial statements of acquiring indirect control of a subsidiary	11
3	Discuss the need for and nature of disclosure of transactions between related parties.	(a)	Discuss the need for and nature of disclosure of transactions between related parties	16
4	Produce the disclosures for earnings per share.	(a)	Produce the disclosures for earnings per share	17
C	**Analysis of financial performance and position**			
1	Evaluate the financial performance, financial position and financial adaptability of an incorporated entity.	(a)	Calculate ratios relevant for the assessment of an entity's profitability, financial performance, financial position and financial adaptability	19
		(b)	Evaluate the financial performance, financial position and financial adaptability of an entity based on the information contained in the financial statements provided	19
		(c)	Advise on action that could be taken to improve an entity's financial performance and financial position	19
2	Discuss the limitations of ratio analysis.	(a)	Discuss the limitations of ratio analysis based on financial statements that can be caused by internal and external factors	19

Studying F2

1   What's F2 about

The Paper F2 syllabus is in three parts:

- Sources of long-term finance
- Financial reporting
- Analysis of financial performance and position

1.1 Sources of long-term finance

This part of the syllabus covers the structure of the financial markets, the different sources of long-term finance available, and how to evaluate the suitability of each source of finance. You will also need to be able to calculate the cost of finance, through cost of equity, cost of debt and weighted average cost of capital calculations.

Weighted at 15% of the syllabus, it's important that you are familiar with the more discursive, concept-based side of the topic, as well as the numerical workings.

1.2 Financial reporting

This is by the biggest component of the syllabus, at a weighting of 60%. Essentially, this component can be divided into two parts: group reporting, and issues in recognition and measurement.

As you work through the progressively advanced topics on **group reporting**, it is vital that you get a good grasp of the basics and the principles. There are a lot of easy marks available for basic consolidation techniques. You should not, however, concentrate on the 'hows' of the calculation to the exclusion of the 'whys', which will always be tested through objective test questions.

The **recognition and measurement** part of the financial reporting component involves explaining the problems of profit measurement. Thus you will need to understand the principles contained in the Conceptual Framework. Very importantly, you will need to apply these principles to relevant accounting standards, all of which are covered in this Study Text.

1.3 Analysis of financial performance and position

With a weighting of 25%, this is an important area, unsurprisingly, given that the title of the paper is Advanced Financial Reporting, rather than Financial Accounting.

Again, discussion is every bit as important as calculation in this section. It is important that you are able not just to calculate the ratios, but also to explain the implication of each ratio. The OTQs will test your understanding in a precise way.

2 What's required

2.1 Knowledge

The exam requires you to demonstrate knowledge as much as application. Bear in mind this comment from the examiner, from her report on an exam under the old syllabus:

At the top end, some candidates scored very highly indeed, producing a full complement of excellent answers. However, a substantial minority of candidates appeared to have virtually no useable knowledge of the syllabus.

2.2 Explanation

As well as stating your knowledge, you will also sometimes be asked to demonstrate the more advanced skill of explaining the requirements of accounting standards. Explaining means providing simple definitions and covering the reasons why regulations have been made and what the problems are that the standards are designed to counter. In an OTQ exam, you will still need to demonstrate your ability to 'explain' – questions may require you to select the correct definitions and make inferences in a short scenario, based on your understanding of the topics.

2.3 Calculations

Calculations are of course an important part of this exam. Make sure you learn the formulas by heart, through repeated practice. It's important (especially when it comes to ratios) that you learn the formulas as provided in this Study Text. The precision of objective testing means that if you use a wrong figure in one part of your workings, and thus choose the wrong answer, you will not gain the allocated marks.

3 How to pass

3.1 Cover the whole syllabus?

Yes! You need to be comfortable with **all areas of the syllabus**, as questions in the objective test exam will cover all syllabus areas.

3.2 Lots of question practise

You can **develop application skills** by attempting questions in the Practice Question Bank. While these might not be in the format that you will experience in your exam, doing the full question will enable you to answer the exam questions. For example, you will only be able to answer a question on an element of a consolidated statement of financial position if you know how to prepare the complete consolidated statement of financial position. Similarly, in the integrated case study exam, you will have to answer questions that combine F2 syllabus areas with E2 and P2. However, by answering questions on F2 you will develop the technical knowledge and skills in order to answer those questions.

However, you should practice exam standards questions, which you will find in the BPP Exam Practice Kit and Integrated Case Study Kit.

3.3 Answering questions in the Integrated Case Study

Well-judged, **clear recommendations** grounded in the scenario will always score well as markers for this paper have a wide remit to reward good answers. You need to be **selective**.

Scenario details should only be used if they support the points you're making, but they should be used when relevant.

Answers should be well-structured, clear and concise. They should demonstrate a clear and logical thought process. If the question asks for a discussion, a list of single-line bullet points will not be an adequate answer.

3.4 The pre-seen

The pre-seen provides an idea of what may be in the integrated case study exam, and enables you to put questions into context. You will be expected to use the information in the pre-seen when answering questions, as well as using the additional unseen information that you will be given in the exam.

3.5 Develop business awareness

Candidates with good business awareness can score well in a number of areas.

- Reading articles in CIMA's *Financial Management* magazine and the business press will help you understand the practical rationale for accounting standards and make it easier for you to apply accounting requirements correctly

- Looking through the accounts of major companies will familiarise you with the contents of accounts and help you comment on key figures and changes from year-to-year

4   Brought forward knowledge

The examiner may test knowledge or techniques you've learnt at lower levels. As F2 is part of the Financial pillar, the content of paper F1 will be significant.

5   The Integrated Case Study and links with E2 and P2

The integrated case study exam is based on the expectation that students are developing a pool of knowledge. When faced with a problem students can appropriately apply their knowledge from any syllabus. Students will avoid a historical problem of partitioning their knowledge and accessing, for example, their knowledge of IFRS only when faced with a set of financial statements.

- **Enterprise operational decisions** will impact upon financial and performance objectives, the financial reports, working capital, and the risks the organisation faces.

- **Financial and performance decisions** will likewise have an impact on enterprise operational decisions.

- At the same time **enterprise operations** will be **constrained** by the finance available and the level of risks the organisation is prepared to bear.

- **Financial operational decisions** will **impact** upon the **risks** the organisation bears and perhaps impose limitations on the plans the organisation can implement.

- **Costing techniques**, particularly in relation to manufacturing, environmental costing and costs of quality, will have an impact on the **choices available** for enterprise operational decisions.

6 What the examiner means

The table below has been prepared by CIMA to help you interpret the syllabus and learning outcomes and the meaning of questions.

You will see that there are 5 levels of Learning objective, ranging from Knowledge to Evaluation, reflecting the level of skill you will be expected to demonstrate. CIMA Certificate subjects only use levels 1 to 3, but in CIMA's Professional qualification the entire hierarchy will be used.

At the start of each chapter in your study text is a topic list relating the coverage in the chapter to the level of skill you may be called on to demonstrate in the exam.

Learning objectives	Verbs used	Definition
1 Knowledge What are you expected to know	• List • State • Define	• Make a list of • Express, fully or clearly, the details of/facts of • Give the exact meaning of
2 Comprehension What you are expected to understand	• Describe • Distinguish • Explain • Identify • Illustrate	• Communicate the key features of • Highlight the differences between • Make clear or intelligible/state the meaning or purpose of • Recognise, establish or select after consideration • Use an example to describe or explain something
3 Application How you are expected to apply your knowledge	• Apply • Calculate/ compute • Demonstrate • Prepare • Reconcile • Solve • Tabulate	• Put to practical use • Ascertain or reckon mathematically • Prove with certainty or to exhibit by practical means • Make or get ready for use • Make or prove consistent/compatible • Find an answer to • Arrange in a table
4 Analysis How you are expected to analyse the detail of what you have learned	• Analyse • Categorise • Compare and contrast • Construct • Discuss • Interpret • Prioritise • Produce	• Examine in detail the structure of • Place into a defined class or division • Show the similarities and/or differences between • Build up or compile • Examine in detail by argument • Translate into intelligible or familiar terms • Place in order of priority or sequence for action • Create or bring into existence
5 Evaluation How you are expected to use your learning to evaluate, make decisions or recommendations	• Advise • Evaluate • Recommend	• Counsel, inform or notify • Appraise or assess the value of • Propose a course of action

 BPP LEARNING MEDIA

Competency Framework

CIMA has developed a competency framework detailing the skills, abilities and competencies that finance professionals need. The CIMA syllabus has been developed to match the competency mix as it develops over the three levels of the professional qualification. The importance of the various competencies at the management level is shown below.

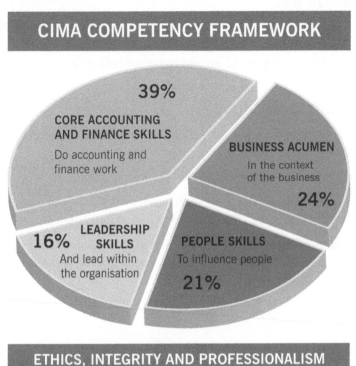

Assessment

The CIMA assessment is a two-tier structure with objective tests for each subject and an integrated case study at each level.

Objective test

The objective tests are computer based and can be taken on demand. The student exam preparation on the CIMA website (www.cimaglobal.com) has additional information and tools to help you become familiar with the test style. Make sure you check back regularly as more information may be added.

Integrated case study

Candidates must pass or receive exemptions from the three objective tests at each level, before attempting the integrated case study exam for that level.

The integrated case studies are available four times a year.

The integrated case study exams will combine the knowledge and learning from all the pillars. They will be set in the context of a pre-seen fictional organisation based on a real business or industry.

The management level will require long and short essays supported by calculations and analysis. The role of the candidate will be that of a manager reporting to the CFO and senior business managers.

LONG-TERM FINANCE

Part A

SOURCES OF LONG-TERM FINANCE

 Entities finance themselves using a mix of different sources of long-term finance. You need to be aware of how an entity can effectively source the long-term finance required to fund its operations.

You will need to understand how finance can be issued via the stock and bond markets and the importance of the role of the advisor in this process

Topic list	learning outcomes	syllabus references
1 The operation of stock and bond markets	A1	A1(b)
2 The role of advisors	A1	A1(a)
3 Shares	A1	A1(a)
4 Long-term debt	A1	A1(a)
5 Other sources of finance	A1	A1(a)

Chapter Overview

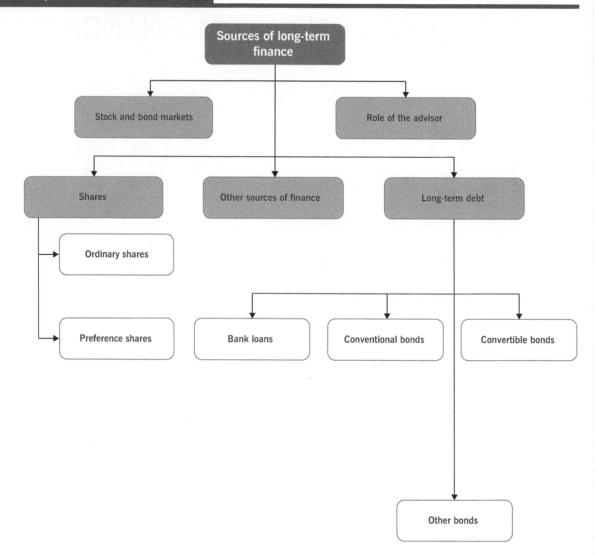

1 The operation of stock and bond markets

1.1 Stock market

Capital markets are markets for trading in **medium- and long-term finance**, in the form of financial instruments such as equities and corporate bonds. In the UK, the principal capital markets are:

(a)   The stock exchange '**main market**' (for companies with a full stock exchange listing)

(b)   The more loosely regulated 'second tier' **Alternative Investment Market (AIM)**

1.1.1 Advantages of a stock market listing

1.1.2 Disadvantages of a stock market listing

The owners of a company seeking a stock market listing must take the following disadvantages into account:

(a)   There will be significantly greater **public regulation, accountability** and **scrutiny**. The legal requirements the company faces will be greater, and the company will also be subject to the rules of the stock exchange on which its shares are listed.

(b)   A **wider circle of investors** with more exacting requirements will hold shares.

(c)   There will be additional costs involved in making share issues, including **brokerage commissions** and **underwriting fees**.

1.1.3 Methods of obtaining a listing

An unquoted company can obtain a listing on the stock market by a variety of means; this is sometimes referred to as 'going public' or 'floating' the company.

Initial public offer (IPO)	Placing	Introduction
A means of selling the shares of a company to the public at large for the first time.	A **placing** is an arrangement whereby the shares are not all offered to the public, but instead, the sponsoring market maker arranges for most of the issue to be bought by a **small number of investors**.	No shares are made available to the market (neither existing nor newly created shares).
An issuing house publishes an invitation to the public to apply for shares, either at a **fixed price** (an offer for sale) or on a **tender basis**.		This will only happen where shares in a large private company are already widely held, so that a market can be seen to exist.
The issuing house will often underwrite the issue ie will, for a fee, guarantee to buy any unsold shares.	Examples are institutional investors such as pension funds and insurance companies.	

1.1.4 The choice between an IPO / offer for sale and a placing

Is a company likely to prefer an IPO of its shares, or a placing?

(a) **Placings** are much **cheaper**. Approaching institutional investors privately is a much cheaper way of obtaining finance. An offer for sale will involve underwriting costs and the costs of advertising the share issue to the public. Thus placings are often used for smaller issues.

(b) Placings are likely to be **quicker**.

(c) Placings are likely to involve **less disclosure** of **information**.

(d) However, most of the shares will be placed with a **relatively small number of (institutional) shareholders**, which means that most of the shares are **unlikely to be available for trading** after the flotation, and that **institutional shareholders** will have control of the **company**.

1.1.5 Rights issues

KEY TERM

A RIGHTS ISSUE is the raising of new capital by giving **existing shareholders** the right to subscribe to new shares in proportion to their current holdings. These shares are usually issued at a **discount to market price**.

The issue price must be set **low enough** to secure **acceptance** of shareholders but **not** so low that **earnings per share is excessively diluted**.

Rights issues are **cheaper** to organise than public share issues but underwriting costs are still significant.

The possible courses of action open to existing **shareholders** are:

(a) Buy the new shares;
(b) Sell their rights to buy the shares;
(c) Sell enough rights to finance their share purchases; or
(d) Do nothing.

After the announcement of a rights issue, share prices typically fall due to uncertainty about the consequences of the issue, future profits and future dividends.

Term	Meaning
Cum rights	When a rights issue is announced, all existing shareholders have the rights to subscribe for new shares and so there **are rights attached to the shares** ie the shares are traded 'cum rights'.
Ex rights	On the first day of dealings in the newly issued shares, the rights no longer exist and the old shares are now traded **without rights attached** ('ex rights').
Theoretical ex rights price (TERP)	A theoretical **weighted average price** after the rights issue assuming that all the newly issued shares are taken up by all of the existing shareholders.

Example: Calculation of TERP

Assume rights issue on a 1 for 5 basis

Share price immediately before exercise of rights $11

Rights price $5

$$
\begin{array}{lr}
 & \$ \\
5 \, @ \, \$11 = & 55 \\
\dfrac{1}{\overline{6}} \, @ \, \$5 & \dfrac{5}{\overline{60}} \\
\end{array}
$$

$$\therefore \text{TERP} = \frac{\$60}{6} = \$10$$

1.2 Bond market

Corporate bonds are most commonly issued on the **primary market**. Typically, the issue of corporate bonds are **underwritten**. As we have seen in relation to share issues, the underwriters – normally financial institutions such as banks – buy the issue of bonds and sell them on to investors.

Bonds are often **traded over-the-counter (OTC)**, that is to say, sold and bought directly through financial institutions, without the supervision of recognised exchanges. Corporate bonds can also be **traded publicly** in bond markets – many of the recognised exchanges also have an associated bond market, such as the London Stock Exchange and the New York Stock Exchange.

The issue of bonds on the exchange resembles the process for share issues: a prospectus must be prepared, which must be approved by the listing authority in order for the bonds to be admitted to trading. Bonds traded on exchanges can then be resold on **secondary markets**.

Question 1.1   Stock market listing

Which ONE of the following statements is CORRECT in relation to a stock market listing?

A   A stock market listing narrows the pool of investors in a company.

B   An introduction combines shares being offered to the public and shares being purchased by institutional investors via the sponsoring market maker.

C   An unquoted company may obtain a listing via an initial public offering, a placing or an introduction.

D   The costs of issuing shares via a placing are greater than for issuing shares via an initial public offer.

2   The role of advisors

Raising finance on the capital market requires input from a wide range of experts.

2.1 Sponsor

A **sponsor**, typically an investment bank or large accountancy firm, acts as the lead advisor in an IPO on the main market.

The sponsor's functions include:

(a) Project managing the IPO process
(b) Co-ordinating the due diligence and the drafting of the prospectus
(c) Ensuring compliance with the applicable rules
(d) Developing the investment case, valuation and offer structure

For listings on AIM, the role of the sponsor is fulfilled by the **nominated advisor** (**Nomad**).

2.2 Bookrunner

A bookrunner is the **main underwriter** of a syndicate (a group of underwriters) for new share and debt issues. It is usually a financial institution, such as an investment bank. The bookrunner typically:

(a) Raises finance from investors on behalf of the company
(b) Helps to determine the appropriate pricing for the shares or debt
(c) Guarantees to buy unsold shares or debt itself if it is unable to find enough investors

2.3 Reporting accountants

The directors bear legal responsibility for the integrity of the listing documents (including the prospectus). The sponsor, as the company's lead advisor, risks considerable damage to its reputation should the prospectus be deficient.

For this reason, the sponsor would usually require the company to engage a **reporting accountant** to review and report on the company's readiness for the transaction.

The reporting accountant would typically report on the following:

(a) **Financial reporting procedures** – whether the company would be able to meet its reporting obligations as a public company

(b) **Financial historical records** – the equivalent of an audit opinion on the company's entire financial track record

(c) **Working capital** – whether the basis for the directors' working capital statement in the prospectus is sound

(d) **Other information** – any other additional information provided in the prospectus, such as profit forecasts and proforma financial information (for example, to illustrate the effects of an IPO).

2.4 Lawyer

In an IPO, a lawyer typically:

(a) Performs legal due diligence
(b) Drafts the prospectus
(c) Provides legal opinions

2.5 Financial public relations firm

The company obtaining a listing may appoint a financial PR firm to develop an appropriate **communication strategy** pre-IPO and post-IPO.

3 Shares

3.1 Ordinary shares

Ordinary shares are issued to the owners of a company. Each share will have a face value (known as '**par value**' or 'nominal value') eg $1. Ordinary shareholders have **rights** as a result of their ownership of the shares:

(a) Shareholders can attend company general meetings and **can vote on important company matters** such as:

  • The appointment and re-election of directors

  • Approving a takeover bid for another company, where the financing arrangements will involve a large new issue of shares

  • The appointment of auditors

  • Approving the company's remuneration policy for senior executives

(b) They are **entitled to receive a share of any agreed dividend**. It is up to the directors to decide whether to pay a dividend and how much the dividend should be.

(c) They will receive a **share of any assets remaining after liquidation**.

(d) They can **participate in any new issue of shares**.

The main benefit of using **equity finance** is that the timing of the dividend payments is **flexible**.

3.2 Preference shares

Preference shareholders **also receive dividends (normally at a fixed rate)**, but they are paid before ordinary shareholders and have **no voting rights**. Preference shares are rare in the UK because they **do not attract tax relief**.

Like ordinary shares, preference shares have a face value (known also as '**par value**' or 'nominal value'). Here is an example of a preference share that Aviva has issued.

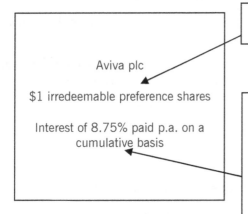

Aviva plc

$1 irredeemable preference shares

Interest of 8.75% paid p.a. on a cumulative basis

Preference shares may be **redeemable** (the entity has to repay the principal) or **irredeemable**.

If **cumulative**, if there are insufficient distributable reserves to pay the dividend in the current year, the entity must pay it in future years when sufficient distributable reserves arise.

If **non-cumulative**, if there are insufficient distributable reserves to pay the dividend in the current year, the entity never has to pay this dividend.

Question 1.2   Difference between ordinary and preference shares

Complete the following statement using the words below. Each word can be used more than once.

| Less | Higher | More | Lower |

Investors in preference shares will expect a _____ return than investors in ordinary shares because they face a _____ risk than investors in ordinary shares and potentially earn _____ of a return as the entity's performance improves.

Equity capital usually refers to finance provided by the owners of the business, and as such refers to the capital invested by **ordinary shareholders**.

However, **non-cumulative irredeemable preference shares** are also treated as **equity** in the financial statements because they do not contain an obligation.

Cumulative irredeemable preference shares and **redeemable preference shares contain an obligation** and are therefore treated as a **liability**.

4 Long-term debt

4.1 Characteristics of long-term debt

The following are characteristics of long-term debt:

(a) The providers of debt finance are **not owners** of the business.

(b) The entity **normally** has an obligation to **pay interest** to the debt-holders, and to **repay the principal**.

(c) On liquidation, the debt-holders would have **priority access** to **the assets of the** entity before any shareholders. Because debt-holders are taking **less risk** than ordinary shareholders, **the expected return on debt is lower** than the expected return on shares.

(d) The cost of debt will also be cheaper than ordinary or preference shares because the **interest** is **tax deductible** (unlike preference or ordinary dividends).

(e) If the entity has little or no existing debt finance, it may be **easier to raise debt finance** rather than equity finance, particularly if the entity is unquoted (ie cannot issue shares to the public).

4.2 Types of long-term debt

4.2.1 Bank loans

A bank loan will be for a **fixed amount**, for an **agreed period of time** on pre-arranged terms.

The **interest** rate may be **fixed** (for the period of the loan), **variable** (set at a fixed percentage above the bank base lending rate) or **capped** (the bank guarantees a maximum rate of interest).

A **repayment structure** will be put in place eg monthly, quarterly or annually.

The bank may require **security** for the loan.

A **loan covenant** may be set by the bank. This is a condition that the borrower must comply with and if they do not, the loan can be considered to be in default and the bank can demand repayment. Examples of debt covenants include:

(a)   Positive covenants

(i)   Often involve maintaining certain levels of particular financial ratios. Examples of financial ratios that banks may watch are the debt to equity (gearing), debt to asset ratio, and the company's net working capital.

(b)   Negative covenants

(i)   Limit the borrower's behaviour eg not to borrow any money from any other lender.

4.2.2 Conventional bonds

Conventional bonds are **fixed rate debt** issued by companies to institutional investors. They are sometimes referred to as loan stock, loan notes, or debentures.

Here is an example of a bond that was issued in 2013 by BP.

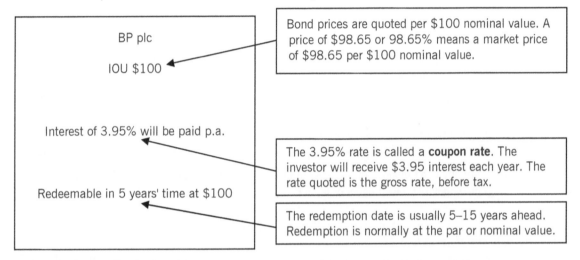

Features of bonds	
Issued **at par** (unless deep discounted – see later)	The coupon rate is fixed at the time of issue, and will be set according to **prevailing market conditions** given the **credit rating** of the company issuing the debt.
Marketable	The ability to sell the debt can mean that investors accept a lower return compared to the return demanded by a bank on a term loan.
Redeemable	Bonds are normally redeemable. Some bonds do not have a redemption date, and are **'irredeemable'** or 'undated'. These are sometimes called perpetual or undated bonds. These are normally issued by banks.

4.2.3 Convertible bonds

Convertible bonds give the holders the right (but not an obligation) to convert their bonds at a specified future date into new equity shares of the company, at a conversion rate that is also specified when the bonds are issued. **If bondholders choose not to convert their bonds into shares, the bonds will be redeemed at maturity, usually at par.**

A typical example of a transaction is that of J Sainsbury, which raised £190 million in 2009 by issuing a 5 year bond with a coupon of 4.25% and a conversion price set 35% above the share price at time of issue.

Convertible bonds issued at par normally have a **lower coupon rate of interest** than conventional fixed return bonds. This is a key reason why the issue of convertible bonds is attractive to a company.

4.2.4 Other types of bonds

Deep discount bonds	Zero coupon bonds
• Bonds or loan notes issued at a price which is at a **large discount** to the nominal value of the notes, and which will be redeemable at par (or above par) when they eventually mature. • Deep discount bonds will carry a much **lower rate of interest** than other types of bond. However, the issuer of the bonds will have to pay a much larger amount at maturity than it borrowed when the bonds were issued.	• Bonds that are issued at a discount to their redemption value, but **no interest** is paid on them. • Zero coupon bonds are an extreme form of deep discount bond.

4.2.5 Security

Bonds may be secured and bank loans are often secured. **Security** may take the form of either a **fixed charge** or a **floating charge**.

Fixed charge	Floating charge
Security relates to specific asset/group of assets (eg land and buildings).	Security relates to a certain group of assets which will be constantly changing (eg trade receivables or inventory).
Company **can't dispose** of assets without providing substitute/consent of lender.	Company **can dispose** of assets until default takes place.
	In event of default, lenders **appoint receiver** rather than lay claim to assets.

Investors are likely to expect a **higher yield** with **unsecured** bonds to compensate them for the extra risk. Similarly, a bank may charge higher interest for an unsecured loan compared with a similar secured loan.

Question 1.3	Characteristics of debt

Which of the following are true in relation to long-term debt? (Tick as appropriate)

	Tick
It is up to the directors to determine the return that they pay debt-holders	
The expected return on debt is typically lower than the expected return on equity as debt-holders are exposed to greater risk than equity holders	
Interest is usually payable on debt and may be fixed, variable or capped	
On liquidation, debt-holders only have access to assets remaining after shareholders have been repaid	
Debt has to be secured with either a fixed or floating charge	
Bank loans, bonds, debentures and loan notes are all possible types of long-term debt	

5 Other sources of finance

Type of finance	Suitable for	Features
Retained earnings	N/A	Accumulated profits (after dividends) – needed for future growth but **cannot be used to fund investment projects.** Cash is needed instead.
Sale and leaseback	Entity with significant amounts of property, plant and equipment	Sell an asset with long useful life and lease it back. **Releases funds** without loss of use of assets.
Grants/government assistance	Small and medium unlisted entities	Governments (local and national) or larger bodies (eg the European Union) may provide grant or assistance to business. Usually **conditional** on certain requirements relating to technology, job creation, asset purchase or regional policy. Does **not normally** need to be **repaid.**
Debt with warrants attached	An entity wishing to raise debt finance and attract investors by offering a 'sweetener'	A warrant is an **option to buy shares** at a specified point in the future at a specified ('exercise') price. Holder will benefit from capital gain if share prices rises above exercise price but could sell warrant before exercise date.
Venture capital	Young, unquoted entities wishing to expand	**Usually equity** finance but can be mixture of debt and equity. Venture capitalists usually **accept low dividends** hoping to make their **return** as a **capital gain** on exit via an IPO or flotation.
Business angels	Small businesses	**Wealthy investors** providing **equity** finance.

Question 1.4	Other sources of finance

AB is a large well-established listed entity operating in the retail sector. AB owns a significant portfolio of valuable high street properties. AB would like to invest in a new product line.

Required

Which ONE of the following would be the most appropriate source of finance for AB to use to fund its investment in the new product line? (Tick the correct answer).

Sources of finance	Tick
Venture capital	
Retained earnings	
Government grant	
Sale and leaseback	

Chapter Summary

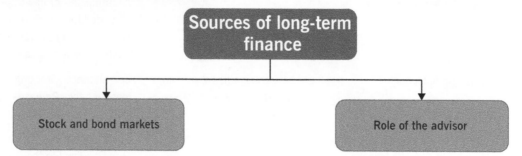

Sources of long-term finance

Stock and bond markets

Obtaining a listing

- Initial public offering (IPO)
  (selling to public for first time; issuing house publishes invitation to public at fixed price or on tender)
- Placing
  (shares not all offered to public; most of issue bought by small number of investors)
- Introduction
  (no shares made available to public)

Stock market listing

- Pros:
  Access to a wider pool of finance
  Improved marketability of shares
  Enhanced public image
  Easier to grow by acquisition
- Cons:
  Greater regulation
  Wider circle of investors
  Additional costs when issuing shares

Rights issue

- Offer to existing shareholders to subscribe to new shares in proportion to the current holding (usually at a discount to market price)
- Cheaper than public share issue
- Shareholders may buy new shares, sell rights, sell some rights to finance share purchase or do nothing
- TERP = weighted average price after rights issue

Corporate bond market

- Primary market
- Underwritten
- Traded OTC or publicly

Role of the advisor

Sponsors

- Project manage IPO
- Draft prospectus
- Ensure compliance
- Develop valuation

Reporting accountants

report on:

- Financial reporting procedures
- Financial historical records
- Working capital
- Other information

Bookrunner

Main underwriter:

- Raises finance from investors
- Helps determine pricing
- Guarantees to buy unsold shares or debt

Lawyer

- Performs legal due diligence
- Drafts the prospectus
- Provides legal opinions

Financial PR firm

Develops communication strategy pre- and post-IPO.

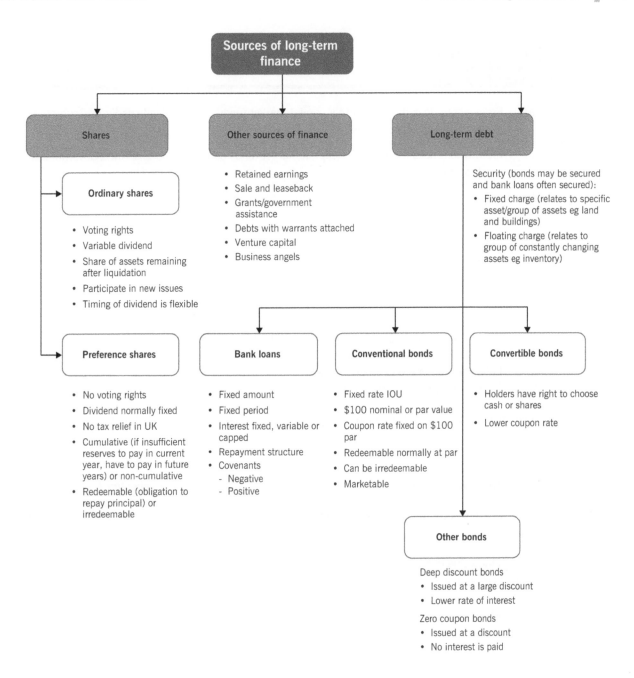

Quick Quiz

1   (a)   From whom does the **demand** for capital market funds come: Individuals/Firms/Government? (Delete any that do not apply).

      (b)   From whom does the **supply** of capital market funds come: Individuals/Firms/Government? (Delete any that do not apply).

2   Which of the following types of investment carries the highest level of risk?

      A   Corporate bonds
      B   Preference shares
      C   Government bonds
      D   Ordinary shares

3   Which of the following is least likely to be a reason for seeking a stock market flotation?

      A   Improving the existing owners' control over the business
      B   Access to a wider pool of finance
      C   Enhancement of the company's image
      D   Transfer of capital to other uses

4   A company has 12% debentures in issue, which have a market value of $135 per $100 nominal value. What is:

      (a)   The coupon rate?   12%.
      (b)   The amount of interest payable per annum per $100 (nominal) of debenture?   100 × 12% = $12.

5   Convertible securities are fixed-rate securities that may be converted into zero coupon bonds/ordinary shares/warrants. (Delete as appropriate.)

6   What is the value of $100 12% debt redeemable in three years at a premium of 20c per $ if the loanholder's required return is 10%?

        1 – 3   Inte $ DF(10%)
                                12   2.487   29.84
        3   Red prem.   120   0.751   90.12
       Value of debt   119.96

Answers to Quick Quiz

1   (a) and (b): You should have deleted none.

2   D   Ordinary shares

3   A   Flotation is likely to involve a significant loss of control to a wider circle of investors.

4   (a)   12%
     (b) $12

5   Ordinary shares

6

Years		$	Discount factor 10%	Present value $
1–3	Interest	12	2.487	29.84
3	Redemption premium	120	0.751	90.12
Value of debt				119.96

Answers to Questions

1.1 Stock market listing

The correct answer is:

C   An unquoted company may obtain a listing via an initial public offering, a placement or an introduction.

Tutorial note. A is incorrect as a stock market listing widens (rather than narrows) the pool of investors. B is incorrect because an introduction does not involve any shares being issued to the public. D is incorrect because a placement is cheaper than an initial public offering.

1.2 Difference between ordinary and preference shares

Investors in preference shares will expect a **LOWER** return than investors in ordinary shares because they face a **LOWER** risk than investors in ordinary shares and potentially earn **LESS** of a return as the entity's performance improves.

1.3 Characteristics of debt

The statements which have been ticked below are **true**:

	Tick
It is up to the directors to determine the return that they pay debt-holders **This is true of ordinary shares but with long-term debt, the return is normally predetermined in the contract**	
The expected return on debt is typically lower than the expected return on equity as debt-holders are exposed to greater risk than equity holders **It is true that the expected return on debt is typically lower than equity but it is because debt-holders are exposed to less risk than equity holders**	
Interest is usually payable on debt and may be fixed, variable or capped	✓
On liquidation, debt-holders only have access to assets remaining after shareholders have been repaid **Debt-holders have priority access to assets over shareholders**	
Debt has to be secured with either a fixed or floating charge **Debt may be secured but it does not have to be**	
Bank loans, bonds, debentures and loan notes are possible types of long-term debt	✓

1.4 Other sources of finance

The correct answer is:

Sources of finance	Tick
Venture capital **Venture capital is typically provided to young, unquoted profit-making entities. Since AB is a well-established listed entity, it is not appropriate here.**	
Retained earnings **Retained earnings represent accumulated profits not cash so in themselves, they cannot be used to fund a new product.**	
Government grant **Government grants are typically offered to small and medium-sized unlisted entities in return for specific conditions. As AB is a large listed entity, it is unlikely to be eligible for a government grant.**	
Sale and leaseback **Since AB has a large valuable property portfolio, it would be able to likely to be able to raise a significant amount of long term finance through sale and leaseback of its property. This is the most appropriate of the four sources of finance provided to fund the investment in the new product line.**	✓

Now try these questions from the Practice Question Bank	Number	Level	Marks	Time
	Q1	Introductory	N/A	15 mins
	Q2	Introductory	15	27 mins

COST OF CAPITAL

Organisations need to be able to calculate the cost of the finance they are using so that they can:

- Compare the cost to alternative sources of finance; and

- Ascertain whether an investment undertaken using that finance would earn a high enough return to cover the cost.

You will need to be able to calculate costs of equity, different types of debt and an overall weighted average cost of capital for an incorporated entity.

Topic list	learning outcomes	syllabus references
1 Investment appraisal techniques	A2	A2(a)
2 The cost of finance	A2	A2(c)
3 The cost of equity – the dividend valuation model	A2	A2(a)
4 Cost of debt – bank loan	A2	A2(b)
5 Cost of debt – irredeemable bonds	A2	A2(b)
6 Cost of debt – redeemable bonds	A2	A2(b)
7 Cost of debt – convertible bonds	A2	A2(b)
8 Weighted average cost of capital	A2	A2(b)

Chapter Overview

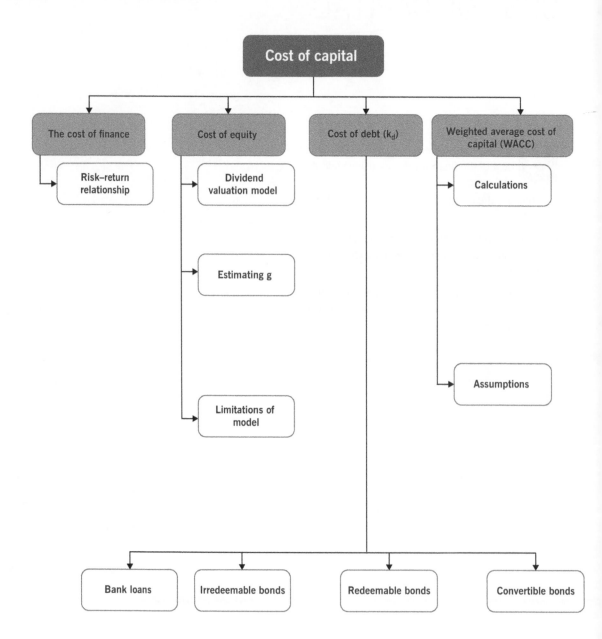

1 Investment appraisal techniques

1.1 Discounted cash flow (DCF) techniques

Which would you prefer? $1,000 today or $1,000 1 year from today? It is common sense to prefer to receive $1,000 today. The **logic** behind rejecting the $1,000 in 1 year's time is that you would be better off if you put $1,000 into a bank account for a year.

This is the meaning of the term '**time value of money**'.

DCF techniques take into account the time value of money. This is critical when cash flows are going to be spread across several years.

1.2 Purpose of discounting

To establish what a future cash flow is worth to an investor today, given information about their required rate of return (or cost of capital).

Many projects involve investing money now and receiving returns in the future. A project's cash flows need to be analysed to see if they offer a better return than an investor could get by investing elsewhere.

The process of adjusting a project's cash flows to reflect the return that investors could get elsewhere is known as discounting the cash flows or DCF.

The value of a future cash flow today is the **present value**.

KEY TERMS

COST OF CAPITAL: The return required by the providers of finance. This is the discount rate. The calculations of cost of capital are explained in the main body of the chapter.

ANNUITY: A series of identical cash flows that occur every year for a number of years.

PERPETUITY: A series of identical cash flows that occur every year for ever.

1.2.1 DCF formulae

EXAM

$$\text{Present value} \quad = \quad \frac{1}{[1+r]^n}$$

r = discount rate
n = time period of cash flow

$$\text{Present value of an annuity} \quad = PV = \frac{1}{r}\left[1 - \frac{1}{[1+r]^n}\right]$$

- For **equal annual cash flows** starting at time 1, for a number of years, n.

- For annuities starting after time 1 use the appropriate annuity factor and then subtract the annuity figure for the periods before the annuity starts.

1.2.2 Present value/cumulative present value factors

Tables given in the exam give both the present value for $1 to be received after n years **and** the present value of a constant inflow of $1 starting after 1 year and continuing for n years.

Example: Technique demonstration

Required

(a) What is the present value of $60,000 at year 6, if a return of 15% per annum is obtainable?

(b) What is the present value of $1,000 in contribution earned each year from years 1–10, when the required return on investment is 11%?

Solution

(a) Present value = $60,000 × 0.432 = $25,920
(b) Present value = $1,000 × 5.889 = $5,889

1.3 Net present value (NPV)

KEY TERM

NPV: The sum of the present values of all the relevant cash flows of a project discounted at an appropriate cost of capital.

The NPV represents the change in wealth of the investor as a result of investing in the project.

1.4 Decision rule

Accept all projects with a positive NPV.

1.5 Internal rate of return (IRR)

KEY TERM

IRR: The annual percentage return generated by a project, taking into account the time value of money.

The IRR is a cost of capital at which the NPV of a project would be $0.

1.5.1 Calculation

LEARN

Steps:

 Calculate NPV at given cost of capital.

 Calculate NPV using a second discount rate.

 Calculate the IRR using the formula:

$$IRR = a + \frac{NPVa}{NPVa - NPVb} (b - a)$$

Where   a is the first discount rate giving NPVa
          b is the second discount rate giving NPVb

1.5.2 Decision rule

Accept all projects with an IRR above the cost of capital.

2 The cost of finance

An understanding of the cost of using any type of finance will help an organisation to:

*   Compare the relative costs of different potential sources of finance

*   Estimate its overall cost of capital in order to assess the net present value of potential investments (this area is developed in Paper P2)

2.1 Risk–return relationship

Risk is the main driving force behind the return that is expected by investors ie the higher the risk faced by the investor, the higher the return they will expect. This is the **risk–return relationship**.

In the event of a company being unable to pay its debts and going into liquidation, there is an order in which it has to repay its creditors and investors.

Increasing risk

1. Creditors with a fixed charge

2. Creditors with a floating charge

3. Unsecured creditors

4. Preference shareholders

5. Ordinary shareholders

2.2 Implications and terminology

The cheapest form of finance is debt (especially if secured).

*   The cost of debt is **referred to as k_d**.

The **most expensive form of finance is equity** (ordinary shares).

*   The cost of equity is **referred to as k_e**.

3 The cost of equity – the dividend valuation model

The cost of equity is the rate of return a shareholder requires for their investment in a business. A simple way of estimating the return that is expected by shareholders is to compare the price that they are paying for a share to the dividend that they are expecting.

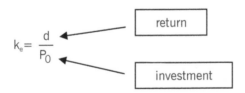

$$k_e = \frac{d}{P_0}$$

return

investment

This is the formula used for **preference shares** as there is no growth of dividends since they pay a fixed dividend each year (eg 5% preference shares pay 5% of the par value of the shares as a dividend annually).

Example: Cost of equity with no dividend growth

WR has just paid a dividend of 60c and has a market value of $5.50. No dividend growth is expected.

Required

What is its cost of equity?

Solution

The cost of equity is $k_e = \dfrac{d}{P_0}$

$k_e = 60/550 = $ **10.9%**

If a dividend is about to be paid and the share price is cum-div, then the share price needs to be adjusted by stripping the dividend out of the share price. This is because the ex-div price shows the actual net investment that is being made.

3.1 Dividend growth

Shareholders will normally expect the dividend to grow in the future (g). Again, by looking at how much shareholders are prepared to pay for this share (P_0), it is possible to estimate the return that they are expecting.

EXAM

As before, this shows the return provided by comparing the next dividend to the amount being invested

$$k_e = \dfrac{d_1}{P_0} + g$$

In addition, further dividend growth is expected

If a company fails to provide this return to shareholders, then **its share price will fall**.

Example: Cost of equity with dividend growth

WR is **about to pay** a dividend of 60c and has a market value of $6.10 cum-div. Dividend growth of 8% is expected.

Required

What is its cost of equity?

Solution

$$k_e = \dfrac{d_1}{P_0} + g$$

$P_0 = 610c - 60c = 550c$

$d_1 = 60 \times 1.08 = 64.8c$

$g = 0.08$

$k_e = 64.8/550 + 0.08 = $ **19.8%**

3.2 Limitations of the model

$$k_e = \frac{d_1}{P_0} + g$$

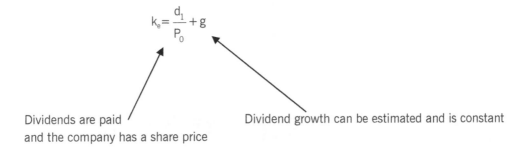

Dividends are paid and the company has a share price

Dividend growth can be estimated and is constant

3.3 Estimating dividend growth

There are two methods of estimating dividend growth.

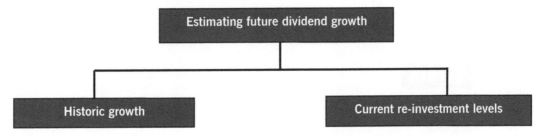

Estimating future dividend growth

Historic growth

Current re-investment levels

3.4 Historic growth

EXAM

By comparing the most recent dividend to a dividend paid in the past it is possible to identify the annual growth rate in dividends. It could then be *assumed* that this will continue into the future.

$$\text{past dividend} \times (1 + g)^n = \text{latest dividend}$$

This can re-arranged to:

$$g = \sqrt[n]{\left(\text{latest dividend} \Big/ \text{past dividend}\right)} - 1$$

Question 2.1   Cost of equity: historic growth method

PB has just paid a dividend of 32.21c per share. Five years ago the dividend was 20c per share. PB's share price is 832.21c *ex div*.

Required

Using the historic growth method to calculate 'g', what is PB's cost of equity?

A   14.3%
B   13.9%
C   14.4%
D   14.0%

3.5 Current re-investment levels

The current reinvestments method assumes that:

growth = **r**eturn on investment × **b**alance of profits reinvested

EXAM

> This is often abbreviated to $g = r \times b$

Example: Cost of equity: current reinvestment method

XF has just paid a dividend per share of 20c. This was 40% of earnings per share. XF's return on investment is 30%. The current share price is 200c.

Required

Using the current reinvestment levels method to calculate 'g', calculate XF's cost of equity to one decimal place:

Solution

29.8%

Workings

$g = 0.3 \times 0.6 = 0.18$

$k_e = (20 \times 1.18)/200 + 0.18 = 0.298$ or 29.8%

4   Cost of debt – bank loan

The simplest type of debt is a bank loan. The interest rate on a loan will be agreed at the outset of the loan. The only adjustment that may be required is to reflect that a company may save tax as it makes loan interest repayments.

LEARN

> **Post-tax cost of a loan = pre-tax cost × (1 – tax rate)**

5   Cost of debt – irredeemable bonds

After making an investment in bonds/debentures/loan stock (nominal value $100), debt-holders receive fixed interest only.

5.1 Irredeemable bonds (no tax)

Similar to the dividend growth model.

$$k_d = \frac{I}{P_0} \qquad I = \text{interest paid} \qquad P_0 = \text{market value of the debt}$$

Example: Cost of debt

CHP has 8% bonds quoted at 82%.

Required

What is the cost of debt (ignore tax)?

Solution

Cost pre-tax = 8/82 = **9.8%**

5.2 Tax on profits

Paying interest reduces taxable profits which reduces the tax charge, so the cost of debt to the company is reduced.

5.3 Irredeemable bonds (with tax)

$$k_d = \frac{I(1-t)}{P_0}$$ where P_0 is the market value of debt ex-interest

Example: Cost of debt with tax

Required

Recalculate the cost of debt for CHP (see previous example) assuming tax on profits is 30%.

Solution

Cost of debt to the company = $\dfrac{\$8\,(1-0.30)}{\$82}$ = **6.8%**

6 Cost of debt – redeemable bonds

If an investor invests money in a bond now and receives returns in the future, then the bond's cash flows can be analysed to determine the percentage return that the bond holder receives. This is called the **internal rate of return of the bond**.

The return to the bond holder will be **similar** to the cost of the bond to the company.

Estimating the internal rate of return requires an understanding of the concept of discounting. This is covered in detail in other papers (for example P2), but the basics are recapped in the following examples and in Section 1.

STEP 1   Calculate the net present value of the project at <u>any</u> rate eg 5%

STEP 2   Calculate the net present value of the project at any other rate eg 10%

STEP 3   Estimate the internal rate of return

Example: Illustrating Step 1

WL has $100,000 5% redeemable bonds in issue. Interest is paid annually on 31 December. The ex-interest market value of a bond now (1 January 20X5) is $90 and the bonds are redeemable at a 10% premium on 31 December 20X9.

Required

What is the net present value if the bond holder wants a 5% return?

Solution

Time	0	1	2	3	4	5
Per $100	−90	5	5	5	5	115
Discount factor at 5%	1.0	0.952	0.907	0.864	0.823	0.784
Present value	−90	4.76	4.535	4.32	4.115	90.16
NPV	= (−90 + 4.76 + 4.535 + 4.32 + 4.115 + 90.16) = **17.89**					

or

Time	0	1 to 5	5
Per $100	−90	5	110
Discount factor at 5%	1.0	4.329	0.784
Present value	−90	21.65	86.24
NPV	= −90 + 21.65 + 86.24 = **17.89**		

ie the investment delivers a return of over 5%

Example: Illustrating Step 2

Required

Using the same information as in the previous example, calculate the net present value if the bond holder wants a 10% return.

Solution

Time	0	1 to 5	5
Per $100	−90	5	110
Discount factor at 10%	1	3.791	0.621
Present value	−90.00	18.96	68.31

Net present value	= −90 + 18,96 + 68.31 = **−2,73**

ie the investment delivers a return of less than 10%

Example: Illustrating Step 3

Required

Using the following formula, estimate the internal rate of return of the above bond.

$$IRR = a + \frac{NPVa}{NPVa - NPVb}(b - a)$$

Solution

NPVa = 17.89	NPVb = −2.73	a = 5	b = 10

$$IRR = 5 + \frac{17.89}{17.89 - \text{-}2.73}(10 - 5) = 5 + 4.3 = \underline{\mathbf{9.3\%}}$$

6.1 Cost to the company

Having worked out the return to the investor, the **same approach** can now be applied to working out the cost to the company. **The only difference is that the company gets tax relief on interest payments.**

Example: Steps 1–3 from the company's view

WL has $100,000 5% redeemable bonds in issue. Interest is paid annually on 31 December. The ex-interest market value of a bond now (1 January 20X5) is $90 and the bonds are redeemable at a 10% premium on 31 December 20X9. **Tax on profits is 30%.**

Required

What is the **cost** of debt?

New information

Solution

Time	0	1 to 5	5
Per $100	−90	3.5	110
		(5 × (1−0.3))	
Discount factor at 5%	1	4.329	0.784
Present value	−90.00	15.15	86.24
NPV	= − 90 + 15.15 + 86.24 = **11.39**		

ie the investment delivers a return of over 5%

Time	0	1 to 5	5
Per $100	–90	3.5	110
Discount factor at 10%	1	3.791	0.621
Present value	–90.00	13.27	68.31

NPV = –90 + 13.27 + 68.31 = **–8.42**

ie the investment delivers a return of less than 10%

IRR = 5 + (11.39/19.81 × 5) = **7.9%**

7 Cost of debt – convertible bonds

Convertible bonds are redeemable bonds that can be converted into shares at a future date. Its cost in interest terms tends to be lower than straight debt, but at the date of redemption the debt-holders may, at their discretion, convert their debt into shares.

An IRR approach will need to be used to identify the cost of the bond, **replacing the redemption value of the bond with the value of the shares if conversion is likely to happen**.

Example: Steps 1–3 for convertible debt

WL plc has $100,000 5% **convertible** bonds in issue. The market value of a bond now (1 January 20X5) is $90 and the bonds are redeemable at a 10% premium on 31 December 20X9 **or can be converted into shares at a ratio of $100 nominal value of debt to 20 shares**. Tax is 30%. **It is estimated that the share price will be $6 by December 20X9.**

Required

What is the **cost** of debt?

Solution

Time	0	1 to 5	5
Per $100	–90	3.5	120
		(5 × (1–0.3))	
Discount factor at 5%	1	4.329	0.784
Present value	–90.00	15.15	94.08
NPV	= –90 + 15.15 + 94.08 = **19.23**		

ie the investment delivers a return of over 5%

Time	0	1 to 5	5
Per $100	–90	3.5	120
Discount factor at 10%	1	3.791	0.621
Present value	–90.00	13.27	74.52
NPV	= –90 + 13.27 + 74.52 = **–2.21**		

ie the investment delivers a return of less than 10%

IRR = 5 + (19.23/21.44 × 5) = **9.48%**

8 Weighted average cost of capital

8.1 Introduction

In the examination, you may be required to calculate the weighted average cost of capital for the business by **combining together the costs of two or more of the types of capital covered above**.

8.2 WACC formula

EXAM

$$WACC = k_{eg} \frac{Ve}{Ve + Vd} + k_d (1-t) \frac{Vd}{Ve + Vd}$$

Where V_e = total market value (ex-div) of shares **ie market capitalisation**

V_d = total market value (ex-interest) of debt

k_{eg} = cost of equity in a geared company

k_d = cost of debt

A third source of finance may have to be added into the formula.

Example: WACC

CP is financed by 10 million $1 ordinary shares and $8,000,000 8% redeemable bonds having market values of $1.60 ex-div and $90% ex-interest respectively. A dividend of 30c has just been paid and future dividends are expected to grow by 5%. The bonds are redeemable at par in 5 years' time; the cost of this debt has been estimated as 8.3% using an IRR approach.

Required

If taxation is 30%, calculate the WACC.

Solution

$$k_e = \frac{d_0(1+g)}{P_0} + g = \frac{30(1.05)}{160} + 0.05$$

$$= 24.69\%$$

Ve = 10m × $1.60 = $16m

k_d: 8.3%

Vd = $8m × 90% = $7.2m

$$WACC = (24.69\% \times \frac{16}{(16+7.2)}) + (8.3\% \times \frac{7.2}{(16+7.2)}) = \underline{\underline{19.6\%}}$$

Question 2.2   Continuation introducing a third type of finance

If, in the previous example, the company also had a $1.8m bank loan costing 12% pre-tax, what would be the new weighted average cost of capital?

8.3 Use of weighted average cost of capital (WACC)

WACC is often used as a discount rate in **project appraisal** when performing net present value or internal rate of return calculations. If the project has a positive NPV when discounted using the WACC, it should be accepted.

However, this is only appropriate if the following conditions are met:

(a)   There is **no change to financial risk** ie the capital structure is constant. If the capital structure changes, the weightings in the WACC will also change.

(b)   There is **no change to business risk** ie the new investment has the same business risk profile as the entity's existing operations.

(c)   The **new investment is marginal** to the entity. If the investment is small, none of k_e, k_d or WACC will change materially. If the investment is substantial it will usually cause these values to change.

The WACC calculation is **dependent on having a market value** for the shares and debt. If the shares or debt are unquoted, estimates of market value will have to be used instead, reducing the reliability of the WACC figure.

Question 2.3	Use of WACC

CD has a gearing ratio of 40% and a weighted average cost of capital (WACC) of 10%. CD is considering expanding its business.

Required

In which ONE of the following circumstances would it be most appropriate to use CD's WACC when calculating net present values for project evaluation purposes?

A   Expansion into a new industry at the same split of equity to debt
B   Expansion into a new project at different levels of equity and debt
C   Expansion within existing operations at the same split of equity to debt
D   Expansion within existing operations at different levels of equity and debt

Chapter Summary

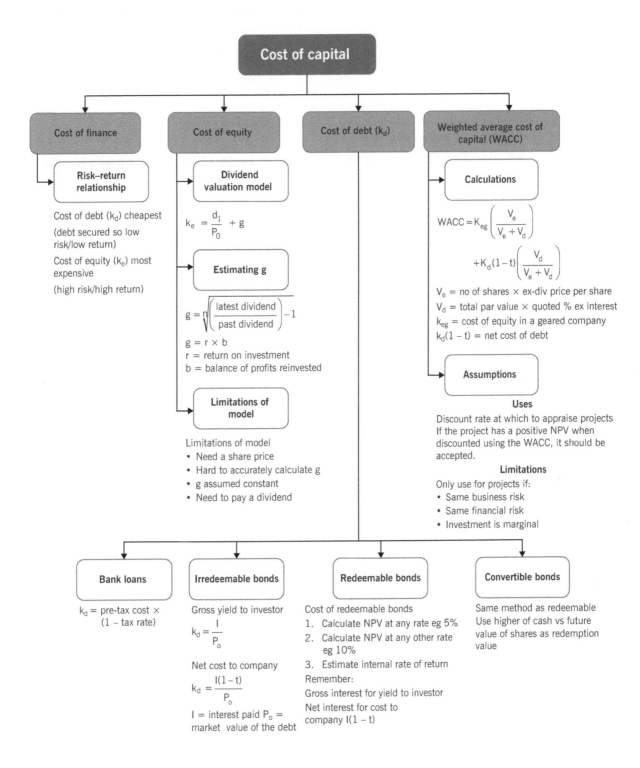

Cost of capital

Cost of finance

Risk–return relationship

Cost of debt (k_d) cheapest
(debt secured so low risk/low return)

Cost of equity (k_e) most expensive
(high risk/high return)

Cost of equity

Dividend valuation model

$$k_e = \frac{d_1}{P_0} + g$$

Estimating g

$$g = \sqrt[n]{\left(\frac{\text{latest dividend}}{\text{past dividend}}\right)} - 1$$

$g = r \times b$
r = return on investment
b = balance of profits reinvested

Limitations of model

Limitations of model
• Need a share price
• Hard to accurately calculate g
• g assumed constant
• Need to pay a dividend

Cost of debt (k_d)

Weighted average cost of capital (WACC)

Calculations

$$\text{WACC} = K_{eg}\left(\frac{V_e}{V_e + V_d}\right)$$
$$+ K_d(1-t)\left(\frac{V_d}{V_e + V_d}\right)$$

V_e = no of shares × ex-div price per share
V_d = total par value × quoted % ex interest
k_{eg} = cost of equity in a geared company
$k_d(1 - t)$ = net cost of debt

Assumptions

Uses

Discount rate at which to appraise projects
If the project has a positive NPV when discounted using the WACC, it should be accepted.

Limitations

Only use for projects if:
• Same business risk
• Same financial risk
• Investment is marginal

Bank loans

k_d = pre-tax cost × (1 – tax rate)

Irredeemable bonds

Gross yield to investor
$$k_d = \frac{I}{P_0}$$

Net cost to company
$$k_d = \frac{I(1-t)}{P_0}$$

I = interest paid P_0 = market value of the debt

Redeemable bonds

Cost of redeemable bonds
1. Calculate NPV at any rate eg 5%
2. Calculate NPV at any other rate eg 10%
3. Estimate internal rate of return
Remember:
Gross interest for yield to investor
Net interest for cost to company I(1 – t)

Convertible bonds

Same method as redeemable
Use higher of cash vs future value of shares as redemption value

Quick Quiz

1   What is the formula for calculating the future value of an investment plus accumulated compound interest after n time periods?

2   What is the formula for calculating the present value of a future sum of money at the end of n time periods?

3   What is the formula for the present value of a perpetuity?

4   A share has a current market value of 120c and the last dividend was 10c. If the expected annual growth rate of dividends is 5%, calculate the cost of equity capital.

5   Identify the variables k_{eg}, k_d, V_E and V_D in the following weighted average cost of capital formula.

$$WACC = K_{eg}\left(\frac{V_E}{V_E + V_D}\right) + K_d\,(1-t)\left(\frac{V_D}{V_E + V_D}\right)$$

6   When calculating the weighted average cost of capital, which of the following is the preferred method of weighting?

A   Book values of debt and equity
B   Average levels of the market values of debt and equity (ignoring reserves) over five years
C   Current market values of debt and equity
D   Book value of debt and current market value of equity

7   What is the cost of $1 irredeemable debt capital paying an annual rate of interest of 7% and having a current market price of $1.50?

Answers to Quick Quiz

1    $FV = PV (1 + r)^n$

2    $PV = FV \dfrac{1}{(1+r)^n}$

3   PV = Annual cash flow/discount rate

4    $\dfrac{10(1+0.05)}{120} + 0.05 = 13.75\%$

5   k_{eg} is the cost of equity

    k_d is the cost of debt

    V_E is the market value of equity in the firm

    V_D is the market value of debt in the firm

6   C   Current market values of debt and equity

7   Cost of debt $= \dfrac{0.07}{1.50} = 4.67\%$

Answers to Questions

2.1 Cost of equity: historic growth method

A   14.3%

$$g = \sqrt[5]{\left(32.21\big/20\right)} - 1 = 0.1 \text{ (or 10\%)}$$

$$k_e = \frac{32.21(1.1)}{832.21} + 0.1 = 0.143 \text{ or } \underline{\mathbf{14.3\%}}$$

13.9% is the answer if you forget to multiply the dividend per share of 32.21 by (1+g) to get the dividend expected in 1 year.

The other 2 answers are the result of subtracting the dividend from the share price – this is unnecessary here because the share price is already ex div.

2.2 Continuation introducing a third type of finance

k_e = 24.69% as before

Ve = 10m × $1.60 = $16m

k_{d1}: 8.3%

Vd1 = $8m × 90% = $7.2m

Loan cost = 12 × (1 − 0.3) = 8.4%

Vd2 = $1.8m

Ve + Vd1 + Vd2 = $16m + $7.2m + $1.8m = $25m

WACC $= (24.69\% \times \dfrac{16}{25}) + (8.3\% \times \dfrac{7.2}{(25)}) + (8.4\% \times \dfrac{1.8}{25}) = \underline{\underline{\textbf{18.8\%}}}$

2.3 Use of WACC

C   Expansion within existing operations at the same split of equity to debt

This is the correct answer because it would not involve any change to business risk (as expanding within existing operations) nor financial risk (as maintaining the same capital structure ie split of equity to debt).

A is incorrect because although there is no change in financial risk (same split of equity to debt), expanding into a new industry would change the business risk and WACC is only appropriate when there is no change to business risk.

B is incorrect because there would be a change in financial risk (different levels of equity and debt) and WACC is only appropriate when there is no change to financial risk.

D is incorrect because although there would be no change to business risk, there would be a change in financial risk (different levels of equity and debt) making use of WACC inappropriate.

Now try these questions from the Practice Question Bank	Number	Level	Marks	Time
	Q3	Introductory	N/A	16 mins

ACCOUNTING STANDARDS

Part B

FINANCIAL INSTRUMENTS

The term financial instruments covers a range of assets, liabilities and equity. It is very important that such items are correctly categorised and accounted for to ensure that the gearing ratio in the financial statements is accurate.

You will need to be able to define, classify and determine the correct recognition and measurement treatment for the main types of financial instrument.

3

Topic list	learning outcomes	syllabus references
1 Definition (IAS 32)	B1	B1(c)
2 Classification (IAS 32)	B1	B1(c)
3 Recognition (IFRS 9)	B1	B1(d)
4 Derecognition (IFRS 9)	B1	B1(d)
5 Measurement (IFRS 9)	B1	B1(d)
6 Impairment of financial assets (IFRS 9)	B1	B1(d)

Chapter Overview

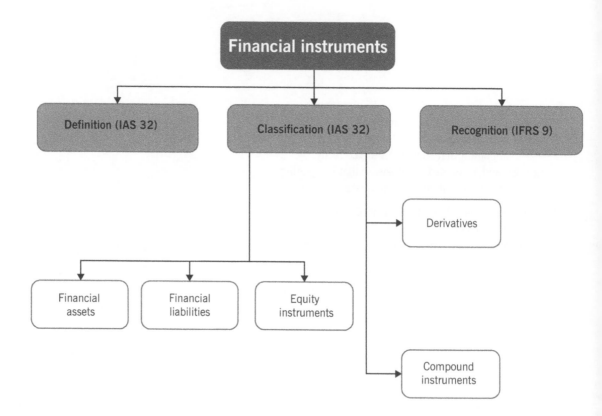

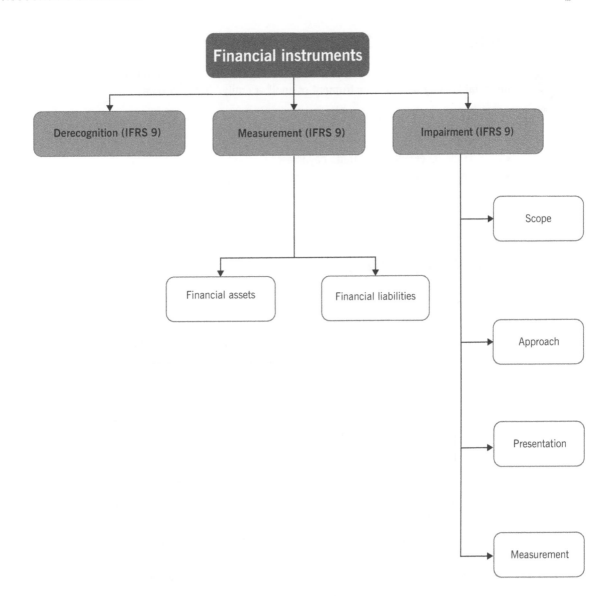

1 Definition (IAS 32)

KEY TERM

'A FINANCIAL INSTRUMENT is any contract that gives rise to both a **financial asset** of one entity and a **financial liability or equity instrument** of another entity.' (IAS 32: para. 11)

For the purposes of F2, this includes:

* Cash
* Trade receivables and trade payables
* Loans (bonds, debentures, loan notes)
* Shares
* Derivatives

2 Classification (IAS 32)

2.1 Categories

Financial instruments fall into three categories, summarised in the diagram below.

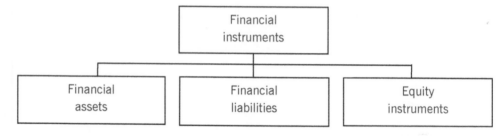

Financial assets

Definition:
* Cash
* An equity instrument of another entity
* A **contractual right** to:
  - Receive cash or another financial asset from another entity
  - Exchange financial assets or liabilities under potentially favourable conditions
* A contract that will or may be settled in the entity's own equity instruments

Examples:
* Investment in shares
* Trade receivables
* Bonds purchased
* Forward standing at a gain

Financial liabilities

Definition:
Any liability that is:
* A **contractual obligation** to:
  - Deliver cash or another financial asset to another entity
  - Exchange financial assets or liabilities under potentially unfavourable conditions
* A contract that will or may be settled in the entity's own equity instruments

Examples:
* Trade payables
* Bonds issued
* Mandatorily redeemable preference shares
* Cumulative irredeemable preference shares
* Forward standing at a loss

Equity instruments

Definition:
* Any contract that evidences a residual interest in the assets of an entity after deducting all of its liabilities

Examples:
* Own ordinary shares
* Non-cumulative irredeemable preference shares

(IAS 32: para 11)

Note. The financial asset and liability definitions are consistent with the *Conceptual Framework* asset and liability definitions.

Question 3.1

Classification

XY issued 60,000 redeemable $1 preference shares on 1 January 20X1 paying an annual (cumulative) dividend of 7% per annum, redeemable in 10 years' time.

Required

How should the shares and the dividends be recorded in the financial statements for the year ended 31 December 20X1? (Tick the correct answer)

Tick	Options
	Equity of $60,000 in the statement of financial position; dividends of $4,200 deducted from retained earnings and shown in the statement of changes in equity
	Financial liability of $60,000 within current liabilities in the statement of financial position; dividends of $4,200 deducted from retained earnings and shown in the statement of changes in equity
✓	Financial liability of $60,000 within non-current liabilities in the statement of financial position; finance cost of $4,200 in the statement of profit or loss and other comprehensive income
	Equity of $60,000 in the statement of financial position; finance cost of $4,200 in the statement of profit or loss and other comprehensive income

2.2 Derivatives

A derivative has three characteristics:

- Its value changes in response to an underlying variable (eg share price or interest rate).
- It requires little or no initial net investment.
- It is settled at a future date. (IFRS 9: Appendix A)

If a derivative is **favourable** at the year end (ie standing at a gain), it is a **financial asset**. The double entry to record this derivative would be:

Dr Financial asset
Cr Profit or loss

If a derivative is **unfavourable** at the year end (ie standing at a loss), it is a **financial liability**. The double entry to record this derivative would be:

Dr Profit or loss
Cr Financial liability

Example: Derivatives

On 1 November 20X1, LM took out a speculative forward contract to buy coffee beans for delivery on 30 April 20X2 at an agreed price of $6,000 intending to settle net in cash. Due to a surge in expected supply, a forward contract for delivery on 30 April 20X2 would have cost $5,000 at 31 December 20X1.

Required

(a) Calculate the value of the forward contract as at 31 December 20X1 and state whether it is a financial asset or liability.

(b) Prepare the accounting entry to record the forward contract in LM's financial statements for the year ended 31 December 20X1.

Solution

(a) *Forward contract at 31 December 20X1*

	$
Market price of contract at 31 December 20X1	5,000
LM's forward price	(6,000)
Loss (as pay more under forward than would at year-end rate) = **Financial liability**	(1,000)

(b) *Accounting entry*

DEBIT	Profit or loss ('finance cost')	$1,000	
CREDIT	Financial liability		$1,000

2.3 Compound financial instruments

Where a financial instrument contains some characteristics of equity and some of financial liability then its separate components need to be classified separately. (IAS 32: para. 28–29)

Convertible debt is an example of a compound financial instrument – in substance, it contains some characteristics of equity (the right to a share) and some of a financial liability (an obligation to pay interest and to repay the principal).

The financial liability and equity components are separated as follows (IAS 32: para 32):

(a) **Financial liability** component:

	$
Present value of principal*	X
Present value of interest*	X
	X

      *Discount using the market interest rate of non-convertible debt

(b) **Equity** component = Proceeds – financial liability component

The journal is as follows.

Dr (↑) Cash
Cr (↑) Financial liability
Cr (↑) Equity

Example: Compound financial instruments

A company issued 3,000 convertible bonds at par on 1 January 20X1. The bonds are redeemable in 4 years' time (on 31 December 20X4) at their par value of $100 per bond.

The bonds pay interest annually in arrears at an interest rate (based on nominal value) of 5%. Each bond can be converted at the maturity date into 5 $1 shares.

The prevailing market interest rate for 4 year bonds that have no right of conversion is 8%.

The annuity factor for 4 years at 8% is 3.312. The present value of $1 receivable in 4 years' time at 8% is 0.735.

Required

Prepare the accounting entry to record the issue of the convertible bonds.

Solution

DEBIT	Cash (3,000 bonds × $100 par value)	$300,000	
CREDIT	Financial liability (W1)		$270,180
CREDIT	Equity (W1)		$29,820

Workings

1   *Split of bond into financial liability and equity components*

	$
Proceeds	300,000
Financial liability component of convertible bond (W2)	(270,180)
Equity component of convertible bond	29,820

2   *Calculation of financial liability component*

	$
Present value of principal (3,000 × $100 = $300,000 × 0.735)	220,500
Present value of interest annuity ((5% × $300,000) × 3.312)	49,680
	270,180

3 Recognition (IFRS 9)

Financial instruments are recognised on the statement of financial position 'when the entity becomes a **party to the contractual provisions of the instrument**.' (IFRS 9: para. 3.1.1)

In practical terms, this usually means:

Type of financial instrument	Recognition
Trade receivable/payable	On delivery of goods or performance of service
Loans (bonds, debentures, loan notes)	On issue
Shares	On issue
Derivatives	On the commitment date

4 Derecognition (IFRS 9)

Derecognition happens:

Financial assets: — when the contractual rights to the cash flows **expire** (eg because a customer has paid their debt or an option has expired worthless); **or**

— the financial asset is **transferred** (eg sold), based on whether the entity has transferred **substantially all** the risks and rewards of ownership of the financial asset. (IFRS 9: para. 3.2.3, 3.2.6)

Financial liabilities: — when the obligation is **discharged** (eg paid off), **cancelled** or **expires**. (IFRS 9: para. 3.3.1)

Question 3.2

Derecognition

On 31 December 20X1, AP sold trade receivables of $100,000 to a factoring company, XY. AP received $80,000 from XY, being 80% of the trade receivables sold. Under the terms of the arrangement, XY administers the collection of the receivables and must remit a residual amount to AP depending on how quickly individual customers pay. Any debts not recovered after 120 days are transferred back to AP for immediate cash repayment.

Required

How should the sale of the trade receivables be accounted for by AP in the year ended 31 December 20X1? (Tick the correct answer)

Tick	Accounting entries			
	DEBIT	Cash	$80,000	
	CREDIT	Trade receivables		$80,000
	DEBIT	Cash	$80,000	
	CREDIT	Liability		$80,000
	DEBIT	Cash	$80,000	
	DEBIT	Bad debt expense	$20,000	
	CREDIT	Trade receivables		$100,000
✓	DEBIT	Cash	$80,000	
	DEBIT	Receivable (from XY)	$20,000	
	CREDIT	Trade receivables		$100,000

5 Measurement (IFRS 9)

5.1 Financial assets

		Initial measurement	Subsequent measurement
1	**Investments in debt instruments** Business model approach:		
	(a) Held to collect contractual cash flows; and cash flows are solely principal and interest	Fair value + transaction costs	Amortised cost
	(b) Held to collect contractual cash flows **and** to sell; and cash flows are solely principal and interest	Fair value + transaction costs	Fair value through other comprehensive income (with reclassification to profit or loss (P/L) on derecognition) NB: interest revenue calculated on amortised cost basis recognised in P/L

	Initial measurement	Subsequent measurement
2 Investments in equity instruments not 'held for trading' (optional irrevocable election on initial recognition)	Fair value + transaction costs	Fair value through other comprehensive income (no reclassification to P/L on derecognition) NB: dividend income recognised in P/L
3 All other financial assets	Fair value (transaction costs expensed in P/L)	Fair value through profit or loss

(IFRS 9: para. 4.1.1 – 4.1.4)

5.2 Financial liabilities

	Initial measurement	Subsequent measurement
1 Most financial liabilities (eg trade payables, loans, preference shares classified as a liability)	Fair value less transaction costs	Amortised cost
2 Financial liabilities at fair value through profit or loss - 'held for trading' (short-term profit making) - derivatives that are liabilities	Fair value (transaction costs expensed in P/L)	Fair value through profit or loss *
3 Financial liabilities arising when transfer of financial asset does not qualify for derecognition (eg debt factoring where risks and rewards are not transferred to the factor)	Consideration received	Measure financial liability on same basis as transferred asset (amortised cost or fair value)

(IFRS 9: para. 4.2.1)

5.3 Amortised cost

This is the amount at which the item was initially recorded, less any principal repayments, plus the cumulative amortisation of the difference between the initial and maturity values.

This difference is amortised using the effective interest rate of the instrument, ie its internal rate of return (as seen in Chapter 2). It includes:

- Transaction costs
- Interest payments
- Any discount on the debt on inception
- Any premium payable on redemption

(IFRS 9: Appendix A)

The proforma and double entries for the amortised cost table is as follows:

Financial asset:

	$		Accounting entries:
Balance b/d	X		Dr (↑) Financial asset Cr (↓) Cash (if initial recognition at start of year)
Finance income (effective interest × b/d)	X	**SPL**	Dr (↑) Financial asset Cr (↑) Finance income
Interest received (coupon × par value)	(X)		Dr (↑) Cash Cr (↓) Financial asset
Balance c/d	X	**SOFP**	

Financial liability:

	$		Accounting entries:
Balance b/d	X		Dr (↑) Cash Cr (↑) Financial liability (if initial recognition at start of year)
Finance cost (effective interest × b/d)	X	**SPL**	Dr (↑) Finance cost Cr (↑) Financial liability
Interest paid (coupon × par value)	(X)		Dr (↓) Financial liability Cr (↓) Cash
Balance c/d	X	**SOFP**	

Example: Amortised cost

PR has a 31 December year end. On 1 January 20X0 PR issued a deep discount bond for $157,963 and incurred transaction costs of $200. Interest of 4% is payable annually on 31 December. The bond will be redeemed on 31 December 20X4 for $200,000 (its par value). The effective interest rate of the bond is 9.5%.

Required

What is the carrying amount of the bond on 31 December 20X1 (rounded to the nearest $)?

Solution

Carrying amount of the bond (financial liability) at 31 December 20X1 = $172,402 (W1)

Working: Carrying amount of bond at 31 December 20X1

	$
1.1.X0 (157,963 - 200)	157,763
Finance cost 20X0 (9.5% × 157,763)	14,987
Interest paid (4% × 200,000)	(8,000)
At 31.12.X0	164,750
Finance cost 20X1 (9.5% × 164,750)	15,651
Interest paid (4% × 200,000)	(8,000)
At 31.12.X1	172,401

5.4 Fair value

KEY TERM

FAIR VALUE: 'The price that would be received to sell an asset or paid to transfer a liability in an orderly transaction between market participants at the measurement date.' (IFRS 13: para. 9)

Example: Fair value

WN anticipates capital expenditure in a few years and so has a policy to invest its excess cash into short and long-term financial assets so it can fund the expenditure when the need arises. WN will hold these assets to collect the contractual cash flows, and, when an opportunity arises, the entity will sell financial assets to re-invest the cash in different financial assets with a higher return. The managers responsible for this portfolio are remunerated on the overall return it generates.

As part of this policy, WN purchased $50,000 par value of loan notes at a 10% discount on their issue on 1 January 20X1. The redemption date for these loan notes is 31 December 20X4. An interest coupon of 3% of par value is paid annually on 31 December. Transaction costs of $450 were incurred on the purchase. The effective interest rate on the loan notes is 5.6%.

At 31 December 20X1, due to a decrease in market interest rates, the fair value of these loan notes increased to $51,000.

Required

For the year ended 31 December 20X1, what amount should WN recognise in profit or loss and other comprehensive income respectively in relation to the loan notes?

Solution

Amount to be recognised in profit or loss:

$ | 2,545 |

Amount to be recognised in other comprehensive income:

$ | 4,505 |

Working: Investment in loan notes

	$
Fair value on 1.1.20X1 ((50,000 × 90%) + 450)	45,450
Finance income 20X1 (to profit or loss) (45,450 × 5.6%)	2,545
Interest received (50,000 × 3%)	(1,500)
	46,495
Revaluation gain (to other comprehensive income) [bal. figure]	4,505
Fair value at 31.12.20X1	51,000

5.5 Treatment of gain or loss on derecognition

On derecognition of a financial asset in its entirety, the difference between:

(a)   the **carrying amount** (measured at the **date of derecognition**) and

(b)   the **consideration received**

is recognised **in profit or loss**. (IFRS 9: para. 3.2.12)

Applying this rule, in the case of **investments in equity instruments** not held for trading where the **irrevocable election has been made** to report changes in fair value in other comprehensive income, **all changes in fair value** up to the point of derecognition are **reported in other comprehensive income**.

Therefore, a gain or loss in **profit or loss** will only arise if the investments in equity instruments are **not sold at their fair value** and for any **transaction costs** on derecognition.

For **investments in debt** held at **fair value through other comprehensive income**, on derecognition, the **cumulative revaluation gain or loss** previously recognised in other comprehensive income is **reclassified** to profit or loss. (IFRS 9: para. 5.7.10)

Example: Measurement, derecognition and accounting entries

LF has a 31 December year end. On 1 July 20X0 LF purchased 12,000 shares in ABC through a broker for $1.25 a share. LF elected to measure this investment at fair value through other comprehensive income. The market price at 31 December 20X0 was $1.32 a share. On 30 September 20X1, LF sold the shares in ABC for their fair value of $17,000. The broker charges transaction costs of 1% purchase/sale price.

Required

What is the accounting entries to record the remeasurement and derecognition of this investment on 30 September 20X1?

Solution

Accounting entries:

Remeasurement:

DEBIT	Investment in equity instruments	$1,160	
CREDIT	Other comprehensive income		$1,160

Derecognition:

DEBIT	Cash (17,000 – (17,000 × 1%))	$16,830	
DEBIT	Profit or loss	$170	
CREDIT	Investment in equity instruments		$17,000

Working: Carrying amount of investment

	$
Fair value on 1.7.X0 ((12,000 × $1.25 = $15,000) + ($15,000 × 1%))	15,150
Fair value gain/(loss) [balancing figure]	(690)
Fair value at 31.12.X0 (12,000 × $1.32)	15,840
Fair value gain/(loss) [balancing figure]	1,160
Fair value at 30.09.X1	17,000

6 Impairment of financial assets (IFRS 9)

6.1 Scope

IFRS 9's impairment rules apply to:

- Investments in debt instruments measured at amortised cost (business model: objective – to collect contractual cash flows of principal and interest)

- Investments in debt instrumentsmeasured at fair value through other comprehensive income (OCI) (business model: objective – to collect contractual cash flows of principal and interest **and** to sell financial assets)

- Lease receivables within the scope of IFRS 16 *Leases*

- Contract assets within the scope of IFRS 15 *Revenue from Contracts with Customers*

(IFRS 9: paras. 5.5.1–5.5.2)

6.2 Approach

IFRS 9's approach uses an 'expected loss' model. Credit losses should be recognised in **three stages**:

	Stage 1	Stage 2	Stage 3
When?	Initial recognition (and subsequently if no significant deterioration in credit risk)	Credit risk increases significantly (rebuttable presumption if > 30 days past due)	Objective evidence of impairment exists at the reporting date
Credit losses recognised	12-month expected credit losses	Lifetime expected credit losses	Lifetime expected credit losses
Calculation of effective interest	On gross carrying amount	On gross carrying amount	On carrying amount net of allowance for credit losses after date evidence exists

(IFRS 9: para. 5.5.3 – 5.5.11)

6.3 Presentation

Type of asset	Treatment of credit loss
All investments in debt instruments except those measured at fair value through other comprehensive income	• Recognised in profit or loss • Credit losses held in a **separate allowance account offset against the carrying amount of the asset**: Financial asset X Allowance for credit losses (X) Carrying amount (net of allowance for credit losses) X
Investments in debt instruments measured at **fair value through other comprehensive income**	• **Portion** of the fall in fair value relating to **credit losses** recognised in **profit or loss** • **Remainder** recognised in **other comprehensive income** • **No allowance account** necessary because already carried at fair value (which is automatically reduced for any fall in value, including credit losses)

(IFRS 9: para. 5.5.2, 5.5.8)

6.4 Measurement

The measurement of expected credit losses should reflect:

(a) an unbiased and **probability-weighted amount** that is determined by evaluating a range of possible outcomes;

(b) the **time value of money**; and

(c) **reasonable and supportable information** that is available without undue cost and effort at the reporting date about past events, current conditions and forecasts of future economic conditions. (IFRS 9: para. 5.5.17)

Lifetime expected credit losses are the expected credit losses that result from **all possible default events** over the expected life of the financial instrument. (IFRS 9: Appendix A)

The **12-month expected credit losses** (recognised in Stage 1) are the **portion of lifetime expected credit losses** that result from **default** events on a financial instrument that are possible **within the 12 months** after the reporting date. (IFRS 9: Appendix A)

They are calculated by multiplying the probability of default in the next 12 months by the present value of the **lifetime** expected credit losses that would result from the default.

Example: Impairment of financial assets

AB has a portfolio of loan assets. Its business model is to collect the contractual cash flows of interest and principal. All loan assets have an effective interest rate of 7.5%. The portfolio was initially recognised on 1 January 20X1 at $840,000 with a separate allowance of $5,000 for 12-month expected credit losses (present value of lifetime expected credit losses of $100,000 × 5% chance of default within 12 months). No repayments are due in 20X1.

At 31 December 20X1, the credit quality of the loan assets was considered to have significantly deteriorated. The present value of lifetime expected credit losses was revised to $120,000.

The discount rate used to calculate the present value of lifetime expected credit losses is 6%.

AB's loan receivables and the related allowance for credit losses are shown below.

(a) Loan receivables (gross carrying amount)

	$
At 01.01.X1	840,000
Finance income (7.5% × 840,000)	63,000
Cash received	–
At 31.12.X5	903,000

(b) Allowance for credit losses

	$
At 01.01.X1 (Stage 1 12-month expected credit losses)	5,000
Finance cost (unwind discount) (6% × 5,000)	300
	5,300
Finance cost (increase in allowance)	114,700
At 31.12.X5 (Stage 2 lifetime expected credit losses)	120,000

Tutorial note. The total finance cost for the year is $115,000 ($300 + $114,700). If an exam question had asked you for the 'finance cost for the year' or the 'charge to profit or loss for the year', you could have taken a shortcut and calculated this figure as the carried forward allowance less the brought forward allowance ($120,000 – $5,000 = $115,000).

(c)   Net carrying amount at 31 December 20X1

	$
Loan receivables	903,000
Allowance for credit losses	(120,000)
Net carrying amount	783,000

Tutorial note. At 31 December 20X1, Stage 2 of IFRS 9's expected loss model has been reached because credit risk has increased significantly. Therefore, the allowance needs to be increased to the present value of the lifetime expected credit losses at that date. In the year ended 31 December 20X2, the effective interest on the loan assets will be calculated on their gross carrying amount of $903,000 but if there had been objective evidence of impairment (Stage 3), interest would have been calculated on the net carrying amount of $783,000.

6.5 Trade receivables, contract assets and lease receivables

A **simplified approach** is permitted for trade receivables, contract assets and lease receivables. For trade receivables or contract assets that **do not have an IFRS 15 financing element**, the loss allowance is measured at the **lifetime expected credit losses**, from initial recognition. (IFRS 9: para. 5.5.15)

For **other** trade receivables and contract assets and for lease receivables, the entity can **choose** (as a separate accounting policy for trade receivables, contract assets and for lease receivables) to apply the **three stage approach** or to recognise an allowance **for lifetime expected credit losses** from initial recognition. (IFRS 9: para. 5.5.15)

Chapter Summary

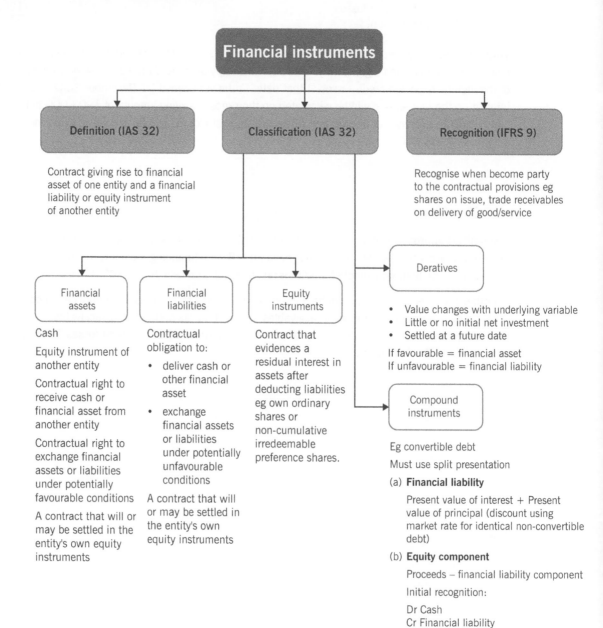

Financial instruments

Definition (IAS 32)

Contract giving rise to financial asset of one entity and a financial liability or equity instrument of another entity

Classification (IAS 32)

Recognition (IFRS 9)

Recognise when become party to the contractual provisions eg shares on issue, trade receivables on delivery of good/service

Financial assets

Cash

Equity instrument of another entity

Contractual right to receive cash or financial asset from another entity

Contractual right to exchange financial assets or liabilities under potentially favourable conditions

A contract that will or may be settled in the entity's own equity instruments

Financial liabilities

Contractual obligation to:
- deliver cash or other financial asset
- exchange financial assets or liabilities under potentially unfavourable conditions

A contract that will or may be settled in the entity's own equity instruments

Equity instruments

Contract that evidences a residual interest in assets after deducting liabilities eg own ordinary shares or non-cumulative irredeemable preference shares.

Deratives

- Value changes with underlying variable
- Little or no initial net investment
- Settled at a future date

If favourable = financial asset
If unfavourable = financial liability

Compound instruments

Eg convertible debt

Must use split presentation

(a) **Financial liability**

Present value of interest + Present value of principal (discount using market rate for identical non-convertible debt)

(b) **Equity component**

Proceeds – financial liability component

Initial recognition:

Dr Cash
Cr Financial liability
Cr Equity

The liability is then measured using amortised cost

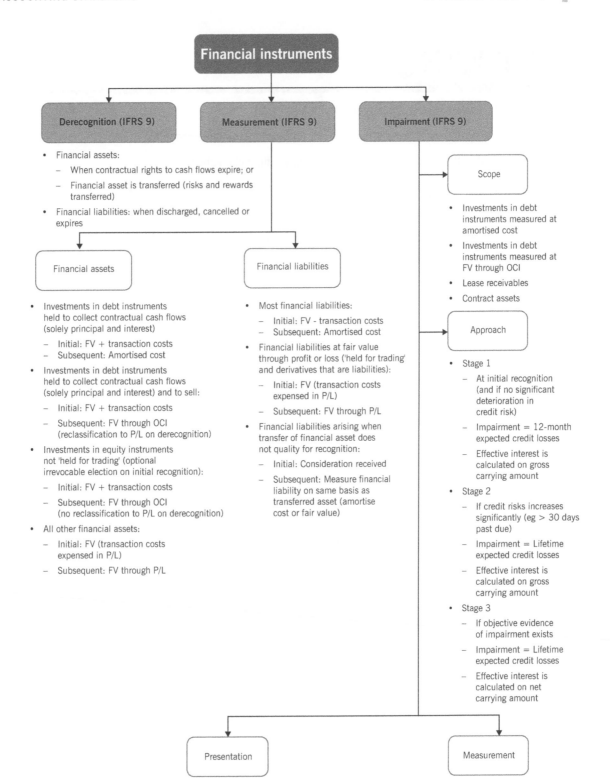

Quick Quiz

1   State two issues which are dealt with by IAS 32.

2   Give examples of items which are not financial instruments according to IAS 32.

3   What is the critical feature used to identify a financial liability?

4   How should compound instruments be presented in the statement of financial position?

5   When should a financial asset be derecognised?

6   How are financial instruments initially measured?

Answers to Quick Quiz

1   Classification and presentation of financial instruments

2   Physical assets, prepaid expenses, non-contractual assets or liabilities, contractual rights not involving transfer of financial assets

3   The contractual obligation to deliver cash or another financial asset to the holder

4   By calculating the present value of the liability component and then deducting this from the instrument as a whole to leave a residual value for the equity component

5   Financial assets should be derecognised when the rights to the cash flows from the asset expire or where substantially all the risks and rewards of ownership are transferred to another party.

6   At fair value plus transaction costs, except when they are designated as at fair value through profit or loss (in which case, at fair value).

Answers to Questions

3.1 Classification

The correct answer is:

Tick	Options
	Equity of $60,000 in the statement of financial position; dividends of $4,200 deducted from dividends in retained earnings and shown in the statement of changes in equity
	Financial liability of $60,000 within current liabilities in the statement of financial position; dividends of $4,200 deducted from dividends in retained earnings and shown in the statement of changes in equity
✓	Financial liability of $60,000 within non-current liabilities in the statement of financial position; finance cost of $4,200 in the statement of profit or loss and other comprehensive income
	Equity of $60,000 in the statement of financial position; finance cost of $4,200 in the statement of profit or loss and other comprehensive income

The preference shares contain an obligation to repay the $60,000 capital and the annual $4,200 dividend. Therefore, they should be treated as a financial liability rather than equity. As they are redeemable 9 years after the year end, they should be classified as a non-current liability. The treatment of the dividends should be consistent with the statement of financial position classification. This is why the dividends are treated as a finance cost in profit or loss rather than an appropriation of profit in the statement of changes in equity.

3.2 Derecognition

The correct answer is:

Tick	Accounting entries			
	DEBIT	Cash	$80,000	
	CREDIT	Trade receivables		$80,000
✓	DEBIT	Cash	$80,000	
	CREDIT	Liability		$80,000
	DEBIT	Cash	$80,000	
	DEBIT	Bad debt expense	$20,000	
	CREDIT	Trade receivables		$100,000
	DEBIT	Cash	$80,000	
	DEBIT	Receivable (from XY)	$20,000	
	CREDIT	Trade receivables		$100,000

The trade receivables cannot be derecognised as AP has not transferred substantially all the risks and rewards of ownership to the factoring company, XY. AP has retained the non-payment risk as AP has to repay the factor for any debts not recovered after 120 days (known as 'recourse'). AP has also retained benefits because some of the $20,000 not advanced by the factor may be received in the future depending on how quickly the customers pay. This means that answers A and C are incorrect.

Instead the proceeds advanced by the factor are recorded as a liability. Both the liability and trade receivable would be derecognised when customers pay the factor, with any difference being expensed in profit or loss.

The final option is incorrect because a receivable in relation to the $20,000 not advanced by the factor cannot be recognised as, at the year-end date of 31 December 20X1, it is not yet clear whether the customers will pay sufficiently quickly for AP to receive an extra payment. Also, a liability should only be recognised for the amount AP might have to repay the factor ie $80,000.

Now try these questions from the Practice Question Bank

Number	Level	Marks	Time
Q4	Introductory	N/A	11 mins
Q5	Introductory	10	18 mins
Q6	Introductory	5	9 mins

LEASES

Many organisations choose leasing as a source of finance. You need to know how to account for leases from the perspective of both the lessee and the lessor.

An entity may also choose to sell an asset then lease it back as a means of raising finance. You need to know the basics of how to account for this sale and leaseback.

Topic list	learning outcomes	syllabus references
1 Lease contracts	B1	B1(c)
2 Lessee accounting	B1	B1(d)
3 Lessor accounting	B1	B1(d)
4 Sale and leaseback transactions	B1	B1(d)

Chapter Overview

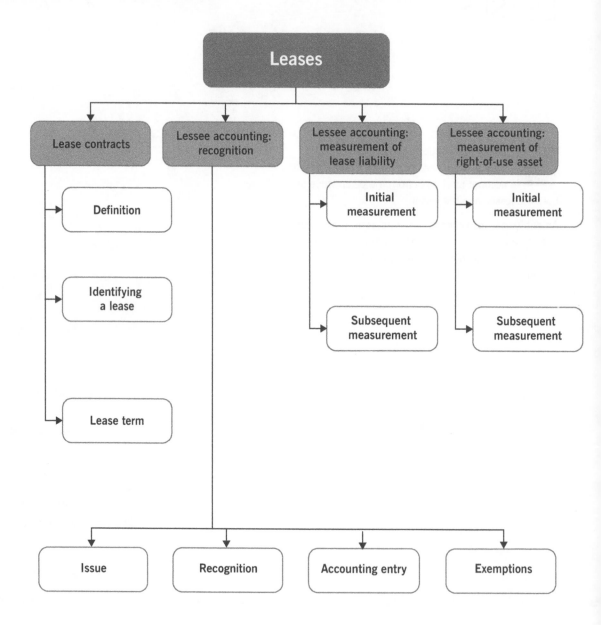

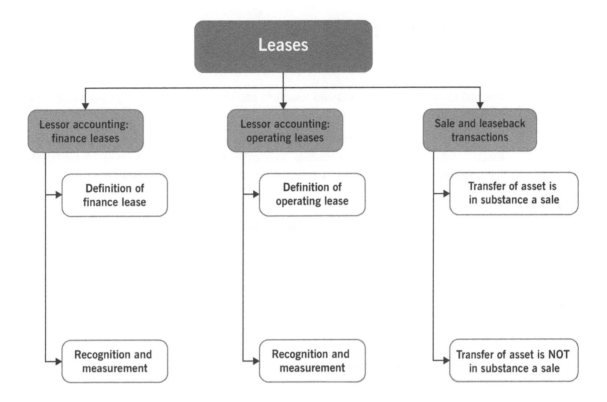

1 Lease contracts

1.1 Issue

IFRS 16 *Leases* requires lessees and lessors to provide relevant information in a manner that faithfully represents those transactions.

The accounting treatment in the lessee's books is driven by the *Conceptual Framework's* definitions of assets and liabilities rather than the legal form of the lease. The legal form of a lease is that the title to the underlying asset remains with the lessor during the period of the lease.

KEY TERMS

LEASE

'A **contract**, or part of a contract, that conveys the **right to use** an asset (the underlying asset) for a period of time **in exchange for consideration**.' (IFRS 16: Appendix A)

LESSEE

'An entity that **obtains the right to use** an underlying asset for a period of time in exchange for consideration'

LESSOR

'An entity that **provides the right to use** an underlying asset for a period of time in exchange for consideration'

(IFRS 16: Appendix A)

A lease arises where the lessee obtains the right to use the **asset**. Where it is the lessor that controls the asset used, a service rather than a lease arises.

1.2 Identifying a lease

An entity must identify whether a contract contains a lease, which is the case if the contract conveys the **right to control** the use of an **identified asset** for a **period of time in** exchange for consideration.

Right to control	Identified asset	Period of time

Present if an entity has the right to:

- Obtain substantially all economic benefits from the use of the asset, within the parameters of the lease; and
- Direct the use of the asset.

- Must be explicitly or implicitly specified in the contract.
- May be a portion of an asset (eg a floor of an office block) if physically distinct.
- Customer does not have right to use an identified asset if supplier has substantive rights to substitute the asset throughout the period of use.

- May be described in terms of use of the underlying asset eg the number of units produced by a leased machine.
- Lease may only be for a portion of the term of the contract (if the right to control an asset exists for only part of the term).

(IFRS 16: para. 9, 10, B9, B13, B14, B20)

Where a contract contains **multiple components**, the consideration is allocated to each lease and non-lease component based on the relative stand-alone prices of each component (the price the lessor or similar supplier would change for the component, or a similar component, separately). (IFRS 16: para.13, 14)

1.3 Lease term

The lease term is 'the **non-cancellable period** for which a lessee has the **right to use** an underlying **asset**, together with both:

(a)   periods covered by an **option to extend** the lease if the lessee is **reasonably certain to exercise** that option; and

(b)   periods covered by an **option to terminate** the lease if the lessee is **reasonably certain not to exercise** the option.'   (IFRS 16: Appendix A)

Example: Lease term

A lease contract is for 5 years with lease payments of $10,000 per annum. The lease contract contains a clause which allows the lessee to extend the lease for a further period of 3 years for a lease payment of $5 per annum (as it is unlikely that the lessor would be able to lease the asset to another party). The economic life of the asset is approximately 8 years.

Required

What is the lease term for this contract?

Solution

The lease term for this contract is 8 years.

Although 5 years is the non-cancellable period for which the lessee has the right to use the underlying asset, the period covered by an option to extend the lease should also be included if the lessee is reasonably certain to exercise that option. Here, two factors indicate that the lessee is likely to exercise the option to extend the lease:

*   At $5 per annum, the rental for the secondary period is substantially below market value ($10,000 per annum), making it an attractive proposition for the lessee; and

*   The underlying asset has an economic life of 8 years, so the lessee is likely to wish to retain use of the asset for another 3 years beyond the 5 year initial lease term.

Therefore, the total lease term here is 8 years – the initial non-cancellable 5 years plus a 3 year extension as the lessee is reasonably certain to exercise this option.

Question 4.1   Lease definition (based on IFRS 16 Illustrative Example 5)

FG enters into a contract with KL, a truck rental company, for the use of a specified truck for one week to transport cargo from City A to City B. KL does not have the right to substitute the truck for any other vehicle. The contract specifies a maximum distance that the truck can be driven. FG is able to choose the details of the journey (speed, route, rest stops, etc) within the parameters of the contract. FG does not have the right to continue using the truck after the specified trip is complete.

The cargo to be transported, and the timing and location of pick-up in City A and delivery in City B, are specified in the contract. FG is responsible for driving the truck from City A to City B.

Required

Does this contract contain a lease?

2   Lessee accounting

2.1 Issue

The **accounting treatment** in the **lessee's books** is driven by the *Conceptual Framework's* **definitions of assets and liabilities** rather than the legal form of the lease.

2.2 Recognition

At the commencement date (the date the lessor makes the underlying asset available for use by the lessee), the lessee recognises:

- A right-of-use asset (the ability to use the underlying asset for the lease term)
- A lease liability (the lessee's obligation to make lease payments to the lessor).

(IFRS 16: para. 22 and Appendix A)

The required accounting entry is:

Dr (↑) Right-of-use asset
Cr (↑) Lease liability

2.3 Initial measurement of lease liability

The lease liability is initially measured at the **present value of lease payments not paid at the commencement date** (IFRS 16: para. 26). This refers to **future lease payments** so should exclude any lease payments made on or before the commencement date (such as a non-refundable deposit or an instalment paid in advance).

The discount factor used in the calculation is the **interest rate implicit in the lease** (or the lessee's incremental borrowing rate if not readily determinable).

Lease payments include:

(a)   Fixed payments

(b)   Variable lease payments that depend on an index or a rate

(c)   Amounts expected to be payable by the lessee under residual value guarantees

(d)   Exercise price of a purchase option if the lessee is reasonably certain to exercise it

(e)   Payments of penalties for terminating the lease if the lease term reflects the option for termination being exercised. (IFRS 16: para. 27)

2.4 Subsequent measurement of lease liability

The lease liability is **subsequently measured** by (IFRS 16: para. 36):

- Increasing it by interest on the lease liability (calculated at a constant periodic rate on the remaining balance of the lease liability):

  Dr (↑) Finance costs
  Cr (↑) Lease liability

- Reducing it by lease payments (instalments) made:

  Dr (↓) Lease liability
  Cr (↓) Cash

The calculation of the lease liability depends on whether the instalments are paid in arrears or in advance (based on a lease commencing on 1 January 20X1):

		Payments in arrears $
1.1.X1	Present value of future lease payments	X
1.1.X1–31.12.X1	Finance cost (interest % × balance at 1.1.X1)	X
31.12.X1	Instalment 1 (in arrears)	(X)
31.12.X1	**Liability c/d**	X
1.1.X2–31.12.X2	Finance cost (interest % × balance at 1.1.X2)	X
31.12.X2	Instalment 2 (in arrears)	(X)
	Non-current liability	X

Current liability = Liability c/d at 31.12.X1 – Non-current liability

		Payments in advance $	
1.1.X1	Present value of future lease payments *	X	Can be analysed
1.1.X1–31.12.X1	Finance cost (interest % × balance at 1.1.X1)	Ⓧ	→ separately as
31.12.X1	**Liability c/d**	X	interest payable
1.1.X2	Instalment 2 (in advance)	(X)	as not paid at y/e,
	Non-current liability	X	but no IFRS 16 requirement to do so

Current liability = Liability c/d at 31.12.X1 – Non-current liability

* For payments in advance, as instalment 1 is paid at the lease commencement date, the initial lease liability will only include instalment 2 onwards (discounted to present value).

Example: Lease liability

PQ leases an asset on 1 January 20X1. The terms of the lease are to pay a non-refundable deposit of $575 on 1 January 20X1, followed by 7 annual instalments of $2,000 payable in arrears. The present value of the lease payments not paid on 1 January 20X1 is $10,000.

The interest rate implicit in the lease is 9.2%.

Required

(a) In relation to this lease, what is the finance cost in PQ's statement of profit or loss for the year ended 31 December 20X1? (Round your answer to the nearest $)

(b) In relation to the lease, what are the current and non-current liability balances included in PQ's statement of financial position as at 31 December 20X1? (Round your answer to the nearest $)

Solution

(a) Finance cost: $920

(b) Current liability: $1,179

Non-current liability: $7,741

Working: Lease liability

		$
1.1.X1	Present value of future lease payments	10,000
1.1.X1–31.12.X1	Finance cost (9.2% × 10,000)	920
31.12.X1	Instalment 1 (in arrears)	(2,000)
31.12.X1	**Liability c/d**	8,920
1.1.X2–31.12.X2	Finance cost (9.2% × 8,920)	821
31.12.X2	Instalment 2 (in arrears)	(2,000)
	Non-current liability	7,741

Current liability = Liability c/d $8,920 – Non-current liability $7,741 = $1,179

Note. The present value of lease payments of $10,000 given in the question comprises the present value of the *future* lease payments not paid at the commencement date, so automatically excludes the $575 deposit. This is correct figure to use to measure the initial lease liability under IFRS 16. However, the $575 deposit would be included in the amount capitalised as a right-of-use asset, but this is not asked for here.

2.5 Initial measurement of right-of-use asset

The right-of-use asset is initially measured at cost (IFRS 16: para. 23, 24):

	$
Initial measurement of lease liability (present value of future lease payments)	X
Lease payments made at/before commencement date	X
Initial direct costs incurred by lessee	X
Estimated dismantling and restoration costs (where an obligation exists) *	X
Lease incentives received	(X)
Cost of right-of-use asset	**X**

* Likely to be discounted to present value as IAS 37 *Provisions, Contingent Assets and Contingent Liabilities* requires discounting of provisions where the effect of the time value of money is material.

2.6 Subsequent measurement of right-of-use asset

Subsequently, the right-of-use asset is normally measured using the **cost model** of IAS 16 *Property, Plant and Equipment*, unless it is an investment property or the revaluation model applies. (IFRS 16: para. 29, 34, 35)

The right-of-use asset is **depreciated** from the commencement date to the **earlier of** the **end of its useful life** and the **end of the lease term** (end of its useful life if ownership is expected to be transferred) (IFRS 16: para. 31, 32):

Dr (↑) Depreciation expense
Cr (↑) Accumulated depreciation (offset against the cost of right-of-use asset)

Example: Right-of-use asset and lease liability

ZX prepares its accounts to 31 December each year. It enters into a lease (as lessee) to lease an item of equipment with the following terms:

Commencement date	1 January 20X1
Lease term	6 years
Annual lease payments (commencing 1 January 20X1)	$600,000
Interest rate implicit in the lease	7%
Present value of future lease payments	$2,460,000

On 1 January 20X1, ZX paid $50,000 of direct costs in setting up the lease. The useful life of the asset to ZX is five years and there is no residual value.

Required

(a)   What is the accounting entry to initially record the lease and associated costs in ZX's accounting records at 1 January 20X1?

(b)   What is the value of the right-of-use asset in ZX's statement of financial position as at 31 December 20X2? (Round your answer to the nearest $)

(c)   What are the current and non-current liability balances in ZX's statement of financial position as at 31 December 20X2? (Round your answer to the nearest $)

Solution

(a)

DEBIT	Right-of-use asset	$3,110,000	
CREDIT	Lease liability		$2,460,000
CREDIT	Cash		$650,000

The right-of-use asset is calculated as the initial measurement of the lease liability (the present value of future lease payments of $2,460,000) plus the lease payments made at/before the commencement date (the first instalment of $600,000 paid on 1 January 20X1) plus initial direct costs incurred by the lessee of $50,000. This amounts to $3,110,000 as shown in (W1).

The initial measurement of the lease liability is the present value of future lease payments of $2,460,000.

The remaining credit is to cash of $650,000, comprising the instalment paid on 1 January 20X1 of $600,000 and the direct costs incurred by the lessee on the same date of $50,000.

(b)   Right-of-use asset: $2,488,000   (W1)

(c)   Current liability: $600,000   (W2)

Non-current liability: $2,032,200   (W2)

Workings

1   *Right-of-use asset*

	$
Initial measurement of lease liability	2,460,000
Lease payments made at/before commencement date	600,000
Initial direct costs incurred by lessee	50,000
Cost of right-of-use asset	**3,110,000**
Less: Accumulated depreciation (3,110,000 / 5 years*)	**(622,000)**
Carrying amount of right-of use asset	**2,488,000**

* Depreciate asset from the commencement date of the lease to the earlier of the end of its useful life (5 years) and the end of the lease term (6 years)

2   *Lease liability*

		$
1.1.X1	Present value of future lease payments	2,460,000
1.1.X1–31.12.X1	Finance cost (7% × 2,460,000)	172,200
31.12.X1	Liability c/d	2,632,200
1.1.X1	Instalment 2 (in advance)	(600,000)
		2,032,200
1.1.X2–31.12.X2	Finance cost (7% × 2,032,200)	142,254
31.12.X2	**Liability c/d**	**2,174,454**
1.1.X3	Instalment 3 (in advance)	(600,000)
	Non-current liability	**1,574,454**

Current liability = Liability c/d $2,174,454 – Non-current liability $1,574,454 = $600,000

Note. The first lease instalment is not shown in the above table as the instalments are in advance. This means that the first instalment was paid at the commencement date and therefore, is excluded from the initial lease liability which is calculated as the present value of *future* lease payments under IFRS 16.

2.7 Optional recognition exemptions

IFRS 16 provides an optional exemption from the full requirements of the standard for (IFRS 16: para. 5):

- **Short-term leases** (leases with a lease term of 12 months or less) (IFRS 16: Appendix A)

- Leases for which the **underlying asset is low value** (e.g. tablet and personal computers, small items of office furniture and telephones). (IFRS 16: para. B8)

If the entity elects to take the exemption, lease payments are **recognised as an expense** on a **straight-line basis over the lease term** or another systematic basis (if more representative of the pattern of the lessee's benefits) (IFRS 16: para. 6).

Question 4.2	Recognition exemptions

SC is preparing its financial statements for the year ended 30 June 20X6. On 1 May 20X6, SC made an upfront payment in full of $32,000 for an 8-month lease of a machine.

SC wishes to take advantage of IFRS 16's recognition exemption for short-term leases.

Required

What amount would be charged to SC's statement of profit or loss for the year ended 30 June 20X6 in respect of this transaction?

A $0
B $8,000
C $16,000
D $32,000

3   Lessor accounting

3.1 Overview

The approach to lessor accounting classifies leases into two types:

- **Finance leases** (where a lease receivable is recognised as an asset in the statement of financial positon), and

- **Operating leases** (which are accounted for as rental income in the statement of profit or loss).

3.2 Classification of leases for lessor accounting

KEY TERMS

FINANCE LEASE

A *lease* that **transfers substantially all the risks and rewards** incidental to ownership of an underlying asset.

OPERATING LEASE

A *lease* that **does not transfer** substantially all the risks and rewards incidental to ownership of an underlying asset.

(IFRS 16: Appendix A)

IFRS 16 identifies five examples of situations which *would normally* lead to a lease being classified as a finance lease (IFRS 16: para. 63):

(a)   **S** – underlying asset is of such **specialised** nature that only the lessee can use it without major modifications

(b)   **T** – lease **transfers** ownership of the underlying asset to the lessee by the end of the lease term

(c)   **O** – lessee has the **option** to purchase the underlying asset at a price sufficiently lower than fair value at the exercise date, that it is reasonably certain at the inception date, that the option will be exercised

(d)   **M** – lease term is for **major** part of the underlying asset's economic life

(e)   **P** – **present** value of lease payments at the inception date amounts to at least substantially all of the fair value for the underlying asset

3.3 Finance leases

3.3.1 Recognition and measurement

At the commencement date (the date the lessor makes the underlying asset available for the use by the lessee), the lessor **derecognises the underlying asset** and **recognises**:

A receivable at amount equal to the **net investment in the lease** (IFRS 16: para. 67).

The **net investment in the lease** (IFRS 16: Appendix A) is the sum of:

Present value of lease payments receivable by the lessor	X
Present value of any unguaranteed residual value accruing to the lessor	X
	X

The *unguaranteed residual value* is that portion of the residual value of the underlying asset, the realisation of which by a lessor is not assured or is guaranteed solely by a party related to the lessor (IFRS 16: Appendix A).

Finance income is recognised over the lease term based on a pattern reflecting a constant periodic rate of return on the lessor's net investment in the lease (IFRS 16: para. 75).

The **derecognition** and **impairment** requirements of IFRS 9 *Financial Instruments* are applied to the net investment in the lease (IFRS 16: para. 77).

Example: Lessor accounting (finance lease)

AB Leasing arranges financing arrangements for its customers for bespoke equipment acquired from manufacturers. AB Leasing leased an item of equipment to a customer commencing on 1 January 20X5. The expected economic life of the asset is 8 years.

The terms of the lease were 8 annual payments of $4 million, commencing on 31 December 20X5. The lessee guarantees that the residual value of the assets at the end of the lease will be $2 million (although AB Leasing expects to be able to sell it for its parts for $3 million). The present value of the lease payments including the residual value guarantee (discounted at the interest rate implicit in the lease of 6.2%) was $25.9 million. This was equivalent to the purchase price.

Required

How should this lease be presented in the financial statements of AB Leasing for the year ended 31 December 20X5? (Round your answer to the nearest $'000)

Solution

Statement of profit or loss	Statement of financial position
Finance income of $1,644,000	Lease receivable of $24,162,000

The arrangement is a finance lease as the lessee uses the asset for all of its economic life and the present value of lease payments is substantially all of the fair value of the asset of $25.9 million.

As AB Leasing is the lessor, it should recognise a lease receivable at 1 January 20X5 comprising the present value of lease payments receivable plus the present value of any unguaranteed residual value. It should then recognise interest income on the lease receivable at the interest rate implicit in the lease of 6.2%. This interest is added to the lease receivable then the lease instalment received in arrears is deducted from the lease receivable to arrive at the year end balance.

Workings

1   *Lease receivable at 1 January 20X5*

	$'000
Present value of lease payments receivable	25,900
Present value of unguaranteed residual value (3m – 2m = 1m × $1/1.062^8$)	618
Lease receivable at 1 January 20X5	26,518

2   *Lease receivable at 31 December 20X5*

		$'000
1.1.X5	Receivable b/d	26,518
1.1.X5 – 31.12.X5	Finance cost (6.2% × 26,518)	1,644
31.12.X5	Instalment 1 (in arrears)	(4,000)
31.12.X5	Receivable c/d	24,162

3.4 Operating leases

3.4.1 Recognition and measurement

Lease payments from operating leases are recognised as **income** on **either a straight-line basis or another systematic basis** (if more representative of the pattern in which benefit from use of the underlying asset is diminished) (IFRS 16: para. 81).

Any initial direct costs incurred in obtaining the lease are added to the carrying amount of the underlying asset. IAS 16 *Property, Plant and Equipment* or IAS 38 *Intangible Assets* then applies to the depreciation or amortisation of the underlying asset as appropriate (IFRS 16: para. 83, 84).

Example: Lessor accounting (operating lease)

On 1 January 20X2, ND leased a property to a LF under an operating lease for 5 years at an annual rate of $100,000. However, the contract stated that the first 6 months are 'rent-free'. In the year ended 31 December 20X2, ND received the $50,000 instalment owed from LF.

Required

What accounting entry is required in ND's accounting records in respect of this lease in the year ended 31 December 20X2?

Solution

DEBIT	Accrued income	$40,000	
DEBIT	Cash	$50,000	
CREDIT	Lease rental income		$90,000

The benefit received from the asset is earned over the 5 years. However, in the first year (the year ended 31 December 20X2), the lessor only receives $100,000 × 6/12 = $50,000. Lease rentals of $450,000 ($50,000 + ($100,000 × 4 years)) are received over the 5 year lease term.

Therefore the lessor recognises income of $90,000 per year ($450,000 / 5 years).

Accrued income of $40,000 is recognised at the end of year 1 ($90,000 – $50,000 cash received).

4 Sale and leaseback transactions

4.1 Concept

A sale and leaseback transaction arises where an entity (the seller-lessee) transfers ('sells') an asset to another entity (the buyer-lessor) and then immediately leases it back.

Imagine Co A sells an asset to Co B then leases it back again:

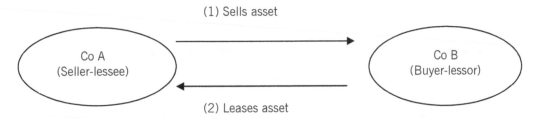

The entity applies the requirements of IFRS 15 *Revenue from Contracts with Customers* to **determine whether in substance a sale occurs** (ie whether a performance obligation is satisfied or not) (IFRS 16: para. 99) (see Chapter 8).

4.2 Transfer of the asset is in substance a sale

4.2.1 Seller-lessee

Note. For the purposes of the F2 exam, it is assumed that the sales proceeds will always be equivalent to the fair value of the asset.

As a sale has occurred, in the seller-lessee's books, the **carrying amount** of the asset must be **derecognised**.

The **seller-lessee** recognises a right-of-use asset measured at the **proportion of the previous carrying amount** that relates to the right of use **retained** (IFRS 16: para. 100). This is calculated as:

$$\text{Carrying amount} \times \frac{\text{Present value of lease payments}}{\text{Fair value of underlying asset}}$$

A **gain/loss** is recognised in the seller-lessee's financial statements in relation to the **rights transferred** to the buyer-lessor (IFRS 16: para. 100). Calculate in three stages:

Stage 1   Calculate the total gain/loss:

	$
Fair value of the asset (= sales proceeds in F2 exam)	X
Less: Carrying amount of the asset	(X)
Total gain/(loss)	X/(X)

Stage 2   Calculate gain/loss that relates to rights retained:

$$\text{Total gain/loss (from Stage 1)} \times \frac{\text{Present value of lease payments}}{\text{Fair value of underlying asset}}$$

Stage 3   Gain/loss relating to rights transferred is calculated as:

	$
Total gain/loss (from Stage 1)	X
Less: Gain/loss related to rights retained (Stage 2)	(X)
Gain/loss relating to rights transferred	X

4.2.2 Buyer-lessor

The **buyer-lessor** accounts for the purchase as a **normal purchase**:

DEBIT   Property, plant and equipment
CREDIT   Cash

The **lease** is then accounted for in accordance in accordance with the **lessor accounting** requirements of **IFRS 16** (IFRS 16: para 100).

Example: Sale and leaseback

On 1 January 20X6, UV sold its head office building to ET for $3 million and immediately leased it back on a 10-year lease. On that date, the carrying amount of the building was $2.6 million and its fair value was $3 million. The present value of the lease payments was calculated as $2.1 million. The remaining economic life of the building at 1 January 20X6 was 15 years. The transaction constituted a sale in accordance with IFRS 15.

Required

(a)   A right-of-use asset must be recognised in respect of the leased building. At what value should this right-of-use asset be recognised on 1 January 20X6 in the financial statements of UV?

(b)   What is the gain on the sale that should be recognised on 1 January 20X6 in the financial statements of UV?

Solution

(a)   Right-of-use asset = $1,820,000

$$\text{Carrying amount} \times \frac{\text{Present value of lease payments}}{\text{Fair value of underlying asset}}$$

= $2.6m × $2.1m/$3m = $1,820,000

(b)   Gain on sale = $400,000

Stage 1   Calculate the total gain/loss:

	$
Fair value of the asset (= sales proceeds)	3,000,000
Less: Carrying amount of the asset	(2,600,000)
Total gain/(loss)	400,000

Stage 2   Calculate gain/loss that relates to rights retained:

$$\text{Total gain/loss (from Stage 1)} \times \frac{\text{Present value of lease payments}}{\text{Fair value of underlying asset}}$$

= $400,000 × $2,100,000/$3,000,000 = $280,000

Stage 3   Gain/loss relating to rights transferred is calculated as:

	$
Total gain/loss (from Stage 1)	400,000
Less: Gain/loss related to rights retained (Stage 2)	(280,000)
Gain/loss relating to rights transferred	120,000

4.3 Transfer of the asset is NOT in substance a sale

4.3.1 Seller-lessee

The **seller-lessee continues to recognise the transferred asset** and recognises a financial liability equal to the transfer proceeds (and accounts for it in accordance with IFRS 9 *Financial Instruments*)
(IFRS 16: para. 103).

4.3.2 Buyer-lessor

The **buyer-lessor** does not recognise the transferred asset and **recognises a financial asset** equal to the transfer proceeds (and accounts for it in accordance with IFRS 9) (IFRS 16: para. 103).

Chapter Summary

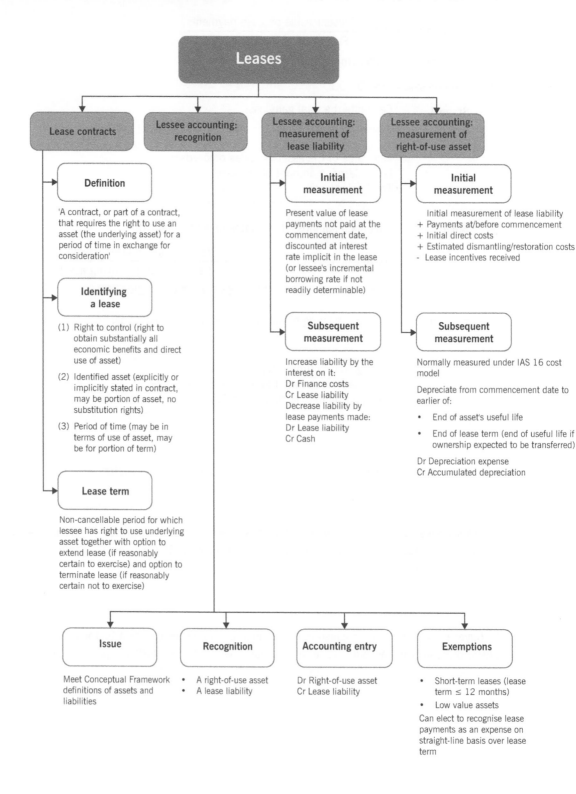

Leases

Lease contracts

Lessee accounting: recognition

Lessee accounting: measurement of lease liability

Lessee accounting: measurement of right-of-use asset

Definition

'A contract, or part of a contract, that requires the right to use an asset (the underlying asset) for a period of time in exchange for consideration'

Identifying a lease

(1) Right to control (right to obtain substantially all economic benefits and direct use of asset)

(2) Identified asset (explicitly or implicitly stated in contract, may be portion of asset, no substitution rights)

(3) Period of time (may be in terms of use of asset, may be for portion of term)

Lease term

Non-cancellable period for which lessee has right to use underlying asset together with option to extend lease (if reasonably certain to exercise) and option to terminate lease (if reasonably certain not to exercise)

Initial measurement

Present value of lease payments not paid at the commencement date, discounted at interest rate implicit in the lease (or lessee's incremental borrowing rate if not readily determinable)

Subsequent measurement

Increase liability by the interest on it:
Dr Finance costs
Cr Lease liability
Decrease liability by lease payments made:
Dr Lease liability
Cr Cash

Initial measurement

Initial measurement of lease liability
+ Payments at/before commencement
+ Initial direct costs
+ Estimated dismantling/restoration costs
- Lease incentives received

Subsequent measurement

Normally measured under IAS 16 cost model

Depreciate from commencement date to earlier of:

- End of asset's useful life

- End of lease term (end of useful life if ownership expected to be transferred)

Dr Depreciation expense
Cr Accumulated depreciation

Issue

Meet Conceptual Framework definitions of assets and liabilities

Recognition

- A right-of-use asset
- A lease liability

Accounting entry

Dr Right-of-use asset
Cr Lease liability

Exemptions

- Short-term leases (lease term ≤ 12 months)
- Low value assets

Can elect to recognise lease payments as an expense on straight-line basis over lease term

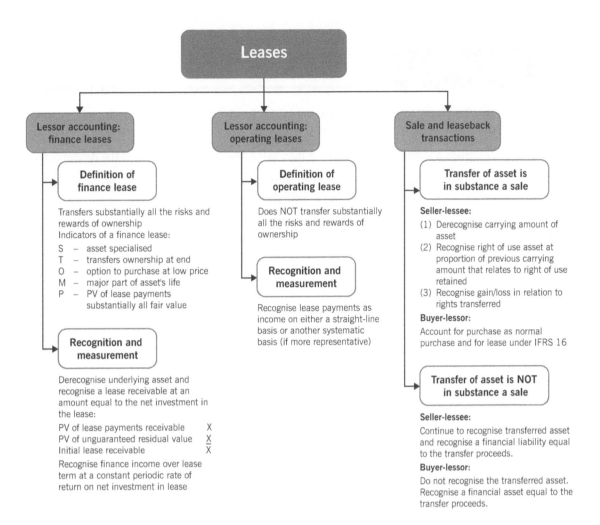

Quick Quiz

1   A contract is, or contains, a lease if the contract conveys the right to _____ an identified asset for a period of time in exchange for _____. *Complete the blanks.*

2   A business acquires an asset under a high-value, five-year lease. What is the double entry?

3   A lorry has an expected useful life of six years. It is acquired under a four year lease with no purchase options. Over which period should it be depreciated?

4   A company leases a tablet computer. How should this lease be treated in its financial statements?

Answers to Quick Quiz

1   A contract is, or contains, a lease if the contract conveys the right to **control the use of** an identified asset for a period of time in exchange for **consideration** (IFRS 16: para. 9).

2   DEBIT   Right-of-use asset account

        CREDIT   Lease liability

3   The four-year term, being the shorter of the lease term and the useful life.

4   This is a low-value lease, so the company should recognise the lease rentals as an expense over the lease term.

Answers to Questions

4.1   Lease definition (based on IFRS 16 Illustrative Example 5)

This contract contains a lease as the relevant IFRS 16 criteria are met:

IFRS 16 criteria	
Right to control	Right to obtain substantially all the economic benefits from the asset during the period of use?
	FG has exclusive use of the truck throughout the period of use (one week). Therefore, FG has the right to obtain substantially all of the economic benefits from the truck through the period of use.
	Right to direct the use of the asset?
	FG has the right to direct the use of the truck because it has the right to operate the truck by driving it and determining details such as the speed, route and rest stops throughout the period of use (one week). How and for what purpose the track will be used for (the transportation of cargo from City A to City B within a specified timeframe) is predetermined in the contract.
Identified asset	*The identified asset is the truck. This is explicitly stated in the contract.*
	KL (the supplier) does not have the right to substitute the truck for a different vehicle, implying that FG (the customer) does have the right to use the identified asset.
Period of time	*This is specified as one week under the contract.*

4.2   Recognition exemptions

The correct answer is: B

The lease is a short term lease (as it has a lease term of 12 months or less) so the IFRS 16 recognition exemption applies. The lease payments should be charged to profit or loss on the straight-line basis. Therefore, the charge for the year ended 30 June 20X6 is $32,000 \times 2/8 = \$8,000$.

Now try these questions from the Exam Question Bank

Number	Level	Marks	Time
Q7	Preparation	10	20 mins

PROVISIONS, CONTINGENT LIABILITIES AND CONTINGENT ASSETS

 A provision is a liability of uncertain timing or amount. Before an organisation can include a provision in the financial statements it must meet certain criteria.

You need to understand the rules for provisions, contingent liabilities and contingent assets and be able to explain and produce the correct accounting entries.

5

Topic list	learning outcomes	syllabus references
1 Provisions	B1	B1(c)(d)
2 Application of the recognition and measurement rules	B1	B1(c)(d)
3 Contingent liabilities	B1	B1(c)(d)
4 Contingent assets	B1	B1(c)(d)

Chapter Overview

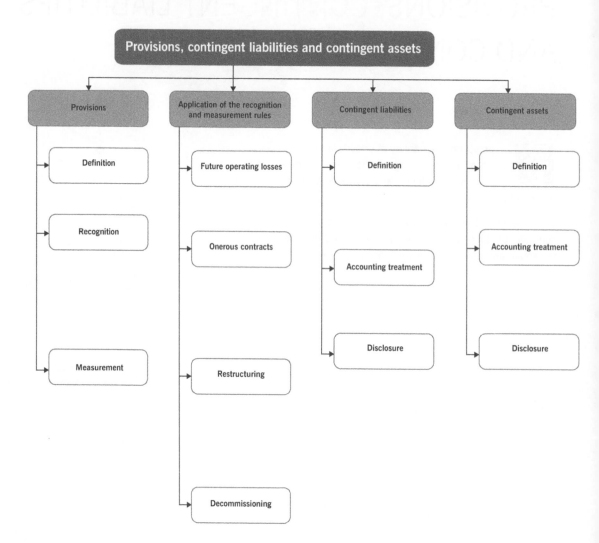

1 Provisions

KEY TERM

A PROVISION is a liability of uncertain timing or amount. (IAS 37: para. 10)

1.1 Recognition

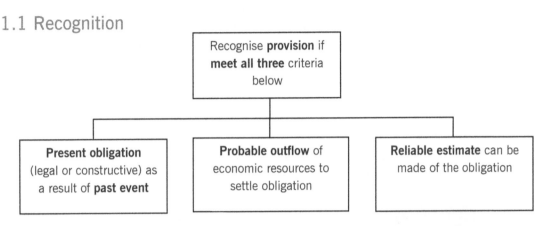

(IAS 37: para. 14)

Provisions should be reviewed each year and adjusted to reflect the current best estimate:

	$
Provision b/d	X
Movement (to P/L)	X/(X)
Provision c/d	X

The accounting entry for an **increase in provision** (and initial recognition of a provision) is:

Dr (↑) Expense (SPL)
Cr (↑) Provision (SOFP)

The accounting entry for a **decrease in provision** is:

Dr (↓) Provision (SOFP)
Cr (↓) Expense (SPL)

1.1.1 Present obligations and obligating events

A past event which leads to a present obligation is called an **obligating event**. To be obligating, there must be **no realistic alternative** to settling the obligation. (IAS 37: para. 17)

In rare cases if it is not clear whether there is a present obligation, a past event is deemed to give rise to a present obligation if it is **more likely than not** that a present obligation exists at the statement of financial position date. (IAS 37: para. 15)

1.1.2 Legal and constructive obligations

An obligation can either be **legal** or **constructive**.

(a)   A **legal obligation** is one that derives from a **contract**, **legislation** or any other operation of law.

(b)   A **constructive obligation** is an obligation that derives from the actions of an entity where:

     (i)   By an established pattern of **past practice**, **published policies** or a specific statement the entity has indicated to other parties that it will accept certain responsibilities; and

     (ii)   As a result the entity has created a **valid expectation** in other parties that it will discharge those responsibilities. (IAS 37: para. 10)

Example: Provision criteria

On 28 December 20X1 Gunge Co has been fined $10,000 for causing unlawful environmental damage. A new law is also highly likely to be passed which will make companies like Gunge responsible for cleaning up any damage they have caused and would make it necessary for Gunge to alter its machines in order to be permitted to carry on using them lawfully. The expected cost of the clean-up is $1,000,000 and of the machines $50,000.

Required

At the year ended 31 December 20X1 how would you account for the:

(a)   Fine
(b)   Costs of rectifying the damage
(c)   Cost of modifying machines?

Solution

(a)   The $10,000 fine will be an expense in the statement of profit or loss and an accrual in the statement of financial position. There is no uncertainty.

(b)   The obligating event is the environmental damage caused. Since it is more likely than not that there will be an outflow of economic resources in respect of this past event, a provision should be recognised in the statement of financial position and an expense in the statement of profit or loss for the expected amount of the clean-up.

(c)   These costs will have no effect in the accounts because there is no obligating event – the obligation would only arise if there was no commercial alternative to the alteration of the machines. It could be avoided by ceasing to operate the machinery altogether.

1.2 Measurement

The amount recognised as a provision is the **best estimate** of the expenditure required to settle the obligation at the end of the reporting period. (IAS 37: para. 36)

Provisions are **discounted** where the effect of the time value of money is material. (IAS 37: para. 45)

1.2.1 Uncertainties

Where the provision involves a large population of items:

•   Use expected values, taking into account the probability of all expected outcomes

Where a single obligation is being measured:

•   The individual most likely outcome may be the best evidence of the liability

(IAS 38: para. 39–40)

Example: Calculation of provision

An entity sells goods with a one year warranty. The customer does not have the option to purchase the warranty separately. The warranty provides assurance that the product complies with agreed-upon specifications and will operate as promised one year from the date of purchase.

If all goods required minor repairs this would cost $1m whereas if all goods required major repairs the cost would be $6m.

The entity expects that 75% of the goods will have no faults, 20% will need minor repairs and 5% major repairs.

Required

What provision should be made for warranty claims?

Solution

The entity should use expected values to calculate the provision.

($1m × 20%) + ($6m × 5%) = $0.5m.

2 Application of the recognition and measurement rules

2.1 Future operating losses

Provisions are **not** recognised for future operating losses.

Future operating losses do not meet the definition of a liability or the *Conceptual Framework* recognition criteria. (IAS 37: para. 63–64)

2.2 Onerous contracts

IAS 37 *Provisions, contingent liabilities and contingent assets* defines an onerous contract as one in which the unavoidable **costs** of completing the contract **exceed the benefits** expected to be received under it. (IAS 37: para. 10)

If an entity has a contract that is onerous a provision must be made for the **least net cost** of exiting from the contract (IAS 37: para. 66, 68), which is:

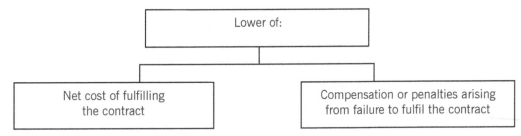

A lease can only be accounted for as an onerous contract if:

(a)   It becomes onerous before the lease commencement date; or

(b)   It has been accounted for under the IFRS 16 recognition exemptions and has become onerous. (IAS 37: para. 5)

Example: Onerous contract

On 1 January 20X2, JK leased an asset from PQ under a 12-month lease at a rental of $2,000 per month. Under the contract, if JK cancels the lease, it will have to pay PQ compensation of $600 for each month remaining on the lease. As this qualifies as a short-term lease, JK elected to account for the lease in accordance with the IFRS 16 recognition exemptions.

On 31 August 20X2, JK ceased the operations of the division that had been using the asset as it had become loss-making. JK did not have an alternative use for the leased asset and it became surplus to requirements. JK could sub-let the asset to another company for the remaining four months of the lease at a monthly rental of $1,200.

Required

What is the amount of the provision that should be recognised in relation to this contract?

Solution

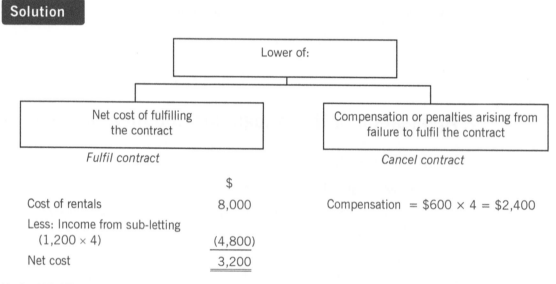

	$	
Cost of rentals	8,000	Compensation $= \$600 \times 4 = \$2,400$
Less: Income from sub-letting (1,200 × 4)	(4,800)	
Net cost	3,200	

Under IAS 37, when a contract is onerous, an entity must provide for the least net cost of exiting from the contract. This is defined as the lower of the net cost of fulfilling the contract ($3,200) and any compensation arising from failure to fulfil the contract ($2,400). Therefore, here, a provision is required for $2,400 with a corresponding expense in profit or loss.

2.2.1 Restructuring

A provision for restructuring costs is recognised only when the entity has a constructive obligation to restructure. Such an obligation only arises where an entity:

(a)   Has a **detailed formal plan** for the restructuring

(b)   Has raised a **valid expectation** in those affected that it will carry out the restructuring by starting to implement the plan or announcing its main features to those affected by it (IAS 37: para. 72)

A restructuring provision should include only direct expenditures arising from the restructuring and which are:

(a)   Necessarily entailed by the restructuring
(b)   Not associated with the ongoing activities of the entity (IAS 37: para. 80)

A restructuring provision does not include such costs as:

- Retraining or relocating continuing staff
- Marketing
- Investment in new systems and distribution networks (IAS 37: para. 81)

Question 5.1   Restructuring provision

On 12 December 20X1 the board of an entity decided to close down a division. The detailed plan was agreed by the board on 20 December 20X1, and letters sent to notify customers. By the year end of 31 December 20X1, the staff had received redundancy notices.

Required

Explain the appropriate accounting treatment for the closure for the year ended 31 December 20X1.

2.2.2 Decommissioning costs

Often in industries such as the oil and other extraction industries, entities are only granted licences to extract raw materials provided that they 'make good' any damage made during the extraction process.

An entity should provide for decommissioning costs from the date on which the **obligating event occurs**. These costs will be added onto the cost of the non-current asset:

Dr (↑) Property, plant and equipment (SOFP)
Cr (↑) Provision (SOFP)

(IAS 37: Illustrative Example 3)

Example: Decommissioning provision with discounting

A company built an oil rig at a cost of $80m. The oil rig came into operation on 1 January 20X2. The operating licence is for 20 years from 1 January 20X2, after which time the company is obliged to dismantle the oil rig and dispose of the parts in an environmentally friendly way. At 1 January 20X2, the cost of dismantling was estimated at $10m.

An appropriate discount rate is 6%. The present value of $1 receivable in 20 years' time at 6% is 0.312.

Required

(a)   What is the accounting entry to record the provision on 1 January 20X2?

(b)   What is the carrying amount of the oil rig at 31 December 20X2?

(c)   What is the carrying amount of the provision at 31 December 20X2?

(d)   Explain the treatment of any environmental damage arising through operating the oil rig (assuming the company is legally required to clean it up at the end of the rig's life).

Round your answer to the nearest $'000.

Solution

(a)   The provision should be discounted to its present value as the time value of money is material = $10m × 0.312 = $3,120,000. (IAS 37: para 45)

The entry would be:

DEBIT	Property, plant and equipment	$3,120,000	
CREDIT	Provision		$3,120,000

(b) Carrying amount of oil rig

	$'000
Cost	80,000
Provision ($10m × 0.312)	3,120
	83,120
Depreciation ($83.12m × 1/20)	(4,156)
Carrying amount at 31 December 20X2	78,964

(c) Provision for dismantling costs

	$'000
At 1 January 20X2	3,120
Interest ($3.12m × 6%)	187
At 31 December 20X2	3,307

(d) Treatment of environmental damage

The obligation to rectify damage caused by extraction of the oil only arises as the extraction progresses.

Therefore the provision is increased year on year for the discounted expected future costs related to rectifying the damage caused by extraction of the oil each year and the amount charged to profit or loss.

3 Contingent liabilities

KEY TERM

A CONTINGENT LIABILITY is either:

(a) A **possible obligation** arising from past events whose existence will be confirmed only by the occurrence of one or more uncertain future events not wholly within the control of the entity; or

(b) A **present obligation** that arises from past events but is not recognised because:

(i) It is **not probable** that an outflow of economic benefit will be required to settle the obligation; or

(ii) The amount of the obligation **cannot be measured** with sufficient **reliability**.

(IAS 37: para.10)

3.1 Accounting treatment

A contingent liability is **not** recognised in the financial statements as the *Conceptual Framework* definition of a liability has not been met. It is disclosed in a note to the financial statements unless the possibility of an outflow of economic benefits is remote. (IAS 37: para. 27–28)

Users of the financial statements need to be made aware of the **potential adverse impact on cash flows and profit** should the contingent liability require settlement.

3.2 Disclosure

For each class of contingent liability, an entity should disclose, at the statement of financial position date, all of the following.

(a)   The nature of the contingent liability
(b)   An estimate of its financial effect
(c)   An indication of the uncertainties relating to the amount or timing of any outflow
(d)   The possibility of any reimbursement (IAS 37: para. 86)

Question 5.2	Contingent liabilities

Your company sold eggs to Cuisine Co that it used in baking cakes. The cakes were then sold to the public. Unfortunately, five people are now in hospital suffering from food poisoning after eating the cakes and Cuisine Co believe that it is due to the eggs.

Cuisine Co is now suing your company and your solicitor advises you that there is a 35% chance that you will lose the case. If you do lose the case you will be liable to pay $100,000.

Required

(a)   What kind of obligation, if any, exists?
(b)   Does a contingent liability exist?

4   Contingent assets

KEY TERM

A CONTINGENT ASSET is a **possible asset** arising from past events whose existence will only be confirmed by the occurrence of one or more uncertain future events not wholly within the control of the entity. (IAS 37: para. 10)

4.1 Accounting treatment

An entity should not recognise a contingent asset because it could result in the recognition of profits that may never be realised. However, where the realisation of profit is **virtually certain**, then the related asset is not a contingent asset and **recognition** is appropriate. (IAS 37: para. 31, 33)

4.2 Disclosure

A contingent asset is **disclosed** where an inflow of economic benefits is **probable**. (IAS 37: para. 34)

The following should be disclosed:

(a)   A brief description of the nature of the contingent asset at the statement of financial position date
(b)   Where practicable, an estimate of the financial effect (IAS 37: para. 89)

Users of the financial statements need to be aware of the potential **positive impact on cash flows and profits** should the contingent asset become receivable.

Question 5.3

DE sells electronic goods with a warranty. Shortly before the year end, DE discovered a serious fault with its goods and had to recall all items sold for repair or replacement. However, DE believed the fault was due to a defective component purchased from its manufacturers, FG.

DE has instructed its lawyers to sue FG for compensation. The lawyers believe that there is a 60% chance of success.

Required

How should DE account for this compensation?

A   Record an asset in the statement of financial position
B   Disclose a contingent asset in the financial statements
C   Disclose a contingent liability in the financial statements
D   Do nothing

Chapter Summary

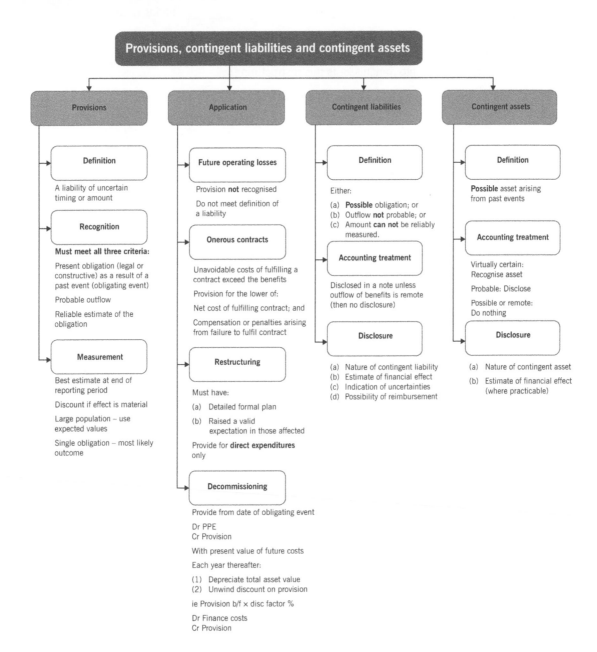

Provisions, contingent liabilities and contingent assets

Provisions

Definition

A liability of uncertain timing or amount

Recognition

Must meet all three criteria:

Present obligation (legal or constructive) as a result of a past event (obligating event)

Probable outflow

Reliable estimate of the obligation

Measurement

Best estimate at end of reporting period

Discount if effect is material

Large population – use expected values

Single obligation – most likely outcome

Application

Future operating losses

Provision **not** recognised

Do not meet definition of a liability

Onerous contracts

Unavoidable costs of fulfilling a contract exceed the benefits

Provision for the lower of:

Net cost of fulfilling contract; and

Compensation or penalties arising from failure to fulfil contract

Restructuring

Must have:

(a) Detailed formal plan

(b) Raised a valid expectation in those affected

Provide for **direct expenditures** only

Decommissioning

Provide from date of obligating event

Dr PPE
Cr Provision

With present value of future costs

Each year thereafter:

(1) Depreciate total asset value
(2) Unwind discount on provision

ie Provision b/f × disc factor %

Dr Finance costs
Cr Provision

Contingent liabilities

Definition

Either:

(a) **Possible** obligation; or
(b) Outflow **not** probable; or
(c) Amount **can not** be reliably measured.

Accounting treatment

Disclosed in a note unless outflow of benefits is remote (then no disclosure)

Disclosure

(a) Nature of contingent liability
(b) Estimate of financial effect
(c) Indication of uncertainties
(d) Possibility of reimbursement

Contingent assets

Definition

Possible asset arising from past events

Accounting treatment

Virtually certain: Recognise asset

Probable: Disclose

Possible or remote: Do nothing

Disclosure

(a) Nature of contingent asset
(b) Estimate of financial effect (where practicable)

Quick Quiz

1   A provision is a _____ of _____ timing or amount.
Complete the blanks.

2   A programme is undertaken by management which converts the previously wholly owned chain of restaurants they ran into franchises. Is this restructuring?

3   Define contingent asset and contingent liability.

Answers to Quick Quiz

1   Liability, uncertain

2   Yes. The manner in which the business is conducted has changed.

3   Contingent asset: A possible asset that arises from past events and whose existence will be confirmed by the occurrence of one or more uncertain future events not wholly within the entity's control.

Contingent liability:

- A **possible obligation** that arises from past events and whose existence will be confirmed only by the occurrence or non-occurrence of one or more uncertain future events not wholly within the entity's control, or

- A **present obligation** that arises from past events, but is not recognised because:

  - It is **not probable** that a transfer of economic benefits will be required to settle the obligation, or

  - The amount of the obligation **cannot be measured** with sufficient reliability

Answers to Questions

5.1 Restructuring provision

The communication of the decision to the customers and employees gives rise to a constructive obligation because it creates a valid expectation that the division will be closed. The outflow of resources embodying economic benefits is probable so, at 31 December 20X1, a provision should be recognised for the best estimate of the direct costs of closing the division.

5.2 Contingent liabilities

(a)   Possible legal obligation: the existence of the obligation will be decided by the outcome of the court case.

(b)   Yes, because there is a possible outflow of resources (35% chance of having to pay $100,000). The contingent liability will therefore be disclosed given that the possibility of outflow is not remote.

5.3 Contingent assets

The correct answer is:

B   Disclose a contingent asset in the financial statements because IAS 37 *Provisions, contingent liabilities and contingent assets* defines probable as more likely than not and therefore a 60% chance of success qualifies as probable. It is an asset rather than a liability as there is a probable inflow rather than outflow.

Now try these questions from the Practice Question Bank	Number	Level	Marks	Time
	Q8	Introductory	N/A	7mins

DEFERRED TAXATION

 Certain transactions and balances are treated differently for tax and accounting purposes. Where this difference is temporary an adjustment needs to be made in the financial statements for deferred taxation. This is to ensure that the tax expense shown in the financial statements is logically matched to accounting profit.

Topic list	learning outcomes	syllabus references
1 Concept	B1	B1(c)
2 Deferred tax liabilities	B1	B1(d)
3 Deferred tax assets	B1	B1(d)
4 Measurement	B1	B1(d)

Chapter Overview

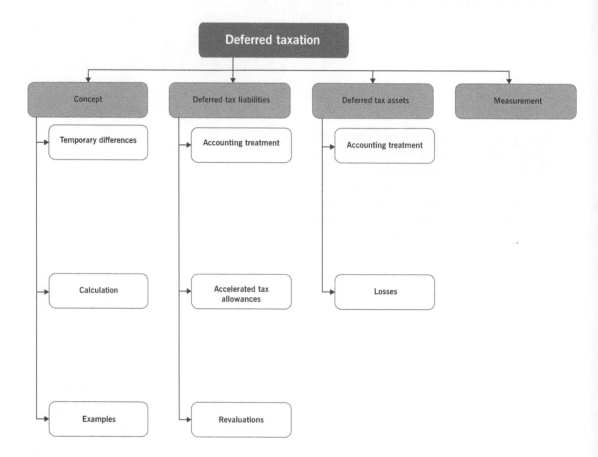

1   Concept

Deferred tax is not a tax which is paid, but rather an accounting adjustment. It deals with situations where the accounting treatment of a transaction is different from the tax treatment. Some differences are **permanent** (eg customer entertaining), while others are **temporary** differences because of timing.

Deferred tax is the tax attributable to **temporary differences**.

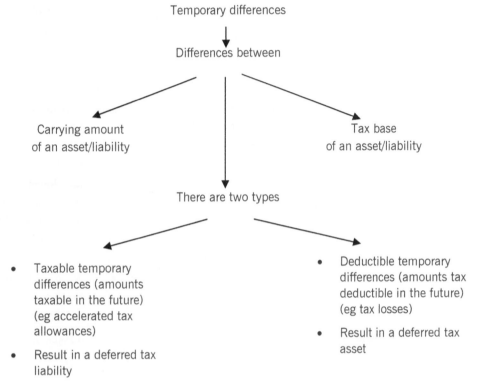

(IAS 12: para. 15, 24)

The temporary difference is calculated as follows (IAS 12: para. 5):

	$
Carrying amount of asset/(liability) [in accounting SOFP]	X/(X)
Less tax base [value for tax purposes]	(X)/X
Temporary difference	X/(X)
Deferred tax (liability)/asset [always opposite sign to temporary difference] (tax rate % × temporary difference)	(X)/X

Temporary differences:

Item	Carrying amount in the statement of financial position	Tax base in 'tax accounts'
Non-current asset	**Carrying amount** = Cost – accumulated depreciation	**Tax written down value** = Cost – Tax depreciation Temporary difference is cumulative tax depreciation less cumulative financial statement depreciation.

Item	Carrying amount in the statement of financial position	Tax base in 'tax accounts'
Accrued income	Included in financial statements on an accruals basis ie when **receivable**	If only included in tax accounts when **received, tax base will be nil** at reporting date. The temporary difference is equal to the accrued income in the financial statements.
		If included in tax accounts on an accruals basis, the tax base is also the accrued income and there is no temporary difference so no deferred tax adjustment.
Accrued expenses and provisions	Included in financial statements on an accruals basis ie when **payable**	If included in tax accounts when **paid, tax base is nil** at reporting date. The temporary difference is equal to the accrual or provision in the financial statements.
		If included in tax accounts on an accruals basis, the tax base is also the accrual or provision and there is no temporary difference so no deferred tax adjustment.
Income received in advance	When the cash is received, it will be in the financial statements as deferred income ie a liability	If included in tax accounts when cash received the income will already have been taxed so **tax base is nil**. The temporary difference is equal to the liability.
Trading losses	Reported 'profit' is negative	Taxable profit is nil. Temporary difference will equal cumulative losses.

1.1 Link to IASB's *Conceptual Framework*

Definition of asset and liability

As a result of a past transaction or event, the entity has an **obligation** to pay tax or **right** to future tax relief. Therefore, the *Conceptual Framework* definition of a liability or asset has been met and if no current tax charge or credit has been recorded, a deferred tax liability or asset should be recognised.

Accruals concept

To achieve matching in statement of profit or loss and other comprehensive income, the **tax should be recorded in the accounts in the same period as the item that the tax relates to is recorded**. If the tax arises in a different period than the item is recorded in the accounts, a deferred tax adjustment is required.

Question 6.1	Temporary differences

(a)   Interest receivable has a carrying amount of $300. The related interest revenue will be taxed on a cash basis.

(b)   A machine cost $400. For tax purposes, depreciation of $250 has already been deducted in current and prior periods and the remaining cost will be deductible in future periods, either as depreciation or through a deduction on disposal. Carrying amount is $240.

(c)   Current liabilities include accrued expenses with a carrying amount of $100. The related expense will be deducted for tax purposes on a cash basis.

(d)   Current liabilities include accrued expenses with a carrying amount of $100. The related expense has already been deducted for tax purposes.

(e)   Dividends receivable have a carrying amount of $200. The dividends are not taxable.

Required

Using the table below, for each of the above items, state: .

(i)   Is there a difference in the tax and accounting treatment?
(ii)   Is the difference temporary or permanent?
(iii)   The amount of the temporary difference and the tax on this (assume a tax rate of 25%)
(iv)   Whether this is a deferred tax asset or a tax liability

Work to the nearest $.

2   Deferred tax liabilities

2.1 Accounting treatment

Taxable temporary differences result in a **deferred tax liability**. (IAS 12: para. 15)

2.2 Accounting entries

To create or increase a deferred tax liability:

DEBIT   Deferred tax expense*

CREDIT   Deferred tax liability

To reverse or decrease a deferred tax liability:

DEBIT   Deferred tax liability

CREDIT   Deferred tax expense*

*This is reported in the statement of profit or loss and other comprehensive income in the same place as the income or expense it relates to. Normally this will be in profit or loss but for a revaluation of property, plant and equipment, it will be in other comprehensive income. (IAS 12: para. 61A)

2.3 Accelerated tax allowances

A taxable temporary difference arises where tax (or 'capital') allowances or tax depreciation rates are available at a rate higher than the accounting depreciation rates applied to the same assets.
(IAS 12: para. 17(b))

Example: Calculation of deferred tax

A company buys an item of equipment on 1 January 20X1 for $1,000,000. It has a useful life of 10 years and an estimated residual value of $100,000. The equipment is depreciated on a straight-line basis. For tax purposes, a tax expense can be claimed on a 20% reducing balance basis.

The rate of income tax can be taken as 30%.

Required

In respect of the above item of equipment, calculate the deferred tax charge/credit in the company's profit or loss for the year to 31 December 20X2 and the deferred tax balance in the statement of financial position at that date.

Solution

Movement in the deferred tax liability for the year ended 31 December 20X2

	$'000
Deferred tax liability b/d	33
∴Profit or loss charge	21
Deferred tax liability c/d	54

Workings

1   **Deferred tax liability**

	Carrying amount	Tax base	Temporary differences	Deferred tax liability @ 30%
20X1	$'000	$'000	$'000	$'000
Cost	1,000	1,000	–	–
Depreciation	(W2) (90)	(W3) (200)		
c/d	910	800	110	(33)
20X2				
b/d	910	800		
Depreciation	(90)	(W3) (160)		
c/d	820	640	180	(54)

2   *Depreciation*

$1,000,000 cost − $100,000 residual value / 10 years = $90,000 per annum.

3   *Tax depreciation/capital allowances*

20X1: $1,000,000 × 20% = $200,000
20X2: $800,000 Carrying amount b/d × 20% = $160,000

2.4 Revaluations of non-current assets

A taxable temporary difference occurs when an asset is revalued and no equivalent adjustment is made for tax purposes. The gain arising on the increase in the value of an asset will be taxable on the use or sale of the asset and therefore a **deferred tax liability** is recognised since the gain itself has been recognised. (IAS 12: para. 20)

IAS 12 *Income taxes* requires **deferred tax on revaluations** to be charged to **other comprehensive income** (because the gain is reported in other comprehensive income). This is simply an application of the accruals (matching concept).

Example: Deferred tax on revaluation gain

A company purchased some land on 1 January 20X7 for $400,000. On 31 December 20X8 the land was revalued to $500,000. In the tax regime in which the company operates, revaluations do not affect either the tax base of the asset or taxable profits.

The income tax rate is 30%.

Required

Prepare the accounting entry to record the deferred tax in relation to this revaluation for the year ended 31 December 20X8.

Solution

| DEBIT | Other comprehensive income (and revaluation surplus) | $30,000 | |
| CREDIT | Deferred tax liability | | $30,000 |

Working: Deferred tax

	$
Carrying amount of asset	500,000
Less Tax base	(400,000)
Temporary difference	100,000
Deferred tax (liability) (30% × 100,000)	(30,000)

3 Deferred tax assets

3.1 Accounting treatment

Deductible temporary differences result in a **deferred tax asset** on the statement of financial position. (IAS 12: para. 24)

3.2 Accounting entries

To record or increase a deferred tax asset:

| DEBIT | Deferred tax asset |
| CREDIT | Deferred tax expense* |

To reverse or decrease a deferred tax asset:

| DEBIT | Deferred tax expense* |
| CREDIT | Deferred tax asset |

*This is reported in the statement of profit or loss and other comprehensive income in the same place as the item it relates to. Normally this will be in profit or loss but for a revaluation of property, plant and equipment, it will be in other comprehensive income. (IAS 12: para. 61A)

3.3 Losses that can be carried forward

Losses that can be carried forward to reduce current tax on future profits represent a future tax saving. Therefore a **deferred tax asset** is recognised in respect of tax losses to the extent that it is probable that the losses can be used before they expire. (IAS 12: para. 34)

Example: Deferred tax on losses

BG incurs $80,000 of tax losses in the year ended 31 December 20X1 which it can carry forward for 2 accounting periods before they expire. The company expects to make a loss in 20X2 and to return to profitability in 20X3, expecting to make a profit of $50,000 in that year. The company pays tax at 20%.

Required

Calculate the amount of any deferred tax asset or liability and show the accounting entry BG should make to account for deferred tax on the tax losses for the year ended 31 December 20X1.

Solution

A deferred tax asset is recognised in 20X1 for the portion of the losses for which relief is likely to be granted: $50,000 × 20% = $10,000:

DEBIT	Deferred tax asset (SOFP)	$10,000	
CREDIT	Deferred tax (P/L)		$10,000

In 20X3 the deferred tax asset is reversed resulting in a charge to profit or loss when the profits that the tax losses are used against are earned.

4 Measurement

4.1 Measurement

Deferred tax assets and liabilities are measured at the tax rates expected to apply to the period when the asset is realised or liability settled, based on tax rates (and tax laws) that have been **enacted (or substantively enacted) by the end of the reporting period**. (IAS 37: para 47)

Changes in tax rates after the year end are therefore non-adjusting events after the reporting period.

An entity is likely to have a brought down deferred tax asset or liability from the previous year. Therefore, an **accounting entry** will only be required for the **movement in the deferred tax asset or liability** (rather than for the whole carried down balance):

	$
Deferred tax asset/liability b/d	X
Movement (to SPLOCI) [accounting entry]	X/(X)
Deferred tax asset/liability c/d	X

Example: Accounting entry

TF had a net deferred tax liability of $11,000 at 31 December 20X1. At 31 December 20X2, the following temporary differences exist:

- TF created a provision for warranties of $30,000 on 31 December 20X2 but tax relief will not be granted until the costs are incurred.

- TF purchased an item of equipment for $500,000 on 1 January 20X2. It has a useful life of 10 years. Tax depreciation is charged on a 20% reducing balance basis.

The income tax rate is 30%.

Required

Prepare the accounting entry to record the movement in the net deferred tax asset or liability for the year ended 31 December 20X2.

Solution

DEBIT	Deferred tax liability	$5,000	
CREDIT	Deferred tax expense (in P/L)		$5,000

Workings

1   *Movement in deferred tax liability*

	$
Deferred tax liability at 1 January 20X2	11,000
∴ Profit or loss charge/(credit)	(5,000)
Deferred tax liability at 31 December 20X2 (W2)	6,000

2   *Deferred tax liability at 31 December 20X2*

	Carrying amount $	Tax base $	Temporary difference $	Tax rate $	Deferred tax asset/(liability) $
Provision	(30,000)	–	(30,000)	× 30%	9,000
Equipment	500,000 × 9/10 = 450,000	500,000 × 80% = 400,000	50,000	× 30%	(15,000)
Net deferred tax liability					(6,000)

Chapter Summary

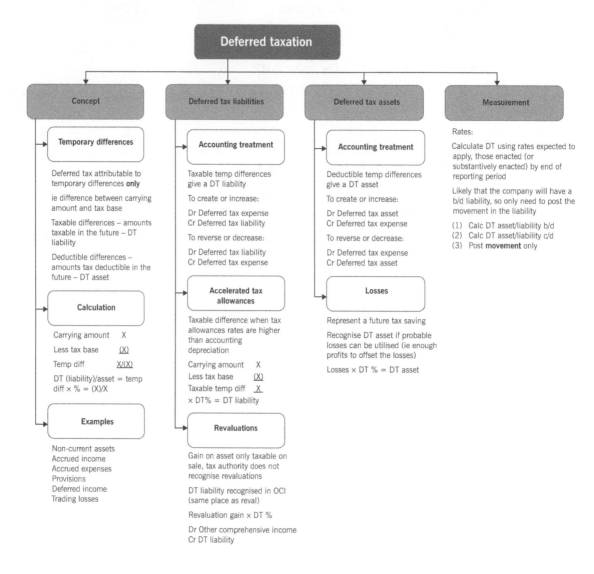

Deferred taxation

Concept

Temporary differences

Deferred tax attributable to temporary differences **only**

ie difference between carrying amount and tax base

Taxable differences – amounts taxable in the future – DT liability

Deductible differences – amounts tax deductible in the future – DT asset

Calculation

Carrying amount   X
Less tax base   (X)
Temp diff   X/(X)

DT (liability)/asset = temp diff × % = (X)/X

Examples

Non-current assets
Accrued income
Accrued expenses
Provisions
Deferred income
Trading losses

Deferred tax liabilities

Accounting treatment

Taxable temp differences give a DT liability

To create or increase:

Dr Deferred tax expense
Cr Deferred tax liability

To reverse or decrease:

Dr Deferred tax liability
Cr Deferred tax expense

Accelerated tax allowances

Taxable difference when tax allowances rates are higher than accounting depreciation

Carrying amount   X
Less tax base   (X)
Taxable temp diff   X

× DT% = DT liability

Revaluations

Gain on asset only taxable on sale, tax authority does not recognise revaluations

DT liability recognised in OCI (same place as reval)

Revaluation gain × DT %

Dr Other comprehensive income
Cr DT liability

Deferred tax assets

Accounting treatment

Deductible temp differences give a DT asset

To create or increase:

Dr Deferred tax asset
Cr Deferred tax expense

To reverse or decrease:

Dr Deferred tax expense
Cr Deferred tax asset

Losses

Represent a future tax saving

Recognise DT asset if probable losses can be utilised (ie enough profits to offset the losses)

Losses × DT % = DT asset

Measurement

Rates:

Calculate DT using rates expected to apply, those enacted (or substantively enacted) by end of reporting period

Likely that the company will have a b/d liability, so only need to post the movement in the liability

(1) Calc DT asset/liability b/d
(2) Calc DT asset/liability c/d
(3) Post **movement** only

Quick Quiz

1   The tax expense related to the profit from ordinary activities should be shown in the statement of profit or loss.

True ☐

False ☑ ✗

2   Deferred tax liabilities are the amounts of income taxes payable in future periods in respect of _____. *Complete the blanks.*

3   Give three examples of taxable temporary differences. ~~tax base~~ *deductible temp / taxable temp.*

4   Current tax is the amount of income tax payable in respect of the _____ _____ for a period. *Complete the blanks.*

5   Deductible temporary differences give rise to a:

Ⓐ   Deferred tax asset
B   Deferred tax liability

Answers to Quick Quiz

1   True

2   Taxable temporary differences

3   Examples are:

- Interest revenue
- Depreciation
- Development costs
- Prepayments
- Sale of goods revenue

4   Taxable profit

5   A

Answers to Questions

6.1 Temporary differences

	Is there a difference?	Temporary or permanent?	Carrying amount	Tax base	Difference	Tax at 25%	Asset or liability?
(a)	Yes	Temporary	$300	$0	$300	($75)	Liability
(b)	Yes	Temporary	$240	$150	$90	($23)	Liability
(c)	Yes	Temporary	($100)	$0	($100)	$25	Asset
(d)	No	N/A	($100)	($100)	–	–	N/A
(e)	Yes	Permanent	$200	$200*	–	–	N/A

*For permanent differences, make the tax base the same as the carrying amount so that the temporary difference comes to zero.

Now try these questions from the Practice Question Bank	Number	Level	Marks	Time
	Q9	Introductory	N/A	7 mins

SHARE-BASED PAYMENTS

In recent years there has been an increase in the use of share-based payments particularly with regard to employees. Accounting treatment has improved to ensure these payments are reflected correctly in the financial statements.

You need to be able to discuss and prepare the accounting entries for the main types of share-based payment.

Topic list	learning outcomes	syllabus references
1 Types of share-based payment	B1	B1(c)(d)
2 Recognition	B1	B1(c)(d)
3 Measurement	B1	B1(c)(d)
2 Deferred tax implications	B1	B1(d)

Chapter Overview

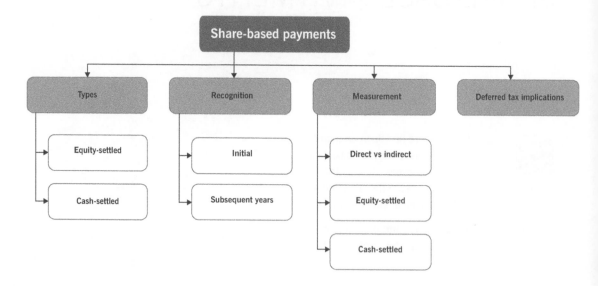

1 Types of share-based payment

Introduction

The use of share-based payment has increased in recent years. Until the issue of this standard there was no IFRS on this topic, other than disclosures formerly required for 'equity compensation benefits' under IAS 19 *Employee benefits*.

Improvements in accounting treatment were called for. In particular, the omission of expenses arising from share-based payment transactions with employees was believed to cause economic distortions and corporate governance concerns.

1.1 Types of transaction

IFRS 2 *Share-based payment* applies to **all** share-based payment transactions (IFRS 2: para. 2):

(a)   **Equity-settled share-based payment**

The entity receives goods or services as consideration for equity instruments of the entity (including shares or share options). (IFRS 2: Appendix A)

(b)   **Cash-settled share-based payment**

The entity acquires goods or services by incurring liabilities to the supplier of those goods or services for amounts that are based on the price (or value) of the entity's shares or other equity instruments. (IFRS 2: Appendix A)

Question 7.1	Distinction between equity and cash settled

Are the following equity-settled or cash-settled share-based payments? (Tick as appropriate)

	Equity-settled?	Cash-settled?
An entity grants share options to its employees	✓	
An entity grants share appreciation rights to its employees (amount payable based on increase in share price)		✓
An entity buys property, plant and equipment and the supplier agrees to take payment in shares		✓
An entity grants a director the right to receive a cash payment equal to the current value of 10,000 shares at the settlement date	✓	✓

2 Recognition

DEBIT   Staff costs [within profit or loss]
CREDIT   Other components of equity (if equity-settled)
CREDIT   Liability (if cash-settled)

(IFRS 2: para. 7–8)

Where performance by the counterparty is not immediate the expense is **spread** over the period until the counterparty becomes entitled to receive the share-based payment (the 'vesting' period).
(IFRS 2: para. 15, 32)

Eg   Employee services where a minimum period of service must be completed before entitlement to the share-based payment.

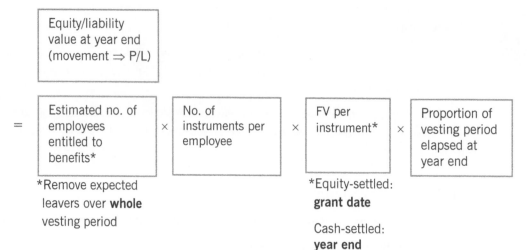

*Remove expected leavers over **whole** vesting period

*Equity-settled: **grant date**

Cash-settled: **year end**

Where the share-based payment was in existence in the prior year, the accounting entry is made with the movement in the equity or liability:

Equity/liability:
B/d	X
Cash paid	(X)
(cash-settled only)	
Expense (balancing figure)	X
C/d	X

Question 7.2

Preparation question – accounting entry

AB granted share options to each of its employees on 1 January 20X3. These options are not conditional on future employment.

Required

From the list below, select and enter the relevant account reference for the debit and credit in the journal entry.

Account reference
DEBIT
CREDIT

Options:

- Profit or loss
- Non-current liabilities
- Share capital
- Other components of equity

3 Measurement

The entity measures the expense using the method that provides the most reliable information:

(a)   **Direct method**

Use the fair value of goods or services received. (IFRS 2: para. 10, 30)

(b)   **Indirect method** (often for employee services)

By reference to the fair value of the equity instruments (eg options or share appreciation rights) granted:

Equity-settled ⇒ use fair value at **grant date** and do not update for subsequent changes (IFRS 2: para. 11)

Cash-settled ⇒ update the fair value at each **year end** (changes recognised in profit or loss) (IFRS 2: para. 33)

Any changes in estimates of expected number of employees being entitled to receive share-based payment are treated as a change in accounting estimate and recognised in the period of the change. (IFRS 2: para. 19, 20)

3.1 Equity-settled share-based payment

Example: Accounting entry and calculation for each year:

An entity grants 100 share options on its $1 shares to each of its 500 employees on 1 January 20X5. Each grant is conditional upon the employee working for the entity over the next 3 years. The fair value of each share option as at 1 January 20X5 is $15.

On the basis of a weighted average probability, the entity estimates on 1 January that 20% of employees will leave during the 3 year period and therefore forfeit their rights to share options.

Required

Show the accounting entries which will be required over the 3 year period in the event of the following:

- 20 employees leave during 20X5 and the estimate of total employee departures over the 3 year period is revised to 15% (75 employees).

- 22 employees leave during 20X6 and the estimate of total employee departures over the 3 year period is revised to 12% (60 employees).

- 15 employees leave during 20X7, so a total of 57 employees left and forfeited their rights to share options. A total of 44,300 share options (443 employees × 100 options) are vested at the end of 20X7.

Solution

20X5

	$
Equity c/d and P/L expense ((500 − 75) × 100 × $15 × 1/3)	212,500

DEBIT	Staff costs	$212,500
CREDIT	Other components of equity		$212,500

20X6

	$
Equity b/d	212,500
∴ Profit or loss expense	227,500
Equity c/d ((500 − 60) × 100 × $15 × 2/3) =	440,000

DEBIT	Staff costs	$227,500	
CREDIT	Other components of equity		$227,500

20X7

	$
Equity b/d	440,000
∴ Profit or loss expense	224,500
Equity c/d (443 × 100 × $15) =	664,500

DEBIT	Staff costs	$224,500	
CREDIT	Other components of equity		$224,500

3.2 Cash-settled share-based payment

(a) This could arise where a company grants share appreciation rights to employees as part of their pay package. The employees will become entitled to a future cash payment based on the increase in the entity's share price from a specified level over a specified period of time.

(b) The company must recognise the services received and the related liability **as the services are rendered**. The liability must be recognised at **fair value** using an option pricing model, with all changes in fair value being recognised in profit or loss up to the date of settlement.
(IFRS 2: para. 30–33)

Example: Accounting entry and calculation for each year:

On 1 January 20X4 an entity grants 100 cash share appreciation rights (SARs) to each of its 500 employees on the condition that the employees remain in its employ for the next 2 years. The SARs vest on 31 December 20X5 and may be exercised at any time up to 31 December 20X6. The fair value of each SAR at the grant date is $7.40.

Year ended	Leavers	No. of employees exercising rights	Outstanding SARs	Estimated further leavers	Fair value of SARs $	Intrinsic value (ie cash paid) $
31 December 20X4	50	–	450	60	8.00	
31 December 20X5	50	100	300	–	8.50	8.10
31 December 20X6	–	300	–	–	–	9.00

Required

Show the expense and liability which will appear in the financial statements in each of the three years and the relevant accounting entries.

Solution

20X4			$
Liability c/d and P/L expense ((500 – 110) × 100 × $8.00 × ½)			156,000

DEBIT	Staff costs	$156,000	
CREDIT	Liability		$156,000

20X5		$
Liability b/d		156,000
∴ Profit or loss expense		180,000
Less cash paid on exercise of SARs by employees (100 × 100 × $8.10)		(81,000)
Liability c/d (300 × 100 × $8.50)		255,000

DEBIT	Staff costs	$180,000	
CREDIT	Cash		$81,000
CREDIT	Liability ($255,000 – $156,000)		$99,000

20X6		$
Liability b/d		255,000
∴ Profit or loss expense		15,000
Less cash paid on exercise of SARs by employees (300 × 100 × $9.00)		(270,000)
Liability c/d		–

DEBIT	Staff costs	$15,000	
DEBIT	Liability	$255,000	
CREDIT	Cash		$270,000

4 Deferred tax implications

Deferred tax will arise on share-based payments if a **tax deduction** is granted by the tax authorities in a **different period** to when the expense is recognised in profit or loss.

For example, for share options granted to employees:

Accounting treatment	Measure expense at **fair value** at grant date and spread **over vesting period**
Tax treatment (will be given in question)	Eg tax deduction granted **on exercise** of the options based on the **intrinsic value** (fair value of share – exercise price) at date of exercise
Temporary difference	Arises because **expense** recognised in profit or loss in **different period** to when **tax relief** granted

This gives rise to a **deferred tax asset** as the entity will get **tax relief** on exercise of the options.

As the **amount** recognised in **profit or loss** (fair value) **differs** from the **amount** that the **tax relief** will be granted on (intrinsic value), when calculating the temporary difference and deferred tax, the amount that the tax authorities will use as their basis for the tax deduction must be used ie **the intrinsic value**.

In the above share options example, the **temporary difference** is calculated as:

	Estimated no. of employees entitled to benefits *	×	No. of instruments per employee	×	**Intrinsic value** per instrument at year end	×	Proportion of vesting period elapsed at year end

*Remove expected leavers over **whole** vesting period

The **deferred tax asset** is calculated by **multiplying** the temporary difference **by the tax rate**.

(IAS 12: para. 68A–68C)

Question 7.3	Deferred tax on share-based payments

On 1 January 20X2 an entity granted 5,000 share options to an employee vesting 2 years later on 31 December 20X3. The fair value of each option measured at the grant date was $3.

Tax law in the jurisdiction in which the entity operates allows a tax deduction of the intrinsic value of the options on exercise. The intrinsic value of the share options was $1.20 on 31 December 20X2.

Assume a tax rate of 30%.

Required

Which THREE of the following statements are correct in relation to deferred tax on the share options for the year ended 31 December 20X2? (Tick the correct answers)

Tick	Options
	No deferred tax should be recognised because there is no temporary difference
	A deferred tax asset of $2,250 should be recognised with a corresponding debit to profit or loss
	A temporary difference has arisen because the expense and tax deduction are recognised in different periods
	The share-based payment expense to be recognised in profit or loss for the year ended 31 December 20X2 is $7,500
	The temporary difference as at 31 December 20X2 is $6,000
	A deferred tax asset of $900 should be recognised at 31 December 20X2 with a corresponding credit to profit or loss

Chapter Summary

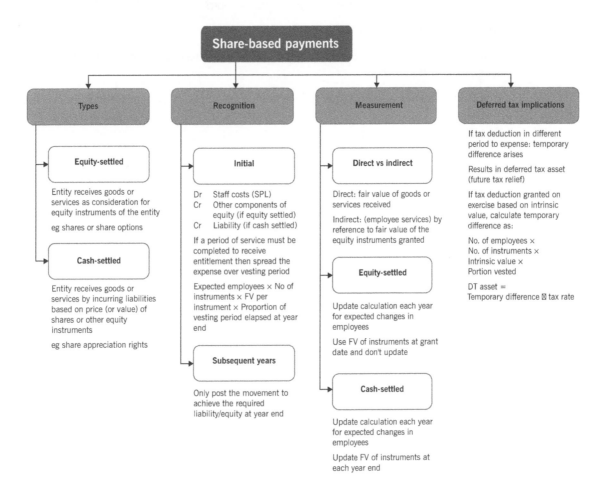

Share-based payments

Types

Equity-settled

Entity receives goods or services as consideration for equity instruments of the entity

eg shares or share options

Cash-settled

Entity receives goods or services by incurring liabilities based on price (or value) of shares or other equity instruments

eg share appreciation rights

Recognition

Initial

Dr Staff costs (SPL)
Cr Other components of equity (if equity settled)
Cr Liability (if cash settled)

If a period of service must be completed to receive entitlement then spread the expense over vesting period

Expected employees × No of instruments × FV per instrument × Proportion of vesting period elapsed at year end

Subsequent years

Only post the movement to achieve the required liability/equity at year end

Measurement

Direct vs indirect

Direct: fair value of goods or services received

Indirect: (employee services) by reference to fair value of the equity instruments granted

Equity-settled

Update calculation each year for expected changes in employees

Use FV of instruments at grant date and don't update

Cash-settled

Update calculation each year for expected changes in employees

Update FV of instruments at each year end

Deferred tax implications

If tax deduction in different period to expense: temporary difference arises

Results in deferred tax asset (future tax relief)

If tax deduction granted on exercise based on intrinsic value, calculate temporary difference as:

No. of employees ×
No. of instruments ×
Intrinsic value ×
Portion vested

DT asset =
Temporary difference ⊠ tax rate

BPP
LEARNING MEDIA

Quick Quiz

1   What is a cash-settled share-based payment transaction?

2   What does grant date mean?

3   If an entity has entered into an equity-settled share-based payment transaction, what should it recognise in its financial statements?

4   Where an entity has granted share options to its employees in return for services, how is the transaction measured?

Answers to Quick Quiz

1 A transaction in which the entity receives goods or services in exchange for amounts of cash that are based on the price (or value) of the entity's shares or other equity instruments of the entity.

2 The date at which the entity and another party (including an employee) agree to a share-based payment arrangement, being when the entity and the other party have a shared understanding of the terms and conditions of the arrangement.

3 The goods or services received and a corresponding increase in equity.

4 By reference to the fair value of the equity instruments granted, measured at grant date.

Answers to Questions

7.1 Distinction between equity and cash settled

	Equity-settled?	Cash-settled?
An entity grants share options to its employees	✓	
An entity grants share appreciation rights to its employees (amount payable based on increase in share price)		✓
An entity buys property, plant and equipment and the supplier agrees to take payment in shares	✓	
An entity grants a director the right to receive a cash payment equal to the current value of 10,000 shares at the settlement date		✓

7.2 Accounting entry

	Account reference
DEBIT	Profit or loss
CREDIT	Other components of equity

7.3 Deferred tax on share-based payments:

Tick	Options
	No deferred tax should be recognised because there is no temporary difference
	A deferred tax asset of $2,250 should be recognised with a corresponding debit to profit or loss
✓	A temporary difference has arisen because the expense and tax deduction are recognised in different periods
✓	The share-based payment expense to be recognised in profit or loss for the year ended 31 December 20X2 is $7,500
	The temporary difference as at 31 December 20X2 is $6,000
✓	A deferred tax asset of $900 should be recognised at 31 December 20X2 with a corresponding credit to profit or loss

The expense in profit or loss is calculated as:

5,000 options × $3 fair value at the grant date × ½ vested = $7,500

As the expense is recognised over the vesting period but the tax deduction is not granted until exercise of the options, a temporary difference has arisen. The temporary difference is calculated as:

5,000 options × $1.20 intrinsic value × ½ vested = $3,000

This gives rise to a deferred tax asset because tax relief will be granted on exercise. It is calculated by multiplying the temporary difference by the tax rate: $3,000 × 30% = $900. The accounting entry is:

DEBIT	Deferred tax asset	$900	
CREDIT	Deferred tax expense (in P/L)		$900

<table>
<tr><td rowspan="4">Now try these questions from the Practice Question Bank</td><td>Number</td><td>Level</td><td>Marks</td><td>Time</td></tr>
<tr><td>Q10</td><td>Introductory</td><td>N/A</td><td>5 mins</td></tr>
<tr><td>Q11</td><td>Introductory</td><td>10</td><td>18 mins</td></tr>
</table>

REVENUE

Modern organisations enter into a wide range of complex sales transactions. It is vital that the revenue from these transactions is accounted for correctly and within the correct time period. IFRS 15 *Revenue from Contracts with Customers* gives guidance on revenue recognition.

You need to be able to explain the correct accounting treatment for certain revenue transactions and be able to produce the accounting entries.

Topic list	learning outcomes	syllabus references
1 Approach to revenue recognition	B1	B1(c)(d)
2 Satisfaction of performance obligation at a point in time	B1	B1(c)
3 Satisfaction of performance obligation over time	B1	B1(c)
4 Contract costs	B1	B1(c)(d)
5 Presentation and accounting entries	B1	B1(c)(d)
6 Specific guidance	B1	B1(c)(d)

Chapter Overview

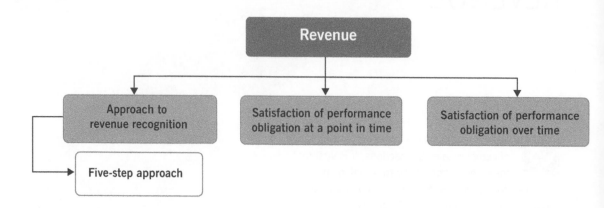

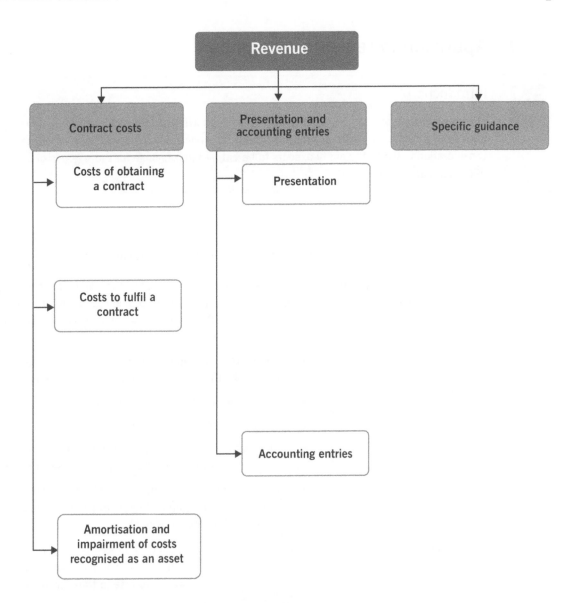

1   Approach to revenue recognition

Introduction

The core principle of IFRS 15 *Revenue from Contracts with Customers* is that an entity recognises revenue to depict the **transfer of promised goods or services to customers** in an **amount that reflects the consideration** to which the entity **expects to be entitled** in exchange for those goods or services (IFRS 15: para. IN7).

1.1   Five-step approach

IFRS 15 requires an entity to recognise revenue by applying the five steps below (IFRS 15: para. IN7):

(1)	Identify **contract with the customer**	The model applies where a **contract** (an **agreement** between two or more parties that creates **enforceable rights and obligations**) exists (IFRS 15: para. 10) and all of the following criteria are met (IFRS 15: para. 9):

- The parties have approved the contract (in writing, orally or implied by the entity's customary business practices)
- The entity can identify each party's rights
- The entity can identify payment terms
- The contract has commercial substance (risk, timing or amount of future cash flows expected to change as a result of the contract)
- It is probable that the entity will collect the consideration (customer's ability and intention to pay that amount of consideration when it is due).

(2)	Identify **performance obligation(s)**	At contract inception, an entity shall assess the goods and services promised in a contract with a customer and shall identify as a performance obligation each **promise to transfer** to the customer either (IFRS 15: para. 22):

- **A good or service** (or a bundle of goods or services) that is **distinct** (ie the customer can benefit from the good or service on its own or together with other readily available resources and the entity's promise is separately identifiable from other promises in the contract); or
- A **series of distinct goods or services** that are **substantially the same** and that have the same pattern of transfer to the customer.

Note. If a promised good or service is not distinct, an entity shall combine that good or service with other promised goods and services until it identifies a bundle of goods or services that is distinct. (IFRS 15: para. 30)

(3)	Determine **transaction price**	The amount to which the entity expects to be 'entitled' (IFRS 15: para. 47).
		Includes **variable consideration** if highly **probable** that significant **reversal** of cumulative revenue will **not occur** (IFRS 15: para. 56). Measure variable consideration at (IFRS 15: para. 53):
		• Probability-weighted expected value (eg if large number of contracts with similar characteristics); or
		• Most likely amount (eg if only two possible outcomes).
		Discounting is not required where consideration is due in less than one year (where discounting is applied, present interest separately from revenue) (IFRS 15: para. 63, 65).
(4)	**Allocate transaction price** to performance obligations	**Multiple deliverables**: transaction price allocated to each separate performance obligation in proportion to the **stand-alone selling price** at contract inception of each performance obligation (IFRS 15: para. 73–75).
(5)	Recognise revenue when (or as) **performance obligation satisfied**	A performance obligation is **satisfied** when the entity **transfers** a promised good or service (ie an asset) to a customer (IFRS 15: para 31).
		An asset is considered transferred when (or as) the customer obtains control of that asset (IFRS 15: para 31).
		Control of an asset refers to the **ability to direct the use of**, and **obtain substantially** all of the **remaining benefits** from, the asset (IFRS 15: para 33).

Example: Step 2 (based on IFRS 15 Illustrative Example 11)

A software developer enters into a contract with a customer to transfer a software licence, perform an installation service and provide unspecified software updates and technical support (online and telephone) for a two-year period. The entity sells the licence, installation service and technical support separately. The installation service includes changing the web screen for each type of user. The installation service is routinely performed by other entities and does not significantly modify the software. The software remains functional without the updates and the technical support.

Required

Under IFRS 15 *Revenue from Contracts with Customers,* how many performance obligations are there under this contract?

Solution

There are four performance obligations:

(a)   The software licence
(b)   An installation service
(c)   Software updates
(d)   Technical support

This is because these goods and services are distinct. The software is delivered before the other goods and service and remains functional without the updates and technical support. The installation services do not significantly affect the customer's ability to use and benefit from the software licence because the installation services are routine and could be obtained from alternative providers. The customer can benefit from the software updates together with the software at the start of the contract so this meets the IFRS 15 criteria of the customer benefitting from the goods and services together with other goods and

services that are readily available. The software updates do not significantly affect the customer's ability to use and benefit from the software licence during the licencing period. In conclusion, the software and services are not highly interdependent because the entity would be able to fulfil its promise to transfer the initial software licence independently from its promise to subsequently provide the installation service, software updates or technical support.

Example: Step 3 (variable consideration)

In January 20X6, CPL, a construction company enters into a contract to build a warehouse for a customer in exchange for an agreed fee of $40 million. The contract terms require completion by 30 September 20X6. The price will decrease by $100,000 for each day after this that the project remains incomplete. At the year-end of 30 June 20X6, CPL expects that there is a 75% chance of the project being completed on time, a 15% chance of it being completed a day late, a 6% chance of it being completed two days late and a 4% chance of it being completed three days late.

Required

Using the probability-weighted expected value approach, what is the estimated transaction price at the year-end of 30 June 20X6?

Solution

The estimated transaction price is $39,961,000.

The consideration is variable due to the price concession, i.e. the fact that CPL will accept an amount that is less than the price stated in the contract if the project overruns.

Here the calculation of transaction price is based on expected values.

	$
75% × $40,000,000	30,000,000
15% × $39,900,000	5,985,000
6% × $39,800,000	2,388,000
4% × $39,700,000	1,588,000
Transaction price	39,961,000

Example: Step 3 (discounting)

CD sold some goods to EF on 1 January 20X2 for $220,500 payable on 31 December 20X3. EF cannot return the goods.

The relevant discount rate is 5%.

Required

What are the amounts that should be recognised in CD's financial statements for the year ended 31 December 20X2 as revenue from the sale of goods and interest?

Solution

	$
Revenue from sale of goods ($220,500 \times 1/1.05^2$)	200,000
Interest income ($200,000 \times 5\%$)	10,000
	210,000

Example: Step 4 (allocating the transaction price to multiple deliverables)

JC sells a car including servicing for 2 years for $21,000. The car is also sold without servicing for $20,520 and annual servicing is sold for $540.

Required

Under IFRS 15 *Revenue from Contracts with Customers,* how should the $21,000 transaction price be split between the difference performance obligations?

Solution

Car: $ 19,950
Servicing: $ 1,050

Performance obligation	Stand-alone selling price	% of total	Transaction price allocated
Car	$20,520	95%	$19,950 (21,000 × 95%)
Servicing	$1,080	5%	$1,050 (21,000 × 5%)
Total	$21,600	100%	$21,000

2 Satisfaction of performance obligation at a point in time

To determine the point in time when a customer obtains control of a promised asset and an entity satisfies a performance obligation, the entity would consider indicators of the transfer of control that include, but are not limited to, the following indicators (IFRS 15: para. 38):

(a)   The entity has a **present right to payment** for the asset;

(b)   The customer has **legal title** to the asset;

(c)   The entity has **transferred physical possession** of the asset;

(d)   The customer has the **significant risks and rewards of ownership** of the asset; and

(e)   The customer has **accepted** the asset.

| Question 8.1 | Satisfaction of performance obligation at a point in time |

TW is a wholesaler. It sells goods to retailers on credit with no right of return. TW delivers goods to its customers premises.

Required

At what point should TW recognise revenue from goods sold to retailers?

A   When the customer places the order
B   When the goods are delivered to the customer
C   When an invoice is raised
D   When the customer settles the invoice

3 Satisfaction of performance obligation over time

An entity transfers control of a good or service over time and, therefore, satisfies a performance obligation and recognises revenue over time if one of the following criteria is met (IFRS 15: para. 35):

(a)   The customer **simultaneously receives and consumes the benefits** provided by the entity's performance as the entity performs;

(b)   The entity's **performance creates or enhances an asset** (eg work in progress) that **the customer controls** as the asset is created or enhanced; or

(c)   The entity's **performance** does **not create an asset with an alternative use** to the entity and the entity has an **enforceable right to payment** for performance completed to date.

For each performance obligation satisfied over time, revenue should be recognised by measuring **progress towards complete satisfaction** of that performance obligation (IFRS 15: para. 39).

Appropriate methods of measuring progress include output methods and input methods (IFRS 15: para. 41, B14, B15, B18):

Method	Explanation	Examples
Output	On basis of direct measurements of the **value to the customer** of the goods or services transferred to date relative to the remaining goods or services promised under the contract	• Surveys of performance completed to date • Appraisals of results achieved • Time elapsed • Units produced • Units delivered
Input	On the basis of the **entity's efforts or inputs** to the satisfaction of a performance obligation relative to the total expected inputs	• Resources consumed • Labour hours expended • Costs incurred • Time elapsed • Machine hours used

If an entity **cannot reasonably measure the outcome** of a performance obligation (eg in the early stages of a contract) but the entity expects to recover the costs incurred in satisfying the performance obligation, it should recognise **revenue** only to the extent of **costs incurred**. This applies until it can reasonably measure the outcome of the performance obligation (IFRS 15: para. 45).

Example: Satisfaction of performance obligation over time

MN entered into the following transactions in the year ended 31 December 20X2:

(1) A 6 month contract to undertake training for a customer over the period 1 September 20X2 to 28 February 20X3. The value of services performed to date amounts to $45,000 out of a total contract value of $60,000. All costs are expected to be recoverable.

(2) Performed advertising services for a customer costing $6,000 relating to a fixed price $20,000 contract covering the period 1 December 20X2 to 31 March 20X3. Due to fluctuating advertising costs, the expected total cost cannot be reliably measured at the year end, but MN is certain that the customer will pay the costs incurred to date.

Required

How much revenue should be recognised in MN's financial statements for the year ended 31 December 20X2?

Solution

	$
Training (Note 1)	45,000
Advertising services	6,000
Revenue to be recognised in year ended 31 December 20X2	51,000

Notes

1   The output method of measuring progress towards satisfaction of the performance obligation is appropriate here as the value of services performed to date has been identified as $45,000.

2   Since MN cannot reliably measure the outcome of the performance obligation due to the fluctuating advertising costs but still expects to recover the costs incurred, MN should only recognise revenue to the extent of the costs incurred of $6,000.

Example: Satisfaction of performance obligation over time

On 1 January 20X7, SH, a construction company, entered into a two-year contract to build a factory for a customer on the customer's land. The contract specifies that control of the factory is transferred to the customer as it is constructed. The agreed contract price is $35 million. During the year ended 31 December 20X7, costs incurred amounted to $9.1 million. The total cost of the project is estimated to be $26 million. Work certified at the year-end amounted to $14 million.

Required

How much revenue should be recognised in SH's statement of profit or loss for the year ended 31 December 20X7 if an input method is used to assess progress?

Solution

$12,250,000

Under the input method, progress towards satisfaction is calculated as:

$$\frac{\text{Costs incurred to date}}{\text{Total expected costs}} = \frac{\$9.1m}{\$26m} = 35\%$$

Revenue = 35% × $35 million contract price = $12,250,000

If an output method had been used, revenue would have amounted to the work certified of $14 million.

4 Contract costs

4.1 Costs of obtaining a contract

Incremental costs of **obtaining** a contract are recognised as an asset if the entity expects to recover them (IFRS 15: para. 91).

4.2 Costs to fulfil a contract

If the costs to fulfil a contract are not within the scope of another Standard (eg IAS 2 *Inventories*, IAS 16 *Property, Plant and Equipment* or IAS 38 *Intangible Assets*), they should be recognised as an asset only if they meet all of the following criteria (IFRS 15: para. 95):

(a)   the costs relate directly to a contract or an anticipated contract that the entity can specifically identify;

(b)   the costs generate or enhance resources of the entity that will be used in satisfying (or in continuing to satisfy) performance obligations in the future; and

(c)   the costs are expected to be recovered.

4.3 Amortisation and impairment of costs recognised as an asset

The asset should be amortised to profit or loss on a systematic basis consistent with the pattern of transfer of the goods or services to which the asset relates (IFRS 15: para. 99).

For the costs of obtaining a contract, if the amortisation period is estimated to be one year or less, the costs may be recognised as an expense when incurred (IFRS 15: para. 94).

An impairment loss should be recognised in profit or loss to the extent that the carrying amount exceeds (IFRS 15: para. 101):

(a)   the remaining amount of consideration that the entity expects to receive in exchange for the goods or services to which the asset relates; less

(b)   the costs that relate directly to providing those goods or services that have not yet been recognised as expenses.

Contract costs

VB, a provider of consulting services, wins a competitive bid to provide consulting services to a new customer. VB incurred the following costs to obtain the contract:

	$
External legal fees for due diligence	30,000
Travel costs to deliver proposal	50,000
Commissions to sales employees	20,000
	100,000

VB expects to recover these costs through future fees for consulting services.

Required

What is the amount of costs that VB should recognise as an asset in relation to obtaining this contract?

$ [   ]

5 Presentation and accounting entries

5.1 Presentation

In the statement of financial position, a contract with a customer may be presented as any of (IFRS 15: para. 105):

Receivable	If an entity's **right to consideration is unconditional** (only the passage of time is required before payment is due), it should recognise a receivable (IFRS 15: para. 108).
Contract asset	If the **entity transfers goods or services before the customer pays**, it should present the contract as a 'contract asset' if the entity's right to consideration is **conditional** on something other than the passage of time (eg the entity's performance) (IFRS 15: para. 107).
Contract liability	If a customer **pays consideration** or the entity has a right to an amount of consideration that is unconditional (ie a receivable) **before the entity transfers the goods or services** to the customer, the entity should present the contract as a 'contract liability' when the payment is made or is due (whichever is earlier) (IFRS 15: para. 106).

5.2 Accounting entries

The entity transfers goods or services to a customer on credit and the entity's right to consideration is unconditional:

Dr (↑) Trade receivable

Cr (↑) Revenue

The entity transfers goods or services before the customer pays and the entity's right to consideration is conditional on something other than the passage of time:

Dr (↑) Contract asset

Cr (↑) Revenue

A customer pays consideration before the entity transfers the goods or services to the customer:

(1)   Dr (↑) Cash

        Cr (↑) Contract liability

        When the customer pays

(2)   Dr (↓) Contract liability

        Cr (↑) Revenue

        When the entity transfers the goods or services to the customer

Question 8.3   Accounting entries

AB enters into a cancellable contract with a customer on 18 August 20X6, agreeing to transfer goods to the customer on 30 September 20X6. The contract requires the customer to pay AB $120,000 on 31 August 20X6; the customer pays on 7 September 20X6.

Required

What is the accounting entry to record the receipt of $120,000 from the customer on 7 September 20X6? (Tick the correct answer)

Tick	Accounting entries		
	DEBIT Cash	$120,000	
	CREDIT Revenue		$120,000
	DEBIT Cash	$120,000	
	CREDIT Contract liability		$120,000
	DEBIT Cash	$120,000	
	CREDIT Contract asset		$120,000
	DEBIT Cash	$120,000	
	CREDIT Trade receivable		$120,000

6   Specific guidance

Appendix B of IFRS 15 gives specific guidance on how to account for revenue in certain circumstances. Some of these are outlined below:

Type	Guidance
Sale with right of return	• Recognise all of (IFRS 15: para. B21): (a) **revenue** for the transferred products in the amount **of consideration** to which the entity **expects to be entitled** (ie revenue not recognised for products expected to be returned); (b) a **refund liability**; and (c) an **asset** (and corresponding adjustment to cost of sales) for its **right to recover products** from customers on settling the refund liability.
Warranties	• If customer has the **option to purchase** a warranty **separately**, treat as **separate performance obligation** under IFRS 15 (IFRS 15: para. B29) • If customer **does not have the option to purchase** a warranty **separately**, account for warranty **in accordance with IAS 37** Provisions, Contingent Liabilities and Contingent Assets (IFRS 15: para. B30) • If warranty provides the customer with **a service in addition** to the assurance that the product complies with agreed-upon specifications, the **promised service is a performance obligation** (IFRS 15: para. B32)

Principal versus agent	• If the entity **controls** the specified goods or service before transfer to a customer, it is a **principal** (IFRS 15: para. B35)
	   ⟹ Revenue = gross amount of consideration
	
	• If the entity **arranges for goods or services to be provided by the other party**, it is an **agent** (IFRS 15: para. B36)
	   ⟹ Revenue = fee or commission
	
	• Indicators that an entity controls the goods or service before transfer and therefore is a principal include (IFRS 15: para. B37):
	
	(a) the entity is primarily responsible for fulfilling the promise to provide the specified good or service
	
	(b) the entity has inventory risk
	
	(c) the entity has discretion in establishing the price for the specified good or service.

Non-refundable upfront fees	• If it is an **advance payment** for future goods and services, recognise **revenue** when **future goods and services provided** (IFRS 15: para. B49)

Chapter Summary

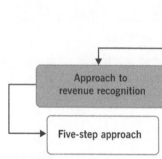

```
                                    ┌─────────────────┐
                                    │     Revenue     │
                                    └─────────────────┘
```

Approach to revenue recognition	Satisfaction of performance obligation at a point in time	Satisfaction of performance obligation over time

Approach to revenue recognition

Five-step approach

(1) Identify contract with the customer
- Contract = agreement between 2 or more parties that creates enforceable rights and obligations
- Parties have approved contract (in writing, orally or implied)
- Entity can identify each party's rights
- Entity can identify payment terms
- Contract has commercial substance
- Probable that entity will collect consideration

(2) Identify performance obligation(s)
Performance obligation is each promise to transfer to the customer either:
- A good or service (or bundle of goods or services) that is distinct; or
- A series of distinct goods or services that are substantially the same and have the same pattern of transfer to the customer

(3) Determine transaction price
= the amount to which the entity expects to be 'entitled'
- Includes variable consideration if highly probable that significant reversal will not occur
- Measure variable consideration at probability-weighted expected value or most likely amount
- Discounting not required where consideration due in < 1 year
- Where discounting is applied, present interest separately from revenue

(4) Allocate transaction price to performance obligations
Multiple deliverables: transaction price allocated based on stand-alone selling price of each performance obligation

(5) Recognise revenue as performance obligation satisfied
= when entity transfers promised good or service to a customer ie when or as customer obtains control (ability to direct use of, and obtain substantially all the benefits from, the asset)

Satisfaction of performance obligation at a point in time

To determine point in time customer obtains control of the asset, the entity should consider the following indicators:
- Entity has present right to payment for the asset
- Customer has legal title of the asset
- Entity has transferred physical possession of the asset
- Customer has significant risks and rewards of ownership
- Customer has accepted the assets

Satisfaction of performance obligation over time

An entity transfers control of a good or service over time if ONE of the following criteria is met:
- The customer simultaneously receives and consumes the benefits;
- The entity's performance creates or enhances an asset that the customer controls as the asset is created or enhanced; or
- The entity's performance does not create an asset with an alternative use to the entity and the entity has an enforceable right to payment

Revenue should be recognised by measuring progress towards complete satisfaction using methods such as:
- Output methods (based on value to customer)
- Input methods (based on entity's efforts or inputs)

If entity cannot reasonably measure the outcome of a performance obligation but expects to recover costs, revenue = costs incurred.

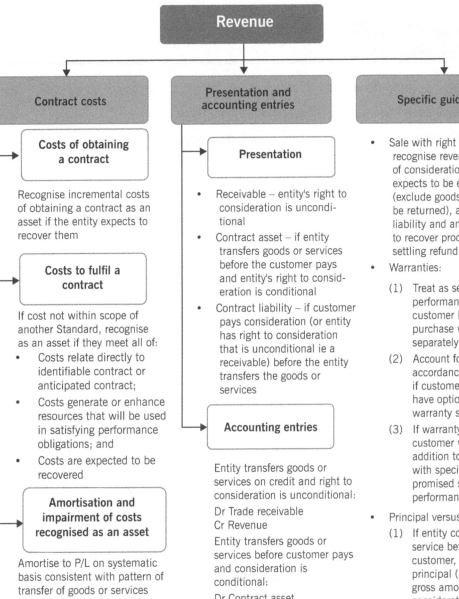

Revenue

Contract costs

Costs of obtaining a contract

Recognise incremental costs of obtaining a contract as an asset if the entity expects to recover them

Costs to fulfil a contract

If cost not within scope of another Standard, recognise as an asset if they meet all of:

- Costs relate directly to identifiable contract or anticipated contract;
- Costs generate or enhance resources that will be used in satisfying performance obligations; and
- Costs are expected to be recovered

Amortisation and impairment of costs recognised as an asset

Amortise to P/L on systematic basis consistent with pattern of transfer of goods or services which asset relates to
For costs of obtaining contract, if amortisation period is ≤ 1 year, can recognise costs as expense when incurred
Recognise impairment loss in P/L to extent carrying amount exceeds:

- Remaining amount of consideration entity expects to receive in exchange for goods or services to which asset relates; less
- Costs that directly relate to providing those goods and services not yet recognised as expenses

Presentation and accounting entries

Presentation

- Receivable – entity's right to consideration is unconditional
- Contract asset – if entity transfers goods or services before the customer pays and entity's right to consideration is conditional
- Contract liability – if customer pays consideration (or entity has right to consideration that is unconditional ie a receivable) before the entity transfers the goods or services

Accounting entries

Entity transfers goods or services on credit and right to consideration is unconditional:
Dr Trade receivable
Cr Revenue
Entity transfers goods or services before customer pays and consideration is conditional:
Dr Contract asset
Cr Revenue
Customer pays before entity transfers goods or services:
(1) Dr Cash
    Cr Contract liability
    When customer pays
(2) Dr Contract liability
    Cr Revenue
    When entity transfers goods or services

Specific guidance

- Sale with right of return – recognise revenue for amount of consideration that entity expects to be entitled to (exclude goods expected to be returned), a refund liability and an asset for right to recover products on settling refund liability
- Warranties:
  (1) Treat as separate performance obligation if customer has option to purchase warranty separately
  (2) Account for warranty in accordance with IAS 37 if customer does not have option to purchase warranty separately
  (3) If warranty provides customer with service in addition to complying with specifications, promised service is a performance obligation
- Principal versus agent
  (1) If entity controls goods or service before transfer to customer, entity = principal (revenue = gross amount of consideration)
  (2) If entity arranges for goods or services to be provided by another party, entity = agent (revenue = fee or commission)
- Non-refundable fees – if it is an advance payment for future goods and services, recognise revenue when future goods and services provided

Quick Quiz

1 What are **output methods** of measuring satisfaction of performance obligations? ⤷ surveys, units of work.

2 What are the two types of contract dealt with in IFRS 15?
⤷ satisfied a point in time / over time.

3 What is the transfer that must take place before revenue can be recognised?
⤷ control

4 What is a repurchase agreement? Sells + promise to repurch

5 List the five steps for recognising revenue under IFRS 15.

Answers to Quick Quiz

1   Methods of measurement based on value to the customer of goods or services transferred. Examples would be surveys of work performed.

2
- Contracts where performance obligations are satisfied at a point in time
- Contracts where performance obligations are satisfied over time

3   **Control** must be transferred before revenue can be recognised.

4   A repurchase agreement is one in which an entity sells an asset and promises, or has the option, to repurchase it.

5   1   Identify the contract with the customer

           2   Identify the separate performance obligations

           3   Determine the transaction price

           4   Allocate the transaction price to the performance obligations

           5   Recognise revenue when (or as) a performance obligation is satisfied

Answers to Questions

8.1 Satisfaction of performance obligation at a point in time

The correct answer is:

B   When the goods are delivered to the customer

The performance obligation is satisfied at a point in time in this example. This point in time that the performance obligation is satisfied and therefore, when revenue should be recognised, is when TW has transferred physical possession of the goods by delivering them to the customer. Once the goods have been delivered to the customer, TW has established its right to payment, the customer has legal title and the significant risks and rewards have been transferred to the customer.

8.2 Contract costs

The correct answer is:

$ | 20,000 |

Only the incremental costs of obtaining a contract should be recognised as an asset if the entity expects to recover them. The legal fees and travel costs would have been incurred regardless of whether the contract was won. Therefore, these costs are not incremental and should be recognised as an expense rather than an asset. However, sales commissions are only paid on the successful bidding for a contract (i.e. if the contract is won) so they do qualify as incremental costs and should be recognised as an asset.

8.3 Accounting entries

The correct answer is:

Tick	Accounting entries		
	DEBIT Cash	$120,000	
	CREDIT Revenue		$120,000
	This is incorrect as revenue can only be recognised when the performance obligation is satisfied and this will not occur until 30 September 20X6 when the goods are transferred to the customer.		
✓	DEBIT Cash	$120,000	
	CREDIT Contract liability		$120,000
	This is correct because the customer has paid consideration before the entity (AB) transfers the goods.		
	DEBIT Cash	$120,000	
	CREDIT Contract asset		$120,000
	This is incorrect as no contract asset exists to derecognise. A contract asset is only recognised if the entity transfers the goods before the customer pays.		
	DEBIT Cash	$120,000	
	CREDIT Trade receivable		$120,000
	This is incorrect. No trade receivable has been recorded because the contract is cancellable meaning that there is no unconditional right to consideration.		

BPP
LEARNING MEDIA

Now try these questions from the Practice Question Bank

Number	Level	Marks	Time
Q12	Introductory	N/A	8 mins

SIMPLE GROUPS

Part C

BASIC GROUPS

In addition to preparing individual financial statements there is a requirement to prepare group accounts if an entity holds certain types of investments. This is to ensure that the shareholders are aware of the performance of the group as a whole since this has a significant impact on the value of their investment and any economic decisions surrounding it.

Chapter 9 is mainly revision of group topics covered at F1.

Topic list	learning outcomes	syllabus references
1 Definition of subsidiary	B1	B1(a)
2 Types of investment	B1	B1(a)
3 Consolidated statement of financial position	B1	B1(a)
4 Key consolidation adjustments	B1	B1(a)
5 Consolidated statement of profit or loss and other comprehensive income	B1	B1(a)
6 Fair values (IFRS 3)	B1	B1(a)

Chapter Overview

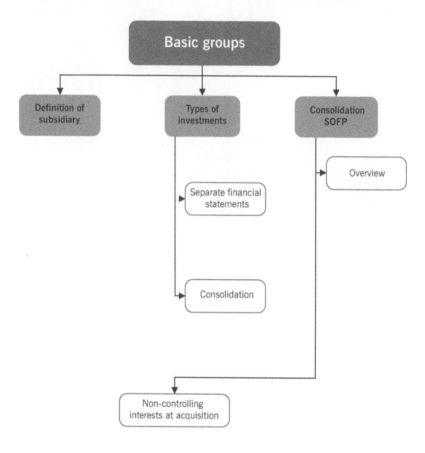

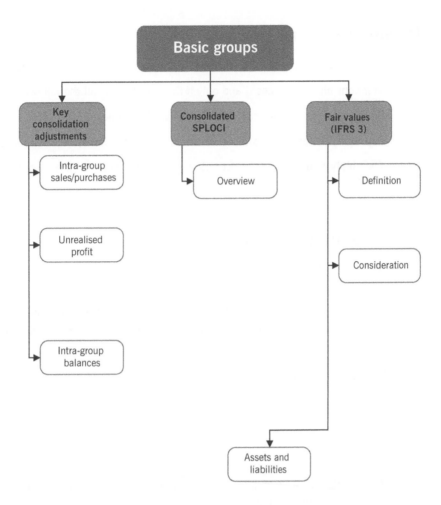

1 Definition of subsidiary

KEY TERM

A SUBSIDIARY is 'an entity that is **controlled** by another entity' (IFRS 10: Appendix A).

An investor **controls** an investee if and only if the investor has **all** the following:

(a) **Power** over the investee to direct the **relevant activities**;

(b) **Exposure, or rights, to variable returns** from its involvement with the investee; and

(c) The **ability to use its power** over the investee to **affect** the amount of the investor's **returns** (IFRS 10: para. 7).

2 Types of investment

The three types of investment in the consolidated financial statements are each governed by an IAS/IFRS:

- Subsidiaries (IFRS 10 *Consolidated financial statements*)
- Associates (IAS 28 *Investments in associates and joint ventures*) [see Chapter 10]
- Joint ventures (IAS 28 and IFRS 11 *Joint arrangements*) [see Chapter 10]

2.1 Accounting treatment in the separate financial statements of the investor

In all three cases, under IAS 27 *Separate financial statements* the investment can be carried in the investor's separate financial statements (IAS 27: para. 10):

- At **cost**; or
- At **fair value** (as a financial asset under IFRS 9 *Financial Instruments*).
- Using the **equity method** as described in IAS 28.

The **equity method** will apply in the **individual financial statements** of the investor when the entity has investments in associates and joint ventures but does not prepare consolidated financial statements as it has **no investments in subsidiaries**.

2.2 Cancellation of investment in the consolidated financial statements

If the investment has been carried at **cost**, the **investment** must be **cancelled** on consolidation.

If the investment has been carried at **fair value**, both the **investment** (at fair value) and the **revaluation gains or losses** on the investment must be **cancelled** on consolidation.

3 Consolidated statement of financial position

IFRS 10 requires full consolidation of a subsidiary (as outlined below) (IFRS 10: para. B86).

(a) **Assets and liabilities:**   Always add P and 100% of S line by line providing P controls S

      Reason: To show the assets and liabilities that the parent **controls**

(b) **Goodwill:**
Consideration transferred		X
Non-controlling interests (see Section 3.3)		X

Less net fair value of identifiable assets acquired
and liabilities assumed:

Share capital	X
Share premium	X
Retained earnings at acquisition	X
Other reserves at acquisition	X
Fair value adjustments at acquisition	X̲

	(X)
	X̲
Less impairment losses on goodwill to date	(X)
	X̲

Reason: Shows the excess paid for reputation etc of subsidiary acquired at acquisition date

(c) **Share capital/ premium:**   P only

Reason: Consolidated financial statements prepared for shareholders of the parent so must only show equity attributable to them

(d) **Retained earnings:**   P plus group share of post-acquisition retained earnings of S, plus/less consolidation adjustments:

	Parent	Subsidiary	Assoc/JV
At the year end	X	X	X
Provision for unrealised profit	(X)	(X)	
Fair value adjustments movement		X/(X)	
At acquisition		(X)	(X)
		Y̲	Z̲

Share of post acq'n ret'd earnings:	
Subsidiary (Y × %)	X
Associate/Joint venture (Z × %)	X
Less impairment of goodwill of subsidiary	(X)
Less impairment of investment in associate	(X)
	X̲

Reason: To show the extent to which the group actually **owns** the net assets included in the consolidated statement of financial position

Note. Other reserves are treated in a similar way.

(e) **Non-controlling interests:**
NCI at acquisition (fair value)/[(SC + SP + reserves + FV adjs) × NCI%]	X
NCI share of post-acquisition reserves (Y × NCI %)	X
Less NCI share of impairment losses (if NCI at FV at acq'n)	(X)
	X̲

Reason: To show the portion of the subsidiary's net assets and goodwill consolidated that belongs to third-party shareholders.

3.1 Measuring non-controlling interests at acquisition

IFRS 3 *Business combinations* allows the non-controlling interests in a subsidiary to be measured **at the acquisition date** in one of two ways **(eg if a parent acquires an 80% subsidiary)** (IFRS 3: para. 19):

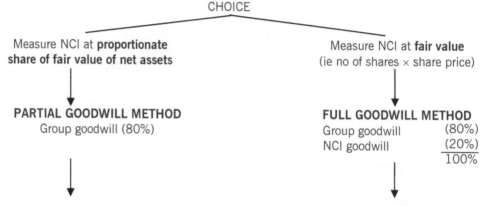

CHOICE

Measure NCI at proportionate share of fair value of net assets

PARTIAL GOODWILL METHOD
Group goodwill (80%)

Consol SOFP
- Deduct **all** of cumulative impairment in **goodwill working**

- Deduct **all** of cumulative impairment losses on recognised goodwill **to retained earnings working**

Consol SPLOCI
- Add **all** of impairment loss for year to expenses

Measure NCI at fair value
(ie no of shares × share price)

FULL GOODWILL METHOD
Group goodwill   (80%)
NCI goodwill   (20%)
                       ───────
                        100%

Consol SOFP
- Deduct **all** of cumulative impairment in **goodwill working**

- Deduct **group share (80%)** of cumulative impairment losses **to retained earnings working**

- Deduct **NCI share** of cumulative impairment losses (20%) in **NCI working**

Consol SPLOCI
- Add **all** of impairment loss for year to expenses

- Deduct impairment loss for year from sub's PFY and TCI in **NCI working**

4 Key consolidation adjustments

(a)   *Cancellation of intra-group sales/purchases:*

Dr (↓) Group revenue   X

Cr (↓) Group cost of sales   X

(b)   *Elimination of unrealised profit on inventories/PPE:*

Dr (↑) Cost of sales*/(↓) ret'd earnings of seller   X

Cr (↓) Group inventories/PPE   X

* if the subsidiary is the seller, adjust subsidiary's profit for year and total comprehensive income in NCI (SPLOCI) working

(c)   *Cancellation of intra-group balances:*

Dr (↓) Payables   X

Cr (↓) Receivables   X

(d)   *Cash in transit:*

Dr (↑) Cash   X

Cr (↓) Receivables   X

(e)   *Goods in transit:*

Dr (↑) Inventories   X

Cr (↑) Payables   X

(IFRS 10: para. B86(c))

| **Question 9.1** | Consolidated statement of financial position |

The statements of financial position for two entities for the year ended 31 December 20X9 are presented below:

STATEMENTS OF FINANCIAL POSITION AS AT 31 DECEMBER 20X9

	BC $'000	HJ $'000
Non-current assets		
Property, plant and equipment	2,300	1,900
Investment in HJ (at cost)	720	–
	3,020	1,900
Current assets	3,340	1,790
	6,360	3,690
Equity		
Share capital	1,000	500
Retained earnings	3,430	1,800
	4,430	2,300
Non-current liabilities	350	290
Current liabilities	1,580	1,100
	6,360	3,690

Additional information:

(1)   BC acquired a 60% investment in HJ on 1 January 20X6 for $720,000 when the retained earnings of HJ were $300,000.

(2)   On 30 November 20X9, HJ sold goods to BC for $200,000, one-quarter of which remain in BC's inventories at 31 December. HJ earns a 25% mark-up on all items sold.

(3)   An impairment review was conducted at 31 December 20X9 and it was decided that the goodwill on acquisition of HJ was impaired by 10%.

Required

Prepare the consolidated statement of financial position for the BC group as at 31 December 20X9 under the following assumptions:

(a)   It is group policy to value non-controlling interest at fair value at the date of acquisition. The fair value of the non-controlling interest at 1 January 20X6 was $480,000.

(b)   It is group policy to value non-controlling interest at the proportionate share of the fair value of the net assets at acquisition.

5 Consolidated statement of profit or loss and other comprehensive income

5.1 Consolidated statement of profit or loss and other comprehensive income

5.1.1 Overview

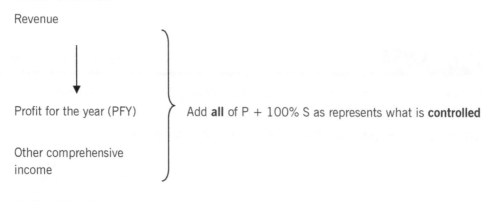

Revenue

Profit for the year (PFY)   Add **all** of P + 100% S as represents what is **controlled**

Other comprehensive income

Profit attributable to:

    Owners of parent   β – balancing figure
    NCI   S's PFY × NCI%

                                                               Ownership reconciliation

Total comprehensive income attributable to:

    Owners of parent   β – balancing figure
    NCI   S's TCI × NCI%

Question 9.2	Consolidated statement of profit or loss and other comprehensive income

The statements of profit or loss and other comprehensive income for two entities for the year ended 31 December 20X5 are presented below:

STATEMENTS OF PROFIT OR LOSS AND OTHER COMPREHENSIVE INCOME FOR THE YEAR ENDED 31 DECEMBER 20X5

	CV $'000	SG $'000
Revenue	5,000	4,200
Cost of sales	(4,100)	(3,500)
Gross profit	900	700
Distribution and administrative expenses	(320)	(180)
Profit before tax	580	520
Income tax expense	(190)	(160)
PROFIT FOR THE YEAR	390	360
Other comprehensive income		
Items that will not be reclassified to profit or loss		
Gain on revaluation of property (net of deferred tax)	60	40
TOTAL COMPREHENSIVE INCOME FOR THE YEAR	450	400

Additional information:

(1) CV acquired an 80% investment in SG on 1 April 20X5. It is group policy to measure non-controlling interests at fair value at acquisition. Goodwill of $100,000 arose on acquisition. The fair value of the net assets was deemed to be the same as the carrying value of net assets at acquisition.

(2) An impairment review was conducted on 31 December 20X5 and it was decided that the goodwill on the acquisition on SG was impaired by 10%.

(3) On 31 October 20X5, SG sold goods to CV for $300,000. Two-thirds of these goods remain in CV's inventories at the year end. SG charges a mark-up of 25% on cost.

(4) Assume that the profits and other comprehensive income of SG accrue evenly over the year.

Required

Prepare the consolidated statement of profit or loss and other comprehensive income for the CV group for the year ended 31 December 20X5.

6 Fair values (IFRS 3)

6.1 Goodwill

We calculate goodwill as (IFRS 3: para. 32):

LEARN

Goodwill	
	$
Consideration transferred (investment)	X
Non-controlling interests (NCI)	X
Less net acquisition-date **fair value** of identifiable assets acquired and liabilities assumed	(X)
	X

Both the consideration transferred and the net assets at acquisition must be measured at fair value to arrive at true goodwill.

Normally goodwill is a **positive** balance which is recorded as an **intangible non-current asset**. Occasionally it is **negative** and arises as a result of a 'bargain purchase'. In this instance, IFRS 3 requires reassessment of the calculations to ensure that they are accurate and then any remaining negative goodwill should be recognised as a **gain in profit or loss** and therefore also recorded in group retained earnings. (IFRS 3: para. 34, 36)

KEY TERM

Fair value – definition (IFRS 13)

FAIR VALUE is 'the price that would be received to sell an asset or paid to transfer a liability in an orderly transaction between market participants at the measurement date.' (IFRS 13: para. 9)

6.2 Fair value of consideration transferred

The consideration transferred is measured at fair value, calculated as the acquisition-date fair values of:

- The assets transferred by the parent;
- The liabilities incurred by the parent (to former owners of the subsidiary); and
- Equity interests (shares) issued by the parent. (IFRS 3: para. 37–40)

Specifically:

Item	Treatment
(a) Deferred consideration	• Discounted to present value to measure its fair value
(b) Contingent consideration (to be settled in cash or shares) (IFRS 3: para. 39, 58)	• Measured at fair value at acquisition date • *Subsequent measurement:*

Additional info
re facts at
acq'n date

Any other change
(eg targets met)

Liability   Equity

Adjust goodwill
(if within one year
from acquisition date)

Gain/loss
to P/L

Not
adjusted

Costs involved in the transaction are **charged to profit or loss**.

However, costs to issue debt or equity instruments are treated in accordance with IAS 32 *Financial instruments: presentation* /IFRS 9 *Financial Instruments*, ie deducted from the financial liability or equity. (IFRS 3: para. 53)

Question 9.3   Fair value of consideration transferred

BW acquired all of GF's 400,000 ordinary shares during the year ended 28 February 20X5. GF was purchased from its directors who will remain directors of the business. BW incurred legal and professional fees as a result of the acquisition of $75,000.

The purchase consideration comprised:

- $250,000 in cash payable at acquisition
- $100,000 payable 1 year after acquisition
- $100,000 payable in 2 years' time if profits exceed $2m
- New shares issued in BW on a 1 for 4 basis

The consideration payable in 2 years after acquisition is a tough target for the directors of GF and so its fair value (taking into account the time value of money) has been measured at only $30,750.

The market value of BW's shares on the acquisition date was $7.35.

An appropriate discount rate for use where relevant is 7% and the 1 year 7% discount factor is 0.935.

Required

Calculate the consideration transferred to acquire GF at the date of acquisition.

6.3 Fair value of identifiable assets acquired and liabilities assumed

6.3.1 Principle

Assets and liabilities in an entity's own financial statements are often not stated at their fair value, eg where the entity's accounting policy is to use the cost model for assets.

If the subsidiary's financial statements are not adjusted to their fair values, goodwill will be over- or understated.

Under IFRS 3 the identifiable **assets acquired and liabilities assumed** of subsidiaries are therefore required to be brought into the consolidated financial statements **at their *fair value* rather than their book value**.

The **difference** between fair values and book values is a **consolidation adjustment** made only for the purposes of the consolidated financial statements.

6.3.2 Detailed rules

The fair value of identifiable net assets of the subsidiary at acquisition may include items that have not been recognised in the subsidiary's individual financial statements:

(a)   **Intangible assets** such as brands, licences, trade names, domain names, customer relationships (not in subsidiary's individual accounts as internally generated and not reliably measureable). (IFRS 3: para B31–B34)

(b)   **Contingent liabilities** (not in subsidiary's individual accounts as IAS 37 *Provisions, contingent liabilities and contingent assets* requires them to be disclosed rather than recognised). (IFRS 3: para. 22, 23)

6.3.3 Working proforma

When preparing a consolidated SOFP, the fair value adjustment working would be:

	Acq'n date	Movement	Year end	
Inventories	X	(X)	X	Adjust figures in SOFP
Property, plant and equipment	X	(X)	X	
Intangible assets	X	(X)	X	
Contingent liabilities	(X)	(X)/X	*X)	
	X	(X)	X	

Goodwill   Ret'd earnings

Example: Fair values

ER acquired 750,000 of BN's 1,000,000 $1 ordinary shares on 1 January 20X2 for $3,800,000 when BN's retained earnings were $3,200,000. It is group policy to value non-controlling interest at fair value at the date of acquisition. The fair value of the non-controlling interest at 1 January 20X2 was $1,600,000. As at 31 December 20X3, there had been no impairment of goodwill.

At 1 January 20X2, the fair value of the net assets acquired was the same as the book value with the following exceptions:

- The fair value of property, plant and equipment was $800,000 higher than book value. These assets were assessed to have a remaining useful life of 16 years from the date of acquisition.

- The fair value of inventories was estimated to be $200,000 higher than the book value. All of these inventories were sold by 31 December 20X2.

- BN had a customer list which it had not recognised as an intangible asset because it was internally generated. However, on acquisition, external experts managed to establish a fair value for the list of $150,000. Customers are typically retained for an average of 5 years.

- A contingent liability, which had a fair value of $220,000 at the date of acquisition. This liability was settled in the year ended 31 December 20X2.

At 31 December 20X3, the retained earnings of ER and BN were $7,500,000 and $4,000,000 respectively. BN's profit for the year and total comprehensive income for the year ended 31 December 20X3 was $500,000.

Required

(a) Calculate the amounts that will appear in the consolidated statement of financial position of the ER group as at 31 December 20X3 for:

    (i)   Goodwill
    (ii)   Consolidated retained earnings
    (iii)   Non-controlling interest

(b) Calculate the non-controlling interest in the profit of BN for inclusion in the consolidated statement of profit or loss and other comprehensive income for the year ended 31 December 20X3.

Solution

(a)   (i)   **Goodwill**

	$'000	$'000
Consideration transferred		3,800
Non-controlling interests (at fair value)		1,600
Less fair value of identifiable net assets at acquisition:		
Share capital	1,000	
Retained earnings	3,200	
Fair value adjustment (W2)	930	
		(5,130)
		270

  (ii)   **Consolidated retained earnings**

	ER $'000	BN $'000
At the year end	7,500	4,000
Fair value movement (W2)		(140)
At acquisition		(3,200)
		660
Share of BN post-acquisition's retained earnings (75% × 660)	495	
	7,995	

  (iii)   **Non-controlling interest (in SOFP)**

	$'000
NCI at acquisition	1,600
NCI share of post-acquisition reserves	165
	1,765

(b)   **Non-controlling interests (in SPLOCI)**

	PFY $'000
Per question	500
Fair value depreciation on property, plant and equipment for the year (W2)	(50)
Fair value amortisation on intangible asset for the year (W2)	(30)
	420
NCI share	× 25%
	= 105

Workings

1   *Group structure*

ER

1.1.X2 750/1,000 = 75%

BN

PAR = $3.2m

2   *Fair value adjustment*

	Acq'n date 1.1.X2 $'000	Movement X2, X3 $'000	Year end 31.12.X3 $'000	
Inventories	200	(200)	-	Adjust
Property, plant and equipment	800	(100)*	700	figures
Intangible assets	150	(60)**	90	in
Contingent liabilities	(220)	220	-	SOFP
	930	(140)	790	

Goodwill   Ret'd
                earnings

*extra depreciation on PPE = 800 × 1/16 = 50 per annum × 2 years = 100
**amortisation of intangibles = 150 × 1/5 = 30 per annum × 2 years = 60

Chapter Summary

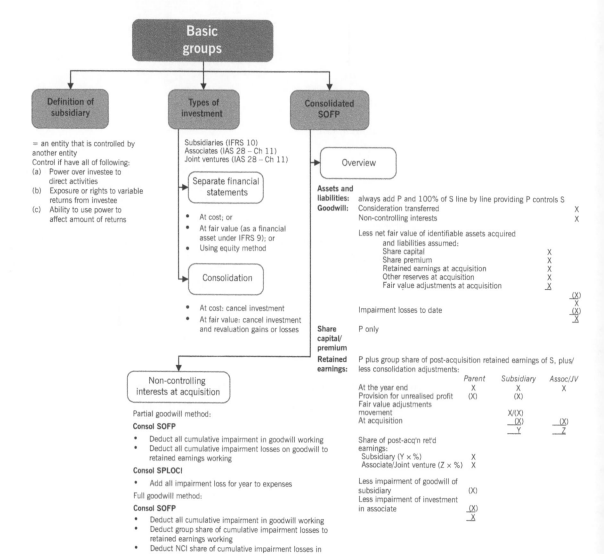

Basic groups

Definition of subsidiary

= an entity that is controlled by another entity
Control if have all of following:
(a) Power over investee to direct activities
(b) Exposure or rights to variable returns from investee
(c) Ability to use power to affect amount of returns

Types of investment

Subsidiaries (IFRS 10)
Associates (IAS 28 – Ch 11)
Joint ventures (IAS 28 – Ch 11)

Separate financial statements

- At cost; or
- At fair value (as a financial asset under IFRS 9); or
- Using equity method

Consolidation

- At cost: cancel investment
- At fair value: cancel investment and revaluation gains or losses

Non-controlling interests at acquisition

Partial goodwill method:

Consol SOFP

- Deduct all cumulative impairment in goodwill working
- Deduct all cumulative impairment losses on goodwill to retained earnings working

Consol SPLOCI

- Add all impairment loss for year to expenses

Full goodwill method:

Consol SOFP

- Deduct all cumulative impairment in goodwill working
- Deduct group share of cumulative impairment losses to retained earnings working
- Deduct NCI share of cumulative impairment losses in NCI working

Consol SPLOCI

- Add all impairment loss for year to expenses
- Deduct impairment loss for year from NCI PFY and TCI

Consolidated SOFP

Overview

Assets and liabilities:	always add P and 100% of S line by line providing P controls S	
Goodwill:	Consideration transferred	X
	Non-controlling interests	X
	Less net fair value of identifiable assets acquired and liabilities assumed:	
	Share capital	X
	Share premium	X
	Retained earnings at acquisition	X
	Other reserves at acquisition	X
	Fair value adjustments at acquisition	X
		(X)
		X
	Impairment losses to date	(X)
		X

Share capital/ premium   P only

Retained earnings: P plus group share of post-acquisition retained earnings of S, plus/less consolidation adjustments:

	Parent	Subsidiary	Assoc/JV
At the year end	X	X	X
Provision for unrealised profit	(X)	(X)	
Fair value adjustments movement		X/(X)	
At acquisition		(X)	(X)
		Y	Z

Share of post-acq'n ret'd earnings:
Subsidiary (Y × %)   X
Associate/Joint venture (Z × %)   X

Less impairment of goodwill of subsidiary	(X)
Less impairment of investment in associate	(X)
	X

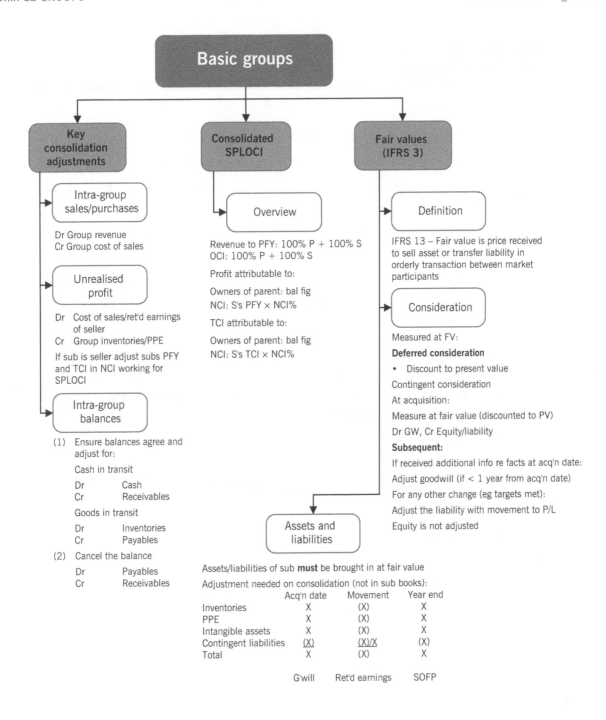

Quick Quiz

1   Define a subsidiary.   *controlled*.

2   What are the three criteria that need to be met under IFRS 10 to determine control?   *–rights –power –affect decis*.

3   What accounting treatment does IFRS 10 require of a parent company?

4   How should an investment in a subsidiary be accounted for in the separate financial statements of the parent?   *cost, FV or equity*

5   Where does unrealised profit on intragroup trading appear in the statement of profit or loss?

6   What are non-controlling interests?   *other 3rd parties unbidlery*

7   Chicken Co owns 80% of Egg Co. Egg Co sells goods to Chicken Co at cost plus 50%. The total invoiced sales to Chicken Co by Egg Co in the year ended 31 December 20X9 were $900,000 and, of these sales, goods which had been invoiced at $60,000 were held in inventory by Chicken Co at 31 December 20X9. What is the reduction in aggregate group gross profit?

8   Major Co, which makes up its accounts to 31 December, has an 80%-owned subsidiary, Minor Co. Minor Co sells goods to Major Co at a mark-up on cost of 33.33%. At 31 December 20X8, Major had $12,000 of such goods in its inventory and at 31 December 20X9 had $15,000 of such goods in its inventory.

     What is the amount by which the consolidated profit attributable to Major Co's shareholders should be adjusted in respect of the above?

     (Ignore taxation)

     A $1,000 Debit
     B $800 Credit
     C $750 Credit
     D $600 Debit

9   What are the components making up the figure of non-controlling interests in a consolidated statement of financial position?

Answers to Quick Quiz

1   An entity that is controlled by another entity.

2   An investor (the parent) controls an investee (the subsidiary) if all of the following IFRS 10 criteria are met:

     –   Power over the investee
     –   Exposure or rights to variable returns from its involvement with the investee
     –   The ability to use its power over the investee to affect the amount of the investor's return

3   The financial statements of parent and subsidiary are combined and presented as a single entity.

4   (a)   At cost, or
     (b)   At fair value, in accordance with IFRS 9; or
     (c)   Using the equity method as described in IAS 28.

5   As an addition to cost of sales.

6   The equity in a subsidiary not attributable, directly or indirectly, to a parent.

7      $\dfrac{\$60,000 \times 50}{150} = \$20,000$

8   D $600 Debit

     $(15,000 - 12,000) \times 33.3/133.3 \times 80\%$

9   The non-controlling interests at acquisition (measured either at their proportionate share of the subsidiary's net assets or at fair value) plus their share of the subsidiary's post-acquisition retained reserves, less impairment of goodwill (if NCI measured at fair value at the date of acquisition)

Answers to Questions

9.1 Consolidated statement of financial position

BC GROUP
CONSOLIDATED STATEMENT OF FINANCIAL POSITION AS AT 31 DECEMBER 20X9

	(a)	(b)
	$'000	$'000
Non-current assets		
Property, plant and equipment (2,300 + 1,900)	4,200	4,200
Goodwill **(W2)**	360	216
	4,560	4,416
Current assets (3,340 + 1,790 – 10 (W5))	5,120	5,120
	9,680	9,536
Equity attributable to owners of the parent		
Share capital	1,000	1,000
Retained earnings **(W3)**	4,300	4,300
	5,300	5,300
Non-controlling interests (W4)	1,060	916
	6,360	6,216
Non-current liabilities (350 + 290)	640	640
Current liabilities (1,580 + 1,100)	2,680	2,680
	9,680	9,536

Workings

1   *Group structure*

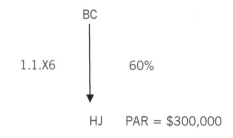

BC

1.1.X6   60%

HJ   PAR = $300,000

2   *Goodwill*

	Part (a)		Part (b)	
	$'000	$'000	$'000	$'000
Consideration transferred		720		720
Non-controlling interests		480	(800 × 40%)	320
Fair value of net assets at acquisition:				
Share capital	500		500	
Retained earnings	300		300	
		(800)		(800)
		400		240
Less impairment losses to date (10%)		(40)		(24)
		360		216

3 *Retained earnings*

	BC $'000	HJ $'000
At the year end	3,430	1,800
Provision for unrealised profit (W5)		(10)
At acquisition		(300)
		1,490
Share of HJ's post-acquisition retained earnings:		
(1,490 × 60%)	894	
Less impairment loss on goodwill:		
Part (a) (40 (W2) × 60%)/**Part (b)** (24 (W2))	(24)	
	4,300	

4 *Non-controlling interests*

	Part (a)	Part (b)
	$'000	$'000
NCI at acquisition (fair value)([500 + 300] × 40%)	480	320
NCI share of post-acquisition reserves	596	596
(1,490 (W3) × 40%)		
NCI share of impairment losses (40 (W2) × 40%)	(16)	(-)
	1,060	916

5 *Provision for unrealised profit*

HJ ⟶ BC

PUP = \$200,000 × ¼ in inventory × 25/125 mark-up = \$10,000

Dr (↓) HJ's retained earnings   \$10,000

Cr (↓) Inventories   \$10,000

9.2 Consolidated statement of profit or loss and other comprehensive income

CV GROUP

CONSOLIDATED STATEMENT OF PROFIT OR LOSS AND OTHER COMPREHENSIVE INCOME FOR THE YEAR ENDED 31 DECEMBER 20X5

	$'000
Revenue (5,000 + [4,200 × 9/12] – 300 (W4))	7,850
Cost of sales (4,100 + [3,500 × 9/12] – 300 (W4) + 40 (W4))	(6,465)
Gross profit	1,385
Distribution and administration expenses (320 + [180 × 9/12] + 10 (W2))	(465)
Profit before tax	920
Income tax expense (190 + [160 × 9/12])	(310)
PROFIT FOR THE YEAR	610
Other comprehensive income	
Items that will not be reclassified to profit or loss	
Gains on property revaluation (net of tax) (60 + [40 × 9/12])	90
TOTAL COMPREHENSIVE INCOME FOR THE YEAR	700
Profit attributable to:	
Owners of the parent (610 – 44)	566
Non-controlling interests (W2)	44
	610
Total comprehensive income attributable to:	
Owners of the parent (700 – 50)	650
Non-controlling interests (W2)	50
	700

Workings

1   *Group structure*

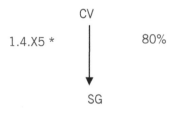

CV

1.4.X5 *   80%

SG

*This is a mid-year acquisition – SG should be consolidated for 9 months.

2   *Non-controlling interests*

	PFY $'000	TCI $'000
Per question (360 × 9/12)/(400 × 9/12)	270	300
Impairment loss on goodwill (W3)	(10)	(10)
PUP (W4)	(40)	(40)
	220	250
NCI share	× 20%	× 20%
	= 44	= 50

3   *Impairment of goodwill*

Impairment of goodwill for the year = $100,000 goodwill × 10% impairment = $10,000

Add $10,000 to 'administration expenses' and deduct from PFY/TCI in NCI working (as full goodwill method adopted here)

4   *Intra-group trading*

SG → CV

- Intra-group revenue and cost of sales:

Cancel $300,000 out of revenue and cost of sales

- PUP = $300,000 × 2/3 in inventories × 25/125 mark-up = $40,000

Increase cost of sales by $40,000 and reduce PFY/TCI in NCI working (as subsidiary is the seller)

9.3 Fair value of consideration transferred

Consideration transferred

	$
Cash	250,000
Deferred consideration (100,000 × 0.935)	93,500
Contingent consideration (measure at fair value)	30,750
Shares in BW (400,000/4 × $7.35)	735,000
	1,109,250

Now try these questions from the Practice Question Bank

Number	Level	Marks	Time
Q13	Introductory	N/A	14 mins
Q14	Introductory	10	18 mins
Q15	Introductory	10	18 mins
Q16	Introductory	10	18 mins
Q17	Introductory	14	25 mins

ASSOCIATES AND JOINT ARRANGEMENTS

In addition to interests in subsidiaries the parent may have interests in associates and joint arrangements. The accounting treatment for these is different.

You need to be able to produce consolidated accounts incorporating associates and joint arrangements in accordance with the provisions of IAS 28 *Investments in associates and joint ventures* and IFRS 11 *Joint arrangements*.

Chapter Overview

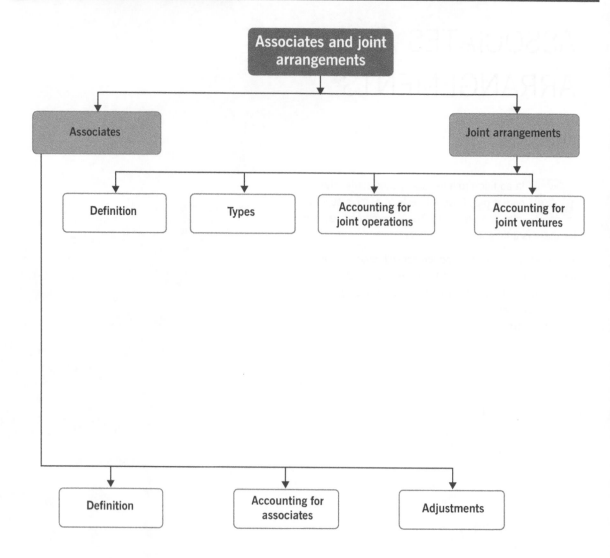

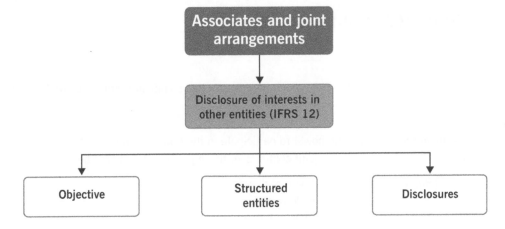

1 Definition of an associate

1.1 Definition

'An ASSOCIATE is an entity over which the investor has **significant influence**.' (IAS 28: para. 3)

Significant influence is the power to participate in the financial and operating policy decisions of the investee but is not control or joint control over those policies. This could be shown by:

(a)   Representation on the board of directors
(b)   Participation in policy-making processes
(c)   Material transactions between the entity and investee
(d)   Interchange of managerial personnel
(e)   Provision of essential technical information

(IAS 28: para. 3, 6)

1.1.1 Presumptions

If an investor holds, directly or indirectly:

(a)   ≥ 20% of voting power

- Presumption of significant influence unless demonstrated otherwise

(b)   < 20% of voting power

- Presumption of no significant influence unless demonstrated otherwise

(IAS 28: para. 5)

2 Accounting for associates

2.1 Parent's separate financial statements

Investments in subsidiaries, associates and joint ventures can be carried in the investor's separate financial statements (IAS 27: para. 10):

- At **cost**; or
- At **fair value** (as a financial asset under IFRS 9 *Financial Instruments*).
- Using the **equity method** as described in IAS 28 *Investments in associates and joint ventures*.

2.2 Consolidated financial statements

An investment in an associate is accounted for in consolidated financial statements using the **equity method**.

2.3 Equity method

STATEMENT OF FINANCIAL POSITION

IAS 28 states the following treatment (IAS 28: para. 10):

Non-current assets

Investment in associates (Working)	X

Working	
Cost of associate	X
Share of post-acquisition retained earnings (and other reserves)	D
Less impairment losses on associate to date	(E)
	X

Consolidated retained earnings

	Parent	Subsidiary	Associate
At the year end	X	X	X
Provision for unrealised profit	(X)	(X)	
Fair value adjustments movement		X/(X)	
At acquisition		(X)	(X)
		B	C
Share of post acq'n ret'd earnings:			
Subsidiary (B × %)	X		
Associate/Joint venture (C × %)	**D**		
Less impairment of goodwill of subsidiary	(X)		
Less impairment of investment in associate	**(E)**		
	X		

Note. A similar working would be prepared for any other reserves (eg revaluation surplus).

STATEMENT OF PROFIT OR LOSS AND OTHER COMPREHENSIVE INCOME

Profit or loss

A's profit for the year × Group %	X

Shown before group profit before tax.

Other comprehensive income

A's other comprehensive income for the year × Group %	X

Points to note

(a)   An associate is not a group company, therefore no cancellation of 'intra-group' transactions should be performed.

However, IAS 28 states that the **investor's share** of unrealised profits and losses on transactions between investor and associate should be eliminated in the same way as for group accounts. (IAS 28: para. 28)

This is done as follows in SOFP:

Dr (↓) Group retained earnings (P's column)	PUP × A%
Cr (↓) Investment in associate	PUP × A% (if A holds the inventories) **or**
Cr (↓) Group inventories	PUP × A% (if P holds the inventories)

And in SPLOCI:

Dr (↑) Cost of sales	PUP × A% (if P = seller) **or**
Dr (↓) Share of associate's profit	PUP × A% (if A = seller)
[Cr (↓) Investment in associate	PUP × A% (if A holds the inventories)] **or**
[Cr (↓) Group inventories	PUP × A% (if P holds the inventories)]

(b)   After application of the equity method, any impairment losses are considered re the investor's net investment in the associate as a whole. (IAS 28: para. 40)

Example: Associates 1

P purchased a 60% holding in S on 1 January 20X0 for $6.1m when the retained earnings of S were $3.6m. The retained earnings of S at 31 December 20X4 were $10.6m. Since acquisition, there has been no impairment of the goodwill in S.

P also has a 30% holding in A which it acquired on 1 July 20X1 for $4.1m when the retained earnings of A were $6.2m. The retained earnings of A at 31 December 20X4 were $9.2m.

An impairment test conducted at the year end revealed that the investment in associate was impaired by $500,000.

During the year A sold goods to P for $3m at a profit margin of 20%. One-third of these goods remained in P's inventories at the year end. The retained earnings of P at 31 December 20X4 were $41.6m.

Required

(a)   Which of the following accounting adjustments would P process in the preparation of its consolidated financial statements for the year ended 31 December 20X4 in relation to unrealised profit? (Tick the correct answer)

Tick	Options
	Dr Cost of sales $60,000, Cr Investment in associate $60,000
	Dr Share of profit of associate $50,000, Cr Inventories $50,000
	Dr Cost of sales $200,000, Cr Investment in associate $200,000
	Dr Share of profit of associate $60,000, Cr Inventories $60,000

(b)   Calculate the following amounts for inclusion in the consolidated statement of financial position of the P group as at 31 December 20X4:

(i)   Investment in associate

(ii)   Consolidated retained earnings

Solution

(a)   **Accounting adjustment**

The following option is correct:

Tick	Options
	Dr Cost of sales $60,000, Cr Investment in associate $60,000
	Dr Share of profit of associate $50,000, Cr Inventories $50,000
	Dr Cost of sales $200,000, Cr Investment in associate $200,000
✓	Dr Share of profit of associate $60,000, Cr Inventories $60,000

Calculation:

Unrealised profit adjustment (A → P)

$$PUP = \$3,000,000 \times \frac{20\%}{100\%} \text{ margin} \times 1/3 \text{ in inventory} \times 30\% \text{ group share} = \$60,000$$

Tutorial note. As the associate is the seller, the share of the profit of associate rather than cost of sales must be reduced. As the parent holds the inventory, inventory can be reduced as normal. If the parent had sold to the subsidiary, the double entry would be Dr Cost of sales, Cr Investment in associate.

(b)   (i)   **Investment in associate**

	$'000
Cost of associate	4,100
Share of post-acquisition retained earnings (9,200 – 6,200) × 30%	900
	5,000
Less impairment losses on associate to date	(500)
	4,500

(ii)   **Consolidated retained earnings**

	P	S	A
	$'000	$'000	$'000
At the year end	41,600	10,600	9,200
Unrealised profit (part (a))	(60)		
At acquisition		(3,600)	(6,200)
		7,000	3,000
S – share of post-acq'n earnings (7,000 × 60%)	4,200		
A – share of post-acq'n earnings (3,000 × 30%)	900		
Less impairment losses on associate to date	(500)		
	46,140		

Tutorial note. Even though the associate was the seller for the intragroup trading, PUP is adjusted in the parent's column so as not to multiply it by the group share twice.

Working: Group structure

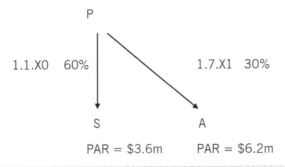

P

1.1.X0   60%   1.7.X1   30%

S   A

PAR = $3.6m   PAR = $6.2m

Example: Associates 2

DE has several subsidiaries. On 1 October 20X2, DE purchased 40% of the equity share capital of FG. FG's profits and other comprehensive income accrue evenly over the year. The summarised statement of profit or loss and other comprehensive income of FG for the year ended 31 December 20X2 is shown below:

	$'000
Profit before tax	10,000
Income tax expense	(3,000)
Profit for the year	7,000
Other comprehensive income (net of tax)	1,000
Total comprehensive income for the year	8,000

On 20 December 20X2, FG sold goods to DE for $25,000 at a mark-up of 25%. All these goods remained in inventory at the year end. As at 31 December 20X2, an impairment test revealed that the investment in the associate had fallen in value by $50,000.

Required

What are the figures in relation to FG for inclusion in the consolidated statement of profit or loss and other comprehensive income for the year ended 31 December 20X2?

Solution

Share of profit of associate: $648,000 (W2)

Share of other comprehensive income of associate: $'100,000 (W3)

Workings

1 Unrealised profit (FG → DE)

$$PUP = \$25,000 \times \frac{25\%}{125\%} \text{ mark-up} \times 40\% \text{ group share} = \$2,000$$

↓ Share of associate's profit (as associate is the seller)

2 *Share of profit of associate*

	$'000
Share of profit for the year (7,000 × 3/12 × 40%)	700
Less provision for unrealised profit (W1)	(2)
Less impairment in investment in associate for the year	(50)
	648

3 *Share of other comprehensive income of associate*

	$'000
Share of other comprehensive income for the year (1,000 × 3/12 × 40%)	100

This is a mid-year acquisition of an associate. It was acquired nine months into the year on 1 October 20X2 which is why we only equity account for three months.

3 Definition of a joint arrangement

3.1 Definitions

KEY TERMS

A JOINT ARRANGEMENT is an arrangement of which **two or more parties** have **joint control**. (IFRS 11: para. 4)

JOINT CONTROL is the contractually agreed sharing of control of an arrangement, which exists only when decisions about the relevant activities require the **unanimous consent** of the parties sharing control. (IFRS 11: para. 7)

A joint arrangement has the following characteristics (IFRS 11: para. 5):

(a) The parties are bound by a contractual arrangement.
(b) The contractual arrangement gives two or more of those parties joint control of the arrangement.

Question 10.1   Power over the arrangement

An arrangement has three parties: A has 50% of the voting rights, B has 30% and C has 20%. The contractual arrangement between A, B and C specifies that at least 75% of the voting rights are required to make decisions about the relevant activities of the arrangement.

Required

Which of the following statements is correct in relation to the power that the entities have over the arrangement? (Tick the correct answer)

Tick	Options
	A, B and C have joint control over the arrangement.
	A and B only have joint control over the arrangement.
	A has outright control over the arrangement.
	A, B and C have significant influence over the arrangement.

2.2 Types

There are two types of joint arrangement:

Joint operations	A joint arrangement whereby the parties that have joint control of the arrangement have **rights to the assets and obligations for the liabilities** relating to the arrangement (IFRS 11: para. 15)
Joint ventures	A joint arrangement whereby the parties that have joint control of the arrangement have **rights to the net assets** of the arrangement (IFRS 11: para. 16)

Under these definitions, accounting treatment is determined based on whether or not the investor has direct rights to assets and obligations for liabilities that should be recognised separately in its financial statements, rather than merely following the legal form of the joint arrangement:

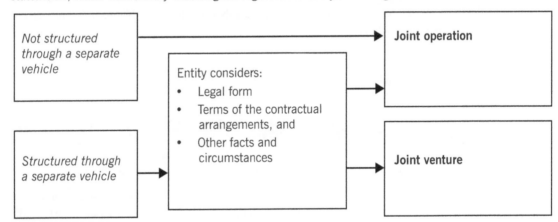

4 Accounting for joint arrangements

4.1 Accounting for joint operations

In its separate financial statements a joint operator recognises (IFRS 11: para. 20):

- Its own assets, liabilities and expenses
- Its share of assets held and expenses and liabilities incurred jointly
- Its revenue from the sale of its share of the output arising from the joint operation
- Its share of revenue from the sale of output by the joint operation itself

No adjustments are necessary on consolidation as the figures are already incorporated correctly into the separate financial statements of the joint operator.

4.2 Accounting for joint ventures

4.2.1 Parent's separate financial statements

Investments in subsidiaries, associates and joint ventures can be carried in the investor's separate financial statements (IAS 27: para. 10):

- At **cost**; or
- At **fair value** (as a financial asset under IFRS 9 *Financial Instruments*).
- Using the **equity method** as described in IAS 28.

4.2.2 Consolidated financial statements

Joint ventures are accounted for using the **equity method** in the consolidated financial statements (IFRS 11: para. 24) in exactly the same way as for associates ie:

Consolidated SOFP	Investment in joint venture
	Share of joint venture's post-acquisition reserves
Consolidated SPLOCI	Share of joint venture's profit for the year
	Share of joint venture's other comprehensive income
Unrealised profit	Cancel **group** share

Question 10.2	Joint arrangements

AB and CD set up EF, an incorporated entity, to extract coal from a surface mine. AB and CD each have a 50% stake and joint control in EF. AB and CD each transfer their own assets to EF on incorporation. A contractual arrangement is signed by both AB and CD such that their own assets would revert to them on liquidation of EF and that they each be individually liable for the liabilities of EF in proportion to their respective shareholdings.

Required

Which of the following is the correct accounting treatment for EF in the financial statements of AB? (Tick the correct option)

Tick	Type of joint arrangement	Accounting treatment in AB's individual financial statements	Accounting treatment in AB's consolidated financial statements
	Joint venture	Investment at cost or fair value	Consolidate
	Joint operation	Include share of joint revenue, expenses, assets and liabilities in addition to the entity's own	No further adjustments (already incorporated in AB's individual financial statements)
	Joint venture	Investment at cost or fair value	Equity account
	Joint operation	Include share of joint revenue, expenses, assets and liabilities in addition to the entity's own	Equity account

5   IFRS 12: Disclosure of interests in other entities

5.1 Objective

The objective of the standard is to require entities to disclose information that enables the user of the financial statements to evaluate the **nature** of, and **risks** associated with, interests in other entities, and the **effects** of those interests on its financial position, financial performance and cash flows.

This is particularly relevant in light of the financial crisis and recent accounting scandals. The IASB believes that better information about interests in other entities is necessary to help users to identify the profit or loss and cash flows available to the reporting entity and to determine the value of a current or future investment in the reporting entity.

IFRS 12 covers disclosures for entities which have interests in:

- Subsidiaries
- Joint arrangements (ie joint operations and joint ventures)
- Associates
- Unconsolidated structured entities

5.2 Structured entities

KEY TERM

STRUCTURED ENTITY: 'An entity that has been designed so that **voting or similar rights** are not **the dominant factor** in **deciding who controls** the entity, such as when any voting rights relate to administrative tasks only and the relevant activities are directed by means of contractual arrangements.' (IFRS 12: Appendix A)

Disclosures are required for structured entities due to their sensitive nature (see below).

5.3 Disclosures

The main disclosures required by IFRS 12 for an entity that has investments in other entities are:

(a)   The **significant judgements and assumptions** made in determining whether the entity has control, joint control or significant influence of the other entities, and in determining the type of joint arrangement (IFRS 12: para. 7)

(b)   Information to understand the **composition of the group** and the interest that non-controlling interests have in the group's activities and cash flows (IFRS 12: para. 10)

(c)   The **nature, extent and financial effects** of interests in **joint arrangements and associates**, including the nature and effects of the entity's contractual relationship with other investors (IFRS 12: para. 20)

(d)   The **nature and extent** of interests in **unconsolidated** structured entities (IFRS 12: para. 24)

(e)   The nature and extent of **significant restrictions** on the entity's ability to **access or use assets and settle liabilities** of the group (IFRS 12: para. 13)

(f)   The nature of, and changes in, the **risks associated with the entity's interests** in consolidated structured entities, joint ventures, associates and unconsolidated structured entities (eg commitments and contingent liabilities) (IFRS 12: para. 14, 21, 29)

(g)   The **consequences of changes in the entity's ownership** interest in a subsidiary that do **not result in loss of control** (ie the effects on the equity attributable to owners of the parent) (IFRS 12: para. 18)

(h)   The **consequences of losing control** of a subsidiary during the reporting period (ie the gain or loss, and the portion of it that relates to measuring any remaining investment at fair value, and the line item(s) in profit or loss in which the gain or loss is recognised (if not presented separately)) (IFRS 12: para. 19)

Question 10.3

IFRS 12 *Disclosures of interests in other entities* was issued in May 2011.

Required

Which ONE of the statements in relation to IFRS 12 is incorrect? (Tick the statement that is incorrect)

Tick	Options
	It requires disclosures in interests in subsidiaries, joint arrangements, associates and unconsolidated structured entities.
	Its objective is to enable users to evaluate the nature of its interest in other entities and the associated risks and effects.
	It requires subsidiaries to be consolidated and associates to be equity accounted in the group financial statements.
	Prior to IFRS 12, the disclosures for subsidiaries, joint arrangements, associates and unconsolidated structured entities were covered in different accounting standards and were inconsistent.

Chapter Summary

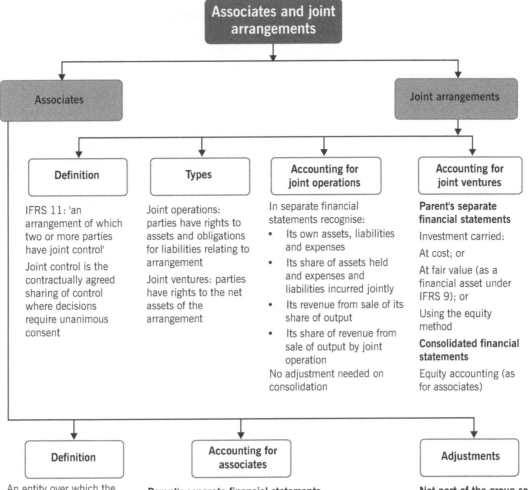

Associates and joint arrangements

Associates

Joint arrangements

Definition

IFRS 11: 'an arrangement of which two or more parties have joint control'

Joint control is the contractually agreed sharing of control where decisions require unanimous consent

Types

Joint operations: parties have rights to assets and obligations for liabilities relating to arrangement

Joint ventures: parties have rights to the net assets of the arrangement

Accounting for joint operations

In separate financial statements recognise:

- Its own assets, liabilities and expenses
- Its share of assets held and expenses and liabilities incurred jointly
- Its revenue from sale of its share of output
- Its share of revenue from sale of output by joint operation

No adjustment needed on consolidation

Accounting for joint ventures

Parent's separate financial statements

Investment carried:

At cost; or

At fair value (as a financial asset under IFRS 9); or

Using the equity method

Consolidated financial statements

Equity accounting (as for associates)

Definition

An entity over which the investor has significant **influence**

Ie power to participate in financial and operating policy decisions of investee.

Shown by:

(a) Representation on board of directors
(b) Participation in policy making processes
(c) Material transactions between entity and investee
(d) Interchange of managerial personnel
(e) Provision of essential technical information

>/ 20% of voting power = presumption of significant influence

Accounting for associates

Parent's separate financial statements

Investment carried:

At cost; or

At fair value (as a financial asset under IFRS 9).Using the equity method

Consolidated financial statements

Use equity method:

SOFP

Non-current assets

Cost of associate	X
Share of post-acquisition retained earnings	X
Less impairment losses on associate to date	(X)
Investment in associate	X

SPLOCI

Profit or loss

A's profit for the year × Group %

Other comprehensive income

A's OCI for the year × Group %

Adjustments

Not part of the group so no cancelling of intra-group

PUP only

SOFP:

Dr Group retained earnings
Cr Investment in associate
　(A holds inventories)
Cr Group inventories
　(P holds inventories)

SPLOCI:

Dr Cost of sales (P is seller)
Dr Share of associate's
　profit
　(A is seller)
Cr Investment in associate
　(A holds inventories)
Cr Group inventories
　(P holds inventories)

Adjust for **group share of PUP only**

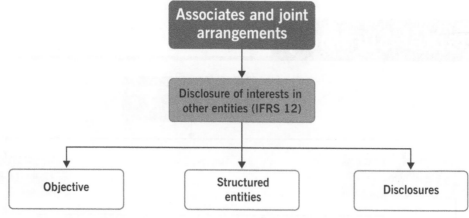

Objective

To require entities to disclose information enabling users to evaluate nature of, and risks associated with, interests in other entities, and the effect of those interests on financial position, financial performance and cash flows.

Structured entities

Designed so voting rights are **not** deciding factor in determining control, but the activities are directed by other means, ie a contract

Disclosures

Significant judgements and assumptions determining control, joint control or sig influence Information to understand composition of group

Nature, extent and financial effects of interests in joint arrangements and associates

Nature and extent of interests in unconsolidated structured entities

Quick Quiz

1   An associate is an ___*× entity*___ over which the investor has *significant influence*
     Complete the blanks.

2   If a company holds 20% or more of the shares of another company, it is presumed that the company has *×*
     significant influence (unless it can be clearly demonstrated that this is not the case). True or false? *F = 3 ✓%*

3   What is significant influence?   *input but not control*

4   What is the effect of the equity method on the statement of profit or loss and other comprehensive income
     and the statement of financial position?   *→ including assoc π*
     → at cost .

5   A joint venture is a joint arrangement whereby the parties that have _*joint control*_ of the
     arrangement have rights to the_____*net assets*_____of the arrangement.
     Complete the blanks.

6   How should a venturer account for its share of a joint operation?   *line by line .*

7   How should a venturer account for its share of a joint venture?   *equity method*

8   A joint arrangement that is structured through a separate vehicle will always be a joint venture. True or
     false?

Answers to Quick Quiz

1   An associate is an **entity** over which the investor has a **significant influence**.

2   True.

3   The power to participate in the financial and operating decisions of the investee but not control or joint control.

4   (a)   Statement of profit or loss and other comprehensive income – investing entity includes its share of the profit for the year of the associate or joint venture

         (b)   Statement of financial position – the investments in associates or joint ventures is initially recorded at cost. This will then increase each year by the group share of the associate/joint venture's post-acquisition reserves. Any impairment losses in the investments in associates to date should be deducted

5   A joint venture is a joint arrangement whereby the parties that have **joint control** of the arrangement have rights to the **net assets** of the arrangement.

6   IFRS 11 requires that a joint operator recognises line by line the following in relation to its interest in a joint operation:

         (a)   Its assets, including its share of any jointly-held assets
         (b)   Its liabilities, including its share of any jointly-incurred liabilities
         (c)   Its revenue from the sale of its share of the output arising from the joint operation
         (d)   Its share of the revenue from the sale of the output by the joint operation, and
         (e)   Its expenses, including its share of any expenses incurred jointly

7   A joint venture is accounted for using the equity method as required by IAS 28 *Investments in associates and joint ventures*.

8   False. Joint arrangements that are structured through a separate vehicle may be either joint ventures or joint operations. The classification will depend on whether the venturer has **rights to the net assets** of the arrangement (joint venture) or **rights to the assets and obligations for the liabilities** (joint operation). This will depend on the terms of the contractual arrangement.

Answers to Questions

10.1 Power over the arrangement

The correct answer is ticked below:

Tick	Options
	A, B and C have joint control over the arrangement.
✓	A and B only have joint control over the arrangement.
	A has outright control over the arrangement.
	A, B and C have significant influence over the arrangement.

Even though A can block any decision, it does not alone control the arrangement because it needs the agreement of B. The terms of their contractual arrangement requiring at least 75% of the voting right to make decisions imply that A and B have joint control of the arrangement because decisions about the relevant activities of the arrangement cannot be made without A and B agreeing. C does not have joint control because A and B (with a combined vote of 80%) can make a joint decision without C's consent.

10.2 Joint arrangements

The following option is correct:

	Type of joint arrangement	Accounting treatment in AB's individual financial statements	Accounting treatment in AB's consolidated financial statements
	Joint venture	Investment at cost or fair value	Consolidate
✓	Joint operation	Include share of joint revenue, expenses, assets and liabilities in addition to the entity's own	No further adjustments (already incorporated in AB's individual financial statements)
	Joint venture	Investment at cost or fair value	Equity account
	Joint operation	Include share of joint revenue, expenses, assets and liabilities in addition to the entity's own	Equity account

Tutorial note. As the joint arrangement is structured as a separate vehicle, EF could be either a joint operation or joint venture. The terms of the contractual arrangement must then be considered to determine which it is. As the contractual arrangement gives AB and CD rights to the assets and obligations for the liabilities of EF, this is a joint operation. If the contractual arrangement had given rights to net assets (rather than rights to assets and obligations for liabilities), it would have been a joint venture.

 BPP LEARNING MEDIA

10.3 IFRS 12

The following statement is **incorrect** in relation to IFRS 12 *Disclosures of interests in other entities*:

Tick	Options
	It requires disclosures in interests in subsidiaries, joint arrangements, associates and unconsolidated structured entities.
	Its objective is to enable users to evaluate the nature of its interest in other entities and the associated risks and effects.
✓	It requires subsidiaries to be consolidated and associates to be equity accounted in the group financial statements.
	Prior to IFRS 12, the disclosures for subsidiaries, joint arrangements, associates and unconsolidated structured entities were covered in different accounting standards and were inconsistent.

Tutorial note. The requirement to consolidate subsidiaries comes from IFRS 10 *Consolidated financial statements* and the requirement to equity account for associates comes from IAS 28 *Investments in associates and joint ventures*. IFRS 12 just covers disclosures of interests in other entities rather than accounting treatment.

Now try these questions from the Practice Question Bank

Number	Level	Marks	Time
Q18	Introductory	N/A	11 mins
Q19	Introductory	20	36 mins
Q20	Introductory	10	18 mins

ADVANCED GROUPS

Part D

CHANGES IN GROUP STRUCTURES

It is common practice for entities to change the level of interest they hold in an investee by purchasing further shares or disposing of all, or part of, their holding.

You need to be able to produce the correct accounting treatment for these changes and understand the impact it will have on the consolidated financial statements.

Topic list	learning outcomes	syllabus references
1 Introduction	B2	B2(a)
2 Acquisitions and disposals where control is retained	B2	B2(a)
3 Acquisitions where control is achieved	B2	B2(a)
4 Disposals where control is lost	B2	B2(a)

Chapter Overview

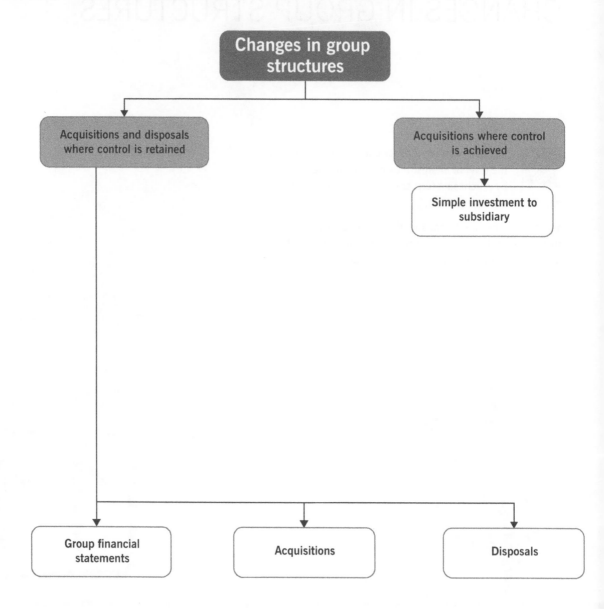

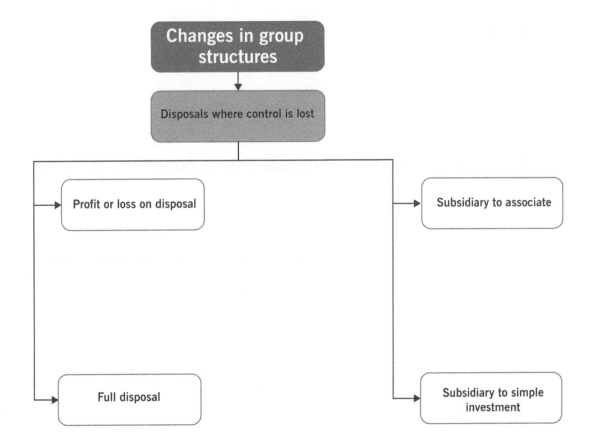

1   Introduction

This chapter covers two main types of changes in group structure:

*   Acquiring additional shareholdings in the period
*   Disposing of all or part of the shareholding in the period

2   Acquisitions and disposals where control is retained

2.1 Group financial statements

Illustration

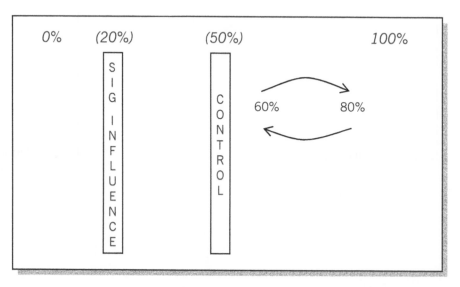

A parent owns 60% of the equity of a subsidiary. The parent buys additional shares from the non-controlling interest so that it now owns 80% of the equity.

In substance, there has been **no acquisition or disposal** as the entity is **still a subsidiary**. Instead, this is a **transaction between group shareholders.** Therefore, it is recorded in equity.

Assume the parent owns 60% of the equity of the subsidiary and buys a further 20% from the non-controlling interest, the accounting is to:

(a)   **Reduce non-controlling interest** in consolidated SOFP

(b)   Record an **adjustment** to **equity** (in the parent's column in the consolidated retained earnings working)

Now assume the parent owns 80% of the equity of the subsidiary and sells 20% to the non-controlling interest. As for an acquisition, this is a **transaction between group shareholders** and it is recorded in equity:

(a)   **Increase non-controlling interest** in consolidated SOFP

(b)   Record an **adjustment** to **equity** (in the parent's column in the consolidated retained earnings working)

(IFRS 10: para. B96)

2.2 Adjustment to equity (for an acquisition)

(a)　Calculation:

	$
Fair value of consideration paid	(X)
Decrease in NCI in net assets [& goodwill*] at acquisition	X
Adjustment to equity	(X)/X

*Will only have an increase or decrease in NCI share in goodwill if NCI measured at fair value at acquisition (full goodwill method)

(b)　How to calculate decrease in NCI:

　　(i)　NCI at fair value *or* NCI at share of net assets at acquisition (full *or* partial goodwill method):

　　　　It is calculated as:

$$\text{NCI at date of step acquisition} \quad \times \quad \frac{\%\,\text{purchased}}{\text{NCI \% before step acquisition}}$$

　　　　NCI at date of step acquisition will either be given in the question or you can calculate it using the consolidated SOFP NCI working.

　　(ii)　NCI at share of net assets at acquisition (partial goodwill method only):

	$
Net assets:	
Share capital	X
Share premium	X
Reserves at date of step acquisition	X
	X
× % purchased	× %
	= X

　　　　This method cannot be used when NCI is measured at fair value at acquisition (full goodwill method) because it does not take into account the goodwill attributable to NCI.

This adjustment should be recorded in the parent's column in the consolidated retained earnings working.

The double entry to record this adjustment is:

Dr (↓) Non-controlling interests	X	
Dr (↓)/Cr (↑) Consolidated retained earnings (with adjustment to equity)	X	
Cr (↓) Cash		X

2.3 Adjustment to equity (for a disposal)

Calculation:

	$
Fair value of consideration received	(X)
Increase in NCI in net assets [& goodwill*] at disposal	X
Adjustment to parent's equity	(X)/X

*Will only have an increase or decrease in NCI share in goodwill if NCI measured at fair value at acquisition (full goodwill method)

As for a step acquisition above, the increase in NCI at disposal is calculated as:

$$\text{NCI at date of disposal} \times \frac{\%\,\text{sold}}{\text{NCI \% before disposal}}$$

Alternatively, for the partial goodwill method, the increase in NCI can be calculated by multiplying the net assets at disposal (share capital, share premium, reserves) by the percentage sold.

This adjustment should be recorded in the parent's column in the consolidated retained earnings working.

The double entry to record this adjustment is:

Dr (↑) Cash	X	
Cr (↑) Non-controlling interests		X
Cr (↑)/Dr (↓) Consolidated retained earnings (with adjustment to equity)		X

2.4 Summary of approach in the consolidated financial statements

For any acquisition or disposal:

(a)   The entity's **status** (subsidiary, associate, simple investment) **during the year** will determine the accounting treatment in the **consolidated statement of profit or loss and other comprehensive income** (pro-rate accordingly).

(b)   The entity's **status** at the **year end** will determine the accounting treatment in the **consolidated statement of financial position** (never pro-rate).

A timeline may be useful.

Consolidated statement of profit or loss and other comprehensive income

- Consolidate subsidiary in full for the whole period
- Non-controlling interests time apportioned based on percentage before and after
- **No profit or loss** on disposal

Consolidated statement of financial position

- **Non-controlling interests decreased** (for step acquisition) or **increased** (for disposal)
- Difference between consideration and change in NCI (above) recorded as an **adjustment to equity**
- **No new goodwill calculation** for new acquisition

Example: Subsidiary to subsidiary acquisition

GZ acquired 60% of the 1,000,000 $1 ordinary shares of TX on 1 January 20X3 for $1,200,000 when TX's retained earnings were $700,000. The group policy is to measure non-controlling interests at fair value at the date of acquisition. The fair value of non-controlling interests at 1 January 20X3 was $800,000. There has been no impairment of goodwill since the date of acquisition.

GZ acquired a further 10% of TX's share capital on 1 October 20X5 for $320,000.

The retained earnings reported in the financial statements of GZ and TX as at 31 December 20X5 were $2,500,000 and $1,800,000 respectively.

Profits of both entities can be assumed to accrue evenly throughout the year. The profits for the year ended 31 December 20X5 for GZ and TX were $600,000 and $400,000 respectively. There was no other comprehensive income in either entity. Neither entity paid any dividends in the year.

Required

Calculate the amounts that will appear in the consolidated financial statements for the year ended 31 December 20X5 for the items listed below.

(i)   Goodwill

(ii)   Consolidated retained earnings

(iii)   Non-controlling interests in the consolidated statement of financial position

(iv)   Non-controlling interests in the consolidated statement of profit or loss and other comprehensive income

Solution

Amounts in consolidated financial statements for year ended 31 December 20X5

(i)   **Goodwill**

	$'000	$'000
Consideration transferred		1,200
Non-controlling interests (at fair value)		800
Less fair value of identifiable net assets at acquisition:		
Share capital	1,000	
Retained earnings	700	
		(1,700)
		300

(ii)   **Consolidated retained earnings**

	GZ	TX	TX
		60%	*70%*
	$'000	$'000	$'000
At the year end/date of increase in control	2,500	1,700	1,800
(1,800 – [3/12 × 400])			
Deduct adjustment to equity (W2)	(20)		
At acquisition/date of increase in control		(700)	(1,700)
		1,000	100
Share of post-acquisition reserves:			
TX – (60% × 1,000)	600		
TX – (70% × 100)	70		
	3,150		

(iii)   **Non-controlling interests (in SOFP)**

	$'000
NCI at acquisition (fair value)	800
NCI share of post-acq'n reserves to mid-year acquisition:	
(40% × 1,000 [part (ii)])	400
	1,200
Decrease in NCI on second acquisition (1,200 × 10%/40%)	(300)
NCI share of post-acq'n reserves from acquisition to year end:	
(30% × 100 [part (ii)])	30
	930

(iv)   **Non-controlling interests (in SPLOCI)**

	$'000
NCI in PFY/TCI from 1 Jan 20X5 to 30 Sep 20X5 (400 × 9/12 × 40%)	120
NCI in PFY/TCI from 1 Oct 20X5 to 31 Dec 20X5 (400 × 3/12 × 30%)	30
	150

Workings

1   *Group structure and timeline*

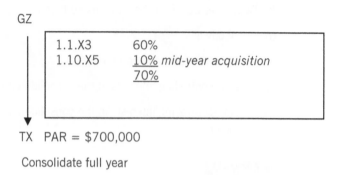

GZ

1.1.X3	60%
1.10.X5	10% *mid-year acquisition*
	70%

TX   PAR = $700,000

Consolidate full year

SPLOCI

NCI (SPLOCI): 9/12 × 40%   NCI (SPLOCI): 3/12 × 30%

1.1.X5   1.10.X5   31.12.X5

Owned 60%
of TX (sub)

Buy 10%
Now own 70%
(still a sub)

SOFP:
Consol TX
with 30%
NCI

2   *Adjustment to equity*

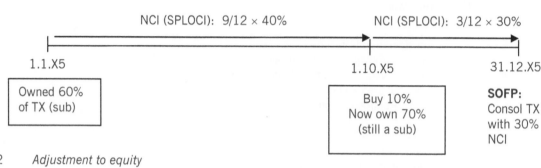

	$'000
Fair value of consideration paid	(320)
Decrease in NCI in net assets and goodwill at acquisition (part (iii))	300
Adjustment to equity	(20)

Question 11.1   Subsidiary to subsidiary disposal

BC acquired 90% of DE's 100,000 $1 shares several years ago. On 1 October 20X8, BC sold 20,000 of its shares in DE for $115,000. At 1 January 20X8, DE's retained earnings were $320,000 and DE made a profit for the year ended 31 December 20X8 of $60,000. It is group policy to measure non-controlling interests at acquisition at the proportionate share of net assets. No fair value adjustments were necessary at acquisition.

Required

Calculate the adjustment to equity that would be recorded in BC's consolidated financial statements for the year ended 31 December 20X8. (Enter your answer into the box below.)

Adjustment to equity: $ [   ]

Solution

Workings

1   *Net assets at disposal*

	$
Net assets:	
Share capital	
Retained earnings at date of disposal	
× % sold	

2   *Adjustment to equity*

	$
Fair value of consideration received	
Increase in NCI at disposal	
Adjustment to equity	

3   Acquisitions where control is achieved

3.1 Group financial statements

Illustration

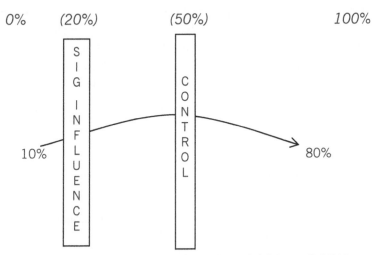

3.2 Simple investment to subsidiary (eg 10% to 80%)

This is the only scenario that will be examined. In substance, as the control and significant influence boundaries have been crossed:

(a)   A 10% investment has been 'sold' – remeasure the previously held investment to fair value at the date of control

(b)   An 80% subsidiary has been purchased' – calculate goodwill on the whole 80% and start consolidating

(IFRS 3: para. 41, 42)

Consolidated statement of profit or loss and other comprehensive income

(a)   Recognise remeasurement gain or loss on investment in profit or loss (or other comprehensive income if irrevocable election had been made under IFRS 9 *Financial Instruments*)

(b)   Consolidate as subsidiary from date of control (pro-rate accordingly).

Consolidated statement of financial position

*   Calculate goodwill at date of control
*   Consolidate as subsidiary at year end

Goodwill is calculated as follows:

	$
Consideration transferred	X
Fair value of acquirer's previously held investment	**X**
Non-controlling interests (at FV or at % FV of net assets)	X
Less: Fair value of identifiable net assets at acquisition	(X)
	X̲

Example: Investment to subsidiary acquisition

AF acquired a 15% investment in BH on 1 January 20X6 for $360,000 when BH's retained earnings were $100,000. AF did not elect to present changes in the fair value of the investment in other comprehensive income.

The fair value of the 15% investment at 31 December 20X8 was $480,000 and at 1 July 20X9 was $510,000.

On 1 July 20X9, AF acquired an additional 65% of the 2 million $1 equity shares of BH for $2,210,000. The retained earnings of BH at that date were $1,100,000. The group policy is to value the non-controlling interest at its fair value at the date of acquisition. The non-controlling interest had a fair value of $680,000 at 1 July 20X9. On 31 December 20X9, an impairment review was conducted and the directors concluded that goodwill on acquisition was impaired by $30,000.

BH's profit for the year ended 31 December 20X9 was $460,000. Profit can be assumed to accrue evenly throughout the year.

Required

(a)   Calculate the goodwill in BH for inclusion in the consolidated statement of financial position of the AF group as at 31 December 20X9.

(b)   Calculate the following figures for inclusion in the consolidated statement of profit or loss of the AF group for the year ended 31 December 20X9:

    (i)   The gain or loss on remeasurement of the 15% investment in BH.

    (ii)   Non-controlling interest in BH's profit for the year.

Solution

(a) **Goodwill**

	$'000	$'000
Consideration transferred (for 65% on 1 July 20X9)		2,210
Non-controlling interests (at fair value)		680
Fair value of previously held investment (15%)		510
Fair value of net assets at acquisition:		
Share capital	2,000	
Retained earnings	1,100	
		(3,100)
		300
Impairment		(30)
		270

(b) (i) **Gain or loss on derecognition of the 15% investment in BH**

	$'000
Fair value at date control achieved (1.7.X9)	510
Original cost of 15% investment	(360)
Gain on derecognition to be recognised in P/L	**150**

Reclassify previous revaluation gains of $120,000 ($480,000 – $360,000) out of OCI

(ii) **Non-controlling interest in BH's profit for the year**

	Profit for year
	$'000
Per question (460 × 6/12)	230
Impairment of goodwill in the year	(30)
	200
NCI share	× 20%
	= 40

(iii) **Profit attributable to the owners of the parent**

	$'000
Consolidated profit for the year:	
AF	1,700
BH (460 × 6/12)	230
Profit on derecognition of investment in BH (part (b) (i))	150
Impairment of goodwill in BH	(30)
	2,050
Profit attributable to:	
Owners of the parent (balancing figure)	**2,010**
Non-controlling interest (part (b)(ii))	40
	2,050

Working: Group structure and timeline

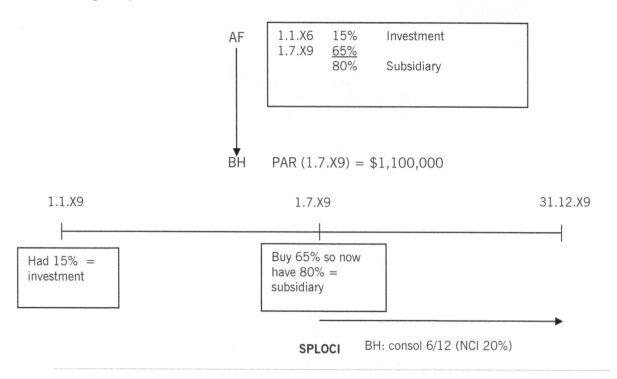

4 Disposals where control is lost

4.1 Group financial statements

Illustration

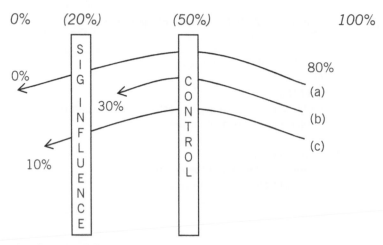

When a boundary is crossed (ie the entity changes status between a subsidiary, associate and financial asset), this triggers two events:

(1)   Calculate group profit or loss on disposal (to be posted to profit or loss) *[in substance, a subsidiary has been sold]*

(2)   Revalue any remaining shareholding to fair value (posting gain or loss to profit or loss as part of the group profit or loss on disposal above) *[in substance, an associate in (b) or simple investment in (c) has been acquired]*

(IFRS 10: para. 25, B97 – B99)

4.2 Full disposal

Consolidated statement of profit or loss and other comprehensive income

- Consolidate income, expenses and non-controlling interests to date of disposal (pro-rate)
- Show profit or loss on disposal

Consolidated statement of financial position

- No consolidation of subsidiary sold (and no non-controlling interests) as no subsidiary at year end

4.3 Subsidiary to associate

Consolidated statement of profit or loss and other comprehensive income

- Consolidate income, expenses and non-controlling interests to date of disposal (pro-rate)
- Show profit or loss on disposal
- Treat as associate thereafter (equity account)

Consolidated statement of financial position

- Fair value of investment remaining at date of disposal
- Equity valuation (as associate) thereafter

4.4 Subsidiary to simple investment

Consolidated statement of profit or loss and other comprehensive income

- Consolidate income, expenses and non-controlling interest up to date of disposal (pro-rate)
- Show profit or loss on disposal
- Show fair value changes (and any dividend income) thereafter

Consolidated statement of financial position

- Fair value of investment remaining at date of disposal
- As an investment in equity instruments (IFRS 9) thereafter

4.5 Calculation of profit or loss on disposal

	$	$
Fair value of consideration received		X
Fair value of any investment retained		X
Less share of consolidated carrying amount at date control lost:		
Net assets	X	
Goodwill	X	
Less non-controlling interests	(X)	
		(X)
Group profit/(loss)		X/(X)

(IFRS 10: para. B98)

Example: Subsidiary to associate disposal

Ted Co bought 240,000 shares in Bill Co (80% of Bill Co's share capital) for $950,000 on 1 October 20X1. At that date Bill Co's retained earnings stood at $510,000. Goodwill of $378,000 arose on acquisition of Bill Co and subsequently there has been no impairment of this goodwill.

Ted Co has several other subsidiaries, which are wholly owned.

The statements of financial position at 30 September 20X8 and the summarised statements of profit or loss to that date are given below.

STATEMENTS OF FINANCIAL POSITION

	Ted Co	
	Group	Bill Co
	$'000	$'000
Property, plant and equipment	2,050	600
Investment in Bill Co	950	–
Current assets	2,700	1,300
	5,700	1,900
Share capital ($1 ordinary shares)	2,000	300
Retained earnings	2,500	1,100
	4,500	1,400
Current liabilities	1,200	500
	5,700	1,900

STATEMENTS OF PROFIT OR LOSS

	$'000	$'000
Profit before interest and tax	1,400	240
Income tax expense	(400)	(40)
Profit for the year	1,000	200

Assume that profits accrue evenly throughout the year.

Ted has a policy of recording investments in subsidiaries at cost in its individual financial statements.

On 30 June 20X8, Ted sold 150,000 of its shares in Bill for $1,350,000. At this date, the non-controlling interest in Bill was measured at $346,000. After the disposal, Ted retained significant influence in Bill. The disposal had not yet been accounted for. As at 30 June 20X8, the fair value of a share in Bill was $9 and the retained earnings of Bill stood at $1,050,000.

(Ignore income taxes arising on the profit on disposal)

Required

(a) Prepare the consolidated statement of profit or loss for the year ended 30 September 20X8.

(b) Prepare the following figures for inclusion in the consolidated statement of financial position as at 30 September 20X8:

    (i) Investment in associate
    (ii) Consolidated retained earnings

Solution

(a) CONSOLIDATED STATEMENT OF PROFIT OR LOSS FOR THE YEAR ENDED 30 SEPTEMBER 20X8

	$'000
Profit before interest and tax (1,400 + (240 × 9/12))	1,580
Profit on disposal of shares in subsidiary (W2)	778
Share of profit of associate (200 × 3/12 × 30%)	15
Profit before tax	2,373
Income tax expense (400 + (40 × 9/12))	(430)
Profit for the year	1,943
Attributable to:	
Owners of parent	1,913
Non-controlling interest (200 × 9/12 × 20%)	30
	1,943

(b)   (i)   **Investment in associate**

	$'000
Fair value at date control lost (90,000 × $9)	810
Share of post-acquisition retained reserves (50 part (b)(ii) × 30%)	15
	825

(ii)   **Consolidated retained earnings**

	Ted	Bill	Bill
		80%	30% ret'd
	$'000	$'000	$'000
At the year end/disposal date (1,100 – [3/12 × 200])	2,500	1,050	1,100
Add group profit on disposal (W2)	778		
At acquisition/date of loss of control		(510)	(1,050)
		540	50
Share of post-acquisition retained earnings:			
Bill – 80% (540 × 80%)	432		
Bill – 30% (50 × 30%)	15		
	3,725		

Workings

1   *Group structure and timeline*

Ted

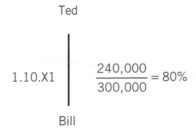

$$\frac{240,000}{300,000} = 80\%$$

1.10.X1

Bill

PAR = $510,000

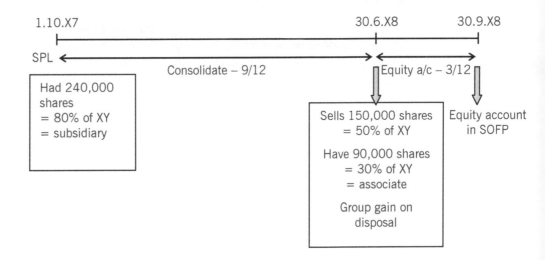

2   *Group profit on disposal of Bill*

	$'000	$'000
Fair value of consideration received		1,350
Fair value of 30% investment retained (90,000 × $9)		810
Less share of consolidated carrying amount when control lost:		
Net assets [(1,400 − (200 × $\frac{3}{12}$)]	1,350	
Goodwill (W3)	378	
Less non-controlling interests (W4)	(346)	
		(1,382)
		778

3   *Goodwill (for group profit on disposal calculation)*

	$'000	$'000
Consideration transferred		950
Non-controlling interests (at fair value)		238
Less fair value of identifiable net assets at acquisition:		
Share capital	300	
Retained earnings	510	
		(810)
		378

4   *Non-controlling interests (SOFP) (for group profit on disposal calculation)*

	$'000
NCI at acquisition (fair value)	238
NCI share of post-acq'n reserves to disposal (1,050 − 510) × 20%	108
	346
Decrease in NCI on loss of control	(346)
	0

Exam context:

The lecture examples in this chapter are longer than you would see in the objective test exam, in order to gain a full understanding of the topic. A single OT would be likely to focus on one of the calculations or workings in each scenario. Timelines have been included in solutions to lecture examples in order to help your understanding but you are unlikely to have time to draw up a timeline in a single OT question.

Chapter Summary

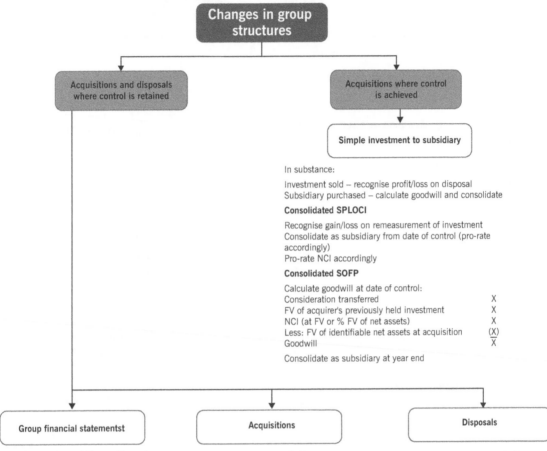

Changes in group structures

Acquisitions and disposals where control is retained

Acquisitions where control is achieved

Simple investment to subsidiary

In substance:

Investment sold – recognise profit/loss on disposal
Subsidiary purchased – calculate goodwill and consolidate

Consolidated SPLOCI

Recognise gain/loss on remeasurement of investment
Consolidate as subsidiary from date of control (pro-rate accordingly)
Pro-rate NCI accordingly

Consolidated SOFP

Calculate goodwill at date of control:

Consideration transferred	X
FV of acquirer's previously held investment	X
NCI (at FV or % FV of net assets)	X
Less: FV of identifiable net assets at acquisition	(X)
Goodwill	X

Consolidate as subsidiary at year end

Group financial statementst

In substance, no acquisition or disposal, no change to the group

Consolidated SPLOCI

Consolidate subsidiary in full whole period

NCI time apportioned (% before/after)

No profit/loss on disposal

Consolidated SOFP

NCI decreased (acq'n) or increased (disposal)

Record adjustment to equity

No new goodwill for new acq'n

Acquisitions

Transaction between group shareholders.

Record in equity:

(i) Reduction in non-controlling interest in SOFP

(ii) Adjustment to equity (in parent's column in consolidated retained earnings working)

Calculation for adjustment:

Fair value of consideration paid	(X)
Decrease in NCI in NA & g'will at acquisition	X
Adjustment to equity	(X)/X

Dr   NCI
Dr/Cr Consolidated retained earnings
Cr   Cash

Disposals

Transaction between group shareholders.

Record in equity:

(i) Increase in non-controlling interest in SOFP

(ii) Adjustment to equity (in parent's column in consolidated retained earnings working)

Calculation for adjustment:

Fair value of consideration received	X
Increase in NCI in NA & g'will at acquisition	(X)
Adjustment to equity	(X)/X

Dr   Cash
Dr/Cr Consolidated retained earnings
Cr   NCI

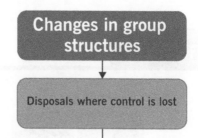

Changes in group structures

Disposals where control is lost

Profit or loss on disposal

FV of consideration received		X
FV of any investment retained		X
Less		
Share of consolidated carrying amount at date control lost:		
Net assets	X	
Goodwill	X	
Less NCI	(X)	
		(X)
Group profit/(loss)		X

Full disposal

Consolidated SPLOCI

Consolidate income, expenses and NCI to date of disposal (pro-rate)

Show profit or loss on disposal

Consolidated SOFP

No consolidation as no sub/NCI at year end

Subsidiary to associate

Consolidated SPLOCI

Consolidate income, expenses and NCI to date of disposal (pro-rate)

Show profit or loss on disposal

Treat as associate thereafter (equity account)

Consolidated SOFP

Fair value of investment remaining at date of disposal

Equity valuation (as associate) thereafter

Subsidiary to simple investment

Consolidated SPLOCI

Consolidate income, expenses and NCI to date of disposal (pro-rate)

Show profit or loss on disposal

After disposal, show fair value changes and any dividend income

Consolidated SOFP

- Fair value of investment remaining at date of disposal

- As an investment in equity instruments (IFRS 9) thereafter

Quick Quiz

1   Control is always lost when there is a disposal. True or false?

2   Why is the fair value of the interest retained used in the calculation of a gain on disposal where control is lost?

3   When is the effective date of disposal of shares in an investment?

4   Subside owns 60% of Diary at 31 December 20X8. On 1 July 20X9 it buys a further 20% of Diary. How should this transaction be treated in the group financial statements at 31 December 20X9?

5   Ditch had a 75% subsidiary, Dodge, at 30 June 20X8. On 1 January 20X9 it sold two-thirds of this investment, leaving it with a 25% holding, over which it retained significant influence. How will the remaining investment in Dodge appear in the group financial statements for the year ended 30 June 20X9?

Answers to Quick Quiz

1   False. Control may be retained if the disposal is from subsidiary to subsidiary, even though the parent owns less and the non-controlling interests own more.

2   It may be viewed as part of the consideration received.

3   When control passes.

4   As a transaction between owners, with a decrease in non-controlling interests (from 40% to 20%) and an adjustment to the parent's equity to reflect the difference between the consideration paid and the decrease in non-controlling interests.

5   It will be equity accounted as an associate. In the consolidated statement of financial position, an investment in associate will be recorded taking its fair value at the date of disposal plus a 25% share of the profits accrued between the date of disposal and the year end, less any impairment at the year end. In the consolidated statement of profit or loss and other comprehensive income, Dodge will be consolidated for the first six months and equity accounted for the remaining six months.

 ## Answers to Questions

11.1 Subsidiary to subsidiary disposal

Adjustment to equity: $ | 22,000 | (W2)

Workings

1   *Net assets at disposal*

	$
Net assets:	
Share capital	100,000
Retained earnings at date of disposal (320,000 + [60,000 × 9/12])	365,000
	465,000
× % sold (20,000 shares sold/100,000 total no. of shares)	× 20%
	= 93,000

2   *Adjustment to equity*

	$
Fair value of consideration received	115,000
Increase in NCI at disposal (W1)	(93,000)
Adjustment to equity	22,000

Now try this question from the Practice Question Bank	**Number**	**Level**	**Marks**	**Time**
	Q21	Introductory	N/A	5 mins

INDIRECT CONTROL OF SUBSIDIARIES

 If a subsidiary holds a controlling interest in another entity the parent will obtain control of this other entity, indirectly giving rise to a vertical group.

You will need to be able to determine the correct consolidation treatment for an indirectly controlled subsidiary.

Topic list	learning outcomes	syllabus references
1 Issues	B2	B2(c)
2 Calculations	B2	B2(c)

Chapter Overview

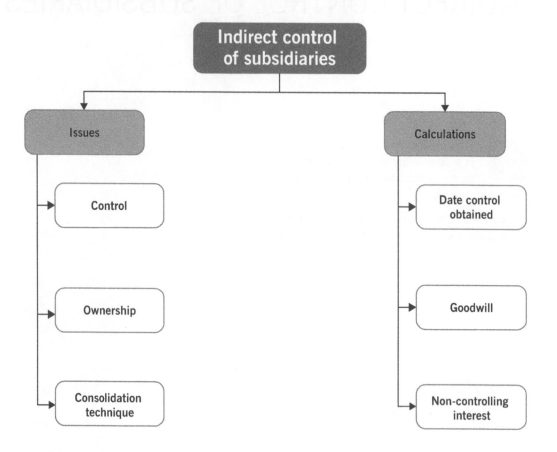

1   Issues

So far we have only considered simple group structures eg

P

80%

S

Here P has direct control of S, its subsidiary.

1.1 Control

P must prepare group accounts including each subsidiary it controls whether directly or indirectly. Consider the following example:

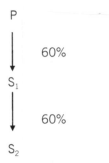

P

60%

S_1

60%

S_2

P controls S_1, S_1 controls S_2; therefore P controls S_2. This is known as a 'vertical group'. S_1 is a subsidiary of P and S_2 is a sub-subsidiary of P.

1.2 Ownership

As S_2 is held via a 60% owned subsidiary (S_1) the ownership of S_2 is 36% (60% × 60%) and the non-controlling interests are 64%.

1.3 Consolidation technique

Statement of financial position:

Assets and liabilities   –   show what group **controls** (P + S_1 + S_2)

Equity section   –   shows the ownership of the assets and liabilities included in the
statement   of financial position

                               –   reserves and NCI are based on **effective** holdings

Statement of profit or loss and other comprehensive income:

Income and expenses   –   show what group **controls** (P + S_1 + S_2)

Non-controlling interests   –   based on **effective** holding

2   Calculations

2.1 Goodwill and post-acquisition profits

When calculating goodwill and post-acquisition profits, the date of the acquisition of the sub-subsidiary by the ultimate parent needs to be considered carefully.

2.2 Date the parent obtains control of the sub-subsidiary

Acquisition of subsidiary then sub-subsidiary

In this case, P first acquires an interest in S_1 only and subsequently the group acquires an interest in S_2. The date P obtains control of S_2 is 1 January 20X7.

Acquisition of pre-existing group

In this case, P acquires **an interest in the S_1 group**. The date P obtains control of S_2 is **1 January 20X5**.

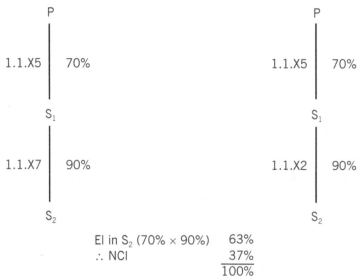

	EI in S_2 (70% × 90%)	63%
	∴ NCI	37%
		100%

CALCULATION OF GOODWILL

	Goodwill in S_1		Goodwill in S_2	
Consideration transferred		X		X × 70%
Non-controlling interests (at % FVNA or at 'full' FV)		X		X
Less Net FV of identifiable assets acquired and liabilities assumed:				
SC and SP	X		X	
Pre-acquisition reserves – **at date P obtains control**	X		X	
FV adjustments	X		X	
		(X)		(X)
		X		X
			X	

CALCULATION OF NON-CONTROLLING INTERESTS

	S_1		S_2	
NCI at acquisition		X		X
NCI share of post-acq'n reserves		X/(X)		X/(X)
Less NCI share of impairment losses (if NCI at FV)		(X)		(X)
Less NCI share of investment in S_2 (X × 30%)		(X)		—
		X		X
			X	

2.3 Consolidated statement of financial position

Example: Each part

On 1 January 20X2, AB acquired 75% of CD's 400,000 $1 ordinary shares for $450,000. On 1 January 20X3, CD acquired 80% of EF's 300,000 $1 ordinary shares for $320,000.

The retained earnings of AB, CD and EF were:

	31 December 20X5 $	1 January 20X3 $	1 January 20X2 $
AB	670,000	540,000	490,000
CD	300,000	100,000	80,000
EF	90,000	60,000	50,000

Handwritten margin notes: AB 1.1.X2 ↓ 75%; CD X 1.1.X3 ↓ 80%; EF = 60%; 40% NCI

AB elected to measure the non-controlling interest in CD and EF at acquisition at fair value. The fair value of the non-controlling interest in CD at 1 January 20X2 was $150,000. The fair value of one equity share in EF at 1 January 20X3 was $1.30.

AB conducted its annual impairment review on 31 December 20X5 and concluded that the goodwill of EF was impaired by $12,000 and that all of this impairment had arisen in the year ended 31 December 20X5. No other impairments of goodwill have arisen.

Required

Calculate the amounts that will be shown in the consolidated statement of financial position of the AB group for the year ended 31 December 20X5 for the items listed below.

(i)   Goodwill   → Consideration t/fred

$

(ii)   Consolidated retained earnings

$

(iii)   Non-controlling interests

$

Solution

(i)   Goodwill = $144,000

(ii)   Consolidated retained earnings = $845,800

(iii) Non-controlling interests = $288,200

Workings

1   Group structure

AB

| |
| 1.1.X2   75% |

CD   PAR (1.1.X2) = $80,000

| |
| 1.1.X3   80% |

EF   PAR (1.1.X3) = $60,000

AB owns in EF (effective interest) = 75% × 80% =   60%

NCI in EF   40%

   100%

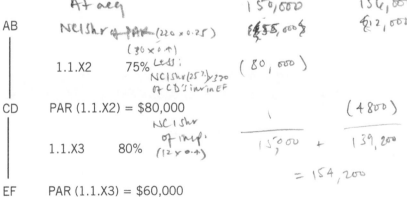

2 *Goodwill*

	CD		EF	
	$	$	$	$
Consideration transferred		450,000		
(320,000 × 75%)				240,000
Non-controlling interests		150,000		
(300,000 × 40% × $1.30)				156,000
FV of net assets at acquisition:				
Share capital	400,000		300,000	
Retained earnings (W1)	80,000		60,000	
		(480,000)		(360,000)
		120,000		36,000
Impairment losses		-		(12,000)
		120,000		24,000

Total goodwill = $120,000 + $24,000 = $144,000

3 *Consolidated retained earnings*

	AB	CD	EF
	$	$	$
At the year end	670,000	300,000	90,000
At acquisition (W2)		(80,000)	(60,000)
		220,000	30,000
Share of post-acquisition retained earnings:			
CD (220,000 × 75%)	165,000		
EF (30,000 × 60%)	18,000		
Impairment losses to date (12,000 × 60%)	(7,200)		
	845,800		

4 *Non-controlling interests*

	CD	EF
	$	$
NCI at acquisition	150,000	156,000
NCI share of post-acquisition reserves:		
CD (220,000 × 25%)	55,000	
EF (30,000 × 40%)		12,000
Less NCI share of impairment losses		
(12,000 × 40%)		(4,800)
Less NCI share of investment in EF		
(320,000 × 25%)	(80,000)	
	125,000	163,200

Total NCI = $125,000 + $163,200 = $288,200

Example: Goodwill under partial method

On 31 December 20X7, KL purchased 60% of MN's 200,000 $1 equity shares for $500,000. At that date, MN already owned 90% of OP's 100,000 $1 equity shares which it had purchased on 1 January 20X5 for $390,000.

The reserves of MN and OP were:

	31 December 20X7	1 January 20X5
	$	$
MN	550,000	320,000
OP	250,000	190,000

It is group policy to measure the non-controlling interest at the proportionate share of the fair value of net assets at acquisition.

Required

Calculate the goodwill of MN and OP for inclusion in KL's consolidated statement of financial position at 31 December 20X7, using the proforma workings below to help you.

$

Proforma workings

1   *Group structure*

2   *Goodwill*

	MN		OP	
	$	$	$	$
Consideration transferred				
Non-controlling interests				
FV of net assets at acquisition:				
Share capital				
Reserves				

Total goodwill =

Solution

Goodwill $95,000

Workings

1   Group structure

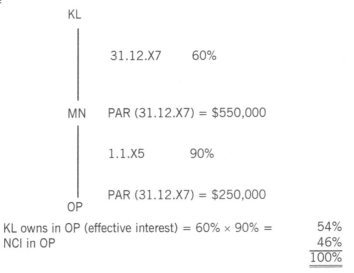

KL

31.12.X7   60%

MN   PAR (31.12.X7) = $550,000

1.1.X5   90%

PAR (31.12.X7) = $250,000

OP

KL owns in OP (effective interest) = 60% × 90% =   54%
NCI in OP   46%
    100%

Tutorial note. KL does not gain control of OP until it purchases its shareholding in MN on 31.12.X7. Therefore, the date of OP's pre-acquisition reserves is 31.12.X7.

2 *Goodwill*

	MN		OP	
	$	$	$	$
Consideration transferred		500,000		
(390,000 × 60%)				234,000
Non-controlling interests				
(750,000 × 40%)		300,000		
(350,000 × 46%)				161,000
FV of net assets at acquisition:				
Share capital	200,000		100,000	
Reserves	550,000		250,000	
		(750,000)		(350,000)
		50,000		45,000

Total goodwill = $50,000 + $45,000 = $95,000

Consolidation adjustments for a sub-subsidiary (such as intra-group trading, intra-group balances, unrealised profit, impairment of goodwill and fair value adjustments) are accounted for in the group accounts in exactly the same way as they would be for a subsidiary.

Example: Consolidation adjustments

QR purchased 70% of ST on 1 January 20X1. ST purchased 60% of UV on 1 January 20X3. At the date of acquisition, all book values were equivalent to their fair values with the exception of UV's property which had a fair value of $50,000 in excess of its book value and a remaining useful life of 10 years.

On 31 December 20X6, the property, plant and equipment of QR, ST and UV was $970,000, $650,000 and $420,000 respectively. Inventory was $120,000, $85,000 and $67,000 respectively.

During the year ended 31 December 20X6, UV sold goods to QR for $30,000 at a margin of 20%. At the year end, QR held half of these goods in inventory.

Required

Calculate the following figures for inclusion in the consolidated statement of financial position of the QR group as at 31 December 20X6:

(i) Property, plant and equipment
(ii) Inventories

Solution

(i) Property, plant and equipment

$970,000 + $650,000 + $420,000 + $30,000 (W2) = $2,070,000

(ii) Inventories

$120,000 + $85,000 + $67,000 - $3,000 (W3) = $269,000

Workings

1   *Group structure*

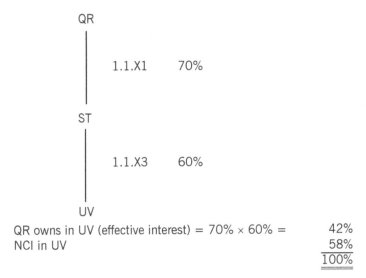

QR owns in UV (effective interest) = 70% × 60% =   42%
NCI in UV   58%
100%

2   *Fair value adjustment*

	Acquisition date 1.1.X3	Movement X3, X4, X5, X6	Year end 31.12.X6
	$	$	$
Property	50,000	(20,000)	30,000

Extra depreciation = $50,000 × 1/10 × 4 years (20X3, 20X4, 20X5, 20X6) = $20,000

3   *Unrealised profit*

UV ⟶ QR

PUP = $30,000 × ½ in inventory × 20/100 margin = $3,000

2.4 Consolidated statement of profit or loss and other comprehensive income

Example: NCI in consolidated SPLOCI

GH owns 75% of JK and JK owns 80% of LM. Both holdings were acquired three years ago. It is group policy to measure non-controlling interests at fair value at acquisition.

In the year ended 31 December 20X4, JK and LM made profits for the year of $190,000 and $140,000 respectively. Total comprehensive income amounted to $220,000 for JK and $150,000 for LM.

An impairment review at 31 December 20X4 revealed an impairment loss of $15,000 on the goodwill of JK. No impairment was deemed necessary for the goodwill of LM.

At acquisition, the fair value of the net assets of both JK and LM was considered to the the same as the book value with the exception of the brands of LM. These brands were not in LM's statement of financial position but at acqustion, they were considered to have a fair value of $40,000 and remaining useful life of five years.

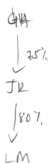

Required

Calculate the following figures for inclusion in the consolidated statement of profit or loss and other comprehensive income of the GH group as at 31 December 20X4:

(i)   Non-controlling interests in profit for the year
(ii)   Non-controlling interest in total comprehensive income for the year

Solution

(i)   Non-controlling interests in profit for the year = $96,550
(ii)   Non-controlling interests in total comprehensive income for the year = $108,050

Workings

1   *Group structure*

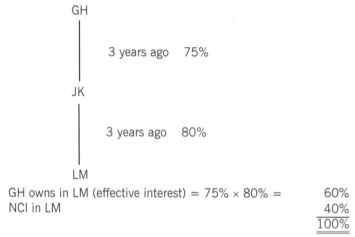

	60%
GH owns in LM (effective interest) = 75% × 80% =	60%
NCI in LM	40%
	100%

2   *Non-controlling interests*

In profit for year:

	JK $	LM $
Per question	190,000	140,000
Adjustments:		
Impairment of goodwill (as full goodwill method)	(15,000)	
Fair value amortisation of brands (40,000 × 1/5)		(8,000)
	175,000	132,000
NCI share	× 25%	× 40%
	= 43,750	= 52,800

Total NCI in profit for year = $43,750 + $52,800 = $96,550

In total comprehensive income for the year:

	JK $	LM $
Per question	220,000	150,000
Adjustments:		
Impairment of goodwill (as full goodwill method)	(15,000)	
Fair value amortisation of brands (40,000 × 1/5)		(8,000)
	205,000	142,000
NCI share	× 25%	× 40%
	= 51,250	= 56,800

Total NCI in TCI for year = $51,250 + $56,800 = $108,050

Question 12.1   Extracts from consolidated SPLOCI

CE owns 60% of SM. SM owns 70% of PV. Both holdings have been owned for several years.

In the year ended 31 December 20X2, cost of sales of CE, SM and PV was $510,000, $430,000 and $380,000 respectively.

During the year ended 31 December 20X2, SM sold goods to PV for $60,000 at a mark up of 25%. At the year end, one third of these goods were still in PV's inventory.

Required

Calculate the cost of sales figure for inclusion in the consolidated statement of profit or loss and other comprehensive income of the CE group for the year ended 31 December 20X2.

$ [   ]

Solution

Workings

1   *Group structure*

2   *Unrealised profit*

Chapter Summary

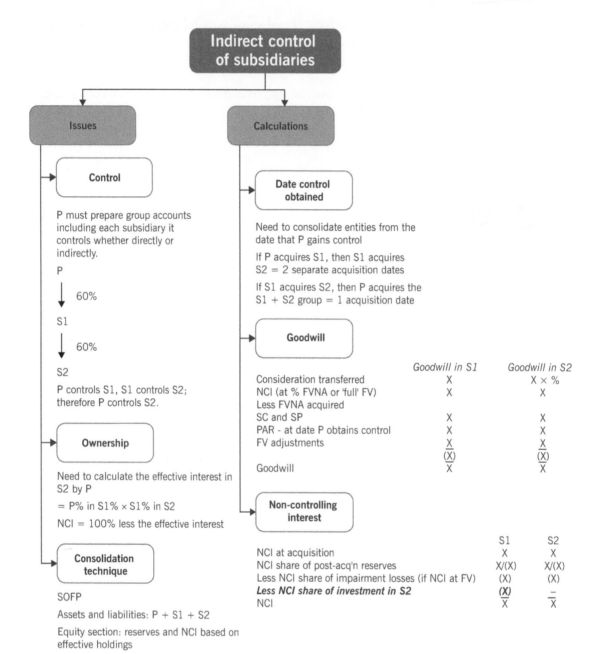

Indirect control of subsidiaries

Issues

Control

P must prepare group accounts including each subsidiary it controls whether directly or indirectly.

P

↓ 60%

S1

↓ 60%

S2

P controls S1, S1 controls S2; therefore P controls S2.

Ownership

Need to calculate the effective interest in S2 by P

= P% in S1% × S1% in S2

NCI = 100% less the effective interest

Consolidation technique

SOFP

Assets and liabilities: P + S1 + S2

Equity section: reserves and NCI based on effective holdings

SPLOCI

Income and expenses: P + S1 + S2

NCI: based on effective holding

Calculations

Date control obtained

Need to consolidate entities from the date that P gains control

If P acquires S1, then S1 acquires S2 = 2 separate acquisition dates

If S1 acquires S2, then P acquires the S1 + S2 group = 1 acquisition date

Goodwill

	Goodwill in S1	Goodwill in S2
Consideration transferred	X	X × %
NCI (at % FVNA or 'full' FV)	X	X
Less FVNA acquired		
SC and SP	X	X
PAR - at date P obtains control	X	X
FV adjustments	X	X
	(X)	(X)
Goodwill	X	X

Non-controlling interest

	S1	S2
NCI at acquisition	X	X
NCI share of post-acq'n reserves	X/(X)	X/(X)
Less NCI share of impairment losses (if NCI at FV)	(X)	(X)
Less NCI share of investment in S2	*(X)*	–
NCI	X	X

Quick Quiz

1 B Co owns 60% of the equity of C Co which owns 75% of the equity of D Co. What is the total non-controlling interests' percentage ownership in D Co?

2 What is the basic consolidation method for sub-subsidiaries in the consolidated statement of financial position?

Answers to Quick Quiz

1   B

| 60%

C

| 75%

D

Effective interest in D = 60% x 75%   = 45%
Therefore, non-controlling interests   = 55%
                                                              100%

(Alternatively, you could calculate it as 25% + (40% of 75%) = 55%)

2   • Net assets: show what the group controls
     • Equity (capital and reserves): show who owns the net assets

Answers to Questions

12.1 Extracts from consolidated SPLOCI

Consolidated cost of sales:

$ | 1,264,000 | ($510,000 + $430,000 + $380,000 - $60,000 intra-group + $4,000 PUP (W2))

Workings

1   *Group structure*

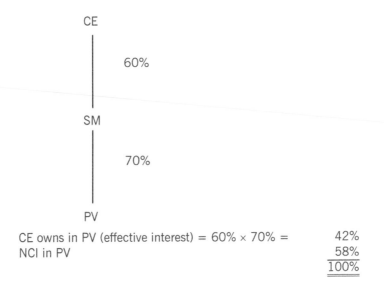

CE owns in PV (effective interest) = 60% × 70% =   42%
NCI in PV   58%
                                                      100%

2   *Unrealised profit*

SM ⟶ PV

$$PUP = \$60,000 \times \frac{1}{3} \text{ in inventory} \times \frac{25}{125} \text{ mark up} = \$4,000$$

Now try these questions from the Practice Question Bank	Number	Level	Marks	Time
	Q22	Introductory	N/A	5 mins

FOREIGN SUBSIDIARIES

 A foreign subsidiary may present its financial statements in a different currency to the parent. The financial statements will, therefore, require translating prior to consolidation.

You will need to be able to correctly consolidate a foreign subsidiary according to IAS 21 *The effects of changes in foreign exchange rates*.

Topic list	learning outcomes	syllabus references
1 Currency concepts	B2	B2(b)
2 Translation and consolidation of foreign subsidiaries	B2	B2(b)

Chapter Overview

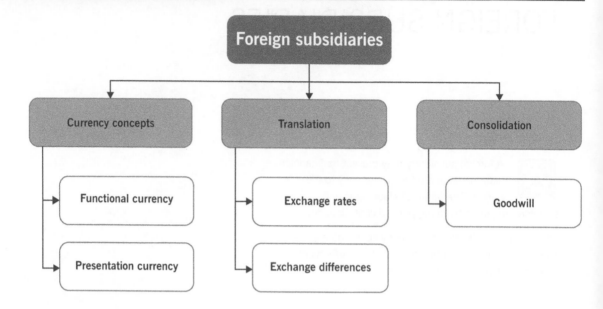

1   Currency concepts

1.1 Two currency concepts

FUNCTIONAL
CURRENCY

PRESENTATION
CURRENCY

- Currency of the **primary economic environment** in which an entity operates
- The currency used for measurement in the financial statements
- Other currencies treated as a foreign currency

(IAS 21: para. 8)

- Can be **any** currency
- The currency in which the year-end financial statements are presented
- Special rules apply to translation from functional currency to presentation currency

1.2 Determining an entity's functional currency

An entity considers the following factors in determining its functional currency (IAS 21: para. 9–10):

(a)   The currency:

   (i)   That mainly influences **sales prices** for goods and services (often the currency in which sales prices for its goods and services are denominated and settled); and

   (ii)   Of the **country** whose competitive forces and regulations mainly determine the sales prices of its goods and services.

(b)   The currency that mainly influences **labour, material and other costs** of providing goods or services (this will often be the currency in which such costs are denominated and settled).

(c)   The currency in which **funds from financing activities** are generated.

(d)   The currency in which **receipts** from operating activities are usually **retained**.

1.3 Determining a foreign subsidiary's functional currency

The following additional factors are considered in determining the functional currency of a foreign subsidiary, and whether its functional currency is the same as that of its parent (IAS 21: para. 11):

(a)   Whether the activities of the foreign subsidiary are carried out as an **extension of the parent**, rather than being carried out with a **significant degree of autonomy**.

(b)   Whether **transactions with the parent** are a **high or a low** proportion of the foreign subsidiary's activities.

(c)   Whether **cash flows** from the activities of the **foreign subsidiary directly affect** the cash flows of the parent and are readily available for remittance to it.

(d)   Whether **cash flows** from the activities of the **foreign subsidiary** are **sufficient** to **service** existing and normally expected debt obligations without funds being made available by the parent.

Question 13.1   Identifying the functional currency

JK prepares its financial statements in dollars. JK acquired 75% of the equity share capital of PQ on 1 January 20X5. PQ operates in country L where the local currency is the 'lander'. JK sources the raw materials for PQ from one of its suppliers and the goods purchased are paid for in dollars. PQ recruits a local workforce and pays all wages and operating expenses in landers. The majority of sales income is received in landers. The management of PQ operates with a high degree of independence and is responsible for raising any finance required to fund operations.

Required

Which of the following statements are TRUE?

Tick ALL that apply.

Tick	Statement
	PQ operates autonomously and raises its own finance which indicates that its functional currency should be the lander.
	PQ is a subsidiary of JK and should therefore select the dollar as its functional currency because the entities are part of the same group.
	PQ must adopt the lander as its presentation currency.
	The functional currency of PQ will be determined by the currency that dominates the primary economic environment in which PQ operates.
	The functional currency of PQ will be the dollar as raw materials are purchased in dollars.

2 Translation and consolidation of foreign subsidiaries

2.1 Translation method

The foreign subsidiary prepares its financial statements in its own functional currency.

Where **different to** the **parent's** functional currency, the financial statements need to be translated into the presentation currency of the group accounts (the parent's currency) before consolidation. (IAS 21: para. 39)

2.2 Exchange rates

In practical terms the following approach is used when translating the financial statements of a foreign operation for exam purposes. (IAS 21: para. 39)

(a)   **Statement of financial position**

All assets and liabilities – at closing rate (CR)

Share capital and reserves (for exam purposes):

Share capital and pre acquisition reserves – at historic rate (HR) [ie when subsidiary acquired]

Post acquisition reserves – balancing figure

(b)   **Statement of profit or loss and other comprehensive income**

All items – at actual rate or average rate (AR) as an approximation

2.3 Calculation of exchange differences

Exchange differences result from (IAS 21: para. 41, 47):

(a)   Translating income and expenses at the average rate and assets and liabilities at the closing rate

(b)   Translating the opening net assets at a closing rate that differs from the previous year's closing rate

(c)   Retranslating goodwill on consolidation at the closing rate at each year end

You may be required to calculate the exchange differences recognised in the statement of profit or loss and other comprehensive income during the year. The exam approach is as follows.

	$
Exchange differences in the year:	
On translation of net assets	
Closing net assets at closing rate	X
Less opening net assets at opening rate	(X)
	X
Less total comprehensive income as translated (net of dividends)	(X)
	X/(X)
On goodwill – see Section 2.5	X/(X)
	X/(X)

2.5 Goodwill

Goodwill is treated as an asset of the foreign subsidiary and is therefore translated at the closing rate each year. It must be calculated first in the foreign currency then translated to find the exchange differences. (IAS 21: para. 47)

	FC'000	FC'000	*Rate*	$'000
Consideration transferred		X	HR	X
Non-controlling interests		X	HR	X
Share capital	X			
Retained earnings	X			
		(X)	HR	(X)
At acquisition (1.1.X1)		X	HR	X
Impairment losses 20X1		(X)	X1 AR or X1 CR	(X)
Exchange differences 20X1		–	–	β
At 31.12.20X1		X	X1 CR	X
Impairment losses 20X2		(X)	X2 AR or X2 CR	(X)
Exchange differences 20X2		–	–	β
At 31.12.20X2		X	X2 CR	X

Note. IAS 21 The effect of changes in foreign exchange rates allows impairment losses to be translated at either the average or closing rate for that year. In the exam, follow any instructions you are given.

Question 13.2	Consolidation of a foreign subsidiary

The functional currency of Henley (the parent) is A$. The functional currency of Saar, a foreign company, is B$. Henley acquired 70% of Saar for B$4,500,000 on 31 December 20X4 when the retained reserves of Saar were B$1,125,000. Neither company paid or declared dividends during the year.

It is group policy to measure non-controlling interests at fair value at the date of acquisition. The fair value of non-controlling interests at 31 December 20X4 was B$1,890,000.

An impairment review conducted on 31 December 20X7 resulted in the goodwill of Saar being written down by 10%. No impairment losses were necessary in previous years. It is group policy to translate impairment losses at the closing rate.

SUMMARISED STATEMENTS OF FINANCIAL POSITION AS AT 31 DECEMBER 20X7

	Henley A$'000	Saar B$'000
Property, plant and equipment	4,500	4,000
Investment in Saar (held at cost)	1,000	
Current assets	2,400	3,000
	7,900	7,000
Share capital	2,000	2,250
Reserves	4,400	3,950
	6,400	6,200
Liabilities	1,500	800
	7,900	7,000

SUMMARISED STATEMENTS OF PROFIT OR LOSS AND OTHER COMPREHENSIVE INCOME FOR YEAR ENDED 31 DECEMBER 20X7

	Henley A$'000	Saar B$'000
Revenue	12,000	5,700
Cost of sales and operating expenses	(10,025)	(3,040)
Profit before tax	1,975	2,660
Income tax expense	(500)	(760)
Profit/total comprehensive income for the year	1,475	1,900

Exchange rates

31 December 20X4 (H&= date y acq of Saar)	A$1/B$4.5
31 December 20X6 Y/E	A$1/B$4.3
31 December 20X7 N/E →CN	A$1/B$4
Average exchange rate for year ended 31 December 20X7	A$1/B$3.8

Required

Prepare the consolidated statement of profit or loss and other comprehensive income and statement of financial position for the Henley Group for the year ended 31 December 20X7 (round your answer to the nearest $'000).

Solution

CONSOLIDATED STATEMENT OF FINANCIAL POSITION AS AT 31 DECEMBER 20X7

	A$'000
Property, plant and equipment (4,500	
Goodwill (W4)	
Current assets (2,400	
Share capital	2,000
Reserves (W5)	
Non-controlling interests (W6)	
Liabilities (1,500	

CONSOLIDATED STATEMENT OF PROFIT OR LOSS AND OTHER COMPREHENSIVE INCOME FOR YEAR
ENDED 31 DECEMBER 20X7

	A$'000
Revenue (12,000	
Cost of sales and operating expense (10,025	
Profit before tax	
Income tax expense (500	
Profit for the year	
Other comprehensive income:	
Items that may be reclassified subsequently to profit or loss	
Exchange difference on translating foreign operations (W8)	
TOTAL COMPREHENSIVE INCOME FOR THE YEAR	
Profit attributable to:	
Owners of the parent	
Non-controlling interests (W7)	
Total comprehensive income attributable to:	
Owners of the parent	
Non-controlling interests (W7)	

Workings

1   *Group structure*

Henley

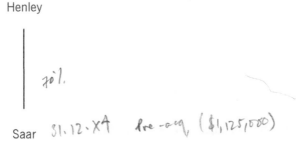

70%

Saar   31.12.X4   Pre-acq ($1,125,000)

2   *Translation of Saar – Statement of financial position*

	B$'000	Rate	A$'000
Property, plant and equipment	4,000	$4 = CR =	1,000
Current assets	3,000	$4 " -	750
	7,000		1,750
Share capital	2,250	$4.50 = HR =	500
Pre-acquisition reserves	1,125	" "	250
			750
Post-acquisition reserves (3,950 – 1,125)	2,825	β	800 ?
	6,200		1,550
Liabilities	800	$4 = CR	200
	7,000		1,750

3   *Saar – Statement of profit or loss and other comprehensive income*

	B$'000	Rate	A$'000
Revenue	5,700	3.8 AR	1500
Cost of sales and operating expenses	(3,040)	3.8 AR	(800)
Profit before tax	2,660		750
Income tax expense	(760)	3.8 AR	(200)
Profit for the year	1,900		560

4   *Goodwill*

	B$'000	B$'000	Rate	A$'000
Consideration transferred		4,500	4.5	1000
Non-controlling interests		1890	4.5	420
Share capital	2250			
Retained reserves	1125			
		(3375)	4.5	(750)
At 31.12.X4		3015	4.5	670
Exchange gain 20X5–20X6 b/d		0	5	31
At 31.12.X6		3015	4.5	701
Impairment losses 20X7 (10%)		(302)	4	(76)
Exchange gain 20X7			8	53
At 31.12.X7		2718	4	678

5   *Retained reserves carried forward*

	Henley A$'000	Saar A$'000
At the year end/(W2)	4400	1050
Pre-acquisition		(250)
		800
Group share of Saar post-acquisition	560	
800 × 70%		
Less group share of impairment losses to date	(53)	
76 × 70%		
Group share of exchange gain on goodwill	59	
31 + 53 × 70%	4966	

6   *Non-controlling interests (SOFP)*

	A$'000
NCI at acquisition (1890 / 4.5	420
NCI share of post-acquisition retained reserves of Saar	240
800 × 30%	
NCI share of impairment loss of goodwill	(23)
76 × 30%	
NCI share of exchange gain on goodwill	25
31 + 53 × 30%	662

7   *Non-controlling interests (SPLOCI)*

	PFY A$'000	TCI A$'000
Profit for the year	500	500
Impairment losses	(76)	(76)
Other comprehensive income: exchange differences	—	103
	424	527
NCI share	× 30%	× 20%
	= 127	= 158

8   *Exchange differences arising during the year*

	A$'000	A$'000
On translation of net assets	1 558	
Closing NA @ CR		
Opening NA @ OR		
Less total comprehensive income as translated		
On goodwill		

Exam context:

This is a comprehensive example to teach you how to compute each figure and working when consolidating a foreign subsidiary. An OT question is more likely to ask you for one or two figures or workings from the consolidated statement of financial position or profit or loss and other comprehensive income for a group incorporating a foreign subsidiary (rather than the whole primary statements).

For example, calculation of the exchange difference for the year is a possible requirement

Chapter Summary

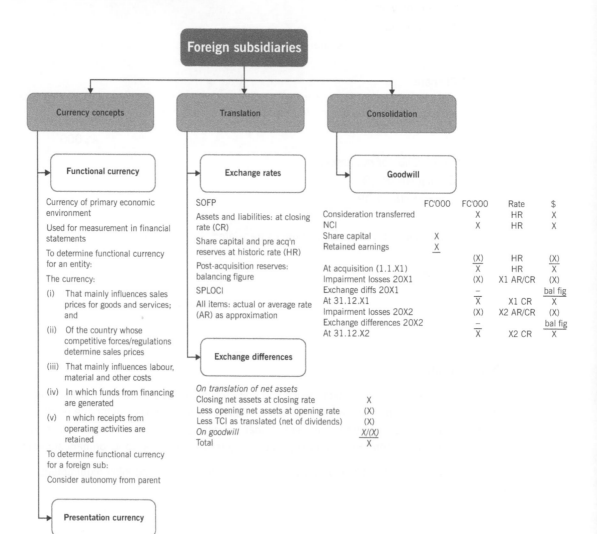

Foreign subsidiaries

Currency concepts

Functional currency

Currency of primary economic environment

Used for measurement in financial statements

To determine functional currency for an entity:

The currency:

(i) That mainly influences sales prices for goods and services; and

(ii) Of the country whose competitive forces/regulations determine sales prices

(iii) That mainly influences labour, material and other costs

(iv) In which funds from financing are generated

(v) n which receipts from operating activities are retained

To determine functional currency for a foreign sub:

Consider autonomy from parent

Presentation currency

Can be any currency
Currency in which financial statements are presented
Special rules for translating from functional to presentation

Translation

Exchange rates

SOFP

Assets and liabilities: at closing rate (CR)

Share capital and pre acq'n reserves at historic rate (HR)

Post-acquisition reserves: balancing figure

SPLOCI

All items: actual or average rate (AR) as approximation

Exchange differences

On translation of net assets

Closing net assets at closing rate	X
Less opening net assets at opening rate	(X)
Less TCI as translated (net of dividends)	(X)
On goodwill	*X/(X)*
Total	X

Consolidation

Goodwill

	FC'000	FC'000	Rate	$
Consideration transferred		X	HR	X
NCI		X	HR	X
Share capital	X			
Retained earnings	X			
		(X)	HR	(X)
At acquisition (1.1.X1)		X	HR	X
Impairment losses 20X1		(X)	X1 AR/CR	(X)
Exchange diffs 20X1		–		bal fig
At 31.12.X1		X	X1 CR	X
Impairment losses 20X2		(X)	X2 AR/CR	(X)
Exchange differences 20X2		–		bal fig
At 31.12.X2		X	X2 CR	X

Quick Quiz

1   What is the difference between conversion and translation?

2   Define monetary items according to IAS 21.

3   How should foreign currency transactions be recognised initially in an individual enterprise's accounts?

4   How should goodwill and fair value adjustments be treated on consolidation of a foreign operation?

Answers to Quick Quiz

1   (a)   Conversion is the process of exchanging one currency for another.
    (b)   Translation is the restatement of the value of one currency in another currency.

2   Units of currency held and assets and liabilities to be received or paid in a fixed or determinable number of units of currency (eg cash, receivables, payables, loans).

3   Use the exchange rate at the date of the transaction. An average rate for a period can be used if the exchange rates did not fluctuate significantly.

4   Treat as assets/liabilities of the foreign operation and translate at the closing rate.

Answers to Questions

13.1   Identifying the functional currency

The statements ticked below are **true**:

Tick	Statement
✓	PQ operates autonomously and raises its own finance which indicates that its functional currency should be the lander.
	PQ is a subsidiary of JK and should therefore select the dollar as its functional currency because the entities are part of the same group.
	PQ must adopt the lander as its presentation currency.
✓	The functional currency of PQ will be determined by the currency that dominates the primary economic environment in which PQ operates.
	The functional currency of PQ will be the dollar as raw materials are purchased in dollars.

Statement (2) is incorrect because the functional currency cannot be chosen. It must be the currency of the primary economic environment. (IAS 21: para. 8)

Statement (3) is incorrect because the presentation currency can be any currency (IAS 21: para. 38). In this case, JK is likely to encourage PQ to select the dollar as its presentation currency as it is the parent's currency and therefore the likely currency of the group financial statements.

Statement (5) is incorrect because the majority of indicators in the scenario point towards the lander as being the currency of the primary economic environment of PQ and therefore its functional currency.

13.2 Consolidation of a foreign subsidiary

CONSOLIDATED STATEMENT OF FINANCIAL POSITION AS AT 31 DECEMBER 20X7

	A$'000
Property, plant and equipment (4,500 + (W2) 1,000)	5,500
Goodwill (W4)	678
Current assets (2,400 + (W2) 750)	3,150
	9,328
Share capital	2,000
Reserves (W5)	4,966
	6,966
Non-controlling interests (W6)	662
	7,628
Liabilities (1,500 + (W2) 200)	1,700
	9,328

CONSOLIDATED STATEMENT OF PROFIT OR LOSS AND OTHER COMPREHENSIVE INCOME FOR THE YEAR ENDED 31 DECEMBER 20X7

	A$'000
Revenue (12,000 + (W3) 1,500)	13,500
Cost of sales and operating expenses (10,025 + (W3) 800 + (W4) 76)	(10,901)
Profit before tax	2,599
Income tax expense (500 + (W3) 200)	(700)
Profit for the year	1,899
Other comprehensive income:	
Items that may be reclassified subsequently to profit or loss	
Exchange difference on translating foreign operations (W8)	103
TOTAL COMPREHENSIVE INCOME FOR THE YEAR	2,002
Profit attributable to:	1,772
Owners of the parent β	127
Non-controlling interests (W7)	1,899
Total comprehensive income attributable to:	
Owners of the parent β	1,844
Non-controlling interests (W7)	158
	2,002

Workings

1   *Group structure*

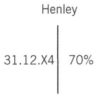

Henley

31.12.X4 | 70%

Saar   Pre-acquisition ret'd reserves B$1,125,000

2   *Translation of Saar – Statement of financial position*

	B$'000	Rate	A$'000	
Property, plant and equipment	4,000	4	1,000	
Current assets	3,000	4	750	
	7,000		1,750	
Share capital	2,250	4.5	500	
Pre-acquisition reserves	1,125	4.5	250	
			750	} 1,050
Post-acquisition reserves				
(3,950 – 1,125)	2,825	β	800	
	6,200		1,550	
Liabilities	800	4	200	
	7,000		1,750	

3   *Translation of Saar –Statement of profit or loss and other comprehensive income*

	B$'000	Rate	A$'000
Revenue	5,700	3.8	1,500
Cost of sales and operating expenses	(3,040)	3.8	(800)
Profit before tax	2,660		700
Income tax expense	(760)	3.8	(200)
Profit for the year	1,900		500

4   *Goodwill*

	B$'000	B$'000	Rate	A$'000
Consideration transferred		4,500	4.5	1,000
Non-controlling interests		1,890	4.5	420
Share capital	2,250			
Retained reserves	1,125			
		(3,375)	4.5	(750)
At 31.12.X4		3,015	4.5	670
Exchange gain 20X5–20X6 b/d		–	β	31
At 31.12.X6		3,015	4.3	701
Impairment losses 20X7 (10%)		(302)	4	(76)
Exchange gain 20X7		-	β	53
At 31.12.X7		2,713	4	678

5   *Retained reserves carried forward*

	Henley A$'000	Saar A$'000
At the year end/(W2)	4,400	1,050
Pre-acquisition (W2)		(250)
		800
Group share of Saar post-acquisition (800 × 70%)	560	
Less group share of impairment losses to date		
((W4) 76 × 70%)	(53)	
Group share of exchange gain on goodwill		
([(W4) 31 + 53)] × 70%)	59	
	4,966	

6   *Non-controlling interests (SOFP)*

	A$'000
NCI at acquisition (1,890/4.5)	420
NCI share of post-acquisition retained reserves of Saar ((W5) 800 × 30%)	240
NCI share of impairment of goodwill ((W4) 76 × 30%)	(23)
NCI share of exchange gain on goodwill ([(W4) 31 + 53] × 30%)	25
	662

7   *Non-controlling interests (SPLOCI)*

	PFY A$'000	TCI A$'000
Profit for the year (W3)	500	500
Impairment losses (W4)	(76)	(76)
Other comprehensive income: exchange differences (W8)	–	103
	424	527
NCI share	× 30%	× 30%
	127	158

8   *Exchange differences arising during the year*

	A$'000	A$'000
On translation of net assets		
Closing NA @ CR (W2)	1,550	
Opening NA @ OR ((B$6,200,000 – 1,900,000) @ 4.3)	1,000	
	550	
Less total comprehensive income as translated (W3)	(500)	
		50
On goodwill (W4)		53
		103

Now try this question from the Practice Question Bank	**Number**	**Level**	**Marks**	**Time**
	Q23	Introductory	N/A	4 mins

CONSOLIDATED STATEMENTS OF CHANGES IN EQUITY

 The statement of changes in equity reconciles the movement in equity in the consolidated statement of financial position at the beginning and end of the period.

You will need to be able to produce a consolidated statement of changes in equity reconciling equity attributable to the owners of the parent and also NCI.

Topic list	learning outcomes	syllabus references
1 Purpose	B1	B1(a)
2 Proforma	B1	B1(a)

Chapter Overview

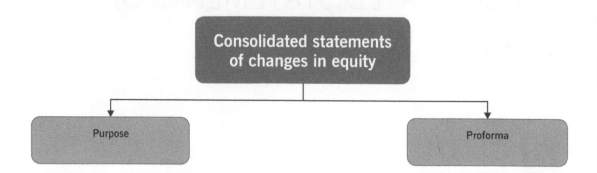

1   Purpose

The statement of changes in equity reconciles the movement in equity in the consolidated statement of financial position at the beginning and end of the period.

Extract from consolidated statement of financial position:

	20X1 $'000	Main reason(s) for movement	20X2 $'000
EQUITY			
Equity attributable to owners of the parent			
Share capital (P only)	X	Share issue by parent (nominal value)	X
Share premium (P only)	X	Share issue by parent (premium)	X
Consolidated reserves	X	P's TCI + Group % of S's TCI – P's dividends	X
	X		X
Non-controlling interest	X	NCI % of S's TCI – NCI % of S's dividends	X
	X		X

2   Proforma

	Equity attributable to owners of the parent $'000	Non-controlling interest $'000	Total $'000	
Balance at 31.12.X1 (from last year's consol SOFP)	X	X	X	(P SC/SP + Group reserves)/ NCI
Share issue	X	–	X	Given in question*
Total comprehensive income for the year	X	X	X	From consolidated SPLOCI
Dividends	(X)	(X)	(X)	P/(S × NCI%)
Adjustment to equity	X/(X)	X/(X)	X/(X)	Disposal/acquisition: control retained
Balance at 31.12.X2 (from this year's consol SOFP)	X	X	X	(P SC/SP + Group reserves)/ NCI

no balance in NCI column as share issue by subsidiary in the year not examinable in F2

(IAS 1: para. IG6)

BPP
LEARNING MEDIA

Example: Simple consolidated SOCIE

The summarised consolidated financial statements of the P group for the year ended 31 December 20X4 are as follows:

CONSOLIDATED STATEMENT OF FINANCIAL POSITION AS AT 31 DECEMBER 20X4

	$'000
Non-current assets	36,900
Current assets	28,200
	65,100
Equity attributable to owners of the parent	
Share capital	12,300
Share premium	5,800
Revaluation surplus	350
Retained earnings	32,100
	50,550
Non-controlling interests	1,750
	52,300
Non-current liabilities	5,200
Current liabilities	7,600
	65,100

CONSOLIDATED STATEMENT OF PROFIT OR LOSS AND OTHER COMPREHENSIVE INCOME FOR THE YEAR ENDED 31 DECEMBER 20X4

	$'000
Profit before tax	16,500
Income tax expense	(5,200)
Profit for the year	11,300
Other comprehensive income	500
Total comprehensive income for the year	11,800
Profit attributable to:	
Owners of the parent	11,100
Non-controlling interests	200
	11,300
Total comprehensive income for the year attributable to:	
Owners of the parent	11,450
Non-controlling interests	350
	11,800

Additional information

The P group is made up of the parent P and a 70% owned subsidiary S. The dividends paid for the year ended 31 December 20X4 by P and S were $800,000 and $500,000 respectively.

Required

Prepare the consolidated statement of changes in equity for the P group for the year ended 31 December 20X4.

Solution

P GROUP – CONSOLIDATED STATEMENT OF CHANGES IN EQUITY

	Equity attributable to owners of the parent $'000	Non-controlling interest $'000	Total $'000
Balance at 1 January 20X4 *(balancing figure)*	39,900	1,550	41,450
Total comprehensive income for the year *(consol SPLOCI)*	11,450	350	11,800
Dividends *(parent)/(NCI % of sub's: 30% × $500,000)*	(800)	(150)	(950)
Balance at 31 December 20X4 *(consol SOFP)*	50,550	1,750	52,300

51,350
39 900

Working: Group structure

P
|
70%
↓
S

Example: Each line of SOCIE

Summarised statements of changes in equity for the year ended 30 June 20X5 for SM and its only subsidiary, CE, are shown below:

Statements of changes in equity for the year ended 30 June 20X5

	SM $'000	CE $'000
Balance at 1 July 20X4	500,000	130,000
Issue of shares	25,000	–
Total comprehensive income for the year	75,000	40,000
Dividends	(16,000)	(10,000)
Balance at 30 June 20X5	584,000	160,000

Notes

1   SM acquired 37.5m of CE's 50m $1 ordinary shares on 1 July 20X2, when CE's total equity was $80m. The first dividend CE has paid since acquisition is the amount of $10m shown in the summarised statement above. The total comprehensive income for the year in SM's summarised statement of changes in equity includes its share of the dividend paid by CE.

2   During the year ended 30 June 20X5, CE sold some goods to SM for $15m at a mark-up of 25% on cost. At the year end, two-thirds of these goods had been sold on to third parties.

3   It is group accounting policy to measure non-controlling interest at acquisition at the proportionate share of the fair value of net assets. There has been no impairment of recognised goodwill in CE to date.

Required

Prepare the consolidated statement of changes in equity for the year ended 30 June 20X5.

Solution

SM GROUP – CONSOLIDATED STATEMENT OF CHANGES IN EQUITY

	Equity attributable to owners of the parent $'000	Non-controlling interest $'000	Total $'000
Balance at 1 July 20X4 (balancing figure)	537,500	32,500	570,000
Issue of shares	25,000	–	25,000
Total comprehensive income for the year (W4)	96,750	9,750	106,500
Dividends (25% × $10m)	(16,000)	(2,500)	(18,500)
Balance at 30 June 20X5 (W5)/(W6)	643,250	39,750	683,000

Workings

1   *Group structure*

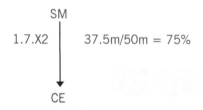

SM

1.7.X2 | 37.5m/50m = 75%

CE

PAR = $80m – $50m = $30m

2   *Unrealised profit*

CE →SM

PUP = $15m × 1/3 in inventory × 25/125 mark-up = $1m
DEBIT   CE's cost of sales (& CE's retained earnings) $1m
CREDIT   Inventories $1m

3   *Intra-group dividend*

Intra-group dividend income = 75% × $10m = $7.5m → Cancel out of SM's profit/total comprehensive income

4   *Consolidated total comprehensive income for the year*

	$'000
Consolidated TCI [($75m – $7.5m (W3)] + [$40m – $1m (W2))]	106,500
Total comprehensive income attributable to:	
Owners of parent (balancing figure)	96,750
Non-controlling interest ($40m – $1m (W2)) × 25%	9,750
	106,500

5   *Consolidated equity at 30 June 20X5*

	SM $'000	CE $'000
At the year end	584,000	160,000
PUP (W2)		(1,000)
At acquisition		(80,000)
		79,000
Share CE post-acquisition (75% × $79m)	59,250	
	643,250	

6   *Non-controlling interest at 30 June 20X5*

	$'000
NCI at acquisition (25% × $80m)	20,000
NCI share of post-acquisition reserves ($79m (W5) × 25%)	19,750
	39,750

7   *Proof of consolidated equity at 1 July 20X4*

	SM $'000	CE $'000
At 1 July 20X4	500,000	130,000
At acquisition		(80,000)
		50,000
Share CE post-acquisition (75% × $50m)	37,500	
	537,500	

8   *Proof of non-controlling interest at 1 July 20X4*

	$'000
NCI at acquisition (W6)	20,000
NCI share of post-acquisition reserves ($50m (W7) × 25%)	12,500
	32,500

Question 14.1   Extract from SOCIE

AB owned 60% of the equity share capital of CD at 31 December 20X4. AB purchased a further 10% of CD's equity shares on 31 December 20X5 for $1,500,000, when the existing non-controlling interest (NCI) in CD was measured at $4,480,000.

Required

Select the correct amounts in respect of the additional purchase from the list below or use 'BLANK' in order to reflect the impact on the consolidated statement of changes in equity for the AB Group for the year ended 31 December 20X5.

EXTRACT FROM THE CONSOLIDATED STATEMENT OF CHANGES IN EQUITY FOR THE AB GROUP FOR THE YEAR ENDED 31 DECEMBER 20X5

	Equity attributable to owners of the parent $'000	Non-controlling interest $'000
Balance at the start of the year	25,000	4,000
Total comprehensive income for the year	6,700	500
Dividends paid	(300)	(20)
Adjustment to NCI for additional purchase of CD shares		
Adjustment to parent's equity for additional purchase of CD shares		

Picklist:

Values	
$'000	
380	(380)
1,120	(1,120)
1,500	(1,500)
2,980	(2,980)
3,360	(3,360)
BLANK	

Workings

Chapter Summary

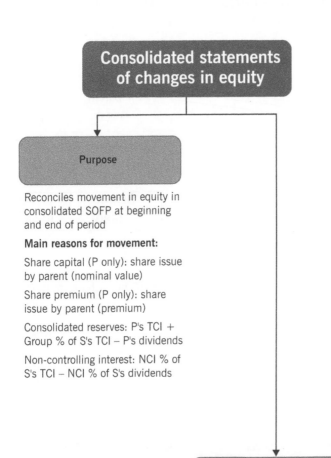

Consolidated statements of changes in equity

Purpose

Reconciles movement in equity in consolidated SOFP at beginning and end of period

Main reasons for movement:

Share capital (P only): share issue by parent (nominal value)

Share premium (P only): share issue by parent (premium)

Consolidated reserves: P's TCI + Group % of S's TCI – P's dividends

Non-controlling interest: NCI % of S's TCI – NCI % of S's dividends

Proforma

	Equity attributable owners of the parent	Non-controlling interest	Total	
	$	$	$	
Balance at 31.12.X1	X	X	X	(P SC/SP + Group reserves)/NCI
Share issue	X	–	X	Given in question
TCI for the year	X	X	X	From consolidated SPLOCI
Dividends	(X)	(X)	(X)	P/(S × NCI%)
Adjustment to equity	X/(X)	X/(X)	X/(X)	Acquisition/disposal: control retained
Balance at 31.12.X2	X	X	X	(P SC/SP + Group reserves)/NCI

Answers to Questions

14.1 Extract from SOCIE

EXTRACT FROM THE CONSOLIDATED STATEMENT OF CHANGES IN EQUITY FOR THE AB GROUP FOR THE YEAR ENDED 31 DECEMBER 20X5

	Equity attributable to owners of the parent $'000	Non-controlling interest $'000
Balance at the start of the year	25,000	4,000
Total comprehensive income for the year	6,700	500
Dividends paid	(300)	(20)
Adjustment to NCI for additional purchase of CD shares	**BLANK**	**(1,120)**
Adjustment to parent's equity for additional purchase of CD shares	**(380)**	**BLANK**

Workings

Adjustment to NCI = $4,480,000 × 10%/40% = $1,120,000 Decrease (as AB buys shares from NCI)

Adjustment to parent's equity:

	$'000
Consideration transferred	(1,500)
Decrease in NCI	1,120
	(380)

Now try these questions from the Practice Question Bank

Number	Level	Marks	Time
Q24	Introductory	N/A	5 mins
Q25	Introductory	12	22 mins
Q26	Introductory	15	27 mins
Q27	Introductory	10	18 mins
Q28	Introductory	17	31 mins
Q29	Introductory	18	32 mins

CONSOLIDATED STATEMENTS OF CASH FLOWS

 A consolidated statement of cash flows will be prepared using the consolidated statement of financial position and consolidated SPLOCI. This means that all intra-group transactions will already have been eliminated. The preparation of a consolidated statement of cash flows is therefore similar to a single entity statement with a few extra lines relevant to groups.

This chapter will focus on the additional group elements.

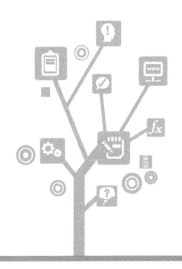

Topic list	learning outcomes	syllabus references
1 Formats	B1	B1(a)
2 Definitions	B1	B1(a)
3 Consolidated statements of cash flows	B1	B1(a)

Chapter Overview

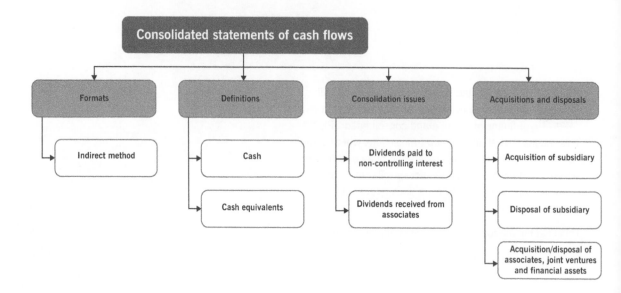

1   Formats

1.1 Indirect method statement of cash flows

Note. New entries for a consolidated statement of cash flows are shaded in grey.

	31.12.X1	
	$'000	$'000
Cash flows from operating activities		
Profit before taxation	3,350	
Adjustment for:		
Depreciation	520	
Profit on sale of property, plant and equipment	(10)	
Share of profit of associate/joint venture	(60)	
Foreign exchange loss	40	
Investment income	(500)	
Interest expense	400	
	3,740	
Decrease in inventories	1,050	
Increase in trade and other receivables	(500)	
Decrease in trade payables	(1,740)	
Cash generated from operations	2,550	
Interest paid *	(270)	
Income taxes paid	(900)	
Net cash from operating activities		1,380
Cash flows from investing activities		
Acquisition of subsidiary X net of cash acquired	(550)	
Purchase of property, plant and equipment	(350)	
Proceeds from sale of equipment	20	
Interest received *	200	
Dividends received (from associates/JVs and other investments)	200	
Net cash used in investing activities		(480)
Cash flows from financing activities		
Proceeds from issue of share capital	250	
Proceeds from long-term borrowings	250	
Payments of lease liabilities	(90)	
Dividends paid * (to owners of parent and NCI)	(1,200)	
Net cash used in financing activities		(790)
Net increase in cash and cash equivalents		110
Cash and cash equivalents at beginning of the period		120
Cash and cash equivalents at end of the period		230

* Interest paid and dividends paid may be reported under 'operating' or 'financing' activities. Interest and dividends received may be reported under 'operating' or 'investing' activities (IAS 7: para. 33).

(IAS 7: Illustrative Examples para. 3)

2 Definitions

KEY TERMS

CASH 'Cash comprises cash on hand and demand deposits'. (IAS 7: para. 6)

CASH EQUIVALENTS 'Cash equivalents are short-term, highly liquid investments that are readily convertible into known amounts of cash and which are subject to an insignificant risk of changes in value'.
(IAS 7: para. 6)

CASH FLOWS 'Cash flows are inflows and outflows of cash and cash equivalents'. (IAS 7: para. 6)

3 Consolidated statements of cash flows

3.1 Issue

A group's statement of cash flows should only deal with flows of cash **external** to the group.

3.2 Non-controlling interests

Only the actual payment of cash, ie **dividends paid to non-controlling interests**, should be reflected in the statement of cash flows. This may be presented either under 'financing activities' or 'operating activities'.

Example: NCI working

CONSOLIDATED STATEMENT OF PROFIT OR LOSS AND OTHER COMPREHENSIVE INCOME
FOR THE YEAR ENDED 31 DECEMBER 20X2

	$'000
Profit before tax	30
Income tax expense	(10)
PROFIT FOR THE YEAR	20
Other comprehensive income	
Items that will not be reclassified to profit or loss	
Gains on property revaluation	12
Income tax expense relating to gain on property revaluation	(4)
TOTAL COMPREHENSIVE INCOME FOR THE YEAR	28
Profit attributable to:	
Owners of the parent	15
Non-controlling interests	5
	20
Total comprehensive income attributable to:	
Owners of the parent	22
Non-controlling interests	6
	28

CONSOLIDATED STATEMENTS OF FINANCIAL POSITION AS AT 31 DECEMBER

	20X2 $'000	20X1 $'000
Non-controlling interests	102	99

Required

Calculate the dividend paid to non-controlling interests.

Solution

Non-controlling interests

	$'000
B/d	99
SPLOCI – TCI	6
	105
Dividends paid to NCI (balancing figure)	(3)
C/d	102

3.3 Associates

Dividends received from associates may be presented either under 'investing activities' or 'operating activities'.

Example: Associate working

CONSOLIDATED STATEMENT OF PROFIT OR LOSS AND OTHER COMPREHENSIVE INCOME FOR THE YEAR ENDED 31 DECEMBER 20X2

	$'000
Profit before interest and tax	60
Share of profit of associates	7
Profit before tax	67
Income tax expense	(20)
PROFIT FOR THE YEAR	47
Other comprehensive income	
Items that will not be reclassified to profit or loss	
Gains on property revaluation	15
Share of gain on property revaluation of associate	3
Income tax relating to items that will not be reclassified	(5)
Other comprehensive income for the year, net of tax	13
TOTAL COMPREHENSIVE INCOME FOR THE YEAR	60

CONSOLIDATED STATEMENTS OF FINANCIAL POSITION AS AT 31 DECEMBER

	20X2 $'000	20X1 $'000
Investment in associates	94	88

Required

Calculate the dividend received from associates and complete the profit before tax and associate lines in the extract from the operating activities section of the cash flow below.

Solution

Investment in associate

	$'000
B/d	88
SPLOCI – share of profit	7
SPLOCI – share of gain on property revaluation	3
	98
Dividends received from associate (balancing figure)	(4)
C/d	94

EXTRACT FROM STATEMENT OF CASH FLOW (OPERATING ACTIVITIES)

Cash flows from operating activities	$'000
Profit before taxation	67
Adjustment for:	
Share of profit of associate	(7)

3.4 Acquisition and disposal of subsidiaries

The acquisition or disposal of a subsidiary should be included under the heading 'Cash flows from **investing** activities'. The following **two cash flows** should be **netted** off and shown in one line (IAS 7: para 39–40, 42):

- Cash paid to buy shares (acquisition) or cash received from selling shares (disposal)

- Cash/overdraft consolidated for the first time on acquisition or cash/overdraft deconsolidated on disposal

3.5 Acquisitions and disposals of associates, joint ventures and financial assets

There are three possible entries to the statement of cash flows:

(a)   Cash paid to acquire associates/joint ventures/simple investments or cash received from selling them (in 'investing activities')

(b)   Dividend income received from associates/joint ventures/simple investments (in 'investing activities' or 'operating activities')

(c)   Under the indirect method, the 'share of the associate or joint ventures profit' must be removed from profit before tax as an adjustment in the 'operating activities' section of the statement of cash flow

(IAS 7: para. 37–38)

Example: Acquisition of subsidiary

On 1 October 20X8 P acquired 90% of S by issuing 100 million shares at an agreed value of $1.60 per share and $140m in cash. At that time the statement of financial position of S (equivalent to the fair value of the assets and liabilities) was as follows:

	$m
Property, plant and equipment	190
Inventories	70
Trade receivables	30
Cash and cash equivalents	10
Trade payables	(40)
	260

Group policy is to measure non-controlling interests at the date of acquisition at the proportionate share of net assets.

The consolidated statements of financial position of P as at 31 December were as follows:

	20X8 $m	20X7 $m
Non-current assets		
Property, plant and equipment	2,642	2,300
Goodwill	60	–
	2,702	2,300
Current assets		
Inventories	1,450	1,200
Trade receivables	1,370	1,100
Cash and cash equivalents	2	50
	2,822	2,350
	5,524	4,650
Equity attributable to owners of the parent		
Share capital ($1 ordinary shares)	1,150	1,000
Share premium account	590	500
Retained earnings	1,778	1,530
Revaluation surplus	74	–
	3,592	3,030
Non-controlling interests	32	–
	3,624	3,030
Non-current liabilities		
Deferred tax	80	40
Current liabilities		
Trade payables	1,710	1,520
Current tax	110	60
	1,820	1,580
	5,524	4,650

The consolidated statement of profit or loss and other comprehensive income for the year ended 31 December 20X8 was as follows:

	$m
Revenue	10,000
Cost of sales	(7,500)
Gross profit	2,500
Administrative expenses	(2,083)

	$m
Profit before tax	417
Income tax expense	(150)
PROFIT FOR THE YEAR	267
Other comprehensive income:	
Items that will not be reclassified to profit or loss	
Gains on property revaluation	115
Income tax relating to items that will not be reclassified	(40)
Other comprehensive income for the year, net of tax	75
TOTAL COMPREHENSIVE INCOME FOR THE YEAR	342
Profit attributable to:	
Owners of the parent	258
Non-controlling interests	9
	267
Total comprehensive income attributable to:	
Owners of the parent	332
Non-controlling interests	10
	342

You are also given the following information:

(1) All other subsidiaries are wholly owned.
(2) Depreciation charged to the consolidated profit or loss amounted to $210m.
(3) There were no disposals of property, plant and equipment during the year.

Required

Prepare a consolidated statement of cash flows for the year ended 31 December 20X8 under the indirect method in accordance with IAS 7 *Statement of cash flows*.

Solution

P GROUP
STATEMENT OF CASH FLOWS FOR THE YEAR ENDED 31 DECEMBER 20X8

	$m	$m
Cash flows from operating activities		
Profit before taxation	417	
Adjustments for:		
Depreciation	210	
Impairment of goodwill (W2)	6	
	633	
Increase in inventories (W3)	(180)	
Increase in trade receivables (W3)	(240)	
Increase in trade payables (W3)	150	
Cash generated from operations	363	
Income taxes paid (W7)	(100)	
Net cash from operating activities		263
Cash flows from investing activities		
Acquisition of subsidiary net of cash acquired (140 – 10)	(130)	
Purchase of property, plant and equipment (W1)	(247)	
Net cash used in investing activities		(377)

	$m	$m
Cash flows from financing activities		
Proceeds from issue of share capital (W4)	80	
Dividends paid to owners of the parent (W5)	(10)	
Dividends paid to non-controlling interests (W6)	(4)	
Net cash from financing activities		66
Net decrease in cash and cash equivalents		(48)
Cash and cash equivalents at the beginning of the year		50
Cash and cash equivalents at the end of the year		2

Workings

1   *Property, plant and equipment*

	$m
B/d	2,300
Revaluation	115
Depreciation	(210)
Acquisition of subsidiary	190
	2,395
Additions (balancing figure)	247
C/d	2,642

2   *Goodwill*

	$m
B/d	–
Acquisition of subsidiary*	66
	66
Impairment loss (balancing figure)	(6)
C/d	60

*Goodwill on acquisition of subsidiary:

	$m
Consideration transferred (140 + (100 × $1.60))	300
NCI (260 × 10%)	26
Less net assets at acquisition	(260)
	66

3   *Inventories, trade receivables and trade payables*

	Inventories $m	Trade receivables $m	Trade payables $m
B/d	1,200	1,100	1,520
Issued on acquisition of subsidiary	70	30	40
	1,270	1,130	1,560
Increase (balancing figure)	180	240	150
C/d	1,450	1,370	1,710

4   Share capital and share premium

	$m
B/d (1,000 + 500)	1,500
Issued on acquisition of subsidiary (100 × $1.60)	160
	1,660
Issue for cash (balancing figure)	80
C/d (1,150 + 590)	1,740

5   Retained earnings (to find dividends paid to owners of the parent)

	$m
B/d	1,530
SPLOCI – profit attributable to owners of parent	258
	1,788
Dividends paid to owners of the parent (balancing figure)	(10)
C/d	1,778

6   Non-controlling interests

	$m
B/d	–
SPLOCI – TCI	10
Acquisition of subsidiary (W2)	26
	36
Dividends paid (balancing figure)	(4)
C/d	32

7   Current and deferred tax

	$m
B/d (40 + 60)	100
SPLOCI – P/L	150
SPLOCI – OCI	40
	290
Tax paid (balancing figure)	(100)
C/d (80 + 110)	190

Question 15.1   Disposal of subsidiary

Below is the consolidated statement of financial position of CD Group as at 30 June 20X5 and the
consolidated statement of profit or loss and other comprehensive income for the year ended
30 June 20X5.

CONSOLIDATED STATEMENT OF FINANCIAL POSITION AS AT 30 JUNE

	20X5 $m	20X4 $m
Non-current assets		
Property, plant and equipment	4,067	3,909
Goodwill (re NW)	–	40
	4,067	3,949

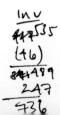

Inv   Rec   Pay

B/d   447535   228417   408
lost on disy (46)   (42)   (28)✓
       441489   375   370
       247   230   10
C/d   736   605   380

	20X5 $m	20X4 $m
Current assets		
Inventories	736	535
Trade receivables	605	417
Cash and cash equivalents	294	238
	1,635	1,190
	5,702	5,139
Equity attributable to owners of the parent		
Share capital	1,000	1,000
Retained earnings	3,637	3,117
	4,637	4,117
Non-controlling interests	482	512
	5,119	4,629
Current liabilities		
Trade payables	380	408
Income tax payable	203	102
	583	510
	5,702	5,139

CONSOLIDATED STATEMENT OF PROFIT OR LOSS AND OTHER COMPREHENSIVE INCOME FOR THE YEAR ENDED 30 JUNE 20X5

	$m
Profit before interest and tax	878
Profit on disposal of shares in subsidiary	36
Profit before tax	914
Income tax expense	(290)
Profit/total comprehensive income for the year	624
Profit/total comprehensive income attributable to:	
Owners of the parent	520
Non-controlling interests	104
	624

You are given the following information.

(1) CD sold its entire interest in NW on 31 March 20X5 for $420m. CD acquired an 80% interest in NW a number of years ago when NW's reserves stood at $80m.

The statement of financial position of NW at the date of disposal showed:

	$m
Property, plant and equipment	370
Inventories	46
Receivables	42
Cash and cash equivalents	20
	478
Share capital	100
Retained earnings	340
	440
Trade payables	38
	478

The non-controlling interests in NW were measured at fair value at the date of acquisition of $44m.

Impairment tests conducted annually since the date of acquisition did not reveal any impairment losses in respect of the consolidated investment in NW.

(2) Depreciation charge for the year was $800m.

There were no disposals of non-current assets other than the disposal of the subsidiary.

Required

(to the nearest $m)

(a) How will the cash flows on disposal of the subsidiary appear on the face of the statement of cash flows? (select from the lists below and enter into the required boxes)

Heading (select from list 1)	Amount in $m (select from list 2)

List 1
Heading
Operating
Investing
Financing

List 2
Amount (in $m)
420
(420)
400
(400)
20
(20)

(b) What are the additions to property, plant and equipment (enter into the box below showing a cash inflow as positive and a cash outflow as negative)?

$m [   ]

(c) What is the dividend paid to non-controlling interests (enter into the box below showing a cash inflow as positive and a cash outflow as negative)? *b/d 44*

TCI att bNCI 104

$m [   ]

c/d

(d) Prepare the reconciliation of profit before tax to cash generated from operations under the indirect method of cash flows (enter into the proforma below).

	$m
Profit before tax	
Adjustments for:	
Depreciation	
Profit on disposal of subsidiary	
Increase in inventories	
Increase in trade receivables	
Increase in trade payables	
Cash generated from operations	

Chapter Summary

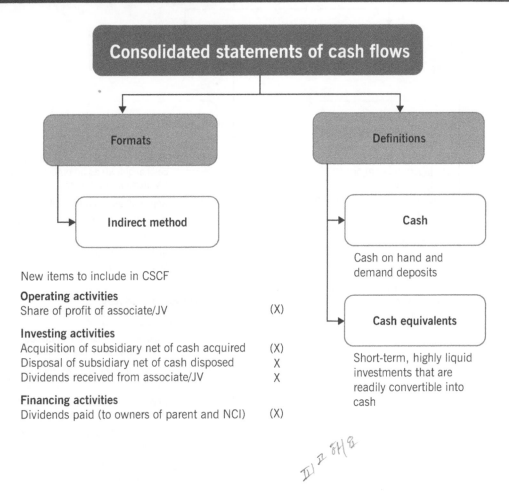

Consolidated statements of cash flows

Formats

Indirect method

New items to include in CSCF

Operating activities
Share of profit of associate/JV   (X)

Investing activities
Acquisition of subsidiary net of cash acquired   (X)
Disposal of subsidiary net of cash disposed   X
Dividends received from associate/JV   X

Financing activities
Dividends paid (to owners of parent and NCI)   (X)

Definitions

Cash

Cash on hand and demand deposits

Cash equivalents

Short-term, highly liquid investments that are readily convertible into cash

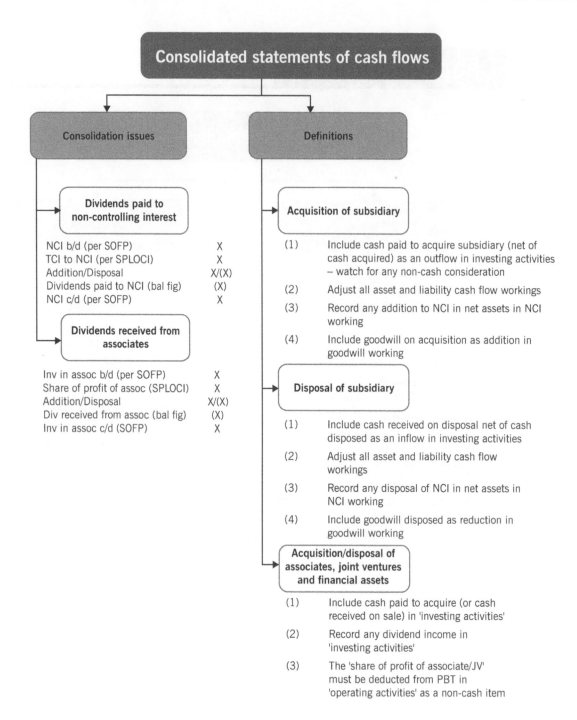

Consolidated statements of cash flows

Consolidation issues

Dividends paid to non-controlling interest

NCI b/d (per SOFP)	X
TCI to NCI (per SPLOCI)	X
Addition/Disposal	X/(X)
Dividends paid to NCI (bal fig)	(X)
NCI c/d (per SOFP)	X

Dividends received from associates

Inv in assoc b/d (per SOFP)	X
Share of profit of assoc (SPLOCI)	X
Addition/Disposal	X/(X)
Div received from assoc (bal fig)	(X)
Inv in assoc c/d (SOFP)	X

Definitions

Acquisition of subsidiary

(1) Include cash paid to acquire subsidiary (net of cash acquired) as an outflow in investing activities – watch for any non-cash consideration

(2) Adjust all asset and liability cash flow workings

(3) Record any addition to NCI in net assets in NCI working

(4) Include goodwill on acquisition as addition in goodwill working

Disposal of subsidiary

(1) Include cash received on disposal net of cash disposed as an inflow in investing activities

(2) Adjust all asset and liability cash flow workings

(3) Record any disposal of NCI in net assets in NCI working

(4) Include goodwill disposed as reduction in goodwill working

Acquisition/disposal of associates, joint ventures and financial assets

(1) Include cash paid to acquire (or cash received on sale) in 'investing activities'

(2) Record any dividend income in 'investing activities'

(3) The 'share of profit of associate/JV' must be deducted from PBT in 'operating activities' as a non-cash item

Quick Quiz

1   What are the standard headings required by IAS 7 to be included in a statement of cash flows?

2   What is the indirect method of preparing a statement of cash flows?

3   How should an acquisition or disposal of a subsidiary be shown in the consolidated statement of cash flows?

Answers to Quick Quiz

1   Operating, investing and financing activities.

2   To determine the cash flow from operating activities, the net profit or loss for the period is adjusted for non-cash items; changes in inventories, receivables and payables from operations; and other items resulting from investing or financing activities.

3   Cash flows from acquisitions and disposals are presented separately under investing activities.

Answers to Questions

15.1 Disposal of subsidiary

(a)   **Disposal of subsidiary**

Heading (select from list 1)	Amount in $ m (select from list 2)
Investing	400 (420 – 20)

(b)   **Additions to property, plant and equipment**

$m   (1,328)   (W1)

(c)   **Dividend paid to non-controlling interests**

$m   (38)   (W2)

(d)   **Reconciliation of profit before tax to cash generated from operations**

Cash flows from operating activities

	$m
Profit before tax	914
Adjustments for:	
Depreciation	800
Profit on disposal of subsidiary	(36)
	1,678
Increase in inventories (W3)	(247)
Increase in trade receivables (W3)	(230)
Increase in trade payables (W3)	10
Cash generated from operations	1,211

Workings

1   *Property, plant and equipment*

	$m
B/d	3,909
Depreciation	(800)
Disposal of subsidiary	(370)
	2,739
Additions (balancing figure)	1,328
C/d	4,067

2   *Non-controlling interests*

	$m
B/d	512
SPLOCI	104
Disposal of subsidiary*	(96)
	520
Dividends paid (balancing figure)	(38)
C/d	482

	$m
*NCI at disposal:	
NCI at acquisition (fair value)	44
NCI share of post-acquisition reserves [(340 − 80) × 20%]	52
	96

3   *Inventories, trade receivables and trade payables*

	Inventories $m	Trade receivables $m	Trade payables $m
B/d	535	417	408
Disposal of subsidiary	(46)	(42)	(38)
	489	375	370
Increase (balancing figure)	247	230	10
C/d	736	605	380

Now try these questions from the Practice Question Bank

Number	Level	Marks	Time
Q30	Introductory	N/A	5 mins
Q31	Introductory	25	45 mins

DISCLOSURES AND ETHICS

Part E

RELATED PARTIES

 Related party relationships are a normal feature of business but related parties could enter into transactions that unrelated parties would not or at different amounts. Since this could have a significant impact on performance and position, it is important to make the user aware of these transactions.

Chapter Overview

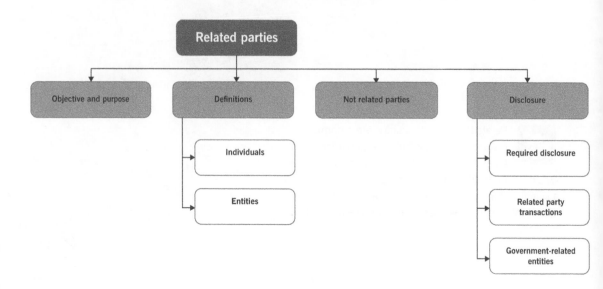

1 Related parties

1.1 Objective of IAS 24 *Related party disclosures*

'To ensure that an entity's financial statements contain the **disclosures** necessary to **draw attention** to the possibility that its **financial position and profit or loss may have been affected** by the **existence** of related parties and by **transactions and outstanding balances,** including commitments with such parties.' (IAS 24: para. 1)

1.2 Purpose of IAS 24

Related party relationships are a normal feature of business but related parties could **enter into transactions that unrelated parties would not or at different amounts**. (IAS 24: para. 5–6)

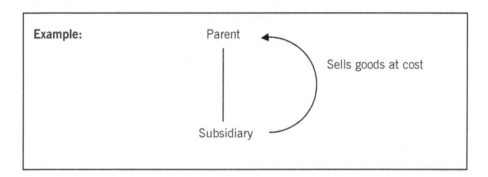

Example:　　　　　　　　　Parent　　　　　Sells goods at cost　　　　　Subsidiary

The profit or loss and financial position of an entity may be affected by a related party relationship even if related party transactions do not occur.

For example, a subsidiary may terminate relations with a trading partner on acquisition by the parent of a fellow subsidiary engaged in the same activity as the former trading partner. (IAS 24: para. 7)

Therefore, knowledge of an entity's transactions, balances, commitments and relationships with related parties **may affect** the **assessment by users** of financial statements **of its operations and of the risks and opportunities** facing the entity. (IAS 24: para. 8)

KEY TERMS

RELATED PARTY **(IAS 24)** A **related party** is a person or entity that is related to the entity that is preparing its financial statements (the 'reporting entity').

(a) A person or a close member of that person's family is related to a reporting entity if that person:

   (i) Has **control** or **joint control** over the reporting entity;

   (ii) Has **significant influence** over the reporting entity; or

   (iii) Is a member of the **key management personnel** of the reporting entity or of a parent of the reporting entity.

(b) An entity is related to a reporting entity if any of the following conditions applies:

   (i) The entity and the reporting entity are **members of the same group** (which means that each parent, subsidiary and fellow subsidiary is related to the others).

   (ii) One entity is an **associate* or joint venture*** of the other entity (or an associate or joint venture of a member of a group of which the other entity is a member).

   (iii) Both entities are **joint ventures* of the same third party**.

   (iv) One entity is a **joint venture* of a third entity** and the other entity is an **associate of the third entity**.

(v)   The entity is a **post-employment benefit plan** for the benefit of employees of either the reporting entity or an entity related to the reporting entity.

(vi)   The entity is **controlled** or **jointly controlled** by a person identified in (a).

(vii)   A person identified in (a)(i) has **significant influence** over the entity or is a member of the **key management personnel** of the entity (or of a parent of the entity).

(viii) The entity, or any member of a group of which it is a part, provides **key management personnel services** to the reporting entity or the parent of the reporting entity.

including subsidiaries of the associate or joint venture

(IAS 24: para. 9)

Close members of the family of a person are defined as 'those family members who may be expected to influence, or be influenced by, that person in their dealings with the entity and include:

- that person's children and spouse or domestic partner;
- children of that person's spouse or domestic partner; and
- dependants of that person or that person's spouse or domestic partner'.

(IAS 24: para. 9)

Key management personnel are 'those persons having authority and responsibility for **planning, directing and controlling the activities** of the entity, directly or indirectly, including any **director** (whether executive or otherwise) of that entity'. (IAS 24: para. 9)

'In considering each possible related party relationship, attention is directed to the **substance** of the relationship, and not merely the legal form'. (IAS 24: para. 10)

2   Not related parties

The following are **not** related parties:

(a)   **Two entities** simply because they have a **director** or other member **of key management personnel in common**, or because a member of key management personnel of one entity has significant influence over the other entity

(b)   **Two venturers** simply because they share joint control over a joint venture

(c)   Simply by virtue of their normal dealings with an entity:

(i)   Providers of finance

(ii)   Trade unions

(iii)   Public utilities

(iv)   Departments and agencies of a government that does not control, jointly control or significantly influence the reporting entity

(d)   A customer, supplier, franchisor, distributor, or general agent with whom an entity **transacts a significant volume of business,** simply by virtue of the resulting economic dependence

(IAS 24: para. 11)

Question 16.1

LM is a private manufacturing company making car parts. The majority of LM's long-term finance is provided by KPG Bank.

LM is 90% owned by XY, a listed entity. XY is a long-established company controlled by the Grassi family through an agreement which pools their voting rights.

LM regularly provides parts at market price to RS, a company in which Francesca Cincetti has a minority (23%) holding and significant influence. Francesca Cincetti is the wife of Roberto Grassi, one of the key Grassi family shareholders that controls XY.

30% of LM's revenue comes from transactions with a major car maker, PQ.

Required

Which of the following are related parties of LM in accordance with IAS 24?

Tick ALL those who are related parties of LM.

Related?	Name of person or entity
	XY
	KPG Bank
	Grassi family
	Francesca Cincetti
	RS
	PQ

3 Disclosure

IAS 24 requires an entity to disclose the following:

(a) The name of its **parent** and, if different, the **ultimate controlling party** irrespective of whether there have been any transactions.

(b) Total **key management personnel compensation** (broken down by category ie short-term benefits, post-employment benefits, other long-term benefits, termination benefits and share-based payment).

(c) **If the entity has had related party transactions**:

    (i) Nature of the related party **relationship**

    (ii) Information about the **amount** of the **transactions and outstanding balances, including commitments, guarantees and bad and doubtful debts** necessary for users to understand the potential effect of the relationship on the financial statements

No disclosure is required of intra-group related party transactions in the consolidated financial statements (since they are eliminated).

Items of a **similar** nature may be disclosed **in aggregate** except where separate disclosure is necessary for understanding purposes.

(IAS 24: para. 4, 13, 17, 18, 24)

3.1 Related party transactions

KEY TERM

RELATED PARTY TRANSACTION (IAS 24) A **transfer of resources, services or obligations** between a reporting entity and a related party, **regardless of whether a price is charged**. (IAS 24: para. 9)

Examples include (IAS 24: para 21):

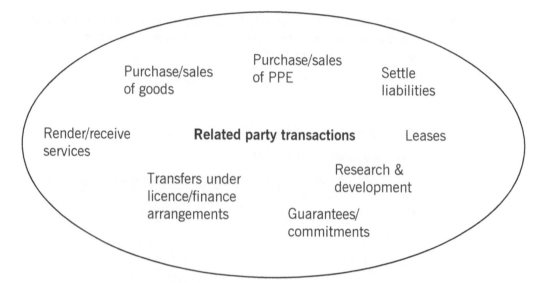

3.2 Government-related entities

If the reporting entity is a **government-related entity** (ie a government has control, joint control or significant influence over the entity), an **exemption** is available from full disclosure of transactions, outstanding balances and commitments with the Government or with other entities related to the same government. (IAS 24: para. 25)

However, if the exemption is applied, disclosure is required of:

(a) The **name of the government** and **nature of the relationship**; and

(b) The nature and amount of each **individually significant transaction** (plus a qualitative or quantitative indication of the extent of other transactions which are collectively, but not individually, significant). (IAS 24: para 26)

Question 16.2	Disclosure

AB is an international supermarket chain with three subsidiaries operating in different geographical areas. AB charges its subsidiaries an annual management services fee of 20% of profit before tax (before accounting for the fee). AB is 100% owned by a holding company EF which in turn is majority owned by a wealthy investor, Mr X.

AB provides interest free loans to its junior employees and also a defined benefit pension plan. AB made contributions of $3m to the pension plan for the year ended 31 December 20X1.

Required

Which of the following should be disclosed in the consolidated financial statements of the AB Group under IAS 24?

Tick which items should be disclosed.

Disclose?	Item
	The management fee from AB's subsidiaries
	The name of the parent, EF
	The name of the ultimate controlling party, Mr X
	The interest free loans to junior employees
	The $3m contributions to the defined benefit pension plan

Question 16.3	Understanding of IAS 24

Which of the following statements is/are CORRECT in relation to IAS 24 *Related party disclosures*?

Tick the statements that are correct.

Correct?	Item
	A transaction with a related party only requires disclosure if it is at below market value.
	The aim of IAS 24 is to make users of financial statements aware of the potential impact of related party transactions on an entity's financial position and profit or loss.
	Two associates in the same group are related parties.
	If an entity has a joint venture and the joint venture has a subsidiary, both the joint venture and its subsidiary are related to the entity.

Chapter Summary

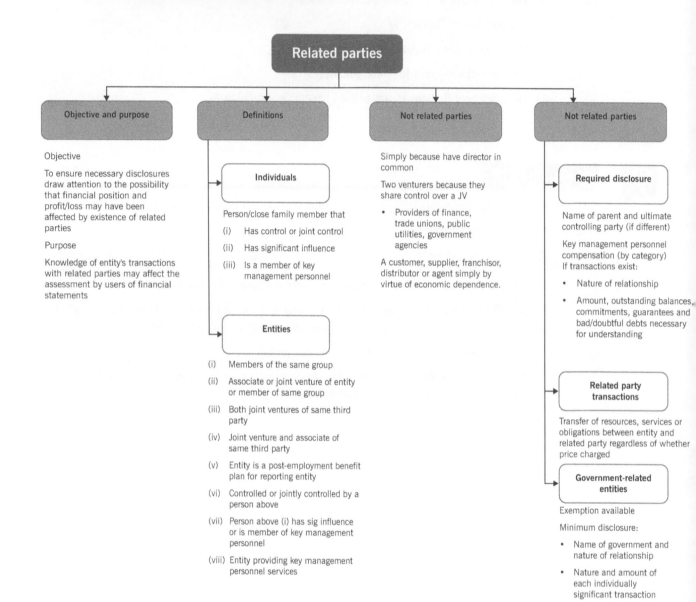

Related parties

Objective and purpose

Objective

To ensure necessary disclosures draw attention to the possibility that financial position and profit/loss may have been affected by existence of related parties

Purpose

Knowledge of entity's transactions with related parties may affect the assessment by users of financial statements

Definitions

Individuals

Person/close family member that

(i) Has control or joint control

(ii) Has significant influence

(iii) Is a member of key management personnel

Entities

(i) Members of the same group

(ii) Associate or joint venture of entity or member of same group

(iii) Both joint ventures of same third party

(iv) Joint venture and associate of same third party

(v) Entity is a post-employment benefit plan for reporting entity

(vi) Controlled or jointly controlled by a person above

(vii) Person above (i) has sig influence or is member of key management personnel

(viii) Entity providing key management personnel services

Not related parties

Simply because have director in common

Two venturers because they share control over a JV

• Providers of finance, trade unions, public utilities, government agencies

A customer, supplier, franchisor, distributor or agent simply by virtue of economic dependence.

Not related parties

Required disclosure

Name of parent and ultimate controlling party (if different)

Key management personnel compensation (by category) If transactions exist:

• Nature of relationship

• Amount, outstanding balances, commitments, guarantees and bad/doubtful debts necessary for understanding

Related party transactions

Transfer of resources, services or obligations between entity and related party regardless of whether price charged

Government-related entities

Exemption available

Minimum disclosure:

• Name of government and nature of relationship

• Nature and amount of each individually significant transaction

Quick Quiz

1   What is a related party transaction?

2   A managing director of a company is a related party of that company. True / False?

Answers to Quick Quiz

1   A transfer of resources, services or obligations between related parties, regardless of whether a price is charged.

2   True. A member of the key management personnel of an entity is a related party of that entity.

Answers to Questions

16.1 Definition of related parties

Related?	Name of person or entity
✓	XY (members of the same group) *[Section 1.5(b)(i)]*
	KPG Bank (providers of finance are not related by virtue of their normal dealings) *[Section 2.1(c)]*
✓	Grassi family (persons who have joint control) *[Section 1.5(a)(i)]*
✓	Francesca Cincetti (close family of a person who has joint control) *[Section 1.5(a)(i)]*
✓	RS (an entity in which close family of a person with joint control has significant influence) *[Section 1.5 (b)(vii)]*
	PQ (a customer with which an entity transacts a significant volume of business is not related simply by virtue of economic dependence) *[Section 2.1(d)]*

(Definition of related parties: IAS 24: para. 9)

16.2 Disclosure

Disclose?	Item
	The management fee from AB's subsidiaries (not disclosed as eliminated in group accounts)
✓	The name of the parent, EF
✓	The name of the ultimate controlling party, Mr X
	The interest free loans to junior employees (not disclosed under IAS 24 as junior employees are not key management personnel and therefore are not related parties)
✓	The $3 million contributions to the defined benefit pension plan

(Related party disclosures: IAS 24: para. 13 - 27)

16.3 Understanding of IAS 24

Correct?	Item
	A transaction with a related party only requires disclosure if it is at below market value
✓	The aim of IAS 24 is to make users of financial statements aware of the potential impact of related party transactions on an entity's financial position and profit or loss
	Two associates in the same group are related parties
✓	If an entity has a joint venture and the joint venture has a subsidiary, both the joint venture and its subsidiary are related to the entity

Statement 1 is incorrect – all material related party transactions must be disclosed regardless of whether they are at market value. (IAS 24: para. 18)

Statement 3 is incorrect – two associates are not related as joint significant influence is not considered to be a close enough relationship (IAS 24: para. 11). An associate and a joint venture are related because the power over a joint venture (joint control) is stronger than that over an associate (significant influence) (IAS 24: para. 9(b)(iv)).

Now try these questions from the Practice Question Bank	Number	Level	Marks	Time
	Q32	Introductory	N/A	7 mins

EARNINGS PER SHARE

Earnings per share is a key shareholder ratio which is reported within the financial statements for quoted companies.
IAS 33 *Earnings per share* governs the preparation and disclosure of basic and diluted EPS.

Topic list	learning outcomes	syllabus references
1 Basic earnings per share	B4	B4(a)
2 Diluted earnings per share	B4	B4(a)

Chapter Overview

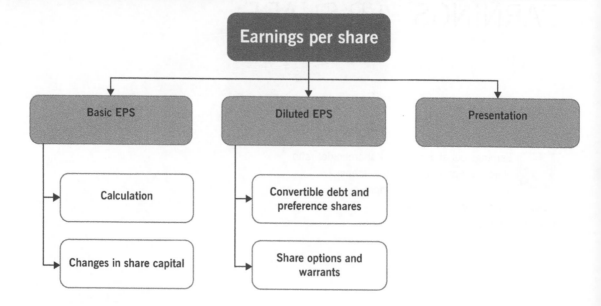

1 Basic earnings per share

1.1 Calculation (IAS 33 *Earnings per share*)

$$EPS = \frac{Earnings}{Weighted\ average\ no.\ of\ equity\ shares\ during\ the\ period}\ cents$$

Earnings

=   Profit or loss for the period attributable to ordinary equity holders of the parent:

ie consolidated profit *after*

- Income taxes

- Non-controlling interests

- Preference dividends (on non-cumulative preference shares where dividends have been declared in respect of the period)*

*Redeemable and cumulative irredeemable preference shares are treated as financial liabilities and their dividends as a finance cost so these dividends will already have been deducted in arriving at the consolidated profit after tax figure (dividends are recognised annually on cumulative preference shares even if they have not been declared).

(IAS 33: para. 10, 13, 14)

Earnings per share (EPS) is only a required disclosure for entities with shares which are **publicly traded**. (IAS 33: para. 2)

1.2 Changes in equity share capital

1.2.1 Issue at full market price

Where a share issue is made at full market price, the company ought to generate **additional profits**, as it has extra funds to generate profits from.

However, if the issue was not at the end of the year, then this will need to be **time apportioned** to reflect the fact that the company will have only been able to generate extra profits from the extra funds for part of the year. (IAS 33: para. 20)

Eg a company has earnings of $100,000 and a year end of 31 December. On 1 October 20X2 the company issued 300,000 shares at full market price. The share capital before the share issue was 600,000 shares.

Weighted number of shares

Date	Narrative	No. shares	Time period	Weighted average
1.1.X2	b/d	600,000	× 9/12	450,000
1.10.X2	Issue at FMP	300,000		
		900,000	× 3/12	225,000
				675,000

$$EPS = \frac{\$100,000}{675,000} = 14.8c$$

1.2.2 Bonus issue (also known as 'scrip' or 'capitalisation' issue)

Bonus shares are issued at no consideration to existing shareholders so the company **cannot be expected to generate the same return** (EPS) per share after a bonus issue.

To avoid the distorting effect of a bonus issue on EPS, the **number of shares is restated** as if the bonus shares had been in issue for all periods prior to the bonus issue.

Eg a company has a 1:1 bonus issue on 1 January 20X2.

	20X2	20X1
Assets (eg cash)	$100,000	$100,000
Earnings	$20,000	$20,000
Shares	200,000	100,000
EPS	10c	20c

To restate the number of shares as if the bonus shares had always been in issue, we use the bonus fraction which is expressed as:

$$\frac{\text{No. of share after bonus issue}}{\text{No. of shares before bonus issue}}$$

The bonus fraction is therefore $\frac{2}{1}$. To make EPS comparable, we need to restate the 20X1 figure as if it had the same share capital as 20X2 ie $\dfrac{\$20,000}{100,000 \times \frac{2}{1}}$

This is algebraically the same as restating the previous EPS by the reciprocal of the bonus fraction, ie 20c × ½ = 10c.

(IAS 33: para. 26–28, 64, Illustrative Example 3)

Rights issue

A rights issue (at below current market price) includes **both** an **issue of shares** and a **bonus issue** which must be accounted for.

The bonus fraction is measured as:

$$\frac{\text{Fair value per share immediately before exercise of rights}}{\text{Theoretical ex rights price (TERP)}}$$

It is applied to all periods (eg months) prior to the issue (ie apply the bonus fraction to the total number of shares for each block of time prior to the rights issue).

Example: Calculation of TERP – Illustration

Assume rights issue on a 1 for 4 basis

Share price immediately before exercise of rights $10

Rights price $6.50

	$
4 @ 10	40.00
1 @ 6.50	6.50
5	46.50

$$\therefore \text{TERP} = \frac{\$46.50}{5} = \$9.30$$

Bonus fraction $= \dfrac{10}{9.3}$ To restate comparatives use reciprocal $\dfrac{9.3}{10}$

(IAS 33: para. 26 – 28, 64, Illustrative Example 4)

Question 17.1   Basic EPS

On 1 January 20X1 Saunders Co had 2,000,000 ordinary shares in issue.

On 30 April 20X1 the company issued at full market price 270,000 ordinary shares.

On 31 July 20X1 the company made a rights issue of 1 for 10 @ $2.00. The fair value of the shares on the last day before the issue of shares from the rights issue was $3.10.

Finally, on 30 September 20X1 the company made a 1 for 20 bonus issue.

Profit for the year was $400,000.

The reported EPS for the year ended 31 December 20X0 was 18.6c.

Required

Calculate the EPS for the year ended 31 December 20X1 and the restated EPS for the year ended 31 December 20X0.

Workings

1   Weighted average number of shares

Date	Narrative	Shares	Time	Bonus fraction	Weighted average

2   Bonus fraction for rights issue

$$= \frac{\text{Fair value per share immediately before exercise of rights}}{\text{Theoretical ex rights price (TERP)}}$$

3   *Theoretical ex rights price*

1.3 Summary

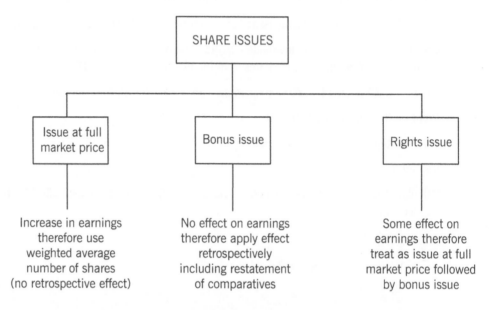

2   Diluted earnings per share

Basic EPS is calculated by comparing earnings with the number of shares currently in issue. If an entity has a **commitment to issue shares in the future** (eg on the conversion of convertible debt or the exercise of options), this may result in a fall in EPS.

IAS 33 refers to such commitments as 'potential ordinary shares'.

Diluted EPS shows **how basic EPS would change** if 'potential ordinary shares' become ordinary shares. It is therefore a **'warning' measure** of what may happen in the future for current ordinary shareholders.

When the potential shares are actually issued, the impact on basic EPS will be two-fold:

(a)   The number of shares will increase
(b)   There may be a change in earnings eg lower interest charges

This potential change in EPS is reflected in the calculation of diluted EPS.

(IAS 33: para 30–32)

2.1 Convertible debt or preference shares

(a)

Earnings	$
Basic earnings	X
Add back interest net of tax (or preference dividends) 'saved'	X
	X̲

(b)

No of shares	No
Basic weighted average	X
Add additional shares on conversion (using terms giving maximum dilution available after the year end)	X
Diluted number	X

(IAS 33: para. 33, 36, 39)

Question 17.2	Diluted EPS for convertible debt

Acorn Co had the same 10 million ordinary shares in issue on both 1 April 20X1 and 31 March 20X2. On 1 April 20X1 the company issued convertible loan stock. Assuming the conversion was fully subscribed, there would be an increase of 4 million ordinary shares. The liability element of the loan stock is $1,200,000 and the effective interest rate is 5%.

The profit before tax for the year ended 31 March 20X2 was $920,000 and the income tax expense for the year was $276,000.

Acorn is subject to income tax at a rate of 30%.

Required

Calculate the basic and diluted earnings per share for the year ended 31 March 20X2.

Solution

Basic EPS

$$\frac{(920,000 - 276,000)}{10,000,000} = 6.4c$$

Diluted EPS

$$\frac{686,000}{14,000,000} = 4.9c.$$

Workings

1   *Diluted earnings*

	$
Basic (920,000 - 276,000)	644,000
Interest saving (1,200,000 @ 5% × 0.7)	42,000
	686,000

2   *Diluted number of shares*

	No. of shares
Basic	10,000,000
On conversion	4,000,000
	14,000,000

2.2 Share options or warrants

Potential shares on the exercise of options or warrants are split as follows:

(a)   Shares that would have been issued if the cash received had been used to buy shares at average market price for the period.

(b)   The remaining shares are treated as having been issued for **no consideration**.

Proforma calculation:

No. shares under option	X
No. that would have been issued at average market price (AMP)	
[(no. options × exercise price)/AMP]	(X)
∴ No. shares treated as issued for nil consideration	X̲

It is **only the shares deemed to have been issued for no consideration** which are added to the number of shares in issue when calculating diluted EPS (shares issued at full market price have **no** dilutive effect). (IAS 33: para. 45)

Question 17.3   Diluted EPS for share options

Galaxy Co has a profit for the year of $3m for the year. 1.4 million ordinary shares were in issue during the year.

Galaxy Co also had outstanding 250,000 options for the whole year with an exercise price of $15. The average market price of one ordinary share during the period was $20.

Required

Calculate the basic and diluted EPS.

Solution

Basic EPS

Diluted EPS

Working: Number of shares for nil consideration

	No. of shares
No. shares under option	
No. that would have been issued at average market price	
∴ No. shares treated as issued for nil consideration	

2.3 Presentation

Basic and diluted EPS are shown on the **face of the statement of profit or loss and other comprehensive income** with equal prominence whether the result is positive or negative for each class of ordinary shares and period presented. (IAS 33: para. 66)

Chapter Summary

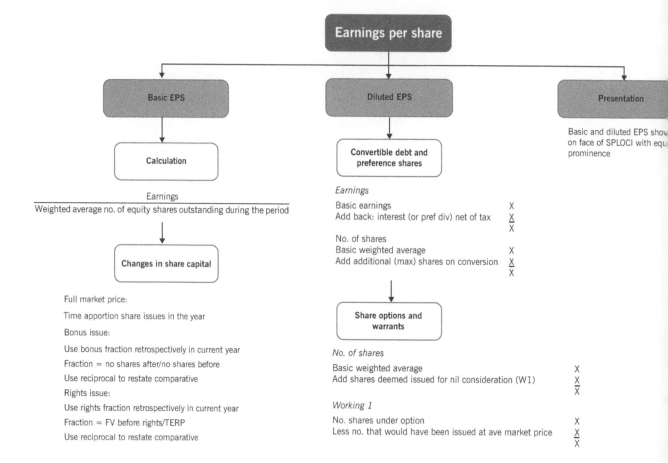

Earnings per share

Basic EPS

Calculation

$$\frac{\text{Earnings}}{\text{Weighted average no. of equity shares outstanding during the period}}$$

Changes in share capital

Full market price:

Time apportion share issues in the year

Bonus issue:

Use bonus fraction retrospectively in current year

Fraction = no shares after/no shares before

Use reciprocal to restate comparative

Rights issue:

Use rights fraction retrospectively in current year

Fraction = FV before rights/TERP

Use reciprocal to restate comparative

Diluted EPS

Convertible debt and preference shares

Earnings

Basic earnings	X
Add back: interest (or pref div) net of tax	X
	X

No. of shares	
Basic weighted average	X
Add additional (max) shares on conversion	X
	X

Share options and warrants

No. of shares

Basic weighted average	X
Add shares deemed issued for nil consideration (W1)	X
	X

Working 1

No. shares under option	X
Less no. that would have been issued at ave market price	X
	X

Presentation

Basic and diluted EPS show on face of SPLOCI with equ prominence

Quick Quiz

1   All entities must disclose EPS. True or false?

2   Why is the numerator adjusted for convertible bonds when calculating diluted EPS?

Answers to Quick Quiz

1   False. Only entities whose ordinary shares are publicly traded need to disclose EPS.

2   Because the conversion of bonds into shares will affect earnings by the interest saving (net of tax).

Answers to Questions

17.1 Basic EPS

EPS for year ended 31.12.X1 $\dfrac{\$400,000}{2,431,509\,(W1)}$ = 16.5 cents

Restated EPS for year ended 31.12.X0

$18.6c \times \dfrac{3.00}{3.10} \times 20/21 = 17.1$ cents

Workings

1   *Weighted average number of shares*

Date	Narrative	Shares	Time	Bonus fraction	Weighted average
1.1.X1	B/d	2,000,000	$\times\dfrac{4}{12}$	$\times\dfrac{3.10}{3.00\,(W3)}\times\dfrac{21}{20}$	723,333
30.4.X1	Full market price	270,000			
		2,270,000	$\times\dfrac{3}{12}$	$\times\dfrac{3.10}{3.00(W3)}\times\dfrac{21}{20}$	615,738
31.7.X1	Rights issue (1/10)	227,000			
		2,497,000	$\times\dfrac{2}{12}$	$\times\dfrac{21}{20}$	436,975
30.9.X1	Bonus issue (1/20)	124,850			
		2,621,850	$\times\dfrac{3}{12}$		655,463
					2,431,509

2   *Bonus fraction for rights issue*

$= \dfrac{\text{Fair value per share immediately before exercise of rights}}{\text{Theoretical ex rights price (TERP)}}$

$= \dfrac{3.10}{3.00\,(W3)}$

3   *TERP*

	$
10 @ $3.10	31.00
1 @ $2.00	2.00
11	33.00

∴ TERP = $33/11 shares = $3.00

17.2 Diluted EPS for convertible debt

Basic EPS

$$\frac{(\$920,000 - \$276,000)}{10,000,000} = 6.4c$$

Diluted EPS

$$\text{Diluted EPS} = \frac{\$686,000 \ (W1)}{14,000,000 \ (W2)} = 4.9c$$

Workings

1   *Diluted earnings*

	$
Basic ($920,000 – $276,000)	644,000
Interest saving 1,200,000 @ 5% × 70%	42,000
	686,000

2   *Diluted number of shares*

	No. of shares
Basic	10,000,000
On conversion	4,000,000
	14,000,000

17.3 Diluted EPS for share options

Basic EPS

$$\frac{\$3,000,000}{1,400,000} = \$2.14$$

Diluted EPS

$$\text{Diluted EPS} = \frac{\$3,000,000}{1,400,000 + 62,500} = \$2.05$$

Working: Number of shares for nil consideration

No. of shares under option	250,000
No. that would have been issued at average market price	(187,500)
[(250,000 × $15)/$20]	
∴ No. shares treated as issued for nil consideration	62,500

Now try these questions from the Practice Question Bank

Number	Level	Marks	Time
Q33	Introductory	N/A	7 mins
Q34	Introductory	14	25 mins

ETHICS IN FINANCIAL REPORTING

The CIMA *Code of Ethics for professional accountants* identifies five fundamental ethical principles. You need to have an understanding of ethical issues in the context of preparation of financial statements.

Chapter Overview

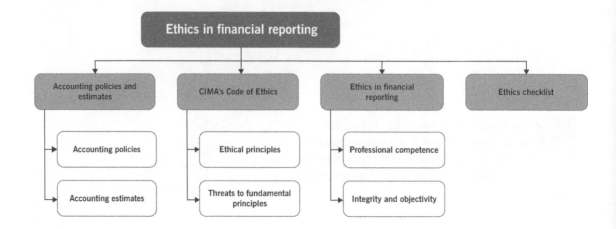

1 Accounting policies and estimates

1.1 Accounting policies

KEY TERM

'ACCOUNTING POLICIES are the specific principles, bases, conventions, rules and practices applied by an entity in preparing and presenting financial statements.' (IAS 8: para. 5)

IAS 8 *Accounting policies, changes in accounting estimates and errors* requires that an entity selects its accounting policies by **applying the relevant IFRS**. (IAS 8: para. 7)

Some standards permit a **choice** of accounting policies (eg cost and revaluation models).

In the absence of an IFRS covering a specific transaction, other event or condition, management uses its judgement to develop an accounting policy which results in information that is **relevant** to the economic decision-making needs of users and **reliable**, considering **in the following order**:

(1)   IFRSs dealing with similar and related issues;

(2)   The *Conceptual Framework* definitions of elements of the financial statements and recognition criteria; and

(3)   The most recent pronouncements of other national GAAPs based on a similar conceptual framework and accepted industry practice (providing the treatment does not conflict with extant IFRSs or the *Conceptual Framework*).

(IAS 8: para. 10)

A **change in accounting policy** is only permitted if the change (IAS 8: para. 14):

*   Is **required by an IFRS**; or
*   Results in financial statements providing **reliable and more relevant information**

The **accounting treatment** for a **change in accounting policy** is (IAS 8: para.19, 22):

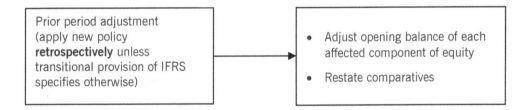

| Prior period adjustment (apply new policy **retrospectively** unless transitional provision of IFRS specifies otherwise) | → | • Adjust opening balance of each affected component of equity

• Restate comparatives |

1.2 Accounting estimates

As a result of the **uncertainties** inherent in business activities, many items in financial statements cannot be measured with precision but can only be estimated. Estimation involves **judgements based on the latest reliable information**. (IAS 8: para. 32)

For example, estimates may be required of (IAS 8: para. 32):

*   Bad debts;

*   Inventory obsolescence;

*   The fair value of financial assets or financial liabilities;

*   The useful lives of, or expected pattern of consumption of the future economic benefits embodied in, depreciable assets; and

*   Warranty obligations.

KEY TERM

'A CHANGE IN ACCOUNTING ESTIMATE is an adjustment of the carrying amount of an asset or a liability, or the amount of periodic consumption of an asset, that results from the assessment of the present status of, and expected future benefits and obligations associated with assets and liabilities.' (IAS 8: para. 5)

'An estimate may need **revision** if **changes occur in the circumstances** on which the estimate was based or as a result of new information or more experience. By its nature, the revision of an estimate does not relate to prior periods and is not the correction of an error.' (IAS 8: para. 34)

The **accounting treatment** for a **change in accounting estimate** is (IAS 8: para. 36–38):

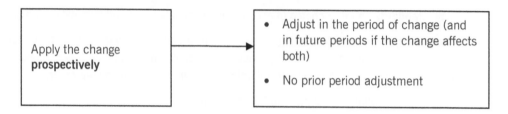

1.3 Creative accounting

Whilst still following international financial reporting standards, there is scope in choice of accounting policy and use of judgement in accounting estimates to select the accounting treatment that presents the financial statements in the best light rather than focusing on the most relevant and reliable accounting policy or estimate.

- **Timing** of transactions may be delayed/speeded up to improve results

- **Profit smoothing** through choice of accounting policy eg inventory valuation

- **Classification** of items eg expenses versus non-current assets

- **Off-balance sheet financing** to improve gearing and return on capital employed eg leases accounted for as an expense under IFRS 16 recognition exemptions

- **Revenue recognition policies** eg through adopting an aggressive accounting policy of early recognition.

When the directors select and adopt the accounting policies and estimates of an entity, they need to apply the principles in CIMA's *Code of Ethics for Professional Accountants.*

2 CIMA's Code of Ethics

2.1 Ethical principles

The CIMA *Code of Ethics for Professional Accountants* (para. 100.5) identifies the fundamental principles:

Principle	Explanation
Integrity	To be straightforward and honest in all professional and business relationships.
Objectivity	To not allow bias, conflict of interest or undue influence of others to override professional or business judgements.
Professional competence and due care	To maintain professional knowledge and skill at the level required to ensure that a client or employer receives competent professional service based on current developments in practice, legislation and techniques and act diligently and in accordance with applicable technical and professional standards.

Principle	Explanation
Confidentiality	To respect the confidentiality of information acquired as a result of professional and business relationships and, therefore, not disclose any such information to third parties without proper and specific authority, unless there is a legal or professional right or duty to disclose, nor use the information for the personal advantage of the professional accountant or third parties.
Professional behaviour	To comply with relevant laws and regulations and avoid any action that discredits the profession.

CIMA's website clearly lays out their commitment to ethics: www.cimaglobal.com/ethics.

2.2 Threats to the fundamental principles

The CIMA *Code of Ethics* (para. 100.12) identifies the following categories of threats to the fundamental principles:

Threat	Explanation
Self-interest	A financial or other interest may inappropriately influence the accountant's judgement or behaviour
Self-review	Where accountant may not appropriately evaluate the results of a previous judgement made or activity or service performed by themselves or others within their firm
Advocacy	Threat that accountant promotes client's or employer's position to the point that their objectivity is compromised
Familiarity	Due to a long or close relationship with a client or employer, an accountant may be too sympathetic to their interests or too accepting of their work
Intimidation	Accountant may not act objectively due to actual or perceived pressures

2.3 Ethics in financial reporting

In the F2 exam, you need an understanding of ethical issues in the context of **preparation of financial statements**.

The following principles and threats are of particular relevance.

2.3.1 Professional competence

Do the financial statements comply with:

- The relevant accounting standard?
- IASB's *Conceptual Framework for Financial Reporting*?

This is most at **risk** in areas of **judgement** (eg estimating the amount of a provision), **choice** (eg measuring non-controlling interests at fair value or share of net assets at acquisition) or **complexity** in accounting standards (eg measurement of financial instruments).

Professional accountants have a duty to **keep up to date** with developments in IFRSs and other relevant regulations.

Circumstances that may **threaten** the ability of accountants in these roles to perform their duties with the appropriate degree of professional competence and due care include:

- Insufficient time
- Incomplete, restricted or inadequate information
- Insufficient experience, training or education
- Inadequate resources

2.3.2 Integrity and objectivity

CIMA's *Code of Ethics* (para. 110.2) clearly states that a professional accountant should **not** be **associated** with reports, returns, communications or other information where they believe that the information:

- Contains a **materially false or misleading** statement;

- Contains statements or information **furnished recklessly**; or

- **Omits or obscures information** required to be included where such omission or obscurity would be misleading.

Circumstances which may threaten integrity and objectivity could include external pressures or the possibility of personal gain such as:

- Financial interests, such as profit-related bonuses or share options
- Threat of dismissal

| Question 18.1 | Accounting policies and estimates |

Required

Which of the following could be considered unethical reasons for revising accounting policies or estimates?

Tick the options which could be perceived to be unethical.

Unethical?	Revision to accounting policy or estimate and reason
	Increasing the useful life of an asset as large profits on disposal in recent years indicate that the previous estimated life was too short
	Reducing the allowance for doubtful debts from 5% to 3% of trade receivables to meet forecast profit targets
	Not equity accounting for an associate in the current year because the finance director failed to realise a relationship of significant influence in the prior year
	Classifying redeemable preference shares as equity to meet the gearing and interest cover loan covenants
	Reclassifying an expense from cost of sales to administrative expenses to align the entity's accounting policy to other entities operating in the same industry

2.4 Ethics checklist

CIMA has developed an ethics checklist to help professional accountants deal with ethical dilemmas:

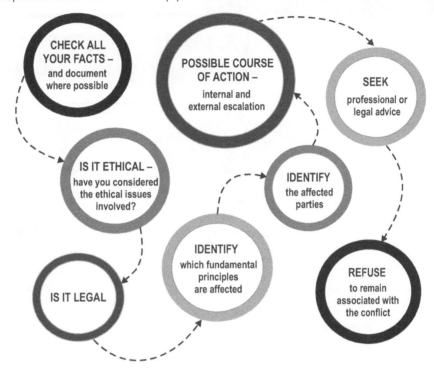

(CIMA, January 2015)

| Question 18.2 | Application of CIMA's Code of Ethics |

The directors of TF receive a bonus if the operating cash flow exceeds a predetermined target for the year. In prior periods, the accounting policy has been to record dividends paid as an operating cash flow. The directors are proposing to change the accounting policy and record dividends paid as a financing cash flow.

When applying the CIMA *Code of Ethics* which of the following statements are appropriate in relation to this scenario? (Tick the appropriate statements)

Appropriate?	Statement
	This accounting treatment is not permitted by IAS 7 and if adopted by the directors, they are not complying with the fundamental principle of professional competence.
	The accounting treatment is permitted by IAS 7 but the change in accounting policy should only be adopted if it results in information that is more reliable and relevant to the decisions of the users of financial statements.
	There is a self-interest threat as the directors are proposing an accounting treatment which will result in their own personal gain and might not be in the best interests of the entity and its stakeholders.
	The directors must contact the CIMA Ethics Helpline before taking any action.

Chapter Summary

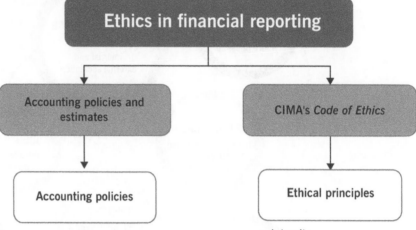

Ethics in financial reporting

Accounting policies and estimates

CIMA's *Code of Ethics*

Accounting policies

Specific principles, bases, conventions applied by an entity in preparing/presenting financial statements

To choose:

(1)   Apply relevant IFRS (choice within IFRS is a matter of accounting policy)

(2)   Consult IFRS dealing with similar issues

(3)   Conceptual Framework

(4)   Other national GAAP

Change in policy:

Apply retrospectively unless transitional provision of IFRS specifies otherwise

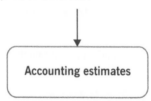

Accounting estimates

Judgements based on latest reliable information

Change in estimate

Apply prospectively ie adjust current and future periods

Ethical principles

- Integrity
- Objectivity
- Professional competence
- Confidentiality
- Professional behaviour

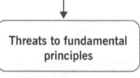

Threats to fundamental principles

- Self-interest
- Self-review
- Advocacy
- Familiarity
- Intimidation

Ensure compliance with relevant standard and Framework.

Therefore:

Remain up to date with developments in IFRSs

Threats:

Insufficient time
Inadequate information
Insufficient experience/training
Inadequate resources

Must not be associated with reports etc where believe info:

- Contains a materially misleading statement
- Contains statements furnished recklessly
- Omits or obscures info where such omission/obscurity misleading

Threats:

Financial interests
Threat of dismissal

Quick Quiz

1   Give the circumstances when a change in accounting policy might be required.

2   Match the fundamental principle to the characteristic.

   (a)   Integrity

   (b)   Objectivity

   (i)   Members should be straightforward and honest in all professional and business relationships.

   (ii) Members should not allow bias, conflict of interest or undue influence of others to override professional or business judgements.

Answers to Quick Quiz

1   **Changes in accounting policy** should be made only if required by one of three things:

    (a)   A new statutory requirement

    (b)   A new accounting standard

    (c)   If the change will result in a more appropriate presentation of events or transactions in the financial statements of the entity

2   (a)   (i)
    (b)   (ii)

Answers to Questions

18.1 Accounting policies and estimates

Unethical?	Revision to accounting policy or estimate and reason
	Increasing the useful life of an asset as large profits on disposal in recent years indicate that the previous estimated life was too short **IAS 16 requires the useful life of an asset to be reviewed at least every financial year end (IAS 16: para. 51) and, if expectations differ from previous estimates, the change should be accounted for as a change in accounting estimate. Here the previous profits on disposal indicate that depreciation in prior years was too high and the useful life of the asset too short. Therefore, the extension of the useful life of the asset is valid under IAS 16 and is considered ethical.**
✓	Reducing the allowance for doubtful debts from 5% to 3% of trade receivables to meet forecast profit targets **There is a self-interest threat here. A change in accounting estimate is only permitted where changes occur in the circumstances on which the estimate is based. Here, there is no evidence that trade receivables payment history has improved. Simply reducing the allowance to meet profit targets would be considered unethical behaviour.**
✓	Not equity accounting for an associate in the current year because the finance director failed to realise a relationship of significant influence in the prior year **There is a self-review threat here because the director appears not to be correcting the accounting treatment of the associate for fear of flagging up his previous mistake. Also, not equity accounting an associate contravenes the requirements of IAS 28 and brings into question the director's professional competence. This proposed accounting treatment is therefore considered unethical.**
✓	Classifying redeemable preference shares as equity to meet the gearing and interest cover loan covenants **This contravenes IAS 32 which requires redeemable preference shares as a financial liability not equity as they contain an obligation to repay the principal (IAS 32: para. 18). Therefore this proposed policy would not demonstrate professional competence. Furthermore, the aim of an accounting policy should be to present financial information that is relevant and reliable (IAS 8: para. 10), not to meet loan covenants. Therefore, this policy can be considered unethical.**

Unethical?	Revision to accounting policy or estimate and reason
	Reclassifying an expense from cost of sales to administrative expenses to align the entity's accounting policy to other entities operating in the same industry **Under IAS 8, it is valid for an entity to change its accounting policy to make it consistent with accepted industry practice (as long as it still complies with the relevant IFRS) (IAS 8: para. 12). Therefore, this is an ethical proposal.**

18.2 Application of CIMA's *Code of Ethics*

Appropriate?	Statement
	This accounting treatment is not permitted by IAS 7 and if adopted by the directors, they are not complying with the fundamental principle of professional competence.
✓	The accounting treatment is permitted by IAS 7 but the change in accounting policy should only be adopted if it results in information that is more reliable and relevant to the decisions of the users of financial statements.
✓	There is a self-interest threat as the directors are proposing an accounting treatment which will result in their own personal gain and might not be in the best interests of the entity and its stakeholders.
	The directors must contact the CIMA Ethics Helpline before taking any action.

Explanation:

IAS 7 *Statement of cash flows* does permit dividends paid to be treated as either an 'operating' or a 'financing' cash flow which makes Statement 1 incorrect (IAS 7: para. 33–34). However, IAS 8 *Accounting policies, changes in accounting estimates and errors* only allows a change in accounting policy which results in information that is more relevant to the economic decision-making needs of users and more reliable (IAS 8: para. 14) rather than simply for the personal gain of the directors, making Statement 2 correct.

The bonus based on the predetermined operating cash flow target represents a self-interest threat because if the directors reclassify the dividends from 'operating' to 'financing', the operating cash flow will be higher and the directors more likely to earn their bonus. This means that Statement 3 is correct.

Statement 4 is incorrect because whilst the directors have the option of contacting the CIMA Ethics Helpline, there is no obligation to do so and in this situation, given that the proposed treatment complies with IAS 7, appears a bit extreme.

Now try these questions from the Practice Question Bank	Number	Level	Marks	Time
	Q35	Introductory	N/A	7 mins

INTERPRETATION OF ACCOUNTS

Part F

ANALYSIS OF FINANCIAL PERFORMANCE AND POSITION

Users of the financial statements need to be able to analyse the performance and position of an entity in order to make economic decisions. This chapter considers the use of ratios to interpret financial statements together with their limitations.

Topic list	learning outcomes	syllabus references
1 Ratio analysis	C1	C1(a)(b)
2 Financial performance ratios	C1	C1(a)(b)(c)
3 Financial position ratios	C1	C1(a)(b)(c)
4 Analysis of statement of cash flows	C1	C1(a)(b)(c)
5 Analysis of segment report	C1	C1(a)(b)(c)
6 Limitations of ratio analysis	C2	C2(a)
7 Action to improve financial performance and position	C2	C2(a)

Chapter Overview

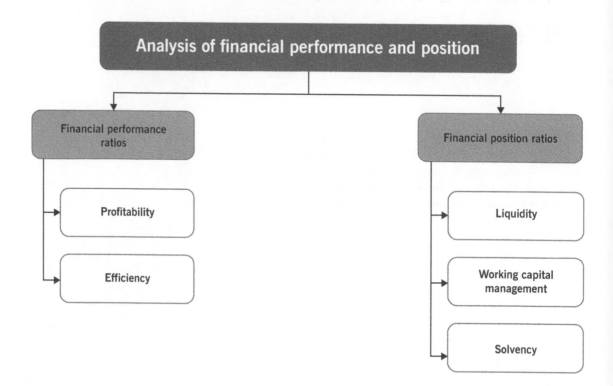

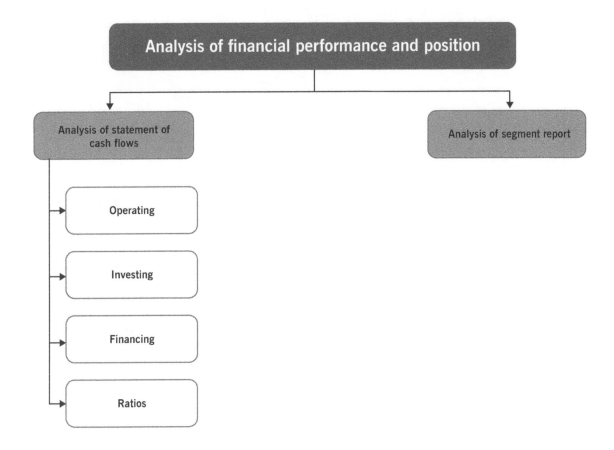

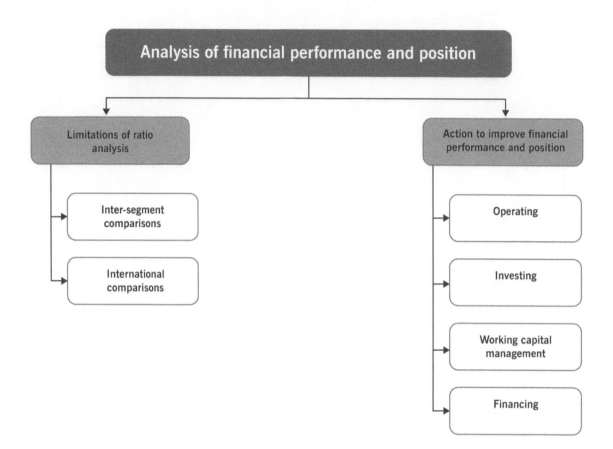

1   Ratio analysis

Ratio analysis is a **useful tool** in the interpretation of financial statements.

To make ratio analysis meaningful, **comparison** is required. For example, to:

- Prior year(s)
- Other companies operating in the same industry
- Industry averages
- Benchmarks
- Budgets or forecasts

1.1 Categories of ratios

Financial performance (focus on statement of profit or loss and other comprehensive income):

- Profitability
- Efficiency

Financial position (focus on statement of financial position):

- Liquidity
- Working capital management (activity)
- Solvency

2   Financial performance ratios

Profitability

$$\text{Return on capital employed} = \frac{\text{Profit before interest and taxation}}{\text{Capital employed}} \times 100\%$$

Notes

1   Capital employed =

Equity (share capital plus reserves) + Interest bearing borrowings − Non-current assets that do not contribute to operating profit (eg financial assets and investment in associates)

2   An overdraft should be included within 'interest bearing borrowings' if it is used as a long-term source of finance (often the case).

3   The PBIT figure should exclude the share of associates' profit or loss and any gains or losses on other investments.

Return on capital employed measures how **efficiently a company uses its capital to generate profits**. A potential investor or lender should compare the return to a target return or a return on other investments/loans.

$$\text{Return on equity} = \frac{\text{Profit after tax and preference dividends}}{\text{Ordinary share capital} + \text{reserves}} \times 100\%$$

Whilst the return on capital employed looks at the overall return on the long-term sources of finance, return on equity focuses on the **return for the ordinary shareholders**.

$$\text{Gross profit margin} = \frac{\text{Gross profit}}{\text{Revenue}} \times 100\%$$

The gross profit margin measures **how well** a company is **running its core operations**.

$$\text{Operating profit margin} = \frac{\text{Profit before interest and tax}}{\text{Revenue}} \times 100\%$$

Note. PBIT should exclude the share of associates' profit or loss because revenue will not include any revenue from the associate.

Profit before interest and taxation (PBIT) is used because it avoids distortion when comparisons are made between two different companies where one is heavily financed by means of loans, and the other is financed entirely by ordinary share capital. The extra consideration for the operating margin over the gross margin is **how well the company is controlling its overheads**.

$$\text{Net profit margin} = \frac{\text{Profit for year}}{\text{Revenue}} \times 100\%$$

The extra considerations for the net margin over the operating margins are **interest and tax**.

2.1 Earnings before interest, tax, depreciation and amortisation (EBITDA)

Many large entities use EBITDA as a key measure of performance on the grounds that depreciation and amortisation should be excluded because they are accounting adjustments involving management judgement (rather than cash flows).

However, critics believe that entities use EBITDA to publish a higher measure of earnings than operating profit and that EBITDA is often misunderstood to be a measure of cash flows when it is not (because financial statements are prepared on an accruals basis).

Question 19.1	Profitability ratios

The following information is available for two potential acquisition targets. The entities have similar capital structures and both operate in the manufacturing sector.

	FG	HI
Revenue	$460m	$420m
Gross profit margin	25%	14%
Net profit margin	10%	9%

Required

Which of the following statements give **realistic conclusions** that could be drawn from the above information?

Tick ALL relevant statements.

Tick	Statements
	HI's management exercises better cost control of the entity's non-production overheads
	HI has sourced cheaper raw materials
	FG operates its production process more efficiently with less wastage and more goods produced per machine hour
	HI operates in the low price end of the market but incurs similar manufacturing costs to FG
	FG's management exercises better cost control of the entity's non-production overheads
	HI has access to cheaper interest rates on its borrowings than FG

Question 19.2

EBITDA

CB has the following statement of profit or loss for the year ended 31 December 20X8:

	$'m
Revenue	390
Cost of sales	(245)
Gross profit	145
Distribution and administrative expenses	(50)
Finance costs	(10)
Profit before tax	85
Income tax expense	(25)
Profit for the year	60

Cost of sales includes depreciation of $12 million on factories, plant and machinery. Administrative expenses includes depreciation of $7 million on the head office premises, fixtures and fittings and amortisation of $8 million on intangibles.

Required

What is CB's EBITDA for the year ended 31 December 20X8?

$'m [   ]

Solution

2.2 Efficiency ratios

LEARN

$$\text{Asset turnover} = \frac{\text{Revenue}}{\text{Capital employed}}$$

Notes

1   Capital employed =

Equity (share capital plus reserves) + Interest bearing borrowings − Non-current assets that do not contribute to operating profit (eg financial assets and investment in associates).

2   An overdraft should be included within 'interest bearing borrowings' if it is used as a long-term source of finance (often the case).

This ratio shows **how much revenue** is produced **per unit of capital** invested.

LEARN

$$\text{Total asset turnover} = \frac{\text{Revenue}}{\text{Total assets}}$$

Total asset turnover is an indication of **how efficiently the entity is using its assets** to generate revenue.

Note. Total assets should exclude any investments in associates because the revenue figure does not include revenue generated from the associate.

LEARN

$$\text{Non-current asset turnover} = \frac{\text{Revenue}}{\text{Non-current assets}}$$

Note. Non-current assets should exclude any investments in associates because the revenue figure does not include revenue generated from the associate.

This ratio specifically examines the **productivity of non-current assets** in generating sales.

Earnings before interest, tax, depreciation and amortisation (EBITDA)

Many large entities use EBITDA as a key measure of performance on the grounds that depreciation and amortisation should be excluded because they are accounting adjustments involving management judgement (rather than cash flows).

However, critics believe that entities use EBITDA to publish a higher measure of earnings than operating profit and that EBITDA is often misunderstood to be a measure of cash flows when it is not (because financial statements are prepared on an accruals basis).

2.2.1 Making sense of profitability and efficiency ratios

Listed below are possible reasons for changes in the above ratios year on year or differences between two entities:

Return on capital employed (ROCE) and asset turnover ratios:

(a)   Type of industry (eg a manufacturing company will have higher assets and therefore lower ROCE/asset turnover typically than a services or knowledge based company)

(b)   Age of assets (eg old asset = low NBV = low capital employed and high ROCE/asset turnover)

(c)   Leased versus owned assets

(d)   Revaluations (increased capital employed = lower ROCE/asset turnover, increased depreciation = lower ROCE)

(e)   Timing of purchase (eg at year end = increased capital employed but no time to affect PBIT/revenue and also a full year's depreciation may be charged depending on the accounting policy)

Gross profit margin

- Change in sales price
- Change in sales mix (eg silver cutlery (high mark-up) versus plastic cutlery (low mark up))
- Change in purchase price and/or production costs (eg due to discounts/efficiencies)
- Inventory obsolescence (written off through cost of sales)

Operating profit margin

- One-off non-recurring expenses
- Rapid expansion
- Relocation
- Efficiency savings (economies of scale)

2.2.2 Link between return on capital employed, operating profit margin and asset turnover

Return on capital employed is a useful primary ratio in analysing **profitability and efficiency** together. However, to sub-analyse ROCE, two secondary ratios can be used to consider profitability and efficiency separately:

- Profitability – operating profit margin
- Efficiency – asset turnover ratio

This is because when the operating profit margin is multiplied by the asset turnover ratio, this results in the ROCE ratio:

LEARN

Operating profit margin × Asset turnover ratio = Return on capital employed

$$\frac{PBIT}{Revenue} \times \frac{Revenue}{Capital\ employed} = \frac{PBIT}{Capital\ employed}$$

Question 19.3   Efficiency ratios

GE is analysing the financial statements of two potential acquisition targets, C and D, that are of a similar size. The non-current asset turnover ratios of the two entities are as follows:

	C	D
Non-current asset turnover	3.8	1.3

Required

Which TWO of the following independent options could realistically explain the difference between the two entities' non-current asset turnover ratios?

Tick	Statements
	During the year, D recorded a revaluation gain on its non-current assets
	D's non-current assets are significantly older than C's
	C operates in the services sector and D operates in the manufacturing sector
	D's non-current assets are operating more efficiently than C's
	C purchased new non-current assets shortly before the year end

3   Financial position ratios

3.1 Liquidity ratios

$$\text{Current ratio} = \frac{\text{Current assets}}{\text{Current liabilities}}$$

This ratio measures a company's **ability to pay its current liabilities out of its current assets**. The industry the company operates in should be taken into consideration. For example, a supermarket has low receivables (mainly cash sales), low inventory (as perishable) and high payables (superior bargaining power) so overall will have a low current ratio.

$$\text{Quick ratio (or acid test)} = \frac{\text{Current assets} - \text{inventories}}{\text{Current liabilities}}$$

This is similar to the current ratio except that it **omits the inventories** figure from current assets. This is because inventories are the **least liquid** current asset that a company has, as it has to be sold, turned into receivables and then the cash has to be collected. This is a more reliable measure as businesses will not be able to use inventories to pay off payables quickly.

3.2 Working capital management (activity) ratios

$$\text{Receivables days} = \frac{\text{Trade receivables}}{\text{Credit sales}} \times 365 \text{ days*}$$

This ratio shows, on average, **how long it takes for the trade receivables to settle their account** with the company. The average credit term granted to customers should be taken into account as well as the efficiency of the credit control function within the company.

$$\text{Inventory days} = \frac{\text{Inventories}}{\text{Cost of sales}} \times 365 \text{ days *}$$

This ratio measures the **number of days inventories are held by a company** on average. This figure will depend on the type of goods sold by the company. A company selling fresh fruit and vegetables should have low inventory holding periods as these goods will quickly become inedible. A manufacturer of aged wine will by default have very long inventory holding periods. It is important for a company to keep its inventory days as low as possible, subject of course to being able to meet its customers' demands.

$$\text{Payables days} = \frac{\text{Trade payables}}{\text{Cost of sales}} \times 365 \text{ days *}$$

This ratio is measuring **the time it takes the company to settle its trade payable balances**. Trade payables provide the company with a valuable source of short-term finance, but delaying payment for too long a period of time can cause operational problems as suppliers may stop providing goods and services until payment is received.

3.2.1 Number of days

365 days is used when calculating working capital ratios for a 12 month period. If a shorter or longer period is being analysed, the number of days must be adjusted. For example, for a 6 month period, 182.5 days is used (365 × 6/12).

3.2.2 Working capital cycle

The working capital cycle (also known as the 'cash operating cycle') includes cash, receivables, inventories and payables. It effectively represents the **time between payment of cash for inventories and eventual receipt of cash from sale of the inventories**.

It shows the number of days for which finance is required. Therefore, ideally the shorter it is, the better. However, it will vary from industry to industry.

The length of the cycle is determined using the working capital management ratios:

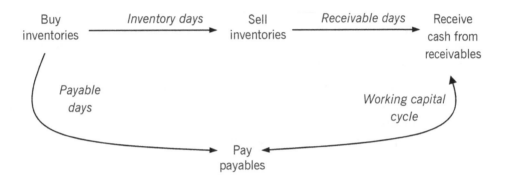

The working capital cycle can be therefore be calculated as:

LEARN

Inventory days + Receivable days − Payable days

Question 19.4	Working capital ratios

FC is a mobile phone manufacturer, selling to both network providers and independent retailers. FC has the following working capital ratios for the years ended 31 December 20X4 and 20X5.

	20X5	20X4
Inventory days	93	98
Receivables days	54	52
Payables days	97	91

Required

Which TWO of the following statements give **realistic conclusions** that could be drawn from the above information?

Tick	Statements
	The risk of inventory obsolescence has increased year on year
	The working capital cycle has decreased year on year
	The number of days' finance required to fund working capital is greater in 20X5 than 20X4
	Overall, FC's working capital management has deteriorated year on year
	There is a slightly higher possibility of bad debts arising in 20X5 than 20X4

3.3 Solvency ratios

Gearing:

LEARN

$$\text{Debt/Equity} = \frac{\text{Long-term debt}}{\text{Equity}} \times 100\% \text{ or}$$

$$\text{Debt/(Debt + Equity)} = \frac{\text{Long-term debt}}{\text{Long-term debt} + \text{Equity}} \times 100\%$$

Note. 'Long-term debt' should include interest-bearing debt such as loans, bonds, lease liabilities, preference shares classified as financial liabilities, pension liabilities and an overdraft if it is being used as a source of long-term finance (often the case).

Gearing is concerned with the **long-term financial stability** of the company. It is looking at how much the company is financed by debt. The advantage of debt is that it is a cheaper source of finance than equity as interest is tax deductible. However, the higher the gearing ratio, the less secure will be the financing of the company and possibly the company's future.

LEARN

$$\text{Interest cover} = \frac{\text{PBIT}}{\text{Interest expense}}$$

Note. PBIT must exclude the share of associates' profit or loss because the interest expense figure will not include any of the associate's interest.

The interest cover ratio considers the **number of times a company could pay its interest payments using its profit from operations**. The main concern is that a company should not have so much debt finance that it risks not being able to settle the debt as it falls due.

| **Question 19.5** | Calculation and interpretation of ratios |

TJF is a national supermarket chain selling food, clothes and household appliances with a 31 December year end. The finance director would like the management accountant to prepare some financial data and analysis to present to the board. He has provided the management accountant with extracts from the financial statements to assist him in his analysis.

EXTRACTS FROM STATEMENT OF PROFIT OR LOSS FOR THE YEAR ENDED 31 DECEMBER 20X5 (WITH COMPARATIVES)

	20X5 $m	20X4 $m
Revenue	20,510	17,835
Cost of sales	18,970	16,835
Gross profit	1,540	1,000
Operating profit	650	530
Finance costs	200	130

EXTRACTS FROM STATEMENT OF FINANCIAL POSITION AS AT 31 DECEMBER 20X5
(WITH COMPARATIVES)

	20X5 $m	20X4 $m
Non-current assets (all property, plant and equipment)	9,100	8,390
Inventories	850	1,000
Total current assets	1,570	1,610
Trade payables	2,100	2,280
Total current liabilities	2,920	2,650
Non-current liabilities (all interest bearing)	3,250	2,530
Equity	4,500	4,820

	20X4
Gross profit margin	5.6%
Operating profit margin	3.0%
ROCE	7.2%
Current ratio	0.61
Inventory holding period	22 days
Payables payment period	49 days
Interest cover	4.08

The finance director has also supplied the following information regarding events in the year ended 31 December 20X5:

(1)   Online food home delivery increased by 25%.

(2)   The number of stores grew by 10% in the year. This was financed by long-term borrowings. TJF does not have an overdraft.

(3)   In the year ended 31 December 20X5, 40% of customers purchased at least one clothing item during the year whereas in the year ended 31 December 20X4, only 20% of customers did.

(4)   A strong marketing campaign took place during the year.

(5)   The new strengthened Grocery Supplier Code of Practice came into force to improve grocery retailers' treatment of suppliers.

Required

(a)   Calculate the ratios below for the year ended 31 December 20X5, state whether it has increased or decreased (or where possible improved or deteriorated) and provide one possible reason for the movement in each ratio:

- Gross profit margin
- Operating profit margin
- Return on capital employed
- Current ratio
- Inventory days
- Payables days
- Interest cover

(b)   Explain why it would not be relevant to calculate receivables days in this example.

4 Analysis of statement of cash flows

4.1 Analysis points

(a)   Overall increase/decrease in cash

(b)   Operating activities:

- Cash inflow or outflow?

- Profit or loss making?

- Depreciation – likely increase or decrease in future? Has PPE been purchased or sold in the year (see 'investing activities')?

- Profit or loss on sale of PPE? Why sold PPE?

- Gain or loss on investments and any investment income? Are investments generating a strong return? Weak or strong treasury management?

- Increases or decreases in trade receivables, inventories and trade payables? Weak or strong working capital management?

- Any interest paid in year? Any borrowings repaid or taken out in the year (see 'financing activities')?

(c)   Investing activities:

- Cash inflow or outflow?

- Any acquisitions of PPE and/or investments in the year? How funded (operating or financing)? Impact on future?

- Any disposals of PPE and/or investments in the year? At a profit or loss (see 'operating activities')? Why sold? Impact on future?

- Interest/dividends received? Assess return on investment and treasury management.

(d)   Financing activities:

- Cash inflow or outflow?

- New finance raised in the year? Debt or equity? Why? Future implications?

- Finance repaid in the year? How afforded to repay?

- Dividends paid in year? Proportion of profit before tax paid out versus proportion reinvested? Assess generosity of directors' dividend policy.

(e)   Ratio analysis (examples of ratios)

$$\text{Cash return on capital employed} = \frac{\text{Cash generated from operations}}{\text{Capital employed}} \times 100\%$$

$$\text{Cash generated from operations to total debt} = \frac{\text{Cash generated from operations}}{\text{Long-term borrowings}}$$

$$\text{Net cash from operating activities to capital expenditure} = \frac{\text{Net cash from operating activities}}{\text{Net capital expenditure}} \times 100\%$$

| Question 19.6 | Cash flow analysis |

The following is an extract from the statement of cash flows for PQ for the year ended 31 December 20X5:

	$m	$m
Cash flow from operating activities		
Profit before taxation	590	
Adjustments	615	
Decrease in trade receivables	560	
Decrease in inventories	230	
Increase in trade payables	890	
Interest paid	(60)	
Tax paid	(165)	
Net cash from operating activities		2,660
Net cash used in investing activities		(1,570)
Net cash used in financing activities		(350)
Net increase in cash and cash equivalents		740

Required

Which THREE of the following statements would be reasonable conclusions about PQ's generation and use of cash and cash equivalents for the year ended 31 December 20X5? (Tick the correct answers)

Tick	Statements
	PQ has used cash generated from operations to fund investing activities
	PQ has raised long-term finance in the year to fund investing activities
	PQ has shown competent stewardship of the entity's resources by generating a profit for the year and a cash inflow in excess of that profit
	PQ has invested in non-current assets in the year, indicating potential for future growth
	PQ must be in decline as there are negative cash flows relating to both investing and financing activities
	PQ has demonstrated poor working capital management in the year

5 Analysis of segment report

The following points may be relevant when analysing segment data.

- Growing segments versus declining segments
- Segments in loss
- Return (and other key indicators) analysed by segment
- The proportion of costs or assets etc that have remained unallocated

IFRS 8 *Operating segments* only requires disclosure of certain financial information by segment. Therefore, it is not possible to calculate all of the financial performance and financial position ratios listed in this chapter. Relevant ratios to calculate might include:

- Growth (% increase or decrease in revenue)
- Margins (segment result/segment revenue)
- Return on assets (segment result/segment assets)
- Return on net assets (segment result/[segment assets − segment liabilities])
- Return on associates (share of associate's profit/investment in associate)

Question 19.7	Analysis of segment report

STV provides haulage and air freight services in several countries. The air freight segment was established in 20X0 whereas the road haulage business has been running since STV's incorporation 15 years ago. An analysis of STV's segment report for the year ended 31 December 20X2 is shown below.

| | Road Haulage | | Air Freight | |
	20X2	20X1	20X2	20X1
Revenue	$653m	$642m	$208m	$150m
Profit margin	31%	33%	6%	−25%
Return on assets	54%	55%	3%	−7%

Required

Which THREE of the following statements would be reasonable conclusions about the performance of STV's segments? (Tick the correct answers)

Tick	Statements
	Road Haulage's performance has improved year on year.
	Air Freight is using its assets more efficiently than Road Haulage to generate profits.
	Air Freight has a lower return on assets than Road Haulage because it has newer assets.
	Air Freight is expanding rapidly whereas Road Haulage has experienced little growth in the year.
	Air Freight's loss in 20X1 is likely to be due to start-up costs since the business was only established in 20X0.
	Road Haulage's return on assets is higher than Air Freight's because it depreciates its assets over a longer useful life.

6 Limitations of ratio analysis

6.1 Issue

A question could require you to identify or select limitations of ratio analysis in a specific scenario. The indicative syllabus content specifically mentions:

* Inter-segment comparisons
* International comparisons

The key is to identify or select limitations that are relevant to the particular scenario.

6.2 Limitations of inter-segment comparisons

Limitation	Example
Different accounting policies	An entity that revalues PPE will have higher depreciation than one that does not revalue, reducing its margins and return on capital employed.
Operating at different ends of the sector	Low price/high volume versus luxury items with high sales prices resulting in different profit margins.
Slightly different range of activities within the business	Supermarkets now often operate in food, retail clothing and financial services. The product mix and therefore margins will vary from entity to entity.
Difference in size of entities	Larger entities may benefit from economies of scale and better margins.
Different classification of costs	Different classification between cost of sales, distribution costs and administrative expenses will impact margins.
Different business decisions	Whether to purchase assets for cash or under leases will reduce comparability. Leases increase capital employed and gearing (because they increase borrowings) whereas cash purchases have no impact on capital employed or gearing.
The age of the business	A new business is likely to make losses in the early years due to start-up costs, impacting profitability ratios.
Age of assets	The older the assets, the lower the capital employed and the lower the depreciation which could result in a higher ROCE for an entity with older assets.

6.3 Limitations of international comparisons

Limitation	Example
Different accounting standards	Different countries will potentially be following different GAAPs. Different measurement rules for major elements (eg PPE, inventories, provisions) are likely to impact profit margins and ROCE.
Different economic environments with different cultural pressures	Examples: minimum wage, quotas, local taxes on goods shipped in or out of country, environmental legislation, strength of local currency and market interest rates.
Listed on stock markets with different levels of liquidity	An entity listed in a country with a highly liquid stock market will find it easier to raise equity finance. This could affect different entities' capital structures and gearing ratios.

Question 19.8	Limitations of inter-segment comparisons

AB and CD are of a similar size and operate in the same sector. The return on capital employed for AB and CD respectively is 29% and 19%.

Required

Which ONE of the following statements could explain the difference between the two entities' return on capital employed? (Tick the correct option)

Tick	Statements
	CD holds its properties under the cost model whilst AB holds its properties under the revaluation model.
	AB classifies its property depreciation as an administrative expense whilst CD classifies it as cost of sales.
	CD purchases its assets under leases whilst AB buys its assets for cash.
	CD sells to the luxury market whereas AB focuses on low cost and high volume products.

7   Action to improve financial performance and position

7.1 Issue

In the exam, you could have to identify action that would be realistically taken by the entity's management to improve financial performance and strengthen financial position, taking into account ethical considerations and internal and external constraints.

The relevant action will depend on the circumstances in the specific scenario but could broadly be broken down into the following four categories:

(1)   Operating
(2)   Investing
(3)   Working capital management
(4)   Financing

Operating

Products	Eg introducing new product, rebranding, product development, added value
Pricing	Eg offering a settlement discount to improve cash flow, lowering the price to sell obsolete inventory, change in sales mix, premium pricing
People	Eg recruiting, training, incentives, appraisals, promotions
Volume	Eg offering bulk discounts to customers to increase sales volume, economies of sale
Cost control	Eg measures to reduce waste in production, freeze wages, source cheaper suppliers, outsourcing/off-shoring
Marketing	Eg advertising to attract new customers, promotions
Markets	Eg entering into new geographical markets, new market sectors

Investing

A business may wish to expand. This can be achieved:

- Internally – through purchase of property, plant and equipment; or
- Externally – through acquisition of another entity.

Working capital management

A business may have cash flow problems which it could improve through better working capital management.

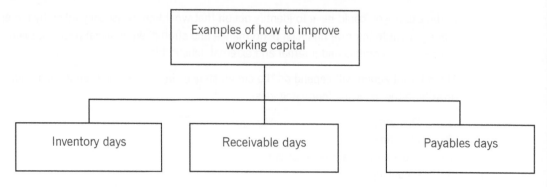

To reduce:

- Just in time ordering system
- Customer discounts on older inventory lines
- Buy inventory on sale or return
- Avoid bulk purchasing

To reduce:

- Offer settlement discount to customers
- Reminder notices to slow payers
- Final demands to very overdue customers
- Prompt invoicing
- Month-end deadlines for cash collection targets
- Regular production and actioning of aged debt analysis
- Switching slow payers to cash only accounts

To increase:

- Take advantage of full credit term
- Negotiate longer credit term
- Consider alternative suppliers with longer credit term

To reduce:

- Take advantage of settlement discounts
- Reduce inventory and receivable days so can pay suppliers more quickly
- Production and monitoring of aged payables analysis

Financing

In order to expand or to survive, the business might need to raise new finance. Considerations should include:

(a) Short-term (eg overdraft, improved working capital management) or long-term need (eg debt or equity)?

(b) Accessibility of finance, for example:

    (i)   Debt – availability of assets for security, existing level of debt, likelihood of meeting covenants, ability to pay interest out of profits?

    (ii)   Equity – listed? Listed companies will find it easier to obtain finance.

    (iii)   Overdraft – size of overdraft compared to current limit, likelihood of renewal, renewal date? Considered expensive and can be withdrawn at short notice.

(c) Ability to repay finance (where applicable)

(d) Ability to service finance (eg interest or dividend payments)

Question 19.9 · · · · · · · · · · · · · · Actions to improve liquidity

KL had a positive cash balance of $150,000 at 30 June 20X4 but an overdraft of $250,000 at 31 December 20X4. The management accountant has calculated the following ratios:

	6 months to 31 December 20X4	6 months to 30 June 20X4
Inventory days	128 days	77 days
Receivable days	90 days	80 days
Payables days	170 days	112 days
Current ratio	1.30	2.06
Quick ratio	0.67	1.38

Required

Which of the following possible actions could be considered both ethical and likely to improve the liquidity of KL?

Tick ALL that apply.

Tick	Statements
	Threaten to take your business elsewhere unless KL's suppliers agree to extend their credit terms
	Introduce a 5% settlement discount for customers who pay within 30 days
	Arrange an end of season sale for older inventory lines with a discount on the normal sales price
	Increase the general allowance for receivables from 2% to 4% in order to decrease receivable days

Chapter Summary

Analysis of financial performance and position

Financial performance ratios

Profitability

ROCE = PBIT/(Equity + long-term debt − investments) × 100%

Return on equity = (PAT − pref divs)/(Ordinary share capital + reserves) × 100%

GP margin = Gross profit/Revenue × 100%

Operating profit margin = PBIT/Revenue × 100%

Net profit margin = PAT/Revenue × 100%

Efficiency

Asset turnover = Revenue/(Equity + long-term debt − investments)

Total asset turnover = Revenue/Total assets

Non-current asset turnover = Revenue/Non-current assets

Financial position ratios

Liquidity

Current ratio = Current assets/Current liabilities

Quick ratio = Current assets − inventories/Current liabilities

Working capital management

Receivables days = Trade receivables/Credit sales × 365 days

Inventory days = Inventories/Cost of sales × 365 days

Payables days = Trade payables/Cost of sales × 365 days

Working capital cycle = Inventory days + Receivables days − Payables days

Solvency

Gearing:

Long-term debt/Equity × 100% or

Long-term debt/(Debt + Equity) × 100%

Interest cover = PBIT/Interest expense

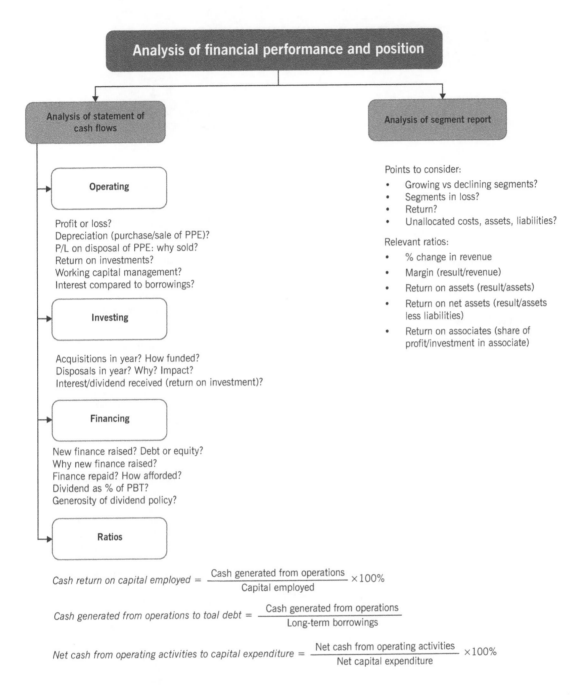

Analysis of financial performance and position

Analysis of statement of cash flows

Operating

Profit or loss?
Depreciation (purchase/sale of PPE)?
P/L on disposal of PPE: why sold?
Return on investments?
Working capital management?
Interest compared to borrowings?

Investing

Acquisitions in year? How funded?
Disposals in year? Why? Impact?
Interest/dividend received (return on investment)?

Financing

New finance raised? Debt or equity?
Why new finance raised?
Finance repaid? How afforded?
Dividend as % of PBT?
Generosity of dividend policy?

Ratios

$$\text{Cash return on capital employed} = \frac{\text{Cash generated from operations}}{\text{Capital employed}} \times 100\%$$

$$\text{Cash generated from operations to toal debt} = \frac{\text{Cash generated from operations}}{\text{Long-term borrowings}}$$

$$\text{Net cash from operating activities to capital expenditure} = \frac{\text{Net cash from operating activities}}{\text{Net capital expenditure}} \times 100\%$$

Analysis of segment report

Points to consider:
- Growing vs declining segments?
- Segments in loss?
- Return?
- Unallocated costs, assets, liabilities?

Relevant ratios:
- % change in revenue
- Margin (result/revenue)
- Return on assets (result/assets)
- Return on net assets (result/assets less liabilities)
- Return on associates (share of profit/investment in associate)

Analysis of financial performance and position

Limitations of ratio analysis

Inter-segment comparisons

Different accounting policies

Operating at different ends of the sector

Slightly different range of activities within the business

Difference in size of entities

Different classification of costs

Different business decisions

The age of the business

Age of assets

International comparisons

Different accounting standards

Different economic environments with different cultural pressures

Listed on stock markets with different levels of liquidity

Action to improve financial performance and position

Operating

Actions that could be taken:
Products ie introduce a new product
Pricing ie change sales mix
People ie training
Volume ie bulk discounts
Cost control ie outsourcing
Marketing ie adverting
Markets ie new geographical location

Investing

Business may want to expand:
Internally ie purchase PPE
Externally ie by acquisition of another entity

Working capital management

Ways to improve working capital:

Reduce inventory days
- Switch to JIT
- Customer discounts on older lines
- Purchase on sale or return
- Avoid bulk purchasing

Reduce receivable days
- Offer settlement discounts
- Reminder notices
- Final demands
- Prompt invoicing
- Aged debt analysis
- Cash only accounts

Reduce payables days
- Negotiate longer terms
- Consider alternative suppliers

Financing

When raising new finance consider:
- Length/maturity
- Accessibility
- Ability to repay
- Ability to service

Quick Quiz

1   What are the main sources of financial information available to external users?

2   Apart from ratio analysis, what other information might be helpful in interpreting a company's accounts?

3   In a period when profits are fluctuating, what effect does a company's level of gearing have on the profits available for ordinary shareholders?

4   Name some accounting standards which allow a choice of accounting policies.

5   The acid test or quick ratio should include:

A	Inventory of finished goods	C	Long-term loans
B	Raw materials and consumables	D	Trade receivables

6   The asset turnover of Taplow Co is 110% that of Stoke Co.

     The ROCE of Taplow Co is 80% that of Stoke Co.

     Calculate Taplow Co's operating profit margin expressed as a percentage of Stoke Co's.

7   Deal Co has the following capital structure:

	$'000
$1 ordinary shares	55,000
Retained earnings	12,000
	67,000
6% $1 cumulative redeemable preference shares	15,000
8% loan notes	30,000
	112,000

What is the most appropriate measure of the debt/equity ratio for a potential equity investor?

Answers to Quick Quiz

1   Published interim financial statements, filed documents, government statistics

2   • Other comments in the accounts, such as Directors' Report
        • Age and nature of the assets
        • Current and future market developments
        • Recent acquisition or disposal of subsidiaries
        • Notes to the accounts, auditors' report, post-reporting date events, etc

3   Profits available for the shareholders will be highly volatile and some years there may not be an ordinary dividend paid.

4   IASs 2, 16, 20 and 38

5   D   Acid test ratio $= \dfrac{\text{CA} - \text{Inventory}}{\text{CL}}$

6       $\dfrac{80}{110} = 73\%$

7   Debt =   15 + 30 = 45
        Equity =   55 + 12 = 67
        ∴ 45/67 × 100 = 67.2%

Answers to Questions

19.1   Profitability ratios

The statements ticked below give realistic conclusions:

Tick	Statements
	HI's management exercises better cost control of the entity's non-production overheads
✓	**HI has a smaller difference between its gross margin and net margin (6%) than FG (15%) which means that HI is controlling the entity's non-production overheads better. One of the differences between gross and net margin is non-production overheads (distribution costs and administrative expense).**
	HI has sourced cheaper raw materials
	This is incorrect as it would make HI's gross margin higher than FG's (whereas FG's is higher).
	FG operates its production process more efficiently with less wastage and more goods produced per machine hour
✓	**This is correct as FG has a higher gross margin than HI and a more efficient production process would cause this.**
✓	HI operates in the low price end of the market but incurs similar manufacturing costs to FG
	This is correct as it would cause HI to have a lower gross margin than FG.

Tick	Statements
	FG's management exercises better cost control of the entity's non-production overheads
	This is incorrect as it would make the difference between FG's gross and net margins less than HI's whereas the opposite is the case.
	HI has access to cheaper interest rates on its borrowings than FG.
✓	**One of the differences between gross and net margin is interest and, as HI has a smaller difference between gross and net margins, this could be explained by HI having lower finance costs than FG.**

19.2 EBITDA

$'m   122

EBITDA (earnings before interest, tax, depreciation and amortisation) is calculated as follows:

	$'m
Profit before tax	85
Add: finance costs	10
Add: depreciation in cost of sales	12
Add: depreciation in administrative expenses	7
Add: amortisation in administrative expenses	8
EBITDA	122

19.3 Efficiency ratios

The correct answers are:

Tick	Statements
✓	During the year, D recorded a revaluation gain on its non-current assets
	D's non-current assets are significantly older than C's
✓	C operates in the services sector and D operates in the manufacturing sector
	D's non-current assets are operating more efficiently than C's
	C purchased new non-current assets shortly before the year end

$$\text{Non-current asset turnover} = \frac{\text{Revenue}}{\text{Non-current assets}}$$

If D has recorded a revaluation gain on its non-current assets, that would increase the denominator of the ratio and make D's non-current asset turnover lower. Therefore this answer is correct.

If D had older non-current assets than C, D would have depreciated its assets more and therefore, its assets would have a lower carrying amount making D's non-current asset turnover higher (rather than lower) than C's. Therefore, this answer is incorrect.

Companies operating in the manufacturing sector typically have more non-current assets (factories, plant and machinery) than companies operating in the services sector (whose main asset is their staff skills which is not recognised in the statement of financial position). Therefore, C operating in the services sector would result in C having lower non-current assets than D and a higher non-current asset ratio. Therefore, this answer is correct.

The more efficiently that assets operate, the more revenue they generate so the higher the non-current asset ratio. Therefore, if D's non-current assets were working more efficiently than C's, it would be expected that D's non-current asset turnover ratio would be higher (not lower) than C's. Thus this answer is incorrect.

If C purchased new assets shortly before the year end, these assets would not yet have had a chance to generate much revenue and as a result, you would expect C's non-current asset turnover to be lower (not higher) than D's. Therefore, this answer is incorrect.

19.4 Working capital ratios

The correct answers are:

Tick	Statements
	The risk of inventory obsolescence has increased year on year
✓	The working capital cycle has decreased year on year
	The number of days' finance required to fund working capital is greater in 20X5 than 20X4
	Overall, FC's working capital management has deteriorated year on year
✓	There is a slightly higher possibility of bad debts arising in 20X5 than 20X4

The working capital cycle is calculated as:

Inventory days + Receivables days – Payable days

In 20X5 = 93 + 54 – 97 = 50 days

In 20X4 = 98 + 52 – 91 = 59 days

Therefore, the working capital cycle has decreased by 9 days year on year, meaning that the number of days' finance required to fund working capital is less (not greater) in 20X5 than 20X4.

The risk of inventory obsolescence has decreased year on year because inventory days have fallen by 5 days meaning that FC is selling its mobile phones faster in 20X5 than 20X4.

Overall, working capital management has improved (not deteriorated) year on year with the working capital cycle decreasing by 9 days. There has been a 5-day improvement in inventory days and a 6 day improvement in payables days (although this is partly offset by a 2-day deterioration in receivables days).

The increase in receivables days from 52 to 54 days implies that the credit control function has been less effective in 20X5 compared to 20X4, thereby increasing the risk of bad debts.

19.5 Calculation and interpretation of ratios

Note. This answer is more comprehensive than was required. You were only required to give one of the reasons listed for the movement in each ratio.

(a) **Ratios**

	20X5	20X4 (given)

Gross profit margin $= \dfrac{\text{Gross profit}}{\text{Revenue}} 100\%$ $\qquad \dfrac{1,540}{20,510} = 7.5\%$ $\qquad$ 5.6%

Gross profit margin has improved.

This appears to be because:

- Online food home delivery increased by 25% in the year and it attracts a higher margin than sales from supermarket visits due to the delivery charge

- There has been a change in sales mix with higher clothes sales in the current year probably attracting a higher margin than food sales

	20X5	20X4 (given)

Operating profit margin $=$

$\dfrac{\text{Profit before interest and taxation}}{\text{Revenue}} 100\%$ $\qquad \dfrac{650}{20,510} = 3.2\%$ $\qquad$ 3.0%

Operating profit margin has improved but not as much as the gross margin.

This appears to be due to:

- New, one-off marketing costs incurred in the year
- Start-up costs associated with the opening of the new stores

	20X5	20X4 (given)

Return on capital employed $=$

$\dfrac{\text{Profit before interest and taxation}}{\text{Capital employed}}$ $\qquad \dfrac{650}{4,500+3,250} = 8.4\%$ $\qquad$ 7.2%

There has only been a small improvement in ROCE despite a significant improvement in gross margin.

This appears to be because:

- The improvements in gross margin due to the higher margin on home delivery and clothes sales have been largely offset by one-off operating costs from marketing and new store start-up costs

- Non-current liabilities have increased due to new borrowings to open new stores; this has largely offset the improvement in profitability

- Any stores opened near the year end will not yet have had a chance to create profits

	20X5	20X4 (given)

Current ratio $= \dfrac{\text{Current assets}}{\text{Current liabilities}}$ $\qquad \dfrac{1,570}{2,920} = 0.54$ $\qquad$ 0.61

The current ratio has deteriorated, meaning that TJF is finding it harder to pay its current liabilities as they fall due.

This appears to be because:

- TJF is holding lower levels of inventories and higher current liabilities although payable days have decreased due to the strengthened Grocery Supplier Code of Practice.

Note. The current ratio is typically low for a supermarket as the receivables are low due to cash sales, inventories are relatively low as the majority are perishable and payables tend to be high due to the strong bargaining power of supermarkets over their smaller suppliers.

	20X5	20X4 (given)
Inventory days $= \dfrac{\text{Inventories}}{\text{Cost of sales}} \times 365$ days	$\dfrac{850}{18,970} \times 365$ days $= 16$ days	22 days

Inventory days have decreased meaning that TJF is selling inventories more quickly and holding lower levels of inventories. This is good for cash flow providing TJF is holding sufficient inventories to meet customer demand.

The decrease appears to be due to:

- An increase in sales volume as a result of the marketing campaign, the growth in online food home delivery, increased clothing sales and the new stores. This increase in demand has resulted in inventory levels being depleted more quickly.

	20X5	20X4 (given)
Payable days $= \dfrac{\text{Trade payables}}{\text{Cost of sales}} \times 365$ days	$\dfrac{2,100}{18,970} \times 365$ days $= 40$ days	49 days

TJF is paying its suppliers more quickly. This is bad for cash flow, as TJF is not taking advantage of the free credit but good for supplier relationships.

The decrease appears to be due to:

- The new strengthened Grocery Supplier Code of Practice coming into force – presumably TJF is paying suppliers more quickly to meet its credit terms and to treat suppliers more fairly in the spirit of the code

	20X5	20X4 (given)
Interest cover $=$ $\dfrac{\text{Profit before interest and taxation}}{\text{Finance costs}}$	$\dfrac{650}{200} = 3.25$	4.08

Interest cover has deteriorated. However, TJF is still easily able to pay its finance costs out of profit.

The deterioration in interest cover appears to be due to:

- Increased borrowings to cover the financing of the new stores opened in the year and due to shorter payable days

(b)   **Why not relevant to calculate receivables days**

In a supermarket, customers have to pay for their purchases immediately. The supermarket will not offer credit to their customers. Therefore, the sales are cash sales rather than credit sales resulting in few if any receivables.

19.6 Cash flow analysis

The statements ticked below give reasonable conclusions:

Tick	Statements
	PQ has used cash generated from operations to fund investing activities
✓	**There is a positive cash inflow from operating activities which is greater than the outflow on investing activities. This, combined with the outflow from financing activities, which implies that investing activities were not funded through raising new long-term finance, makes this first statement a reasonable conclusion.**
	PQ has raised long-term finance in the year to fund investing activities **This appears unlikely given that there is a net cash outflow from financing activities.**

Tick	Statements
	PQ has shown competent stewardship of the entity's resources by generating a profit for the year and a cash inflow in excess of that profit
✓	**The operating activities section shows a profit before tax (rather than a loss before tax) and a net cash inflow from operating activities well in excess of the profit, making this a reasonable conclusion.**
	PQ has invested in non-current assets in the year, indicating potential for future growth
✓	**The net cash outflow from investing activities indicates purchases of non-current assets in the year and these new assets are likely to generate extra revenue and profits in future years, making this a reasonable conclusion.**
	PQ must be in decline as there are negative cash flows relating to both investing and financing activities
	Negative investing and financing cash flows are not a sign of decline. In fact, an investing cash outflow indicates expansion. A negative financing cash flow indicates repayment of long-term finance. This statement is incorrect.
	PQ has demonstrated poor working capital management in the year
	This is untrue as there is an overall cash inflow from the movement in receivables, inventory and payables indicating strong working capital management.

19.7 Analysis of segment report

The statements ticked below give reasonable conclusions:

Tick	Statements
	Road Haulage's performance has improved year on year.
	Whilst Road Haulage has seen an increase in revenue year on year, underlying profitability has declined (profit margin falling from 33% to 31%) making this statement incorrect.
	Air Freight is using its assets more efficiently than Road Haulage to generate profits.
	This is incorrect because Air Freight has a lower return on net assets than Road Haulage.
	Air Freight has a lower return on assets than Road Haulage because it has newer assets.
✓	**This is likely to be true because the Air Freight business was only started three years ago so is likely to have newer assets than the more established Road Haulage business.**
	Air Freight is expanding rapidly whereas Road Haulage has experienced little growth in the year.
✓	**This is true because Air Freight has seen a 39% increase in revenue year on year whereas Road Haulage's revenue has only increased by 2% in the same period.**
	Air Freight's loss in 20X1 is likely to be due to start-up costs since the business was only established in 20X0.
✓	**When a new business is established, start-up costs are usually considerable and losses are common in early years.**
	Road Haulage's return on assets is higher than Air Freight's because it depreciates its assets over a longer useful life.
	This is incorrect because a longer useful life would result in a lower depreciation charge and a higher carrying amount for non-current assets. This would result in a lower return on assets yet Road Haulage has a higher return on assets than Air Freight.

19.8 Limitations of inter-segment comparisons

The ticked statement below could explain the difference between the two entities' return on capital employed:

Tick	Statements
	CD holds its properties under the cost model whilst AB holds its properties under the revaluation model. **If AB held its properties under the revaluation model, it would have higher capital employed due to the revaluation surplus in equity and lower profit due to a higher depreciation charge. This would make AB's ROCE *lower* than CD's, not higher. Therefore this answer is incorrect.**
	AB classifies its property depreciation as an administrative expense whilst CD classifies it as cost of sales. **Different classification of expenses between administrative expenses and cost of sales would have no impact on the ROCE which is calculated on profit after all operating expenses. Therefore this answer is incorrect.**
✓	CD purchases its assets under leases whilst AB buys its assets for cash. **This would cause CD to have higher capital employed than AB due to the lease liability. However, the impact of interest from the lease on CD's profit is irrelevant as ROCE is calculated using profit *before* interest and tax. The higher debt and capital employed of CD should make CD's ROCE lower than AB's. Therefore, this answer is correct.**
	CD sells to the luxury market whereas AB focuses on low cost and high volume products. **If CD sold to the luxury market, CD would be likely to have higher margins and a higher return on capital employed than AB. Here, however, CD has a *lower* ROCE than AB, making this answer incorrect.**

19.9 Actions to improve liquidity

The ticked actions below are consider both ethical and likely to improve the liquidity of CL:

Tick	Statements
	Threaten to take your business elsewhere unless KL's suppliers agree to extend their credit terms **Whilst this would help with cash flow, as it would delay payment to suppliers, it would be considered unethical behaviour.**
✓	Introduce a 5% settlement discount for customers who pay within 30 days **This is both ethical and likely to improve liquidity as it will encourage customers to pay more quickly and reduce receivables days.**
✓	Arrange an end of season sale for older inventory lines with a discount on the normal sales price **This is both ethical and likely to improve liquidity as it will enable KL to sell older inventory lines resulting in a necessary cash inflow, a decrease in inventory days and a reduction in inventory holding costs.**
	Increase the general allowance for receivables from 2% to 4% in order to decrease receivable days **Changing an accounting policy merely to improve the appearance of financial statements would be considered unethical. It is only permitted where required to make the financial statements more relevant and reliable.**

Now try these questions from the Practice Question Bank

Number	Level	Marks	Time
Q36	Introductory	N/A	5 mins
Q37	Introductory	25	45 mins

MATHEMATICAL TABLES & EXAM FORMULAE

Note. Please check the CIMA website for the latest information on what information will be provided in the exams.

Present value table

Present value of £1 = $(1+r)^{-n}$ where r = interest rate, n = number of periods until payment or receipt.

Periods					Discount rates (r)					
(n)	1%	2%	3%	4%	5%	6%	7%	8%	9%	10%
1	0.990	0.980	0.971	0.962	0.952	0.943	0.935	0.926	0.917	0.909
2	0.980	0.961	0.943	0.925	0.907	0.890	0.873	0.857	0.842	0.826
3	0.971	0.942	0.915	0.889	0.864	0.840	0.816	0.794	0.772	0.751
4	0.961	0.924	0.888	0.855	0.823	0.792	0.763	0.735	0.708	0.683
5	0.951	0.906	0.863	0.822	0.784	0.747	0.713	0.681	0.650	0.621
6	0.942	0.888	0.837	0.790	0.746	0.705	0.666	0.630	0.596	0.564
7	0.933	0.871	0.813	0.760	0.711	0.665	0.623	0.583	0.547	0.513
8	0.923	0.853	0.789	0.731	0.677	0.627	0.582	0.540	0.502	0.467
9	0.914	0.837	0.766	0.703	0.645	0.592	0.544	0.500	0.460	0.424
10	0.905	0.820	0.744	0.676	0.614	0.558	0.508	0.463	0.422	0.386
11	0.896	0.804	0.722	0.650	0.585	0.527	0.475	0.429	0.388	0.350
12	0.887	0.788	0.701	0.625	0.557	0.497	0.444	0.397	0.356	0.319
13	0.879	0.773	0.681	0.601	0.530	0.469	0.415	0.368	0.326	0.290
14	0.870	0.758	0.661	0.577	0.505	0.442	0.388	0.340	0.299	0.263
15	0.861	0.743	0.642	0.555	0.481	0.417	0.362	0.315	0.275	0.239
16	0.853	0.728	0.623	0.534	0.458	0.394	0.339	0.292	0.252	0.218
17	0.844	0.714	0.605	0.513	0.436	0.371	0.317	0.270	0.231	0.198
18	0.836	0.700	0.587	0.494	0.416	0.350	0.296	0.250	0.212	0.180
19	0.828	0.686	0.570	0.475	0.396	0.331	0.277	0.232	0.194	0.164
20	0.820	0.673	0.554	0.456	0.377	0.312	0.258	0.215	0.178	0.149

Periods					Discount rates (r)					
(n)	11%	12%	13%	14%	15%	16%	17%	18%	19%	20%
1	0.901	0.893	0.885	0.877	0.870	0.862	0.855	0.847	0.840	0.833
2	0.812	0.797	0.783	0.769	0.756	0.743	0.731	0.718	0.706	0.694
3	0.731	0.712	0.693	0.675	0.658	0.641	0.624	0.609	0.593	0.579
4	0.659	0.636	0.613	0.592	0.572	0.552	0.534	0.516	0.499	0.482
5	0.593	0.567	0.543	0.519	0.497	0.476	0.456	0.437	0.419	0.402
6	0.535	0.507	0.480	0.456	0.432	0.410	0.390	0.370	0.352	0.335
7	0.482	0.452	0.425	0.400	0.376	0.354	0.333	0.314	0.296	0.279
8	0.434	0.404	0.376	0.351	0.327	0.305	0.285	0.266	0.249	0.233
9	0.391	0.361	0.333	0.308	0.284	0.263	0.243	0.225	0.209	0.194
10	0.352	0.322	0.295	0.270	0.247	0.227	0.208	0.191	0.176	0.162
11	0.317	0.287	0.261	0.237	0.215	0.195	0.178	0.162	0.148	0.135
12	0.286	0.257	0.231	0.208	0.187	0.168	0.152	0.137	0.124	0.112
13	0.258	0.229	0.204	0.182	0.163	0.145	0.130	0.116	0.104	0.093
14	0.232	0.205	0.181	0.160	0.141	0.125	0.111	0.099	0.088	0.078
15	0.209	0.183	0.160	0.140	0.123	0.108	0.095	0.084	0.074	0.065
16	0.188	0.163	0.141	0.123	0.107	0.093	0.081	0.071	0.062	0.054
17	0.170	0.146	0.125	0.108	0.093	0.080	0.069	0.060	0.052	0.045
18	0.153	0.130	0.111	0.095	0.081	0.069	0.059	0.051	0.044	0.038
19	0.138	0.116	0.098	0.083	0.070	0.060	0.051	0.043	0.037	0.031
20	0.124	0.104	0.087	0.073	0.061	0.051	0.043	0.037	0.031	0.026

Cumulative present value table

This table shows the present value of £1 per annum, receivable or payable at the end of each year, for *n* years.

Periods					Discount rates (r)					
(n)	1%	2%	3%	4%	5%	6%	7%	8%	9%	10%
1	0.990	0.980	0.971	0.962	0.952	0.943	0.935	0.926	0.917	0.909
2	1.970	1.942	1.913	1.886	1.859	1.833	1.808	1.783	1.759	1.736
3	2.941	2.884	2.829	2.775	2.723	2.673	2.624	2.577	2.531	2.487
4	3.902	3.808	3.717	3.630	3.546	3.465	3.387	3.312	3.240	3.170
5	4.853	4.713	4.580	4.452	4.329	4.212	4.100	3.993	3.890	3.791
6	5.795	5.601	5.417	5.242	5.076	4.917	4.767	4.623	4.486	4.355
7	6.728	6.472	6.230	6.002	5.786	5.582	5.389	5.206	5.033	4.868
8	7.652	7.325	7.020	6.733	6.463	6.210	5.971	5.747	5.535	5.335
9	8.566	8.162	7.786	7.435	7.108	6.802	6.515	6.247	5.995	5.759
10	9.471	8.983	8.530	8.111	7.722	7.360	7.024	6.710	6.418	6.145
11	10.37	9.787	9.253	8.760	8.306	7.887	7.499	7.139	6.805	6.495
12	11.26	10.58	9.954	9.385	8.863	8.384	7.943	7.536	7.161	6.814
13	12.13	11.35	10.63	9.986	9.394	8.853	8.358	7.904	7.487	7.103
14	13.00	12.11	11.30	10.56	9.899	9.295	8.745	8.244	7.786	7.367
15	13.87	12.85	11.94	11.12	10.38	9.712	9.108	8.559	8.061	7.606
16	14.718	13.578	12.561	11.652	10.838	10.106	9.447	8.851	8.313	7.824
17	15.562	14.292	13.166	12.166	11.274	10.477	9.763	9.122	8.544	8.022
18	16.398	14.992	13.754	12.659	11.690	10.828	10.059	9.372	8.756	8.201
19	17.226	15.678	14.324	13.134	12.085	11.158	10.336	9.604	8.950	8.365
20	18.046	16.351	14.877	13.590	12.462	11.470	10.594	9.818	9.129	8.514

Periods					Discount rates (r)					
(n)	11%	12%	13%	14%	15%	16%	17%	18%	19%	20%
1	0.901	0.893	0.885	0.877	0.870	0.862	0.855	0.847	0.840	0.833
2	1.713	1.690	1.668	1.647	1.626	1.605	1.585	1.566	1.547	1.528
3	2.444	2.402	2.361	2.322	2.283	2.246	2.210	2.174	2.140	2.106
4	3.102	3.037	2.974	2.914	2.855	2.798	2.743	2.690	2.639	2.589
5	3.696	3.605	3.517	3.433	3.352	3.274	3.199	3.127	3.058	2.991
6	4.231	4.111	3.998	3.889	3.784	3.685	3.589	3.498	3.410	3.326
7	4.712	4.564	4.423	4.288	4.160	4.039	3.922	3.812	3.706	3.605
8	5.146	4.968	4.799	4.639	4.487	4.344	4.207	4.078	3.954	3.837
9	5.537	5.328	5.132	4.946	4.772	4.607	4.451	4.303	4.163	4.031
10	5.889	5.650	5.426	5.216	5.019	4.833	4.659	4.494	4.339	4.192
11	6.207	5.938	5.687	5.453	5.234	5.029	4.836	4.656	4.486	4.327
12	6.492	6.194	5.918	5.660	5.421	5.197	4.988	4.793	4.611	4.439
13	6.750	6.424	6.122	5.842	5.583	5.342	5.118	4.910	4.715	4.533
14	6.982	6.628	6.302	6.002	5.724	5.468	5.229	5.008	4.802	4.611
15	7.191	6.811	6.462	6.142	5.847	5.575	5.324	5.092	4.876	4.675
16	7.379	6.974	6.604	6.265	5.954	5.668	5.405	5.162	4.938	4.730
17	7.549	7.120	6.729	6.373	6.047	5.749	5.475	5.222	4.990	4.775
18	7.702	7.250	6.840	6.467	6.128	5.818	5.534	5.273	5.033	4.812
19	7.839	7.366	6.938	6.550	6.198	5.877	5.584	5.316	5.070	4.843
20	7.963	7.469	7.025	6.623	6.259	5.929	5.628	5.353	5.101	4.870

Formulae

DVM	Cost of Irredeemable Debt
$$P_0 = \dfrac{d_1}{k_e - g}$$ $$k_e = \dfrac{d_1}{P_0} + g$$ $$g = r \times b$$	$$K_d = \dfrac{I(1-t)}{P_0}$$
WACC $$\text{WACC} = k_{eg}\left[\dfrac{V_E}{V_E + V_D}\right] + k_d[1-t]\left[\dfrac{V_D}{V_E + V_D}\right]$$	

PRACTICE QUESTION AND ANSWER BANK

What the examiner means

The very important table below has been prepared by CIMA to help you interpret exam questions.

Learning objectives	Verbs used	Definition
1 Knowledge		
What you are expected to know	• List	• Make a list of
	• State	• Express, fully or clearly, the details of/facts of
	• Define	• Give the exact meaning of
2 Comprehension		
What you are expected to understand	• Describe	• Communicate the key features of
	• Distinguish	• Highlight the differences between
	• Explain	• Make clear or intelligible/state the meaning of
	• Identify	• Recognise, establish or select after consideration
	• Illustrate	• Use an example to describe or explain something
3 Application		
How you are expected to apply your knowledge	• Apply	• Put to practical use
	• Calculate/ compute	• Ascertain or reckon mathematically
		• Prove with certainty or to exhibit by practical means
	• Demonstrate	
	• Prepare	• Make or get ready for use
	• Reconcile	• Make or prove consistent/compatible
	• Solve	• Find an answer to
	• Tabulate	• Arrange in a table
4 Analysis		
How you are expected to analyse the detail of what you have learned	• Analyse	• Examine in detail the structure of
	• Categorise	• Place into a defined class or division
	• Compare and contrast	• Show the similarities and/or differences between
	• Construct	• Build up or compile
	• Discuss	• Examine in detail by argument
	• Interpret	• Translate into intelligible or familiar terms
	• Prioritise	• Place in order of priority or sequence for action
	• Produce	• Create or bring into existence
5 Evaluation		
How you are expected to use your learning to evaluate, make decisions or recommendations	• Advise	• Counsel, inform or notify
	• Evaluate	• Appraise or assess the value of
	• Recommend	• Propose a course of action

1 Objective test questions: sources of long-term finance

14 mins

1.1 Which of the following is not a benefit, to the borrower, of an overdraft as opposed to a short-term loan?

A   Flexible repayment schedule
B   Only charged for the amount drawn down
C   Easy to arrange
D   Lower interest rates

1.2 According to the creditor hierarchy, list the following from high risk to low risk:

1   Ordinary share capital
2   Preference share capital
3   Trade payables
4   Bank loan with fixed and floating charges

A   1,2,3,4
B   1,3,2,4
C   4,3,2,1
D   4,2,3,1

1.3 Which ONE of the following is issued at a discount to its redemption value and pays its holder no interest during its life?

A   A deep discount bond
B   A gilt-edged security
C   An unsecured loan note
D   A zero coupon bond

1.4 Which of the following is NOT a function that financial intermediaries fulfil for customers and borrowers?

A   Maturity transformation
B   Fund aggregation
C   Dividend creation
D   Pooling of losses

1.5 Which of the following are money market instruments?

1   Certificate of deposit
2   Corporate bond
3   Commercial paper
4   Treasury bill

A   1, 2 and 4 only
B   1 and 3 only
C   1, 3 and 4 only
D   1, 2, 3 and 4

1.6   Which of the following statements about obtaining a full stock market listing is NOT correct?

    A   Compliance costs are likely to increase, but better public profile and access to funds benefit the business. ✓

    B   All else being equal, the value of the business is likely to be unaffected.

    C   It allows owners to realise their investment.

    D   It increases the liquidity of the shares for shareholders.

1.7   Rank the following from highest risk to lowest risk from the investor's perspective.

    1   Preference share
    2   Treasury bill
    3   Corporate bond
    4   Ordinary share

    A   1, 4, 3, 2
    B   1, 4, 2, 3
    C   4, 2, 1, 3
    D   4, 1, 3, 2

1.8   Which ONE of the following statements is incorrect?

    A   Money markets are markets for long-term capital

    B   Money markets are operated by banks and other financial institutions

    C   Money market instruments include interest-bearing instruments, discount instruments and derivatives

    D   Money market instruments are traded over the counter between institutional investors

2 Panda

27 mins

Panda is a large fashion retailer that opened stores in South East Asia three years ago. This has proved to be less successful than expected and so the directors of the company have decided to withdraw from the overseas market and to concentrate on the home market. To raise the finance necessary to close the overseas stores, the directors have also decided to make a one-for-five rights issue at a discount of 30% on the current market value. The most recent statement of profit or loss of the business is as follows.

STATEMENT OF PROFIT OR LOSS FOR THE YEAR ENDED 31 MAY 20X4

	$m
Sales	1,400.00
Net profit before interest and taxation	52.0
Interest payable	24.0
Net profit before taxation	28.0
Company tax	7.0
Net profit after taxation	21.0

Dividends paid are $14 million.

The capital and reserves of the business as at 31 May 20X4 are as follows.

	$m
$0.25 ordinary shares	60.0
Accumulated profits	320.0
	380.0

The shares of the business are currently traded on the Stock Exchange at a P/E ratio of 16 times. An investor owning 10,000 ordinary shares in the business has received information of the forthcoming rights issue but cannot decide whether to take up the rights issue, sell the rights or allow the rights offer to lapse.

Required

(a) Calculate the theoretical ex-rights price of an ordinary share in Panda. **(3 marks)**

(b) Calculate the price at which the rights in Panda are likely to be traded. **(3 marks)**

(c) Evaluate each of the options available to the investor with 10,000 ordinary shares. **(4 marks)**

(d) Discuss, from the viewpoint of the business, how critical the pricing of a rights issue is likely to be. **(5 marks)**

(Total = 15 marks)

3 Objective test questions: cost of capital 16 mins

3.1 GG Co has a cost of equity of 25%. It has 4 million shares in issue, and has had for many years.

Its dividend payments in the years 20X9 to 20Y3 were as follows.

End of year	Dividends $'000
20X9	220
20Y0	257
20Y1	310
20Y2	356
20Y3	423

Dividends are expected to continue to grow at the same average rate into the future.

According to the dividend valuation model, what should be the share price at the start of 20Y4?

A $0.96
B $1.10
C $1.47
D $1.73

3.2 IPA Co is about to pay a $0.50 dividend on each ordinary share. Its earnings per share was $1.50.

Net assets per share is $6. Current share price is $4.50 per share.

What is the cost of equity?

A 31%
B 30%
C 22%
D 21%

3.3 HB Co has in issue 10% irredeemable loan notes, currently traded at 95% cum-interest.

If the tax rate changes from 30% to 20% for the company, the cost of irredeemable debt:

A Increases to 9.4%
B Increases to 8.4%
C Decreases to 9.4%
D Decreases to 8.4%

3.4   BRW Co has 10% redeemable loan notes in issue trading at $90. The loan notes are redeemable at a 10% premium in 5 years' time, or convertible at that point into 20 ordinary shares. The current share price is $2.50 and is expected to grow at 10% per annum for the foreseeable future. BRW Co pays 30% corporation tax.

What is the best estimate of the cost of these loan notes?

A   9.8%
B   7.9%
C   11.5%
D   15.2%

3.5   IDO Co has a capital structure as follows:

	£m
10m $0.50 ordinary shares	5
Reserves	20
13% Irredeemable loan notes	7
	32

The ordinary shares are currently quoted at $3.00, and the loan notes at $90. IDO Co has a cost of equity of 12% and pays corporation tax at a rate of 30%.

What is IDO Co's weighted average cost of capital?

A   10.4%
B   11.1%
C   11.7%
D   11.8%

3.6   An 8% irredeemable $0.50 preference share is being traded for $0.30 cum-div currently in a company that pays corporation tax at a rate of 30%.

What is the cost of capital for these preference shares?

A   10.8%
B   15.4%
C   26.7%
D   18.7%

3.7   ELW Co recently paid a dividend of $0.50 a share. This is $0.10 more than 3 years ago. Shareholders have a required rate of return of 10%.

Using the dividend valuation model and assuming recent dividend growth is expected to continue, what is the current value of a share?

A $23.41
B $5
C $38.48
D $10.48

3.8 Which of the following need to be assumed when using the dividend valuation formula to estimate a share value?

1   The recent dividend, 'D_0', is typical – ie it doesn't vary significantly from historical trends
2   Growth will be constant
3   The cost of equity will remain constant
4   A majority shareholding is being purchased

A   1, 2 and 3 only
B   3 and 4 only
C   1 and 2 only
D   1, 2, 3 and 4

3.9 A 9% redeemable loan note in ATV Co is due to mature in 3 years' time at a premium of 15%, or convertible into 25 ordinary shares at that point. The current share price is $4, expected to grow at 10% per annum. ATV pays corporation tax at a rate of 30%.

What is the current market value of the loan note if loan note holders require a 10% return?

A $108.75
B $115.63
C $102.03
D $122.34

4 Objective test questions: Financial instruments   11 mins

4.1 Which of the following are **not** classified as financial instruments under IAS 32 *Financial instruments: Presentation*?

A   Share options
B   Intangible assets
C   Trade receivables
D   Redeemable preference shares

4.2 An 8% $30 million convertible loan note was issued on 1 April 20X5 at par. Interest is payable in arrears on 31 March each year. The loan note is redeemable at par on 31 March 20X8 or convertible into equity shares at the option of the loan note holders on the basis of 30 shares for each $100 of loan. A similar instrument without the conversion option would have an interest rate of 10% per annum.

The present values of $1 receivable at the end of each year, based on discount rates of 8% and 10%, are:

		8%	10%
End of year	1	0.93	0.91
	2	0.86	0.83
	3	0.79	0.75

What amount will be credited to equity on 1 April 20X5 in respect of this financial instrument?

A $5,976,000
B $1,524,000
C $324,000
D $9,000,000

4.3 A 5% loan note was issued on 1 April 20X0 at its face value of $20 million. Direct costs of the issue were $500,000. The loan note will be redeemed on 31 March 20X3 at a substantial premium. The effective interest rate applicable is 10% per annum.

At what amount will the loan note appear in the statement of financial position as at 31 March 20X2?

A $21,000,000
B $20,450,000
C $22,100,000
D $21,495,000

4.4 How does the *Conceptual Framework* define an asset?

A   A resource owned by an entity as a result of past events and from which future economic benefits are expected to flow to the entity

B   A resource over which an entity has legal rights as a result of past events and from which economic benefits are expected to flow to the entity

C   A resource controlled by an entity as a result of past events and from which future economic benefits are expected to flow to the entity

D   A resource to which an entity has a future commitment as a result of past events and from which future economic benefits are expected to flow from the entity

4.5 Which ONE of the following would be classified as a liability?

A   Dexter's business manufactures a product under licence. In 12 months the licence expires and Dexter will have to pay $50,000 for it to be renewed.

B   Reckless purchased an investment 9 months ago for $120,000. The market for these investments has now fallen and Reckless's investment is valued at $90,000.

C   Carter has estimated the tax charge on its profits for the year just ended as $165,000.

D   Expansion is planning to invest in new machinery and has been quoted a price of $570,000.

4.6 The *Conceptual Framework* identifies four enhancing qualitative characteristics of financial information. For which of these characteristics is **disclosure of accounting policies** particularly important?

A   Verifiability
B   Timeliness
C   Comparability
D   Understandability

5 Amps   18 mins

Learning outcome: B1

Amps is a highly acquisitive company operating in the leisure industry. In order to finance acquisitions, the company has issued a number of financial instruments, both debt and equity, the details of which are given below.

(a) $1 million redeemable bonds were issued on 1 January 20X0, redeemable ten years later for the same amount. The interest rate attached to the bonds is 4% for years 1 to 3, 7% for years 4 to 7 and 10% for the final period. This gives a constant rate of return of 7.5%.

Amps has accounted for 20X0 interest by charging $40,000 to the statement of profit or loss and other comprehensive income.

(b)   Also during 20X0, the company issued $2m convertible debentures carrying interest at 7%. The debentures are convertible into ordinary shares in December 20X1 at the option of the holders.

Amps believe the conversion rights will be exercised and as a result has treated the debentures as part of equity. The annual return to the holders has been treated as a distribution.

Required

Explain how the above matters should be dealt with in the financial statements of Amps for the year ending 31 December 20X0.   **(10 marks)**

6 JKA   9 mins

Learning outcome: B1

JKA entered into the following transaction in the year ended 31 May 20X3: JKA held a portfolio of trade receivables with a carrying amount of $4 million at 31 May 20X3. At that date, the entity entered into a factoring agreement with a bank, whereby it transfers the receivables in exchange for $3.6 million in cash. JKA has agreed to reimburse the factor for any shortfall between the amount collected and $3.6 million. Once the receivables have been collected, any amounts above $3.6 million, less interest on this amount, will be repaid to JKA. JKA has derecognised the receivables and charged $0.4 million as a loss to statement of profit or loss.

Required

(a)   **Explain** how the transfer of the receivables should be accounted for in accordance with principles of the IASB's *Conceptual Framework for Financial Reporting*.   **(3 marks)**

(b)   **Prepare** any journal entries required to correct the accounting treatment for the year to 31 May 20X3.   **(2 marks)**

(Total: 5 marks)

7 Lis   20 mins

On 1 January 20X3 Lis entered into a lease agreement to rent an asset for a six-year period, at which point it will be returned to the lessor and scrapped, with annual payments of $18,420 made in advance. The initial measurement of the lease liability amounts to $65,586, discounted at the implicit interest rate shown in the lease agreement of 12.5%.

Lis expects to sell goods produced by the asset during the first five years of the lease term, but has leased the asset for six years as this is the requirement of the lessor, and in case this expectation changes. Lis has the right to determine the use of the asset during the lease term and will obtain substantially all the economic benefit from its use.

Required

Explain how the above lease would be accounted for the year ending 31 December 20X3 including producing relevant extracts from the statement of profit or loss and statement of financial position.

You are not required to prepare the notes to the financial statements. **(10 marks)**

8 Objective test questions: Provisions, contingent liabilities and contingent assets · 7 mins

8.1 Wick is being sued by a customer for $2 million for breach of contract over a cancelled order. Wick has obtained legal opinion that there is a 20% chance that Wick will lose the case. Accordingly, Wick has provided $400,000 ($2 million × 20%) in respect of the claim. The unrecoverable legal costs of defending the action are estimated at $100,000. These have not been provided for as the case will not go to court until next year.

What is the amount of the provision that should be made by Wick in accordance with IAS 37 *Provisions, contingent liabilities and contingent assets* ?

A $2,000,000
B $2,100,000
C $500,000
D $100,000

8.2 During the year Peterlee acquired an iron ore mine at a cost of $6 million. In addition, when all the ore has been extracted (estimated 10 years' time) the company will face estimated costs for landscaping the area affected by the mining, which have a present value of $2 million. These costs would still have to be incurred even if no further ore was extracted.

How should this $2 million future cost be recognised in the financial statements?

A   Provision $2 million and $2 million capitalised as part of cost of mine.
B   Provision $2 million and $2 million charged to operating costs
C   Accrual $200,000 per annum for next 10 years
D   Should not be recognised as no cost has yet arisen

8.3 Hopewell sells a line of goods under a six-month warranty. Any defect arising during that period is repaired free of charge. Hopewell has calculated that, if all the goods sold in the last six months of the year required repairs, the cost would be $2 million. If all of these goods had more serious faults and had to be replaced the cost would be $6 million.

The normal pattern is that 80% of goods sold will be fault-free, 15% will require repairs and 5% will have to be replaced.

What is the amount of the provision required?

A $2 million
B $1.6 million
C $6 million
D $0.6 million

8.4   Which ONE of the following would NOT be valid grounds for a provision?

A   A company has a policy of cleaning up any environmental contamination caused by its operations, but is not legally obliged to do so.

B   A company is leasing an office building for which it has no further use. However, it is tied into the lease for another year.

C   A company is closing down a division. The Board has prepared detailed closure plans which have been communicated to customers and employees.

D   A company has acquired a machine which requires a major overhaul every three years. The cost of the first overhaul is reliably estimated at $120,000.

9 Objective test questions: Deferred tax   7 mins

9.1   In accounting for deferred tax, which of the following items can give rise to temporary differences?

1   Differences between accounting depreciation and tax allowances for capital expenditure
2   Expenses charged in the statement of profit or loss but disallowed for tax
3   Revaluation of a non-current asset
4   Unrelieved tax losses

A   1, 3 and 4 only
B   1 and 2 only
C   3 and 4 only
D   All four items

9.2   Which of the following are examples of assets or liabilities whose carrying amount is always equal to their tax base?

1   Accrued expenses that will never be deductible for tax purposes

2   Accrued expenses that have already been deducted in determining the current tax liability for current or earlier periods

3   Accrued income that will never be taxable

4   A loan payable in the statement of financial position at the amount originally received, which is also the amount eventually repayable

A   1 and 3 only
B   1 and 2 only
C   2 and 4 only
D   All four items

9.3 Which of the following statements about IAS 12 *Income taxes* are correct?

1 Companies may discount deferred tax assets and liabilities if the effect would be material.

2 The financial statements must disclose an explanation of the relationship between tax expense and accounting profit.

3 Deferred tax may not be recognised in respect of goodwill unless any impairment of that goodwill is deductible for tax purposes.

4 The tax base of an asset or liability is the amount attributed to that asset or liability for tax purposes.

A All the statements are correct
B 2, 3 and 4 only are correct
C 1 and 4 only are correct
D None of the statements is correct.

9.4 The following information relates to an entity.

- At 1 January 20X8, the net book value of non-current assets exceeded their tax written-down value by $850,000.

- For the year ended 31 December 20X8, the entity claimed depreciation for tax purposes of $500,000 and charged depreciation of $450,000 in the financial statements.

- During the year ended 31 December 20X8, the entity revalued a freehold property. The revaluation surplus was $250,000.

- The tax rate was 30% throughout the year.

What is the provision for deferred tax required by IAS 12 *Income taxes* at 31 December 20X8?

A $240,000

B $270,000

C $315,000

D $345,000

10 Objective test questions: Share-based payments 5 mins

10.1 A company grants 500 cash share appreciation rights to each of its 800 employees on 1 January 20X5, vesting on 31 December 20X7, on condition that they remain in its employ until that date. The fair value of each share appreciation right is $4.20 on 1 January 20X5 and $4.30 on 31 December 20X5. At 1 January 20X5 the company estimated that 620 employees would remain employed until the vesting date, adjusted to 610 at 31 December 20X5 as more employees had left than anticipated.

How much should be recognised as an expense in respect of the share appreciation rights for the year ended 31 December 20X5?

A $427,000
B $437,167
C $1,281,000
D $1,311,501

10.2   ABC Plc grants 500 share options to each of its 8 directors on 1 April 20X7, which will vest on 31 March 20X9. The fair value of each option at 1 April 20X7 is $12, and all the options are anticipated to vest on 31 March 20X9.

What is the accounting entry in the financial statements for the year ended 31 March 20X8?

A   Dr Staff expense $24,000 / Cr Other reserves (within equity) $24,000
B   Dr Staff expense $48,000 / Cr Other reserves (within equity) $48,000
C   Dr Asset $24,000 / Cr Liability $24,000
D   Dr Asset $48,000 / Cr Liability $48,000

10.3   On 1 May 20X6, More Shares Plc grants 25 share appreciation rights to each of its 3,500 employees, on the condition that each employee remains in service until 30 April 20X9. 55% of the rights are expected to vest on 30 April 20X9. The fair value of each right on 30 April 20X7 is $18, and their intrinsic value on that date is $12.

What is the accounting entry in the financial statements for the year ended 30 April 20X7?

A   Dr Assets $866,250 / Cr Liability $866,250
B   Dr Staff expense $288,750 / Cr Liability $288,750
C   Dr Staff expense $288,750 / Cr Other reserves (within equity) $288,750
D   Dr Staff expense $433,125 / Cr Liability $433,125

11 Share-based payment   18 mins

Learning outcome: B1

J&B granted 200 options on its $1 ordinary shares to each of its 800 employees on 1 January 20X1. Each grant is conditional upon the employee being employed by J&B until 31 December 20X3.

J&B estimated at 1 January 20X1 that:

(i)   The fair value of each option was $4 (before adjustment for the possibility of forfeiture).

(ii)   Approximately 50 employees would leave during 20X1, 40 during 20X2 and 30 during 20X3, thereby forfeiting their rights to receive the options. The departures were expected to be evenly spread within each year.

The exercise price of the options was $1.50 and the market value of a J&B share on 1 January 20X1 was $3.

In the event, only 40 employees left during 20X1 (and the estimate of total departures was revised down to 95 at 31 December 20X1), 20 during 20X2 (and the estimate of total departures was revised to 70 at 31 December 20X2) and none during 20X3, all spread evenly during each year.

Required

The directors of J&B have asked you to illustrate how the scheme is accounted for under IFRS 2 *Share-based payment.*

(a)   **Prepare** the double entries for the charge to statement of profit or loss for employee services over the three years and for the share issue, assuming all employees entitled to benefit from the scheme exercised their rights and the shares were issued on 31 December 20X3.   **(7 marks)**

(b)   **Explain** how your solution would differ had J&B offered its employees cash-based options on the share value rather than share options.   **(3 marks)**

(Total: 10 marks)

12 Objective test questions: Revenue

8 mins

12.1 Repro Co, a company which sells photocopying equipment, has prepared its draft financial statements for the year ended 30 September 20X4. It has included the following transactions in revenue at the stated amounts below.

Which of these has been correctly included in revenue according to IFRS 15 *Revenue from Contracts with Customers*?

A   Agency sales of $250,000 on which Repro Co is entitled to a commission.

B   Sale proceeds of $20,000 for motor vehicles which were no longer required by Repro Co.

C   Sales of $150,000 on 30 September 20X4. The amount invoiced to and received from the customer was $180,000, which included $30,000 for ongoing servicing work to be done by Repro Co over the next two years.

D   Sales of $200,000 on 1 October 20X3 to an established customer which, (with the agreement of Repro Co), will be paid in full on 30 September 20X5. Repro Co has a cost of capital of 10%.

12.2 Derringdo Co sells a package which gives customers a free laptop when they sign a two-year contract for provision of broadband services. The laptop has a stand-alone price of $200 and the broadband contract is for $30 per month.

In accordance with IFRS 15 *Revenue from Contracts with Customers*, what amount will be recognised as revenue on each package in the first year?

A $439
B $281
C $461
D $158

12.3 Determining the amount to be recognised in the first year is an example of which step in the IFRS 15 five-step model?

A   Determining the transaction price
B   Recognising revenue when a performance obligation is satisfied
C   Identifying the separate performance obligations
D   Allocating the transaction price to the performance obligations

12.4 BX is carrying out a transaction on behalf of another entity and the finance director is unsure whether BX should be regarded as an agent or a principal in respect of this transaction.

Which of the following would indicate that BX is acting as an agent?

A   BX is primarily responsible for fulfilling the contract.
B   BX is not exposed to credit risk for the amount due from the customer.
C   BX is responsible for negotiating the price for the contract.
D   BX will not be paid in the form of commission.

13 Objective test questions: Basic groups

14 mins

13.1 On what basis may a subsidiary be excluded from consolidation?

A   The activities of the subsidiary are dissimilar to the activities of the rest of the group

B   The subsidiary was acquired with the intention of reselling it after a short period of time

C   The subsidiary is based in a country with strict exchange controls which make it difficult for it to transfer funds to the parent

D   There is no basis on which a subsidiary may be excluded from consolidation

13.2 Which of the following is the criterion for treatment of an investment as an associate?

A   Ownership of a majority of the equity shares
B   Ability to exercise control
C   Existence of significant influence
D   Exposure to variable returns from involvement with the investee

13.3 Which of the following statements are correct when preparing consolidated financial statements?

1   A subsidiary cannot be consolidated unless it prepares financial statements to the same reporting date as the parent.

2   A subsidiary with a different reporting date may prepare additional statements up to the group reporting date for consolidation purposes.

3   A subsidiary's financial statements can be included in the consolidation if the gap between the parent and subsidiary reporting dates is five months or less.

4   Where a subsidiary's financial statements are drawn up to a different reporting date from those of the parent, adjustments should be made for significant transactions or events occurring between the two reporting dates.

A   1 only
B   2 and 3
C   2 and 4
D   3 and 4

13.4 IFRS 3 requires an acquirer to measure the assets and liabilities of the acquiree at the date of consolidation at fair value. IFRS 13 *Fair value measurement* provides guidance on how fair value should be established.

Which of the following is **not** one of the issues to be considered according to IFRS 13 when arriving at the fair value of a non-financial asset?

A   The characteristics of the asset

B   The present value of the future cash flows that the asset is expected to generate during its remaining life

C   The principal or most advantageous market for the asset

D   The highest and best use of the asset

13.5 Witch acquired 70% of the 200,000 equity shares of Wizard, its only subsidiary, on 1 April 20X8 when the retained earnings of Wizard were $450,000. The carrying amounts of Wizard's net assets at the date of acquisition were equal to their fair values apart from a building which had a carrying amount of $600,000 and a fair value of $850,000. The remaining useful life of the building at the acquisition date was 40 years.

Witch measures non-controlling interest at fair value, based on share price. The market value of Wizard shares at the date of acquisition was $1.75.

At 31 March 20X9 the retained earnings of Wizard were $750,000. At what amount should the non-controlling interest appear in the consolidated statement of financial position of Witch at 31 March 20X9?

A $195,000
B $193,125
C $135,000
D $188,750

13.6 On 1 June 20X1 Strawberry acquired 80% of the equity share capital of Raspberry. At the date of acquisition the fair values of Raspberry's net assets were equal to their carrying amounts, with the exception of its property. This had a fair value of $1.2 million **below** its carrying amount. The property had a remaining useful life of eight years.

What effect will any adjustment required in respect of the property have on group retained earnings at 30 September 20X1?

A Increase $50,000
B Decrease $50,000
C Increase $40,000
D Decrease $40,000

13.7 On 1 August 20X7, Orange purchased 18 million of the 24 million $1 equity shares of Banana. The acquisition was through a share exchange of two shares in Orange for every three shares in Banana. The market price of a share in Orange at 1 August 20X7 was $5.75. Orange will also pay in cash on 31 July 20X9 (two years after acquisition) $2.42 per acquired share of Banana. Orange's cost of capital is 10% per annum.

What is the amount of the consideration attributable to Orange for the acquisition of Banana?

A $105 million

B $139.5 million

C $108.2 million

D $103.8 million

13.8   Crash acquired 70% of Bang's 100,000 $1 ordinary shares for $800,000, when the retained earnings of Bang were $570,000 and the balance in its revaluation surplus was $150,000. Bang also has an internally developed customer list, which has been independently valued at $90,000. The non-controlling interest in Bang was judged to have a fair value of $220,000 at the date of acquisition.

What was the goodwill arising on acquisition?

A $200,000
B $163,000
C $226,000
D $110,000

14 Group financial statements   **18 mins**

In many countries, companies with subsidiaries have been required to publish group financial statements, usually in the form of consolidated financial statements. You are required to **state** why you feel the preparation of group financial statements is necessary and to **outline** their limitations, if any.

(10 marks)

15 Putney and Wandsworth   **18 mins**

Putney acquired 90% of the share capital of Wandsworth on 1 January 20X1 when Wandsworth's retained earnings stood at $10,000 and there was no balance on the revaluation surplus.

Their respective statements of financial position as at 31 December 20X5 are as follows.

	Putney $	Wandsworth $
Non-current assets		
Property, plant & equipment	135,000	60,000
Investment in Wandsworth	25,000	–
	160,000	60,000
Current assets	62,000	46,000
	222,000	106,000
Equity		
Share capital ($1 ordinary shares)	50,000	15,000
Revaluation surplus	50,000	15,000
Retained earnings	90,000	50,000
	190,000	80,000
Non-current liabilities	14,000	12,000
Current liabilities	18,000	14,000
	222,000	106,000

The group policy is to measure non-controlling interests at acquisition at their proportionate share of the fair value of the identifiable net assets. Impairment losses on goodwill to date have amounted to $1,250.

Required

Prepare the consolidated statement of financial position of Putney and its subsidiary as at 31 December 20X5.   **(10 marks)**

16 Balmes and Aribau

18 mins

Balmes acquired 80% of Aribau's ordinary share capital on 1 July 20X1 for $28.5 million. The balance on Aribau's retained earnings at that date was $24m and $2m on the general reserve.

Their respective statements of financial position as at 30 June 20X3 are as follows.

	Balmes $'000	Aribau $'000
Non-current assets		
Property, plant & equipment	97,300	34,400
Intangible assets	5,100	1,200
Investment in Aribau (note 1)	35,500	–
	137,900	35,600
Current assets		
Inventories	43,400	14,300
Trade and other receivables	36,800	17,400
Cash and cash equivalents	700	-
	80,900	31,700
	218,800	67,300
Equity		
Share capital ($1 ordinary shares)	50,000	5,000
General reserve	4,300	3,000
Retained earnings	118,800	37,100
	173,100	45,100
Non-current liabilities		
Loan notes	10,000	4,000
Current liabilities		
Trade payables	28,400	15,700
Income tax payable	7,300	2,400
Bank overdraft	-	100
	35,700	18,200
	218,800	67,300

Additional information

(a) Balmes' investment in Aribau has been classified as available for sale and is held at fair value. The gains earned on it have been recorded within the retained earnings of Balmes.

(b) At the date of acquisition, Aribau's property, plant and equipment included land and buildings at a carrying value of $12.5m (of which $4.5m related to the land). The fair value of the land and buildings was $14m (of which $5m related to the land). The buildings had an average remaining useful life of 20 years at that date.

(c) The group policy is to value non-controlling interests at acquisition at fair value. The fair value of the non-controlling interests in Aribau on 1 July 20X1 was $7 million.

(d) During June 20X3, Balmes conducted an impairment review of its investment in Aribau in the consolidated financial statements. This revealed impairment losses relating to recognised goodwill of $200,000. No impairment losses had previously been recognised.

Required

Prepare the consolidated statement of financial position for the Balmes Group as at 30 June 20X3.

(10 marks)

17 Reprise

25 mins

Reprise purchased 75% of Encore for $2,000,000 10 years ago when the balance on its retained earnings was $1,044,000. The statements of financial position of the two companies as at 31 March 20X4 are as follows:

	Reprise $'000	Encore $'000
Non-current assets		
Investment in Encore	2,000	–
Land and buildings	3,350	–
Plant and equipment	1,010	2,210
Motor vehicles	510	345
	6,870	2,555
Current assets		
Inventories	890	352
Trade receivables	1,372	514
Cash and cash equivalents	89	51
	2,351	917
	9,221	3,472
Equity		
Share capital - $1 ordinary shares	1,000	500
Retained earnings	4,225	2,610
Revaluation surplus	2,500	–
	7,725	3,110
Non-current liabilities		
10% debentures	500	–
Current liabilities		
Trade payables	996	362
	9,221	3,472

The following additional information is available:

(a)   Included in trade receivables of Reprise are amounts owed by Encore of $75,000. The current accounts do not at present balance, due to a payment for $39,000 being in transit at the year end from Encore.

(b)   Included in the inventories of Encore are items purchased from Reprise during the year for $31,200. Reprise marks up its goods by 30% to achieve its selling price.

(c) $180,000 of the recognised goodwill arising is to be written off due to impairment losses.

(d)   Encore shares were trading at $4.40 just prior to acquisition by Reprise.

Required

Prepare the consolidated statement of financial position for the Reprise group of companies as at 31 March 20X4. It is the group policy to value the non-controlling interests at fair value at acquisition.

(14 marks)

18 Objective test questions: Associates and joint arrangements

11 mins

18.1 On 1 October 20X8 Viardot acquired 30 million of Pauline's 100 million shares in exchange for 75 million of its own shares. The stock market value of Viardot's shares at the date of this share exchange was $1.60 each.

Pauline's profit is subject to seasonal variation. Its profit for the year ended 31 March 20X9 was $100 million. $20 million of this profit was made from 1 April 20X8 to 30 September 20X8.

Viardot has one subsidiary and no other investments apart from Pauline.

What amount will be shown as 'investment in associate' in the consolidated statement of financial position of Viardot as at 31 March 20X9?

A $144 million
B $150 million
C $78 million
D $126 million

18.2 How should an associate be accounted for in the consolidated statement of profit or loss?

A   The associate's income and expenses are added to those of the group on a line-by-line basis.

B   The group share of the associate's income and expenses is added to the group figures on a line-by-line basis.

C   The group share of the associate's profit after tax is recorded as a one-line entry.

D   Only dividends received from the associate are recorded in the group statement of profit or loss.

18.3 Wellington owns 30% of Boot, which it purchased on 1 May 20X7 for $2.5 million. At that date Boot had retained earnings of $5.3 million. At the year end date of 31 October 20X7 Boot had retained earnings of $6.4 million after paying out a dividend of $1 million. On 30 September 20X7 Wellington sold $700,000 of goods to Boot, on which it made 30% profit. Boot had resold none of these goods by 31 October.

At what amount will Wellington record its investment in Boot in its consolidated statement of financial position at 31 October 20X7?

A $2,767,000
B $2,900,000
C $2,830,000
D $2,620,000

18.4 On 1 February 20X1 Picardy acquired 35% of the equity shares of Avignon, its only associate, for $10 million in cash. The post-tax profit of Avignon for the year to 30 September 20X1 was $3 million. Profits accrued evenly throughout the year. Avignon made a dividend payment of $1 million on 1 September 20X1. At 30 September 20X1 Picardy decided that an impairment loss of $500,000 should be recognised on its investment in Avignon.

What amount will be shown as 'investment in associate' in the statement of financial position of Picardy as at 30 September 20X1?

A $9,967,000
B $9,850,000
C $9,200,000
D $10,200,000

18.5 Which of the following statements are true with regards to group financial statements?

1   Under IFRS 11, joint operations are to be accounted for the same way as joint ventures.

2   Goodwill arising on consolidation may be capitalised and amortised, or capitalised and reviewed annually for impairment.

3   Under IFRS 11, joint ventures are to be accounted for using the equity method.

4   Goodwill must always be capitalised and reviewed for impairment annually.

A   Statements 1 and 2
B   Statements 1 and 4
C   Statements 2 and 3
D   Statements 3 and 4

18.6 What, according to IFRS 11, are the characteristics of a joint operation?

1   The parties with joint control have rights to the assets and obligations for the liabilities of the arrangement.

2   The parties with joint control have rights to the net assets of the arrangement.

3   The arrangement is never structured through a separate entity.

4   The arrangement is contractual.

A   1 and 3
B   1 and 4
C   2 and 3
D   2 and 4

19 Hever

36 mins

Hever has held shares in two companies, Spiro and Aldridge, for a number of years. As at 31 December 20X4 they have the following statements of financial position:

	Hever $'000	Spiro $'000	Aldridge $'000
Non-current assets			
Property, plant & equipment	370	190	260
Investments	218	–	–
	588	190	260
Current assets			
Inventories	160	100	180
Trade receivables	170	90	100
Cash	50	40	10
	380	230	290
	968	420	550
Equity			
Share capital ($1 ords)	200	80	50
Share premium	100	80	30
Retained earnings	568	200	400
	868	360	480
Current liabilities			
Trade payables	100	60	70
	968	420	550

You ascertain the following additional information:

(a) The 'investments' in the statement of financial position comprise solely Hever's investment in Spiro ($128,000) and in Aldridge ($90,000).

(b) The 48,000 shares in Spiro were acquired when Spiro's retained earnings balance stood at $20,000.

The 15,000 shares in Aldridge were acquired when that company had a retained earnings balance of $150,000.

(c) When Hever acquired its shares in Spiro, the fair value of Spiro's net assets equalled their book values with the following exceptions:

	$'000
Property, plant and equipment	50 higher
Inventories	20 lower (sold during 20X4)

Depreciation arising on the fair value adjustment to non-current assets since this date is $5,000.

(d) During the year, Hever sold inventories to Spiro for $16,000, which originally cost Hever $10,000. Three-quarters of these inventories have subsequently been sold by Spiro.

(e) No impairment losses on goodwill had been necessary by 31 December 20X4.

(f) It is group policy to value non-controlling interests at fair value. The fair value of the non-controlling interests at acquisition was $90,000.

Required

Prepare the consolidated statement of financial position for the Hever group (incorporating the associate).

(20 marks)

20 Bayonet

18 mins

Learning outcome: A1

Bayonet, a public limited company, purchased 6m shares in Rifle, a public limited company, on 1 January 20X5 for $10m. Rifle had purchased 4m shares in Pistol, a public limited company, for $9m on 31 December 20X2 when its retained earnings stood at $5m. The balances on retained earnings of the acquired companies were $8m and $6.5m respectively at 1 January 20X5. The fair value of the identifiable assets and liabilities of Rifle and Pistol was equivalent to their book values at the acquisition dates.

The statements of financial position of the three companies as at 31 December 20X9 are as follows:

	Bayonet $'000	Rifle $'000	Pistol $'000
Non-current assets			
Property, plant and equipment	14,500	12,140	17,500
Investment in Rifle	10,000		
Investment in Pistol	–	9,000	–
	24,500	21,140	17,500
Current assets			
Inventories	6,300	2,100	450
Trade receivables	4,900	2,000	2,320
Cash	500	1,440	515
	11,700	5,540	3,285
	36,200	26,680	20,785
Equity			
50c ordinary shares	5,000	4,000	2,500
Retained earnings	25,500	20,400	16,300
	30,500	24,400	18,800
Current liabilities	5,700	2,280	1,985
	36,200	26,680	20,785

Group policy is to value non-controlling interests at fair value at acquisition. The fair value of the non-controlling interests in Rifle was calculated as $3,230,000 on 1 January 20X5. The fair value of the 40% non-controlling interests in Pistol on 1 January 20X5 was $4.6m.

Impairment tests in current and previous years did not reveal any impairment losses.

Required

Prepare the consolidated statement of financial position of Bayonet as at 31 December 20X9.

(10 marks)

21 Objective test questions: Changes to group structures

5 mins

21.1 Jalfresi acquired 8 million of the 10 million issued share capital of Dopiaza on 1 October 20X1 for $14.8 million, when the balance on retained earnings was $6 million. On 30 September 20X8 Jalfresi sold 25% of its holding for $4.4 million. It is the group's policy to measure NCI at the proportionate share of the subsidiary's net assets.

Extracts from the statement of financial position of Dopiaza as at 30 September 20X8 is as follows:

	$'000
Share capital	10,000
Retained earnings	8,900
	18,900

What is the gain or loss on disposal/adjustment to parent's equity to be included in the financial statements for the year ended 30 September 20X8?

A $620,000 adjustment to parent's equity.
B $470,000 gain to statement of profit or loss for the year.
C $500,000 adjustment to parent's equity.
D $20,000 gain to statement of profit or loss for the year.

21.2 On 1 September 20X6, BLT held 60% of the ordinary share capital of its only subsidiary CMU. The consolidated equity of the group at that date was $576,600, of which $127,000 was attributable to the non-controlling interest. BLT measures non-controlling interests at acquisition at their proportionate share of the subsidiary's net assets.

On 28 February 20X7, exactly halfway through the financial year, BLT paid $135,000 to buy a further 20% of the ordinary share capital of CMU. In the year ended 31 August 20X7 BLT's profits for the period were $98,970 and CMU's were $30,000. It can be assumed that profits accrue evenly throughout the year.

What is the adjustment to parent's equity as a result of BLT's acquisition of further shares in CMU?

A $68,500 debit
B $68,500 credit
C $2,000 debit
D $2,000 credit

21.3 Bad, whose year end is 30 June 20X9 has a subsidiary, Conscience, which it acquired in stages. The details of the acquisition are as follows:

Date of acquisition	Holding acquired %	Retained earnings at acquisition $m	Purchase consideration $m
1 July 20X7	10	540	120
1 July 20X8	60	800	960

The share capital of Conscience has remained unchanged since its incorporation at $600m. The fair values of the net assets of Conscience were the same as their carrying amounts at the date of the acquisition. Bad did not have significant influence over Conscience at any time before gaining control of Conscience. At 1 July 20X8, the fair value of Bad's 10% holding in Conscience was $160m and the fair value of non-controlling interests was $420m. The group policy is to measure non-controlling interests at acquisition at their fair value.

What is the goodwill on the acquisition of Conscience that will appear in the consolidated statement of financial position at 30 June 20X9?

A $80,000,000
B $140,000,000
C $240,000,000
D $665,000,000

22 Objective test questions: Indirect control of subsidiaries
5 mins

22.1   Rag owns 75% of Tag and Tag owns 40% of Bobtail. Both companies were acquired four years ago. The profit before tax for the year of each company is as follows: Rag $6,000, Tag $5,000 and Bobtail $4,000. Each company has a $1,000 tax expense.

Rag measures non-controlling interests at acquisition at their proportionate share of the subsidiary's net assets.

Goodwill at acquisition of Tag was $1,000 and Bobtail $300. At the date of acquisition the fair value of Bobtail's buildings were $1,000 greater than their book value. The buildings are being depreciated over a remaining useful life of 20 years.

It is estimated that the goodwill at acquisition has suffered impairment losses in the year of $400 for Tag. Goodwill impairments are treated as an operating expense.

What is the figure in the consolidated statement of profit or loss for the non-controlling interests?

A $1,000
B $1,195
C $1,200
D $1,295

22.2   Apricot holds 75% of the issued share capital of Blackcurrant and 40% of the issued share capital of Cranberry.

Blackcurrant holds 60% of the issued share capital of Date.

The receivables balances of the four companies at the statement of financial position date are as follows:

	$'000
Apricot	120
Blackcurrant	110
Cranberry	100
Date	90

What will be the receivables figure to be included in the consolidated statement of financial position of Apricot?

A $230,000
B $320,000
C $340,000
D $420,000

22.3 The following diagram shows the structure of a group:

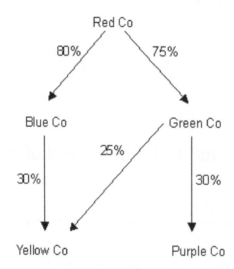

Which of the following are subsidiary undertakings of Red Co?

A   Blue Co and Green Co
B   Blue Co, Green Co and Yellow Co
C   Blue Co, Green Co, Yellow Co and Purple Co

23 Objective test questions: Foreign subsidiaries   4 mins

23.1 Parent has three overseas subsidiaries.

(1)   A is 80% owned. A does not normally enter into transactions with Parent, other than to pay dividends. It operates as a fairly autonomous entity on a day-to-day basis although Parent controls its long-term strategy.

(2)   B is 100% owned and has been set up in order to assemble machines from materials provided by Parent. These are then sent to the UK where Parent sells them to third parties.

(3)   C is 75% owned and is located in France. It manufactures and sells its own range of products locally. It negotiates its own day-to-day financing needs with French banks.

Which of the subsidiaries are likely to have a different functional currency from Parent?

A   A and B
B   A and C
C   B and C
D   all three subsidiaries

23.2 Rat acquired 75% of the equity share capital of Mole, a foreign operation, on 1 January 20X5, when its net assets were Units 720,000. Summarised statements of financial position of the two entities at 31 December 20X6 are shown below:

	Rat $'000	*Mole* Unit'000
Investment in Mole	350	–
Other net assets	2,550	960
	2,900	960
Share capital ($1/Unit1 ordinary shares)	1,000	500
Retained earnings	1,900	460
	2,900	960

Exchange rates were as follows:

	Unit=$1
1 January 20X5	2.0
31 December 20X6	2.5

What are consolidated retained earnings at 31 December 20X6?

A $1,902,000
B $1,918,000
C $1,972,000
D $2,084,000

24 Objective test questions: Consolidated statements of changes in equity
6 mins

24.1 Profits or losses attributable to non-controlling interests should be disclosed in the consolidated statement of profit or loss.

Which of the following statements concerning the presentation of non-controlling interest in the consolidated statement of profit or loss is correct?

A The non-controlling interest share of revenue is deducted on the face of the statement of profit or loss.

B The non-controlling interest share of operating profit before tax and the related taxation charge are separately disclosed.

C The non-controlling interest share of after-tax profits in subsidiaries is shown on the face of the statement of profit or loss.

D Only profits attributable to the group appear in the statement of profit or loss.

24.2 B bought 83% of C on 1 July 20X1. C made a profit after tax of $330,880 for the year ended 31 December 20X1. Profits accrued evenly throughout the year.

What is the profit attributable to non-controlling interests in B's consolidated statement of profit or loss for the year ended 31 December 20X1?

A $18,749
B $28,125
C $56,250
D $66,273

24.3 Which of the following might appear as a separate item in the 'other comprehensive income' section of the statement of profit or loss and other comprehensive income?

A A material irrecoverable debt arising in the year.
B A share issue in the year.
C An impairment loss on assets carried at depreciated historical cost.
D An upward revaluation of the company's assets.

25 Fallowfield and Rusholme

22 mins

Fallowfield acquired a 60% holding in Rusholme three years ago when Rusholme's equity was $56,000 (share capital $40,000 plus reserves $16,000). Both businesses have been very successful since the acquisition and their respective statements of profit or loss and other comprehensive income for the year ended 30 June 20X8 and extracts from their statements of changes in equity are shown below.

	Fallowfield $	Rusholme $
Revenue	403,400	193,000
Cost of sales	(201,400)	(92,600)
Gross profit	202,000	100,400
Distribution costs	(16,000)	(14,600)
Administrative expenses	(24,250)	(17,800)
Dividends from Rusholme	15,000	
Profit before tax	176,750	68,000
Income tax expense	(61,750)	(22,000)
Profit for the year	115,000	46,000
Other comprehensive income (net of tax)	20,000	5,000
Total comprehensive income	135,000	51,000

STATEMENT OF CHANGES IN EQUITY (EXTRACT)

	Fallowfield Total equity $	Rusholme Total equity $
Balance at 30 June 20X7	243,000	101,000
Total comprehensive income for the year	135,000	51,000
Dividends	(40,000)	(25,000)
Balance at 30 June 20X8	338,000	127,000

Additional information

(a) During the year Rusholme sold some goods to Fallowfield for $40,000, including 25% mark-up. Half of these items were still in inventories at the year end.

(b) Group policy is to measure non-controlling interests at acquisition at fair value. The fair value of Rusholme's non-controlling interest at acquisition was $30,000. There has been no impairment in goodwill since acquisition.

Required

Prepare the consolidated statement of profit or loss and other comprehensive income and statement of changes in equity (showing parent and non-controlling interest shares) of Fallowfield Co and its subsidiary for the year ended 30 June 20X8. **(12 marks)**

26 Panther Group

27 mins

Panther operated as a single company, but in 20X4 decided to expand its operations. On 1 July 20X4, Panther paid $2,000,000 to acquire a 60% interest in Sabre, a company to which Panther had advanced a loan of $800,000 at an interest rate of 5% on 1 January 20X4.

The statements of profit or loss and other comprehensive income of Panther and Sabre for the year ended 31 December 20X4 are as follows:

	Panther $'000	Sabre $'000
Revenue	22,800	4,300
Cost of sales	(13,600)	(2,600)
Gross profit	9,200	1,700
Distribution costs	(2,900)	(500)
Administrative expenses	(1,800)	(300)
Finance costs	(200)	(40)
Finance income	50	–
Profit before tax	4,350	860
Income tax expense	(1,300)	(220)
Profit for the year	3,050	640
Other comprehensive income for the year, net of tax	1,600	180
Total comprehensive income for the year	4,650	820

Since acquisition, Sabre purchased $320,000 of goods from Panther. Of these, $60,000 remained in inventories at the year end. Sabre makes a mark-up on cost of 20% under the transfer pricing agreement between the two companies. The fair value of the identifiable net assets of Sabre on purchase were $200,000 greater than their book value. The difference relates to properties with a remaining useful life of 20 years.

Statement of changes in equity (extracts) for the two companies:

	Panther Reserves $'000	Sabre Reserves $'000
Balance at 1 January 20X4	12,750	2,480
Dividend paid	(900)	–
Total comprehensive income for the year	4,650	820
Balance at 31 December 20X4	16,500	3,300

Panther and Sabre had $400,000 and $150,000 of share capital in issue throughout the period respectively.

Required

Prepare the consolidated statement of profit or loss and other comprehensive income and statement of changes in equity (extract for reserves) for the Panther Group for the year ended 31 December 20X4.

No adjustments for impairment losses were necessary in the group financial statements.

Assume income and expenses (other than intragroup items) accrue evenly.   **(15 marks)**

27 SM Group

18 mins

Summarised statements of changes in equity for the year ended 30 June 20X5 for SM and its only subsidiary CE are shown below.

STATEMENTS OF CHANGES IN EQUITY FOR THE YEAR ENDED 30 JUNE 20X5

	SM	CE
	$'000	$'000
Balance at 1 July 20X4	500,000	130,000
Issue of shares	25,000	–
Total comprehensive income for the year	75,000	40,000
Dividends	(16,000)	(10,000)
Balance at 30 June 20X5	584,000	160,000

Notes

1 SM acquired 37.5m of CE's 50m $1 ordinary shares on 1 July 20X2, when CE's total equity was $80m. The first dividend CE has paid since acquisition is the amount of $10m shown in the summarised statement above. The total comprehensive income for the year in SM's summarised statement of changes in equity includes its share of the dividend paid by CE.

2 During the year ended 30 June 20X5, CE sold some goods to SM for $15m at a mark-up of 25% on cost. At the year end two-thirds of these goods had been sold on to third parties.

3 It is group accounting policy to measure non-controlling interests at acquisition at the proportionate share of the fair value of net assets. There has been no impairment of recognised goodwill in CE to date.

Required

Prepare the consolidated statement of changes in equity for the year ended 30 June 20X5. **(10 marks)**

28 Holmes and Deakin

31 mins

Holmes Co has owned 85% of the ordinary share capital of Deakin Co for some years. The shares were bought for $255,000 and Deakin Co's reserves at the time of purchase were $20,000. The group policy is to value non-controlling interests at fair value at the date of acquisition. The fair value of the non-controlling interests in Deakin at acquisition was $45,000.

On 28.2.X3 Holmes Co sold 40,000 of the Deakin shares for $160,000. The only entry made in respect of this transaction has been the receipt of the cash, which was credited to the 'investment in subsidiary' account. No dividends were paid by either entity in the period.

The following draft summarised financial statements are available.

STATEMENTS OF PROFIT OR LOSS AND OTHER COMPREHENSIVE INCOME
FOR THE YEAR TO 31 MAY 20X3

	Holmes Co	Deakin Co
	$'000	$'000
Revenue	1,000	540
Cost of sales and operating expenses	(800)	(430)
Profit before tax	200	110
Income tax expense	(90)	(60)
Profit for the year	110	50
Other comprehensive income (net of tax)	20	10
Total comprehensive income for the year	130	60

STATEMENTS OF FINANCIAL POSITION AS AT 31 May 20X3

	$'000	$'000
Non-current assets		
Property, plant and equipment (NBV)	535	178
Investment in Deakin Co	95	–
	630	178
Current assets		
Inventories	320	190
Trade receivables	250	175
Cash	80	89
	650	454
	1,280	632
Equity		
Share capital ($1 ordinary shares)	500	200
Reserves	310	170
	810	370
Current liabilities		
Trade payables	295	171
Income tax payable	80	60
Provisions	95	31
	470	262
	1,280	632

No impairment losses have been necessary in the group financial statements to date.

Assume that the capital gain will be subject to corporate income tax at 30%.

Required

Prepare:

(a) The consolidated statement of profit or loss and other comprehensive income for Holmes for the year to 31 May 20X3 **(6 marks)**

(b) A consolidated statement of financial position as at 31 May 20X3; and **(9 marks)**

(c) A consolidated statement of changes in equity extract (attributable to owners of the parent **only**) for the year ended 31 May 20X3. **(2 marks)**

(Total: 17 marks)

29 Harvard

32 mins

The draft financial statements of Harvard and its subsidiary, Krakow are set out below.

STATEMENTS OF FINANCIAL POSITION AT 31 DECEMBER 20X5

	Harvard $ '000	Krakow PLN '000
Non-current assets		
Property, plant and equipment	2,870	4,860
Investment in Krakow	840	–
	3,710	4,860
Current assets		
Inventories	1,990	8,316
Trade receivables	1,630	4,572
Cash	240	2,016
	3,860	14,904
	7,570	19,764
Equity		
Share capital ($1/PLN1)	118	1,348
Retained reserves	502	14,060
	620	15,408
Non-current liabilities		
Loans	1,920	–
Current liabilities		
Trade payables	5,030	4,356
	7,570	19,764

STATEMENTS OF PROFIT OR LOSS AND OTHER COMPREHENSIVE INCOME FOR THE YEAR ENDED 31 DECEMBER 20X5

	Harvard $'000	Krakow PLN '000
Revenue	40,425	97,125
Cost of sales	(35,500)	(77,550)
Gross profit	4,925	19,575
Distribution and administrative expenses	(4,400)	(5,850)
Investment income	720	–
Profit before tax	1,245	13,725
Income tax expense	(300)	(4,725)
Profit/total comprehensive income for the year	945	9,000
Dividends paid during the period	700	3,744

The following additional information is given:

(a)   Exchange rates

	Zloty (PLN) to $
31 December 20X2	4.40
31 December 20X3	4.16
31 December 20X4	4.00
15 May 20X5	3.90
31 December 20X5	3.60
Average for 20X5	3.75

(b)   Harvard acquired 1,011,000 shares in Krakow for $840,000 on 31 December 20X2 when Krakow's retained earnings stood at PLN 2,876,000. Krakow operates as an autonomous subsidiary. Its functional currency is the Polish zloty.

The fair value of the identifiable net assets of Krakow were equivalent to their book values at the acquisition date. Group policy is to measure non-controlling interests at acquisition at their proportionate share of the fair value of the identifiable net assets.

(c)   Krakow paid an interim dividend of PLN 3,744,000 on 15 May 20X5. No other dividends were paid or declared by Krakow in the period.

(d)   No impairment losses were necessary in the consolidated financial statements by 31 December 20X5.

Required

(a)   **Prepare** the consolidated statement of financial position at 31 December 20X5.   **(6 marks)**

(b)   **Prepare** the consolidated statement of profit or loss and other comprehensive income and statement of changes in equity (attributable to owners of the parent **only**) for the year ended 31 December 20X5.   **(12 marks)**

(Total = 18 marks)

30 Objective test questions: Consolidated statements of cash flows
                                                                                                5 mins

30.1   The carrying amount of property, plant and equipment was $410 million at 31 March 20X1 and $680 million at 31 March 20X2. During the year, property with a carrying amount of $210 million was revalued to $290 million. The depreciation charge for the year was $115 million. There were no disposals.

What amount will appear on the statement of cash flows for the year ended 31 March 20X2 in respect of purchases of property, plant and equipment?

A $270 million
B $225 million
C $235 million
D $305 million

30.2 The statement of financial position of Beans at 31 March 20X7 showed property, plant and equipment with a carrying amount of $1,860,000. At 31 March 20X8 it had increased to $2,880,000.

During the year to 31 March 20X8, plant with a carrying amount of $240,000 was sold at a loss of $90,000; depreciation of $280,000 was charged and $100,000 was added to the revaluation surplus in respect of property, plant and equipment.

What amount should appear under 'investing activities' in the statement of cash flows of Beans for the year ended 31 March 20X8 as cash paid to acquire property, plant and equipment?

A $1,640,000
B $1,440,000
C $1,260,000
D $1,350,000

30.3 On March 20X4, NS acquired 30% of the shares of TP. The investment was accounted for as an associate in NS's consolidated financial statements. Both NS and TP have an accounting year end of 31 October. NS has no other investments in associates.

Net profit for the year in TP's statement of profit or loss for the year ended 31 October 20X4 was $230,000. It declared and paid a dividend of $100,000 on 1 July 20X4. No other dividends were paid in the year.

What amount will be shown as an inflow in respect of earnings from the associate in the consolidated cash flow statement of NS for the year ended 31 October 20X4?

A $20,000
B $26,000
C $30,000
D $46,000

31 AH Group   45 mins

Learning outcome: A1

Extracts from the consolidated financial statements of the AH group for the year ended 30 June 20X5 are given below.

AH GROUP CONSOLIDATED STATEMENT OF PROFIT OR LOSS
FOR THE YEAR ENDED 30 JUNE 20X5

	20X5 $'000
Revenue	85,000
Cost of sales	59,750
Gross profit	25,250
Operating expenses	5,650
Finance cost	1,400
Disposal of property (note 2)	1,250
Profit before tax	19,450
Income tax	6,250
Profit/total comprehensive income for the year for the year	13,200
Profit/total comprehensive income attributable to:	
Owners of the parent	12,545
Non-controlling interest	655
	13,200

AH GROUP: EXTRACTS FROM STATEMENT OF CHANGES IN EQUITY FOR THE YEAR
ENDED 30 JUNE 20X5

	Share capital $'000	Share premium $'000	Consolidated retained earnings $'000
Opening balance	18,000	10,000	18,340
Issue of share capital	2,000	2,000	
Profit for year			12,545
Dividends			(6,000)
Closing balance	20,000	12,000	24,885

AH GROUP STATEMENT OF FINANCIAL POSITION AT 30 JUNE 20X5

	20X5 $'000	20X5 $'000	20X4 $'000	20X4 $'000
ASSETS				
Non-current assets				
Property, plant and equipment	50,600		44,050	
Intangible assets (note 3)	6,410		4,160	
		57,010		48,210
Current assets				
Inventories	33,500		28,750	
Trade receivables	27,130		26,300	
Cash	1,870		3,900	
		62,500		58,950
		119,510		107,160
EQUITY AND LIABILITIES				
Equity				
Share capital	20,000		18,000	
Share premium	12,000		10,000	
Consolidated retained earnings	24,885		18,340	
		56,885		46,340
Non-controlling interest		3,625		1,920
Non current liabilities				
Interest-bearing borrowings		18,200		19,200
Current liabilities				
Trade payables	33,340		32,810	
Interest payable	1,360		1,440	
Tax	6,100		5,450	
		40,800		39,700
		119,510		107,160

Notes

(1)   Several years ago, AH acquired 80% of the issued ordinary shares of its subsidiary, BI. On
1 January 20X5, AH acquired 75% of the issued ordinary shares of CJ in exchange for a fresh
issue of 2 million of its own $1 ordinary shares (issued at a premium of $1 each) and $2 million
in cash. The net assets of CJ at the date of acquisition were assessed as having the following fair
values.

	$'000
Property, plant and equipment	4,200
Inventories	1,650
Receivables	1,300
Cash	50
Trade payables	(1,950)
Tax	(250)
	5,000

(2)   During the year, AH disposed of a non-current asset of property for proceeds of $2,250,000. The carrying value of the asset at the date of disposal was $1,000,000. There were no other disposals of non-current assets. Depreciation of $7,950,000 was charged against consolidated profits for the year.

(3)   Intangible assets comprise goodwill on acquisition of BI and CJ (20X4: BI only). Goodwill has remained unimpaired since acquisition. Group policy is to measure non-controlling interests at acquisition at their proportionate share of the fair value of the identifiable net assets.

Required

Prepare the consolidated statement of cash flows of the AH Group for the financial year ended 30 June 20X5 in the form required by IAS 7 *Statement of cash flows*, and using the indirect method. Notes to the statement of cash flows are **not** required, but full workings should be shown.

(25 marks)

32 Objective test questions: Related parties   7 mins

32.1   Linney Co is a company specialised in luxury blinds. The majority of Linney Co's long-term finance is provided by KPG Bank.

Linney Co is 90% owned by Corti, a listed entity. Corti is a long-established company controlled by the Benedetti family through an agreement which pools their voting rights.

Linney regularly provides blinds to Venetia Hotels, a company in which Laura McRae has a minority (10%) holding. Laura McRae is the wife of Francesco Benedetti, one of the key Benedetti family shareholders who control Corti.

30% of Linney's revenue comes from transactions with a major supplier, Dreich.

Which of the following are NOT related parties of Linney Co in accordance with IAS 24?

A   KPG Bank only
B   Dreich only
C   KPG Bank and Dreich
D   KPG Bank, Dreich and Laura McRae

32.2   Figleaf operates an international restaurant chain. It charges its subsidiaries an annual management services fee of 20% of profit before tax (before accounting for the fee). Figleaf is 100% owned by a holding company, Tree, which in turn is majority owned by a wealthy investor, Mr Chan.

Figleaf provides interest-free loans to its junior employees and also a defined benefit pension plan. Figleaf made contributions of $3 million to the pension plan for the year ended 31 December 20X1. In the same year, Mr Chan made a loan of $5 million to Figleaf for the acquisition of new restaurants, at an interest rate of 2%.

Which of the following should be disclosed in the consolidated financial statements of the Figleaf Group under IAS 24?

1   The management fee from Figleaf's subsidiaries
2   The name of Figleaf's ultimate controlling party, Mr Chan
3   Details of the interest free loans to junior employees
4   Details of the pension plan
5   Details of the $5 million loan from Mr Chan

A   1, 2, 4 and 5 only
B   1, 2, 3 and 4 only
C   1, 2 and 4 only
D   All of the items should be disclosed

32.3   No disclosure is required of intragroup related party transactions in the consolidated financial statements.

Is this statement true or false?

A   True
B   False

32.4   Which of the following statements is/are CORRECT in relation to IAS 24 *Related party disclosures*?

1   A transaction with a related party only requires disclosure if it is at below market value

2   The aim of IAS 24 is to make users of financial statements aware of the potential impact of related party transactions on an entity's financial position and profit or loss

3   Two associates in the same group are related parties

4   If an entity has a joint venture and the joint venture has a subsidiary, both the joint venture and its subsidiary are related to the entity

A   1 and 3
B   2 and 4
C   3 and 4
D   All of the above

33 Objective test questions: Earnings per share   7 mins

33.1   Barwell had 10 million ordinary shares in issue throughout the year ended 30 June 20X3. On 1 July 20X2 it had issued $2 million of 6% convertible loan stock, each $5 of loan stock convertible into four ordinary shares on 1 July 20X6 at the option of the holder.

Barwell had profit after tax for the year ended 30 June 20X3 of $1,850,000. It pays tax on profits at 30%.

What was the diluted EPS for the year?

A   16.7c
B   18.5c
C   16.1c

33.2 At 1 January 20X8 Artichoke had five million $1 equity shares in issue. On 1 June 20X8 it made a 1 for 5 rights issue at a price of $1.50. The market price of the shares on the last day of quotation with rights was $1.80.

Total earnings for the year ended 31 December 20X8 was $7.6 million.

What was the EPS for the year?

A $1.35
B $1.36
C $1.27
D $1.06

33.3 Waffle had share capital of $7.5 million in 50c equity shares at 1 October 20X6. On 1 January 20X7 it made an issue of 4 million shares at full market price, immediately followed by a 1 for 3 bonus issue.

The financial statements at 30 September 20X7 showed profit for the year of $12 million.

What was the EPS for the year?

A 53c
B 73c
C 48c
D 50c

33.4 Plumstead had four million equity shares in issue throughout the year ended 31 March 20X7. On 30 September 20X7 it made a 1 for 4 bonus issue. Profit after tax for the year ended 31 March 20X8 was $3.6 million, out of which an equity dividend of 20c per share was paid. The financial statements for the year ended 31 March 20X7 showed EPS of 70c.

What is the EPS for the year ended 31 March 20X8 and the restated EPS for the year ended 31 March 20X7?

	20X8	20X7
A	72c	87.5c
B	52c	56c
C	80c	87.5c
D	72c	56c

34 Pilum   25 mins

A statement showing the retained profit of Pilum Co for the year ended 31 December 20X4 is set out below.

	$	$
Profit before tax		2,530,000
Income tax expense		(1,127,000)
		1,403,000
Transfer to reserves		(230,000)
Dividends paid in the period:		
Preference share dividends	276,000	
Ordinary share dividends	414,000	
		(690,000)
Retained profit		483,000

On 1 January 20X4 the issued share capital of Pilum Co was 4,600,000 6% irredeemable non-cumulative preference shares of $1 each and 4,120,000 ordinary shares of $1 each.

Required

Calculate the earnings per share (on basic and diluted basis) in respect of the year ended 31 December 20X4 for each of the following circumstances. (Each of the three circumstances (a) to (c) is to be dealt with separately.)

(a)   On the basis that there was no change in the issued share capital of the company during the year ended 31 December 20X4.   **(3 marks)**

(b)   On the basis that the company made a rights issue of $1 ordinary shares on 1 October 20X4 in the proportion of 1 for every 5 shares held, at a price of $1.20. The market price for the shares at close of trade on the last day of quotation cum rights was $1.78 per share.   **(5 marks)**

(c)   On the basis that the company made no new issue of shares during the year ended 31 December 20X4 but, on 1 January 20X4, issued $1,500,000 5% convertible loan stock with a five-year term. The liability component of the loan stock at 1 January 20X4 was calculated as $1,320,975 using an effective interest rate of 8%. The loan stock may be converted into $1 ordinary shares as follows:

20X5 90 $1 shares for $100 nominal value loan stock

20X6 85 $1 shares for $100 nominal value loan stock

20X7 80 $1 shares for $100 nominal value loan stock

20X8 75 $1 shares for $100 nominal value loan stock   **(6 marks)**

Assume where appropriate that the income tax rate is 30%.

(Total = 14 marks)

35 Objective test questions: Ethics in financial reporting
7 mins

35.1   You are employed in the finance department of Furlong Co. The company is involved in a court case that is ongoing at the year end, which the lawyers believe it is going to lose. The lawyers estimate that there is a 20% of Furlong being ordered to pay a $60,000 fine, a 30% chance of it being ordered to pay a $80,000 fine and a 50% chance of it being ordered to pay a $150,000 fine. The directors propose to make a provision of $75,000.

Would adopting the proposed course of action comply with the CIMA *Code of Ethics*?

A   Yes

B   No

35.2   Which of the following most accurately describes what principle of confidentiality means for a professional accountant?

A   A professional accountant must never, in any circumstance, disclose any information acquired as a result of professional or business relationships to third parties.

B   A professional accountant must never disclose any information acquired as a result of professional or business relationships to third parties, except when requested by the police or tax authorities.

C   A professional accountant may only disclose information acquired as a result of professional or business relationships to third parties with the consent of the parties involved.

D   A professional accountant should not disclose any information acquired as a result of professional or business relationships to third parties without proper and specific authority, unless there is a legal or professional right or duty to disclose.

35.3 John, a professional accountant in business, is asked by the Financial Director of the company he is working for to determine the appropriate accounting treatment for a business combination. Five months previously, he had performed the feasibility study that supported the acquisition decision.

Which of the following ethical threat, if any, does John currently face?

A   Self-interest threat.
B   Self-review threat.
C   Advocacy threat.
D   No ethical threat arises.

35.4 The directors of TF receive a bonus if the operating cash flow exceeds a predetermined target for the year. In prior periods, the accounting policy has been to record dividends paid as an operating cash flow. The directors are proposing to change the accounting policy and record dividends paid as a financing cash flow.

When applying the CIMA *Code of Ethics*, which of the following statements are appropriate in relation to this scenario?

1.   This accounting treatment is not permitted by IAS 7; if adopted by the directors, they are not complying with the fundamental principle of professional competence.

2.   The accounting treatment is permitted by IAS 7, but the change in accounting policy should only be adopted if it results in information that is more reliable and relevant to the decisions of the users of financial statements.

3.   There is a self-interest threat as the directors are proposing an accounting treatment which will result in their own personal gain and might not be in the best interests of the entity and its stakeholders.

4.   The directors must contact the CIMA Ethics Helpline before taking any action.

A   1 and 4
B   2 and 3
C   1 and 3
D   2, 3 and 4

36 Objective test questions: Analysis of financial performance and position
5 mins

36.1 An entity has an average operating profit margin of 23% and an average asset turnover of 0.8, which is similar to the averages for the industry.

The entity is likely to be:

A   An architectural practice
B   A supermarket
C   An estate agent
D   A manufacturer

36.2 Extracts from the financial statements of Persival are as follows:

Statement of profit or loss	$'000		Statement of financial position	$'000
Operating profit	230		Ordinary shares	2,000
Finance costs	(15)		Revaluation surplus	300
Profit before tax	215		Retained earnings	1,200
Income tax	(15)			3,500
Profit for the year	200		10% loan notes	1,000
			Current liabilities	100
			Total equity and liabilities	4,600

What is the return on capital employed?

A   5.1%
B   4.7%
C   6.6%
D   6%

36.3 Which of the following will increase the length of a company's operating cycle?

A   Reducing the receivables collection period
B   Reducing the inventory holding period
C   Reducing the payables payment period
D   Reducing time taken to produce goods

37 DM   **45 mins**

DM, a listed entity, has just published its financial statements for the year ended 31 December 20X4. DM operates a chain of 42 supermarkets in one of the six major provinces of its country of operation. During 20X4, there has been speculation in the financial press that the entity was likely to be a takeover target for one of the larger national chains of supermarkets that is currently under-represented in DM's province. A recent newspaper report has suggested that DM's directors are unlikely to resist a takeover. The six board members are all nearing retirement, and all own significant non-controlling shareholdings in the business.

As an independent financial advisor, you have been approached by a private shareholder in DM. She is concerned that the directors have a conflict of interests and that the financial statements for 20X4 may have been manipulated.

The statement of profit or loss and other comprehensive income and summarised statement of changes in equity of DM, with comparatives, for the year ended 31 December 20X4, and a statement of financial position with comparatives at that date are as follows:

DM STATEMENT OF PROFIT OR LOSS AND OTHER COMPREHENSIVE INCOME
FOR THE YEAR ENDED 31 DECEMBER 20X4

	20X4 $m	20X3 $m
Revenue, net of sales tax	1,255	1,220
Cost of sales	(1,177)	(1,145)
Gross profit	78	75
Operating expenses	(21)	(29)
Finance cost	(10)	(10)
Profit before tax	47	36
Income tax expense	(14)	(13)
Profit/total comprehensive income for the year	33	23

DM SUMMARISED STATEMENT OF CHANGES IN EQUITY FOR THE YEAR ENDED
31 DECEMBER 20X4

	20X4 $m	20X3 $m
Opening balance	276	261
Profit/total comprehensive income for the year	33	23
Dividends	(8)	(8)
Closing balance	301	276

DM STATEMENT OF FINANCIAL POSITION AT 31 DECEMBER 20X4

	20X4 $m	20X4 $m	20X3 $m	20X3 $m
Non-current assets				
Property, plant and equipment	580		575	
Goodwill	100		100	
		680		675
Current assets				
Inventories	47		46	
Trade receivables	12		13	
Cash	46		12	
		105		71
		785		746
Equity				
Share capital	150		150	
Retained earnings	151		126	
		301		276
Non-current liabilities				
Interest-bearing borrowings	142		140	
Deferred tax	25		21	
		167		161
Current liabilities				
Trade and other payables	297		273	
Short-term borrowings	20		36	
		317		309
		785		746

Notes

(a) DM's directors have undertaken a reassessment of the useful lives of property, plant and equipment during the year. In most cases, they estimate that the useful lives have increased and the depreciation charges in 20X4 have been adjusted accordingly.

(b) Six new stores have been opened during 20X4, bringing the total to 42.

(c) Four key ratios for the supermarket sector (based on the latest available financial statements of twelve listed entities in the sector) are as follows:

   (i) Annual sales per store: $27.6m
   (ii) Gross profit margin: 5.9%
   (iii) Net profit margin: 3.9%
   (iv) Non-current asset turnover (including both tangible and intangible non-current assets): 1.93

Required

(a) **Prepare** a report, addressed to the investor, analysing the performance and position of DM, based on the financial statements and supplementary information provided above. The report should also include comparisons with the key sector ratios, and it should address the investor's concerns about the possible manipulation of the 20X4 financial statements. **(20 marks)**

(b) **Explain** the limitations of the use of sector comparatives in financial analysis. **(5 marks)**

(Total: 25 marks)

1 Objective test questions: sources of long-term finance

1.1 **D** Short-term loans are subject to a loan agreement giving the bank security and a definite repayment schedule. This lowers the risk from their perspective, hence the interest rate charged is lower.

1.2 **A** Ordinary shares are most risky from the debt holder's perspective – the company can decide whether to pay a dividend, and how much to pay.

Preference shares are next most risky – dividends are only payable if profit is available to pay dividends from.

Trade payables are next because they have to be paid before shareholders – but are typically unsecured.

Finally, banks with fixed and floating charges face least risk.

1.3 **D** Zero coupon bonds are issued at a discount to their redemption value and do not pay any interest.

1.4 **C** Dividend creation benefits the intermediaries' investors, not their customers/borrowers.

1.5 **C** Money markets focus on short-term financial instruments. A corporate bond is a long-term source of finance, hence is a capital market instrument. Certificates of deposit and commercial paper are short-term private sector lending/borrowing. A treasury bill is short-term government borrowing.

1.6 **B** Increased regulation and transparency reduce the actual and perceived risk from the point of view of shareholders, making the shares more attractive and hence more valuable. In addition, listed company shares are naturally more liquid than an equivalent unlisted company, again adding to their value. The process of listing is, therefore, likely to create value.

1.7 **D** Ordinary shares are riskiest as all other investors are preferential to ordinary shareholders. Preference shares are riskier than corporate bonds as preference shares are paid after corporate bonds – bonds imply a contractual right to receive a pre-defined level of return. Treasury bills are short-term government borrowing hence are the lowest risk of all.

1.8 **A** Money markets are markets for short-term capital, not long-term capital.

2 Panda

> **Top tips.** Remember in (b) that the value of rights is **not** the cost of the rights share. (c) emphasises that taking up and selling the rights should have identical effects.

(a) Current total market value = $21m × 16
                                  = $336m

Market value per share = $336m / (60m × 4)
                        = $1.40

Rights issue price = $1.40 × 0.70
                    = $0.98

Theoretical ex-rights price

		$
5 shares @ $1.40		7.00
1 share @ $0.98		0.98
6 shares		7.98

Theoretical ex-rights price = $7.98 / 6
                             = $1.33

(b) **Rights price**

	$
Theoretical ex-rights price	1.33
Cost of rights share	0.98
Value of rights	0.35

(c) **Take up rights issue**

	$
Value of shares after rights issue (10,000 × 6/5 × $1.33)	15,960
Cost of rights (2,000 × $0.98)	(1,960)
	14,000

Sell rights

	$
Value of shares (10,000 × $1.33)	13,300
Sale of rights (2,000 × $0.35)	700
	14,000

Allow rights offer to lapse

	$
Value of shares (10,000 × $1.33)	13,300

If the investor either takes up the rights issue or sells his rights then his wealth will remain the same. The difference is that if he takes up the rights issue he will maintain his relative shareholding – but if he sells his rights his percentage shareholding will fall, although he will gain $700 in cash.

However, if the investor allows the rights to lapse his wealth will decrease by $700.

(d) Panda clearly needs to raise $47.04, million which is why it was decided to make a 1 for 5 rights issue of 48 million additional shares at a price of $0.98. Provided that this amount is raised it could have been done (for example) by issuing 96 million new shares as a two for five rights issue with the issue price at $0.49 per share.

The **price of the issue** and the **number of shares should not be important** in a competitive market as the value of the business will not change and nor will the shareholders' percentage shareholding.

However, the critical factor about the **price of the rights issue** is that it **must be below the market value** at the time of the rights issue. If the rights issue price is higher than the market value then there is no incentive to shareholders to purchase the additional shares and the rights issue will fail. As far as the business is concerned the details of the rights issue, including the price, must be determined a considerable time before the rights issue actually takes place, therefore there is always the risk that the share price might fall in the intervening period.

3 Objective test questions: cost of capital

3.1 **D** 20X9 to 20Y3 covers four years of growth,

so the average annual growth rate $= \sqrt[4]{(423/220)} - 1 = 0.178 = 17.8\%$

$$K_e = \frac{d_0(1+g)}{P_0} + g$$

$$K_e - g = \frac{d_0(1+g)}{P_0}$$

$$P_0 = \frac{d_0(1+g)}{K_e - g}$$

= (423,000 × 1.178) / (0.25 – 0.178) = $6,920,750 for 4 million shares = $1.73 per share

3.2 **A**   g = retention rate × return on investment.

Retention rate = proportion of earnings retained = ($1.50 – $0.5) / $1.50 = 66.7%

Return on new investment = EPS / net assets per share = $1.5 / $6 = 0.25, so 25%

g = 66.7% × 25% = 16.7%

$$K_e = \frac{d_0(1+g)}{P_0} + g$$

$$= \frac{(\$0.50 \times 1.167)}{(\$4.50 - \$0.50)} + 0.167$$ **Note.** Share price given is cum div

= 31%

3.3 **A** $K_d = I(1\text{-}t) / P_o$

The loan note pays interest of $100 nominal × 10% = 10%. Ex-interest market price is $95 – $10 = $85.

Before the tax cut K_d = 10(1 – 0.3) / 85 = 8.2%

After the tax cut K_d = 10(1 – 0.2) / 85 = 9.4%

Decreasing tax reduces tax saved, therefore increases the cost of debt.

3.4 **C**   Conversion value: Future share price = $2.50 × $(1.1)^5$ = $4.03;

so conversion value = 20 × $4.03 = $80.60. The cash alternative = 100 × 1.1 = $110 therefore investors would not convert and redemption value = $110.

Kd = IRR of the after-tax cash flows as follows:

Time	$	DF 10%	Present value 10% ($)	DF 15%	Present value 15% ($)
0	(90)	1	(90)	1	(90)
1-5	10(1 – 0.3) = 7	3.791	26.54	3.352	23.46
5	110	0.621	68.31	0.497	54.67
			4.85		(11.87)

$$IRR = a + \frac{NPV_a}{NPV_a - NPV_b}(b - a)$$

$$= 10\% + \frac{4.85}{(4.85 + 11.87)}(15\% - 10\%)$$

$$= 11.5\%$$

3.5 **C** $K_d = I(1 - T) / P_0 = 13(1 - 0.3) / 90 = 10.11\%$

$V_d = \$7m \times (90/100) = \$6.3m$

$K_e = 12\%$ (given)

$V_e = \$3 \times 10m$ shares $= \$30m$
Note. reserves are included as part of share price

$V_e + V_d = \$6.3m + \$30m = \$36.3m$

$$WACC = \left[\frac{V_e}{V_e + V_d}\right]k_e + \left[\frac{V_d}{V_e + V_d}\right]k_d$$

$= [30/36.3]12\%\quad +\quad (6.3/36.3)10.11\%\quad = 11.7\%$

3.6 **B**   ex-div share price $= \$0.30 - (8\% \times \$0.50) = \$0.26$

$K_p = \$0.50 \times 8\% / \$0.26 = 15.4\%$

Note. dividends are not tax deductible hence no adjustment for corporation tax is required.

3.7 **A** $P_0 = \dfrac{D_0(1+g)}{(r_e - g)}$ Given on the formula sheet

Growth 'g' – Dividends grew from ($\$0.50 - \$0.10=$) $\$0.40$ to $\$0.50$ in three years. This is an average annual growth rate of:

$\$0.40(1+g)^3 = \$0.50$

$(1+g) = \sqrt[3]{(0.5/0.4)}$

$g = 0.077 = 7.7\%$

$P_0 = \dfrac{\$0.50(1+0.077)}{(0.10 - 0.077)} = \$23.41$

3.8 **A**   Statement 1 needs to be assumed: If D_0 is not typical, a better valuation would include the dividend that would have been paid if D_0 were in line with historical trends.

Statement 2 needs to be assumed: Only one rate for growth is included in the formula.

Statement 3 needs to be assumed: Only one cost of equity is included in the formula.

Statement 4 does not need to be assumed: Minority shareholders are entitled to dividends only, hence this valuation technique is, in fact, best suited to a minority shareholding.

3.9 **D**   Corporation tax is not relevant as investors pay market price and they receive the gross dividend.

Redemption value = ($\$100 \times 1.15=$) $\$115$ cash or conversion value $= P_0(1+g)R = (4 \times 1.1^3 \times 25=) \$133.10$ worth of shares.

Investors would opt to convert, hence the redemption value built into market price will be $\$133.10$.

Time		$	Discount factor 10%	Present value
1-3	Interest	9	2.487	22.383
3	Redemption	133.10	0.751	99.958
				122.341

So current market value = $\$122.34$

4 Objective test questions: Financial instruments

4.1 **B** Intangible assets. These do not give rise to a present right to receive cash or other financial assets. The other options are financial instruments.

4.2 **B**

	$'000
Interest years 1-3 (30m × 8% × (0.91 + 0.83 + 0.75))	5,976
Repayment year 3 (30m × 0.75)	22,500
Debt component	28,476
Equity option (β)	1,524
	30,000

4.3 **D**

	$'000
Proceeds (20m – 0.5m)	19,500
Interest 10%	1,950
Interest paid (20m × 5%)	(1,000)
Balance 30 March 20X1	20,450
Interest 10%	2,045
Interest paid	(1,000)
	21,495

4.4 **C** A resource controlled by an entity as a result of past events and from which future economic benefits are expected to flow to the entity

4.5 **C** This is a valid liability.

The licence payment could be avoided by ceasing manufacture.

The fall in value of the investment is a loss chargeable to the statement of profit or loss.

Planned expenditure does not constitute an obligation.

4.6 **C** Disclosure of accounting policies is particularly important when comparing the results and performance of one entity against another which may be applying different policies.

5 Amps

(a) **Redeemable bonds**

The current treatment accounts for interest on a cash basis. IAS 32 classifies these bonds as financial liabilities since they are not derivatives and they are not held for trading purposes. IFRS 9 states that they should be held at amortised cost, using their effective interest rate – which means that the finance charge in any one year is equal to a constant rate based on the carrying amount. This applies the matching concept. Based upon an effective constant rate of interest of 7½% the charge in 20X0 should be $75,000. The difference between the revised charge of $75,000 and the amount paid to debt holders of $40,000 (ie $35,000) should be added to the statement of financial position liability, giving a total liability at 31 December 20X0 of $1,035,000.

(b) **Convertible debentures**

The convertible debentures are compound instruments, as they have characteristics of both debt (the obligation to pay interest and to repay capital) and equity instruments (the right for the holder to have a share). The debt and equity elements should be classified separately as liability and equity as required by IAS 32. The split is based on measuring the debt element using market rates of return at inception for non-convertible debt of the same maturity date and value and treating the equity element as a balancing figure.

Consequently, the debt element of the convertible debentures should be reallocated as a current liability in this case. The annual return would be treated as finance costs until conversion/redemption.

BPP
LEARNING MEDIA

6 JKA

(a) **Factoring of receivables**

The *Framework* principles include a requirement that financial statements should reflect the substance of transactions. To determine whether the trade receivables should be recognised in JKA's or the factor's financial statements, it needs to be established which entity has the risks and benefits associated with the receivables, ie. which can demonstrate that they meet the *Framework*'s definition of an asset.

JKA retains the bad debt risk of the receivables because JKA has to reimburse the factor for any shortfall between the amounts collected and the $3.6 million transferred by the factor to JKA. JKA also has slow movement risk as, under the terms of the agreement, JKA pays interest to the factor on outstanding balances.

JKA also retains some of the benefits associated with the $4 million receivables as the factor has to pay JKA any amounts received in excess of $3.6 million, less any interest.

Therefore, JKA should not have derecognised the $4 million receivables and recorded a loss of $0.4 million in the statement of profit or loss. As they retain the most significant risks and benefits associated with the trade receivables, they need to reinstate the $4 million receivables in their statement of financial position, reverse the $0.4 million loss and record the proceeds of $3.6 million from the factor as a liability. In substance, JKA has received a loan, secured on its trade receivables.

(b) **Factoring of receivables**

DEBIT	Trade receivables	$4,000,000	
CREDIT	Liabilities		$3,600,000
CREDIT	Profit or loss		$400,000

Being correction of accounting treatment for factored receivables.

7 Lis

The right-of-use asset should be capitalised in the statement of financial position. The asset should be depreciated over the shorter of its useful life (five years) and the lease term (six years).

A lease liability will be shown in the statement of financial position increased by interest calculated using the interest rate implicit in the lease, 12.5%, and reduced by lease payments made in advance.

The lease liability will initially be recognised at $65,586. The right-of-use asset will be measured at $84,006 (the initial lease liability of $65,586 + the first payment of $18,420 made at commencement of the lease).

Financial statement extracts

	$
STATEMENT OF PROFIT OR LOSS (extract)	
Depreciation (W1)	16,801
Finance costs (W2)	8,198

	$
STATEMENT OF FINANCIAL POSITION (extract)	
Non-current assets	
Right-of-use asset (W1)	67,205
Non-current liabilities	
Lease liability (W2)	55,364
Current liabilities	
Lease liability (W2) (73,784 – 55,364)	18,420

Workings

1   *Carrying amount of right-of-use asset*

	$
Initial measurement of right-of-use asset	
Initial lease liability	65,586
Rental payment at commencement of lease	18,420
	84,006
Depreciation of asset: $84,006/5 years useful life	16,801
Carrying amount at year end ($84,006 − $16,801)	67,205

The asset is depreciated over the shorter of its useful life (five years) and lease term (six years).

2   *Lease liability*

		$
1.1.X3	Initial measurement of lease liability	65,586
1.1.X3 − 31.12.X3	Interest at 12.5% ($65,586 × 12.5%)	8,198
31.12.X3	**Lease liability c/d**	**73,784**
1.1.X4	Payment in advance	(18,420)
1.1.X4	**Lease liability c/d after next instalment**	**55,364**

The interest element ($8,198) of the current liability can also be shown separately as interest payable.

Tutorial note. If the lease payments were in arrears, instead of in advance, the calculation of the lease liability would differ to that given above. The initial lease liability would be higher at $74,672, being six payments of $18,420 discounted using a discount rate of 12.5%, as the first lease payment, excluded from the answer above because it is paid at commencement of the lease, would be included. The lease liability would then be calculated as follows:

Lease payments are made in arrears:

		$
1.1.X1	Lease liability (present value of future lease payments)	74,672
1.1.X1 − 31.12.X1	Interest at 12.5%	9,334
31.12.X1	Instalment in arrears	(18,420)
31.12.X1	**Liability carried down**	
1.1.X2 − 31.12.X2	Interest at 12.5%	8,198
31.12.X2	Instalment in arrears	(18,420)
31.12.X2	**Liability due in more than 1 year**	**55,364**

8 Objective test questions: Provisions, contingent liabilities and contingent assets

8.1   **D**   Loss of the case is not 'probable', so no provision is made, but the legal costs will have to be paid so should be provided for.

8.2   **A** $2 million should be provided for and capitalised as part of the cost of the mine. It will then be depreciated over the useful life.

8.3   **D**

	$m
$2 million × 15%	0.3
$6 million × 5%	0.3
	0.6

8.4   **D**   The cost of the overhaul will be capitalised when it takes place. No obligation exists before the overhaul is carried out. The other options would all give rise to valid provisions.

9 Objective test questions: Deferred tax

9.1   **A**   Item 2 consists of permanent differences; all the rest are temporary differences.

9.2   **D**   All four items have a carrying amount equal to their tax base.

9.3   **B**   IAS 12 states that deferred tax assets and liabilities should not be discounted.

9.4   **D**

	$
Taxable temporary differences b/f	850,000
Depreciation for tax purposes	500,000
Depreciation charged in the financial statements	(450,000)
Revaluation surplus	250,000
Taxable temporary differences c/f	1,150,000
Deferred tax at 30%	345,000

10 Objective test questions: Share-based payment

10.1   **B**   Expense recognised at 31 December 20X5 = (610 × 500 × $4.30 × 1/3) = $437,167. The granting of share appreciation rights represent a cash-settled share-based payment transaction, so the fair value of liability must be remeasured at each reporting date.

10.2   **A**   Share options are equity-settled, so credit goes to other reserves within equity. The directors' services do not qualify as assets, so the debit is taken to staff costs within statement of profit or loss. The amount recognised is calculated as 500 options × 8 directors × $12 × 1/2 years = $24,000.

10.3   **B**   As this is a cash-settled payment, we credit liability, not equity. Since the payment relates to the employees' service, it is an expense, not an asset. Only the fair value of the share appreciation right is relevant, and the total cost must be spread over the three years of service to which the expense relates.

25 shares × 3,500 employees × 55% × $18 ×1/3 = $288,750

11 Share-based payment

(a)   **Accounting entries**

31.12.X1 $

DEBIT	Staff costs	188,000	
CREDIT	Other reserves (within equity)		188,000

((800 – 95) × 200 × $4 × 1/3)

Being share-based payment expense for the year ended 31 December 20X1

31.12.X2

DEBIT	Staff costs (W1)	201,333	
CREDIT	Other reserves (within equity)		201,333

Being share-based payment expense for the year ended 31 December 20X2

31.12.X3

DEBIT	Staff costs (W2)	202,667	
CREDIT	Other reserves (within equity)		202,667

Being share-based payment expense for the year ended 31 December 20X3

Issue of shares:

DEBIT	Cash (740 × 200 × $1.50)	222,000	
DEBIT	Other reserves (within equity)	592,000	
CREDIT	Share capital (740 × 200 × $1)		148,000
CREDIT	Share premium (balancing figure)		666,000

Being share issue

Workings

1   *Equity at 31.12.X2*

Equity b/d	188,000
∴ P/L charge	201,333
Equity c/d ((800 – 70) × 200 × $4 × 2/3)	389,333

2   *Equity at 31.12.X3*

Equity b/d	389,333
∴ P/L charge	202,667
Equity c/d ((800 – 40 – 20) × 200 × $4 × 3/3)	592,000

(b)   **Cash-settled share-based payment**

If J&B had offered cash payments based on the value of the shares at vesting date rather than options, the key differences would be recognising a liability in the statement of financial position rather than equity (reflecting the obligation to employees) and measuring it at the fair value at the year end date rather than the grant date (to reflect the best estimate of what will be paid).

In each of the three years a liability would be shown in the statement of financial position representing the expected amount payable based on the following:

No of employees estimated at the year end to be entitled to rights at the vesting date	×	Number of rights each	×	Fair value of each right at year end	×	Cumulative proportion of vesting period elapsed

The movement in the liability would be charged to the statement of profit or loss representing further entitlements received during the year and adjustments to expectations accrued in previous years.

The liability would continue to be adjusted (resulting in a statement of profit or loss charge) for changes in the fair value of the right over the period between when the rights become fully vested and when they are subsequently exercised. It would then be reduced for cash payments as the rights are exercised.

12 Objective test questions: Revenue

12.1   **C**   Sales of $150,000 on 30 September 20X4. The amount invoiced to and received from the customer was $180,000, which included $30,000 for ongoing servicing work to be done by Repro Co over the next two years.

The amount to recognise in revenue is $150,000 as the servicing amount of $30,000 has not yet been earned. This would be recognised as deferred income.

12.2   **A** $439

Year 1			$
Laptop (W)			158
Broadband (562 (W) /2)			281
			439

Working			
Laptop	200	22%	158
Broadband (30 × 12 × 2)	720	78%	562
	920	100%	720

12.3   **B**   Recognising revenue when a performance obligation is satisfied.

12.4   **B**   BX is not exposed to credit risk for the amount due from the customer

The other options would all suggest that BX was the principal.

13 Objective test questions: Basic groups

13.1 **D** There is now no basis on which a subsidiary may be excluded from consolidation.

13.2 **C** A and B give rise to a subsidiary relationship, D is part of the definition of control.

13.3 **B** A subsidiary may prepare additional statements up to the group reporting date and, where statements for a different date are used, adjustments should be made for significant transactions. The allowable gap between reporting dates is three months, not five.

13.4 **B** The present value (of the future cash flows that the asset is expected to generate) measures present value, not fair value. The other items would be considered in determining fair value.

13.5 **B**

	$
Fair value at acquisition (200,000 × 30% × $1.75)	105,000
Share of post-acquisition retained earnings ((750 – 450) × 30%)	90,000
Depreciation on fair value adjustment ((250 / 40) × 30%)	(1,875)
	193,125

13.6 **C** ($1.2 million / 8 × 4/12) × 80% = $40,000

The adjustment will reduce depreciation over the next eight years, so it will *increase* retained earnings.

13.7 **A**

	$'000
Shares (18m × 2/3 × $5.75)	69,000
Deferred consideration (18m × $2.42 × $1/1.1^2$)	36,000
	105,000

13.8 **D**

	$	$
Consideration transferred		800,000
Fair value of non-controlling interest		220,000
		1,020,000
Fair value of net assets:		
Shares	100,000	
Retained earnings	570,000	
Revaluation surplus	150,000	
Intangible	90,000	
		(910,000)
		110,000

14 Group financial statements

Tutorial note. This is a general question to get you thinking about the nature of a group. The question strongly hints that there *are* limitations to group financial statements.

The objective of annual financial statements is to help shareholders exercise control over their company by providing information about how its affairs have been conducted. The shareholders of a parent company would not be given sufficient information from the financial statements of the parent company on its own, because not enough would be known about the nature of the assets, income and profits of all the subsidiary companies in which the parent company has invested. The primary purpose of group financial statements is to provide a true and fair view of the position and earnings of the parent company group as a whole, from the standpoint of the shareholders in the parent company.

However, group financial statements can be argued to have certain limitations.

(a)   Group financial statements may be misleading.

　　(i)   The solvency (liquidity) of one company may hide the insolvency of another.

　　(ii)   The profit of one company may conceal the losses of another.

　　(iii)   They imply that group companies will meet each others' debts (this is certainly not true: a parent company may watch creditors of an insolvent subsidiary go unpaid without having to step in).

(b)   There may be some difficulties in defining the group or 'entity' of companies, although company law and accounting standards have removed many of the grey areas here.

(c)   Where a group consists of widely diverse companies in different lines of business, a set of group financial statements may obscure much important detail unless supplementary information about each part of the group's business is provided.

15 Putney and Wandsworth

CONSOLIDATED STATEMENT OF FINANCIAL POSITION AS AT 31 DECEMBER 20X5

	$
Non-current assets	
Property, plant & equipment (135,000 + 60,000)	195,000
Goodwill (W2)	1,250
	196,250
Current assets (62,000 + 46,000)	108,000
	304,250
Equity attributable to the owners of the parent	
Share capital	50,000
Revaluation surplus (W3)	63,500
Retained earnings (W4)	124,750
	238,250
Non-controlling interests (W5)	8,000
	246,250
Non-current liabilities (14,000 + 12,000)	26,000
Current liabilities (18,000 + 14,000)	32,000
	304,250

Workings

1   *Group structure*

　　Putney

　　　　1.1.X1

　　Wandsworth Pre-acq'n ret'd earnings $10,000

2   *Goodwill*

	$	$
Consideration transferred		25,000
Non-controlling interest at acquisition (25,000 × 10%)		2,500
Net assets at acquisition:		
Share capital	15,000	
Retained earnings at acquisition	10,000	
		(25,000)
Goodwill at acquisition		2,500
Impairment losses to date		(1,250)
Goodwill at 31.12.X5		1,250

3   *Revaluation surplus*

	Putney	*Wandsworth*
Per question	50,000	15,000
Pre-acquisition	–	(0)
	50,000	15,000
Wandsworth – share of post-acquisition revaluation surplus		
(15,000 × 90%)	13,500	
	63,500	

4   *Retained earnings*

	Putney	*Wandsworth*
Per question	90,000	50,000
Pre-acquisition	–	(10,000)
	90,000	40,000
Wandsworth – share of post-acquisition earnings		
(40,000 × 90%)	36,000	
Less: goodwill impairment losses to date	(1,250)	
	124,750	

5   *Non-controlling interests*

NCI at acquisition (W2)	2,500
Share of post-acquisition revaluation surplus (15,000 (W3) × 10%)	1,500
Share of post-acquisition earnings (40,000 (W3) × 10%)	4,000
	8,000

16 Balmes and Aribau

BALMES GROUP

CONSOLIDATED STATEMENT OF FINANCIAL POSITION AS AT 30 JUNE 20X3

	$'000
Non-current assets	
Property, plant & equipment (97,300 + 34,400 + (W6) 1,400)	133,100
Goodwill (W2)	2,800
Other intangible assets (5,100 + 1,200)	6,300
	142,200
Current assets	
Inventories (43,400 + 14,300)	57,700
Trade and other receivables (36,800 + 17,400)	54,200
Cash and cash equivalents	700
	112,600
	254,800
Equity attributable to the owners of the parent	
Share capital	50,000
General reserve (W3)	5,100
Retained earnings (W4)	122,040
	177,140
Non-controlling interests (W5)	9,760
	186,900
Non-current liabilities	
Loan notes (10,000 + 4,000)	14,000
Current liabilities	
Trade payables (28,400 + 15,700)	44,100
Income tax payable (7,300 + 2,400)	9,700
Bank overdraft	100
	53,900
	254,800

Workings

1   *Group structure*

Balmes

|
|

Aribau

1.7.X1   80%

Pre-acquisition retained earnings = $25m
Pre-acquisition general reserve = $2m

2   *Goodwill*

	$'000	$'000
Consideration transferred		28,500
Non-controlling interests at acquisition (fair value)		7,000
Net fair value of identifiable assets acquired:		
Share capital	5,000	
General reserve	2,000	
Retained earnings	24,000	
Fair value adjustments (W6)	1,500	
		(32,500)
		3,000
Impairment losses to date		(200)
		2,800

3 *General reserve*

	Balmes $'000	Aribau $'000
Per question	4,300	3,000
Pre-acquisition		(2,000)
		1,000
Aribau – post-acquisition general reserve (1,000 × 80%)	800	
	5,100	

4 *Retained earnings*

	Balmes $'000	Aribau $'000
Per question	118,800	37,100
Revaluation gain on investment in Aribau cancelled on consolidation (35,500 – 28,500)	(7,000)	
Fair value adjustments movement (W6)		(100)
Pre-acquisition retained earnings		(24,000)
		13,000
Aribau – share of post-acquisition earnings (13,000 × 80%)	10,400	
Less: Group share of goodwill impairment losses to date (80% × 200 (W2))	(160)	
	122,040	

5 *Non-controlling interest*

	$'000
Non-controlling interests at acquisition (W2)	7,000
Share of post-acquisition general reserve (1,000 (W3) × 20%)	200
Share of post-acquisition earnings (13,000 (W4) × 20%)	2,600
NCI share of impairment losses on goodwill (200 (W2) × 20%)	(40)
	9,760

6 *Fair value adjustments*

	At acquisition date $'000	Movement $'000	At y/e date $'000
Land (5,000 – 4,500)	500		500
Buildings ((14,000 – 5,000) – (12,500 – 4,500))	1,000	(100)*	900
	1,500	(100)	1,400

*Extra depreciation ($1,000,000 × 2/20)

17 Reprise

REPRISE GROUP – CONSOLIDATED STATEMENT OF FINANCIAL POSITION AS AT 31 MARCH 20X4

	$'000
Non-current assets	
Land and buildings	3,350.0
Plant and equipment (1,010 + 2,210)	3,220.0
Motor vehicles (510 + 345)	855.0
Goodwill (W2)	826.0
	8,251.0
Current assets	
Inventories (890 + 352 – (W5) 7.2)	1,234.8
Trade receivables (1,372 + 514 – 39 – (W6) 36)	1,811.0
Cash and cash equivalents (89 + 51 + 39)	179.0
	3,224.8
	11,475.8
Equity attributable to owners of the parent	
Share capital	1,000.0
Retained earnings (W3)	5,257.3
Revaluation surplus	2,500.0
	8,757.3
Non-controlling interests (W4)	896.5
	9,653.8
Non-current liabilities	
10% debentures	500.0
Current liabilities	
Trade payables (996 + 362 – (W6) 36)	1,322.0
	11,475.8

Workings

1 Group structure

R

$\Big|$ 75% ∴ non-controlling interests = 25%

E Pre-acquisition retained earnings = $1,044,000

2 *Goodwill*

	$'000	$'000
Consideration transferred		2,000
Non-controlling interests (at fair value)		
(125,000 shares × $4.40)		550
Net assets at acquisition as represented by:		
Share capital	500	
Retained earnings	1,044	
		(1,544)
		1,006
Impairment losses to date		(180)
		826

3   *Consolidated retained earnings*

	Reprise $'000	Encore $'000
Per question	4,225	2,610
PUP (W5)	(7.2)	
Pre-acquisition retained earnings		(1,044)
		1,566
Group share of post-acquisition retained earnings:		
Encore (1,566 × 75%)	1,174.5	
Group share of impairment losses (180 (W2) × 75%)	(135)	
	5,257.3	

4   *Non-controlling interests*

	$'000
NCI at acquisition (W2)	550
NCI share of post-acquisition retained earnings ((W3) 1,566 × 25%)	391.5
NCI share of impairment losses (180 (W2) × 25%)	(45)
	896.5

5   *Unrealised profit on inventories*

Reprise $\longrightarrow$ Encore

Unrealised profit included in inventories is:

$$\$31,200 \times \frac{30}{130} = \$7,200$$

DEBIT ($\downarrow$) Retained earnings of Reprise $7,200

CREDIT ($\downarrow$) Inventories $7,200

6   *Trade receivables/trade payables*

Intragroup balance of $75,000 is reduced to $36,000 once cash-in-transit of $39,000 is followed through to its ultimate destination.

18 Objective test questions: Associates and joint arrangements

18.1 **A**

	$m
Cost (75m × $1.60)	120
Share of post-acquisition retained earnings (100 – 20) × 30%	24
	144

18.2 **C**   The group's share of the associate's profit after tax is recorded as a one-line entry. Option A would be correct for a subsidiary, not an associate. The dividends received from the associate are all that is recorded in the individual entity financial statements of the parent, but in the consolidated financial statements this is replaced by the group share of profit after tax.

18.3 **A**

	$'000
Cost of investment	2,500
Share of post-acquisition profit (6,400 – 5,300) × 30%	330
PUP (700 × 30% ×30%)	(63)
	2,767

18.4 **B**

	$'000
Cost of investment	10,000
Share of post-acquisition profit (3,000 × 8/12) − 1,000) × 35%	350
Impairment	(500)
	9,850

18.5 **D** Joint ventures, like associates, are accounted for using the equity method. Joint operations are accounted for by including the investor's share of assets, liabilities, income and expenses as per the contractual arrangement. Goodwill must always be capitalised and reviewed for impairment annually.

18.6 **B** If the parties with joint control have rights to the net assets of the arrangement, then the arrangement is a joint venture. A joint operation may, in certain cases, be structured through a separate entity.

19 Hever

CONSOLIDATED STATEMENT OF FINANCIAL POSITION AS AT 31 DECEMBER 20X4

	$'000
Non-current assets	
Property, plant & equipment (370 + 190 + (W7) 45)	605
Goodwill (W2)	8
Investment in associate (W3)	165
	778
Current assets	
Inventories (160 + 100 − (W6) 1.5)	258.5
Trade receivables (170 + 90)	260
Cash (50 + 40)	90
	608.5
	1,386.5
Equity attributable to owners of the parent	
Share capital	200
Share premium reserve	100
Retained earnings (W4)	758.5
	1,058.5
Non-controlling interests (W5)	168
	1,226.5
Current liabilities	
Trade payables (100 + 60)	160
	1,386.5

Workings

1   *Group structure*

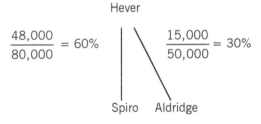

Hever

$$\frac{48,000}{80,000} = 60\% \qquad \frac{15,000}{50,000} = 30\%$$

Spiro   Aldridge

Pre-acq'n reserves = $20k   = $150k

∴ In the absence of information to the contrary, Spiro is a subsidiary, and Aldridge an associate of Hever.

2   *Goodwill on consolidation – Spiro*

	$'000	$'000
Consideration transferred		128
Non-controlling interests (at 'full' fair value)		90
Net assets at acquisition:		
Share capital	80	
Share premium	80	
Retained earnings	20	
Fair value adjustments (W7)	30	
		(210)
Goodwill arising on consolidation		8

3   *Investment in associate*

	$'000
Cost of associate	90
Share of post-acquisition retained reserves (W4)	75
	165

4   *Retained earnings*

	Hever $'000	Spiro $'000	Aldridge $'000
Per question	568	200	400
PUP (W6)	(1.5)	–	–
Fair value movement (W7)		15	
Pre-acquisition retained earnings		(20)	(150)
		195	250
Group share of post-acquisition ret'd earnings:			
Spiro (195 × 60%)	117		
Aldridge (250 × 30%)	75		
	758.5		

5   *Non-controlling interests*

	$'000
NCI at acquisition (W2)	90
NCI share of post-acquisition ret'd earnings ((W4) 195 × 40%)	78
	168

6   *Unrealised profit on inventories*

Hever ⟶ Spiro

Mark-up: $16,000 – $10,000 = $6,000 ∴ PUP = ¼ in inventory × $6,000 = $1,500

↓ Hever's retained earnings $1,500

↓ Inventories $1,500

7   *Fair values – adjustment to net assets*

	At acquisition	Movement	At year end
Property, plant and equipment	50	(5)	45
Inventories	(20)	20	0
	30	15	45

20 Bayonet

BAYONET GROUP
CONSOLIDATED STATEMENT OF FINANCIAL POSITION AS AT 31 DECEMBER 20X9

	$'000
Non-current assets	
Property, plant and equipment (14,500 + 12,140 + 17,500)	44,140
Goodwill (W2)	3,580
	47,720
Current assets	
Inventories (6,300 + 2,100 + 450)	8,850
Trade receivables (4,900 + 2,000 + 2,320)	9,220
Cash (500 + 1,440 + 515)	2,455
	20,525
	68,245
Equity attributable to owners of the parent	
Share capital – 50c ordinary shares	5,000
Retained earnings (W3)	40,680
	45,680
Non-controlling interests (W4)	12,600
	58,280
Current liabilities (5,700 + 2,280 + 1,985)	9,965
	68,245

Workings

1   *Group structure*

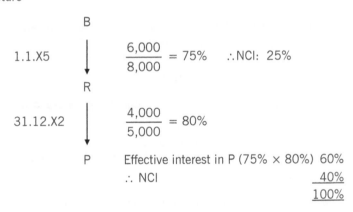

B

1.1.X5 $\frac{6,000}{8,000}$ = 75%   ∴NCI: 25%

R

31.12.X2 $\frac{4,000}{5,000}$ = 80%

P   Effective interest in P (75% × 80%) 60%
    ∴ NCI   40%
    100%

2   *Goodwill*

		Rifle	Pistol	
	$'000	$'000	$'000	$'000
Consideration transferred		10,000	(9,000 × 75%)	6,750
Non-controlling interests (at fair value)		3,230		4,600
Fair value of identifiable net assets at acq'n:				
Share capital	4,000		2,500	
Pre-acquisition retained earnings	8,000		6,500	
		(12,000)		(9,000)
		1,230		2,350
			3,580	

BPP
LEARNING MEDIA

3   *Retained earnings*

	Bayonet $'000	Rifle $'000	Pistol $'000
Per question	25,500	20,400	16,300
Retained earnings at acquisition		(8,000)	(6,500)
		12,400	9,800
Group share of post-acquisition ret'd earnings:			
Rifle (12,400 × 75%)	9,300		
Pistol (9,800 × 60%)	5,880		
	40,680		

4   *Non-controlling interests*

	Rifle $'000	Pistol $'000
NCI at acquisition (W2)	3,230	4,600
NCI share of post-acquisition ret'd earnings:		
Rifle ((W3) 12,400 × 25%)	3,100	
Pistol ((W3) 9,800 × 40%)		3,920
Less: NCI share of investment in Pistol (9,000 × 25%)	(2,250)	
	4,080	8,520
		12,600

21 Objective test questions: Changes in group structure

21.1 **A**

Non-controlling interests

	$'000
NCI at acquisition (($10m share capital + $6m retained earnings) × 20%)	3,200
NCI share of post acq'n reserves to disposal (($8.9m − $6m) × 20%)	580
NCI at disposal	3,780
Increase in NCI on disposal ($3,780k × 20%/20%)	3,780

Adjustment to parent's equity on disposal of 20% of Dopiaza

	$'000
Fair value of consideration received	4,400
Less increase in NCI in net assets and goodwill at disposal (W3)	(3,780)
	620

The $620,000 adjustment is taken to the parent's equity. As control has not been lost, no profit or loss on disposal will be recognised.

21.2 **A**

	$
Fair value of consideration paid	(135,000)
Decrease in NCI in net assets on acquisition (20/40 × 133,000 (W))	66,500
	(68,500)
Workings: NCI at 28.2.20X7	$
NCI b/fwd at 1.8.20X6	127,000
Profits attributable to NCI to 28.2.20X7 (30,000 × 6/12 × 40%)	6,000
	133,000

The complete journal to reflect the transaction would be:

DR Non-controlling interests $66,500
DR Parent's equity $68,500
CR Cash $135,000

21.3 **B**

	$m	$m
Consideration transferred		960
NCI (per question)		420
Fair value of previously held equity interest		160
Fair value of identifiable assets acquired and liabilities assumed		
Share capital	600	
Retained earnings	800	
		(1,400)
		140

22 Objective test questions: Indirect control of subsidiaries

22.1 **D**   NCI share of the profit after tax of Tag ((5,000 – 1,000) × 25%) Plus share of indirect associate's profit after tax (4000 – 1000 – 50 depreciation) × 40% = 1,180 × 25% Note that Rag controls Tag's investment of 40% of Bobtail.

However, it only owns 30% (75% × 40%) in this indirect associate.

The non-controlling interests in Tag own 10% (25% × 40%). As non-controlling interests are measured using the proportionate method, no goodwill or impairments are allocated to the NCI.

22.2 **B**

	$'000
Apricot	120
Blackcurrant	110
Date	90
	320

Apricot does not control Cranberry. Cranberry's assets should therefore not be consolidated in the group financial statements.

22.3 **B**   Blue Co and Green Co are clearly both subsidiaries. Because Red Co controls Blue Co and Green Co, it also controls 55% of the shares in Yellow Co (30% through Blue Co and 25% through Green Co).

23 Objective test questions: Foreign subsidiaries

23.1 **B**   Subsidiary B is clearly an extension of Parent's own activities and therefore it almost certainly has the same functional currency as the parent.

23.2 **A** $1,902,000

	$'000	$'000
Rat		1,900
Mole: closing net assets (960 @ 2.5)	384	
opening net assets (720 @ 2.0)	(360)	
	24	
Group share (75%)		18
Retranslation of goodwill (160 @ 2 – 160 @ 2.5)		(16)
		1,902

	U"000
Goodwill	
Cost of investment (350 × 2)	700
Net assets acquired (75% × 720)	(540)
	160

24 Objective test questions: Consolidated statements of changes in equity

24.1 **C**   The non-controlling interest share of after-tax profits in subsidiaries is shown on the face of the statement of profit or loss. Down to profit after tax, all of the results of the subsidiary are included, in order to show the results arising under group control. Then the non-controlling interest is deducted at that point to leave the profits which are owned by the group.

24.2 **B**   The profits attributable to non-controlling interests, adjusted for mid-year acquisition, is calculated as 17% × 6/12 × $330,880 = $28,125

24.3 **D**   It is the only one of the four options that is a gain or loss accounted for as 'other comprehensive income'.

25 Fallowfield and Rusholme

CONSOLIDATED STATEMENT OF PROFIT OR LOSS AND OTHER COMPREHENSIVE INCOME
FOR THE YEAR ENDED 30 JUNE 20X8

	$
Revenue (403,400 + 193,000 – 40,000)	556,400
Cost of sales (201,400 + 92,600 – 40,000 + (W7) 4,000)	(258,000)
Gross profit	298,400
Distribution costs (16,000 + 14,600)	(30,600)
Administrative expenses (24,250 + 17,800)	(42,050)
Profit before tax	225,750
Income tax expense (61,750 + 22,000)	(83,750)
Profit for the year	142,000
Other comprehensive income (net of tax) (20,000 + 5,000)	25,000
Total comprehensive income for the year	167,000
Profit attributable to:	
Owners of the parent	125,200
Non-controlling interests (W2)	16,800
	142,000
Total comprehensive income attributable to:	
Owners of the parent	148,200
Non-controlling interests (W2)	18,800
	167,000

Tutorial note. Intragroup dividend income from Rusholme has been cancelled out on consolidation.

STATEMENT OF CHANGES IN EQUITY

	Equity attributable to owners of the parent $	Non-controlling interests (W4/W6) $	Total equity $
Balance at 30 June 20X7	270,000 (W3)	48,000	318,000
Total comprehensive income for the year	148,200	18,800	167,000
Dividends (NCI: 25,000 × 40%)	(40,000)	(10,000)	(50,000)
Balance at 30 June 20X8	378,200 (W5)	56,800	435,000

Workings

1   *Group structure*

Fallowfield

| 60%   3 years ago

Rusholme   Pre-acquisition reserves: $16,000

2   *Non-controlling interests (SPLOCI)*

	Profit for the year	Total comprehensive income
	$	$
Per question	46,000	51,000
Less: PUP (W7)	(4,000)	(4,000)
	42,000	47,000
NCI share 40%	16,800	18,800

3   *Equity brought forward*

	Fallowfield	Rusholme
	$	$
Per question	243,000	101,000
Pre-acquisition equity (SC 40,000 + Res 16,000)	–	(56,000)
	243,000	45,000
Rusholme – share of post-acquisition (45,000 × 60%)	27,000	
	270,000	

4   *Non-controlling interest brought forward (SOFP)*

	$
NCI at acquisition (at fair value)	30,000
Share of post-acquisition retained earnings (b/f) (45,000 (W3) × 40%)	18,000
	48,000

5   *Equity carried forward*

	Fallowfield	Rusholme
	$	$
Per question	338,000	127,000
PUP (W7)	–	(4,000)
Pre-acquisition equity (SC 40,000 + Res 16,000)		(56,000)
	338,000	67,000
Rusholme – share of post-acquisition retained earnings (67,000 × 60%)	40,200	
	378,200	

6   *Non-controlling interest carried forward (SOFP)*

	$
NCI at acquisition (at fair value)	30,000
Share of post-acquisition retained earnings (c/f) (67,000 (W5) × 40%)	26,800
	56,800

7   *Provision for unrealised profit*

Rusholme → Fallowfield

PUP = $40,000 × ½ in inventories × 25/125 mark up = $4,000

↑ Rusholme's cost of sales (& adjust NCI (SPLOCI) in (W2))

↓ Rusholme's retained earnings (in (W5))

↓ Group inventories (in SOFP)

26 Panther Group

PANTHER GROUP
CONSOLIDATED STATEMENT OF PROFIT OR LOSS AND OTHER COMPREHENSIVE INCOME
FOR THE YEAR ENDED 31 DECEMBER 20X4

	$'000
Revenue [22,800 + (4,300 × 6/12) – 320]	24,630
Cost of sales [13,600 + (2,600 × 6/12) – 320 + (W3) 10 + (W5) 5]	(14,595)
Gross profit	10,035
Distribution costs (2,900 + (500 × 6/12))	(3,150)
Administrative expenses (1,800 + (300 × 6/12))	(1,950)
Finance costs [200 + (40 × 6/12) – (W4) 20 cancellation]	(200)
Finance income (50 – (W4) 20 cancellation)	30
Profit before tax	4,765
Income tax expense [1,300 + (220 × 6/12)]	(1,410)
Profit for the year	3,355
Other comprehensive income for the year, net of tax [1,600 + (180 × 6/12)]	1,690
Total comprehensive income for the year	5,045
Profit attributable to:	
Owners of the parent (3,355 – 112)	3,229
Non-controlling interests (W2)	126
	3,355
Total comprehensive income attributable to:	
Owners of the parent (5,045 – 162)	4,883
Non-controlling interests (W2)	162
	5,045

CONSOLIDATED STATEMENT OF CHANGES IN EQUITY
FOR THE YEAR ENDED 31 DECEMBER 20X4 (EXTRACT)

	$'000 *Reserves*
Balance at 1 January 20X4 (Panther only)	12,750
Dividend paid	(900)
Total comprehensive income for the year	4,883
Balance at 31 December 20X4 (W6)	16,733

Workings

1   *Group structure and timeline*

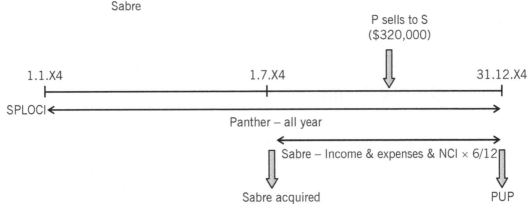

2   *Non-controlling interests*

	PFY $'000	TCI $'000
Per Q (640 × 6/12) / (820 × 6/12)	320	410
Additional depreciation on fair value adjustment (W5)	(5)	(5)
	315	405
NCI share	× 40%	× 40%
	= 126	= 162

3   *Unrealised profit on intragroup trading*

$$\text{Panther to Sabre} = \$60{,}000 \times \frac{20\%}{120\%} = \$10{,}000$$

Adjust cost of sales in books of seller (Panther).

4   *Interest on intragroup loan*

$\$800{,}000 \times 5\% \times 6/12 = \$20{,}000$

Cancel in books of Panther and Sabre.

5   *Fair value adjustments*

	At acq'n 1.7.X4 $'000	Movement $'000	At year end 31.12.X4 $'000
Property	200	(200/20 × 6/12) (5)	195

6   Group reserves carried forward (proof)

	Panther $'000	Sabre $'000
Reserves per question	16,500	3,300
PUP (W3)	(10)	
Fair value movement (W5)		(5)
Pre-acquisition reserves		
[2,480 + (820 × 6/12)]		(2,890)
		405
Group share of post-acquisition reserves:		
Sabre (405 × 60%)	243	
	16,733	

27 SM Group

SM GROUP – CONSOLIDATED STATEMENT OF CHANGES IN EQUITY

	Equity attributable to owners of the parent $'000	Non-controlling interests $'000	Total $'000
Balance at 1 July 20X4 (balancing figure)	537,500	32,500	570,000
Issue of shares	25,000	–	25,000
Total comprehensive income for the year (W4)	96,750	9,750	106,500
Dividends (25% × $10m)	(16,000)	(2,500)	(18,500)
Balance at 30 June 20X5 (W5) / (W6)	643,250	39,750	683,000

Workings

1   *Group structure*

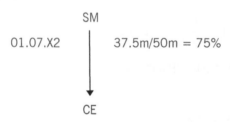

SM
01.07.X2   37.5m/50m = 75%

CE

Pre-acq'n reserves = $80m – $50m = $30m

2   *Unrealised profit*

CE →SM

PUP = $15m × 1/3 in inventory × 25/125 mark-up = $1m
DEBIT   CE's cost of sales (and CE's retained earnings) $1m
CREDIT   Inventories $1m

3   *Intragroup dividend*

Intragroup dividend income = 75% × $10m = $7.5m → Cancel out of SM's profit/total comprehensive income

4   *Consolidated total comprehensive income (TCI) for the year*

	$'000
Consolidated TCI (($75m – $7.5m (W3)) + ($40m – $1m (W2)))	106,500
Total comprehensive income attributable to:	
Owners of parent (balancing figure)	96,750
Non-controlling interests ($40m – $1m (W2)) × 25%	9,750
	106,500

5   *Consolidated equity at 30 June 20X5*

	SM	CE
	$'000	$'000
Per question	584,000	160,000
PUP (W2)		(1,000)
Pre-acquisition equity		(80,000)
		79,000
Share of CE post-acquisition reserves (75% × $79m)	59,250	
	643,250	

6   *Non-controlling interests at 30 June 20X5*

	$'000
NCI at acquisition (25% × $80m)	20,000
NCI share of post-acquisition reserves ($79m (W5) × 25%)	19,750
	39,750

7   *Proof of consolidated equity at 1 July 20X4*

	SM	CE
	$'000	$'000
Per question	500,000	130,000
Pre-acquisition equity		(80,000)
		50,000
Share of CE post-acquisition (75% × $50m)	37,500	
	537,500	

8   *Proof of non-controlling interests at 1 July 20X4*

	$'000
NCI at acquisition (W6)	20,000
NCI share of post-acquisition reserves ($50m (W7) x 25%)	12,500
	32,500

28 Holmes and Deakin

(a) HOLMES CO
CONSOLIDATED STATEMENT OF PROFIT OR LOSS AND OTHER COMPREHENSIVE INCOME
FOR THE YEAR ENDED 31 MAY 20X3

	$'000
Revenue (1,000 + 540)	1,540
Cost of sales and operating expenses (800 + 430)	(1,230)
Profit before tax	310
Income tax expense (90 + 60)	(150)
Profit for the year	160
Other comprehensive income (net of tax) (20 + 10)	30
Total comprehensive income for the year	190

Profit attributable to:	
Owners of the parent β	150
Non-controlling interest $(50 \times \dfrac{9}{12} \times 15\%) + (50 \times \dfrac{3}{12} \times 35\%)$	10
	160

Total comprehensive income attributable to:	
Owners of the parent β	178
Non-controlling interest $(60 \times \dfrac{9}{12} \times 15\%) + (60 \times \dfrac{3}{12} \times 35\%)$	12
	190

(b) HOLMES CO
CONSOLIDATED STATEMENT OF FINANCIAL POSITION AS AT 31 May 20X3

	$'000
Non-current assets	
Property, plant and equipment (535 + 178)	713
Goodwill (W2)	80
	793
Current assets	
Inventories (320 + 190)	510
Trade receivables (250 + 175)	425
Cash (80 + 89)	169
	1,104
	1,897
Equity attributable to owners of the parent	
Share capital $1 ordinary shares	500
Retained earnings (W3)	507.5
	1,007.5
Non-controlling interest (W4)	157.5
	1,165
Current liabilities	
Trade payables (295 + 171)	466
Income tax payable (80 + 60)	140
Provisions (95 + 31)	126
	732
	1,897

(c) STATEMENT OF CHANGES IN EQUITY (ATTRIBUTABLE TO OWNERS OF THE PARENT)
AT 31 MAY 20X3

	$'000
Balance at 31.5.20X2 (500 + (W6) 256.5)	756.5
Total comprehensive income for the year	178
Adjustment to parent's equity on disposal (W5)	73
Balance at 31.5.20X3 (500 + (W3) 507.5)	1,007.5

Workings

1 Group structure and timeline

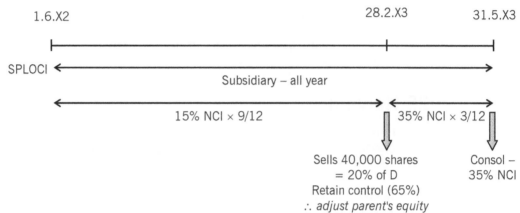

Sells 40,000 shares
= 20% of D
Retain control (65%)
∴ *adjust parent's equity*

Consol –
35% NCI

2 *Goodwill*

	$'000	$'000
Consideration transferred		255
Non-controlling interest (fair value)		45
Fair value of identifiable net assets at acquisition:		
Share capital	200	
Pre-acquisition retained earnings	20	
		(220)
		80

3 *Group reserves at 31 May 20X3*

	Holmes $'000	Deakin 85% $'000	Deakin 65% ret'd $'000
Per question/at date of disposal $(170 - (60 \times \frac{3}{12}))$	310	155	170
Adjustment to parent's equity on disposal (W5)	73		
Reserves at acquisition (W1)/date of disposal		(20)	(155)
		135	15
Group share of post-acquisition reserves:			
Deakin – 85% (135 × 85%)	114.75		
Deakin – 65% (15 × 65%)	9.75		
	507.5		

4 *Non-controlling interests (SOFP)*

	$'000
NCI at acquisition (W2)	45
NCI share of post-acquisition reserves to disposal (135 (W3) × 15%)	20.25
	65.25
Increase in NCI on disposal (65.25 × 20%/15%)	87
NCI share of post-acquisition reserves to year end (15 (W3) × 35%)	5.25
	157.5

5   *Adjustment to parent's equity on disposal of shares in group financial statements*

	$'000
Fair value of consideration received	160
Increase in NCI in net assets at disposal (W4)	(87)
	73

6   *Reserves brought forward*

	Holmes $'000	Deakin $'000
Per question (31.5.X3)	310	170
Less: Total comprehensive income for the year	(130)	(60)
Reserves at acquisition		(20)
	180	90
Deakin – share of post-acquisition earnings (90 × 85%)	76.5	
	256.5	

29 Harvard

(a)   HARVARD GROUP
CONSOLIDATED STATEMENT OF FINANCIAL POSITION AT 31 DECEMBER 20X5

	$'000
Non-current assets	
Property, plant and equipment (2,870 + (W2) 1,350)	4,220
Goodwill (W4)	146.7
	4,366.7
Current assets	
Inventories (1,990 + (W2) 2,310)	4,300
Trade receivables (1,630 + (W2) 1,270)	2,900
Cash at bank and in hand (240 + (W2) 560)	800
	8,000
	12,366.7
Equity attributable to owners of the parent	
Share capital ($1)	118
Retained reserves (W5)	3,018.7
	3,136.7
Non-controlling interests (W6)	1,070.0
	4,206.7
Non-current liabilities	
Loans	1,920
Current liabilities	
Trade payables (5,030 + (W2) 1,210)	6,240
	12,366.7

(b)   CONSOLIDATED STATEMENT OF PROFIT OR LOSS AND OTHER COMPREHENSIVE INCOME
FOR YEAR ENDED 31 DECEMBER 20X5

	$'000
Revenue (40,425 + (W3) 25,900)	66,325
Cost of sales (35,500 + (W3) 20,680)	(56,180)
Gross profit	10,145
Distribution and administrative expenses (4,400 + (W3) 1,560)	(5,960)
Profit before tax	4,185
Income tax expense (300 + (W3) 1,260)	(1,560)
Profit for the year	2,625
Other comprehensive income:	
Exchange differences on translating foreign operations (W7)	316.7
Total comprehensive income for the year	2,941.7

	$'000
Profit attributable to:	
Owners of the parent (2,625 – 600)	2,025
Non-controlling interests ((W3) 2,400 × 25%)	600
	2,625
Total comprehensive income attributable to:	
Owners of the parent (2,941.7 – 675.5)	2,266.2
Non-controlling interests [((W3) 2,400 + (W7) 302) × 25%]	675.5
	2,941.7

Statement of changes in equity for the year ended 31 December 20X5 (extract)

	$'000 Owners of the parent
Balance at 1 January 20X5 (118 + 1,452.5(W5))	1,570.5
Dividends	(700)
Total comprehensive income for the year (per SPLOCI)	2,266.2
Balance at 31 December 20X5 (118 + 3,018.7(W5))	3,136.7

Workings

1   *Group structure*

Harvard

31.12.X2 $\dfrac{1,011}{1,348} = 75\%$

Krakow Pre-acq'n ret'd earnings = PLN 2,876,000

2   *Translation of Krakow – statement of financial position*

	PLN '000	Rate	$'000
Property, plant and equipment	4,860	3.6	1,350
Inventories	8,316	3.6	2,310
Trade receivables	4,572	3.6	1,270
Cash	2,016	3.6	560
	19,764		5,490
Share capital	1,348	4.4	306.4
Retained reserves			
– pre-acquisition	2,876	4.4	653.6
– post-acquisition (14,060 – 2,876)	11,184	β	3,320
	15,408		4,280
Trade payables	4,356	3.6	1,210
	19,764		5,490

3   *Translation of Krakow – statement of profit or loss and other comprehensive income*

	PLN '000	Rate	$'000
Revenue	97,125	3.75	25,900
Cost of sales	(77,550)	3.75	(20,680)
Gross profit	19,575		5,220
Distribution and administrative expenses	(5,850)	3.75	(1,560)
Profit before tax	13,725		3,660
Income tax expense	(4,725)	3.75	(1,260)

Profit for the year	9,000		2,400

4   *Goodwill*

	PLN '000	PLN '000	Rate	$'000
Consideration transferred (840 × 4.4)		3,696		840
Non-controlling interests (4,224 × 25%)		1,056		240
Less: Share of net assets at acquisition:			4.4	
Share capital	1,348			
Retained earnings	2,876			
		(4,224)		(960)
Goodwill at acquisition		528		120
Exchange gain 20X3 – 20X4		–	β	12
Goodwill at 31 December 20X4		528	4.0	132
Exchange gain 20X5		--	β	14.7
Goodwill at year end		528	3.6	146.7

5   *Proof of retained reserves*

(i)   At 31 December 20X5

	Harvard A$'000	Krakow A$'000
Per question/(W2)	502	3,974
Pre-acquisition (W2)		(654)
		3,320
Group share of Krakow post-acquisition (3,320 × 75%)	2,490	
Impairment losses to date	(0)	
Exchange differences on goodwill ((W4) 12 + 15)	27	
	3,019	

(ii)   At 31 December 20X4 *(find as a balancing figure in the exam)*

	Harvard A$'000	Krakow A$'000
Harvard reserves b/d ((502 – (945 – 700))	257	
Krakow net assets b/d (B$15,408 – 9,000 + 3,744) / 4)		2,538
Pre-acquisition net assets (B$ (W2) (1,348 + 2,876) / 4.4)		(960)
		1,578
Group share of Krakow post-acquisition	1,184	
(1,578 × 75%)		
Impairment losses to date	(0)	
Exchange differences on goodwill (W4)	12	
	1,453	

Note. Net assets rather than reserves are used for the foreign subsidiary to incorporate exchange differences.

6   *Non-controlling interests*

	$'000
NCI at acquisition (W4)	240
Add: NCI share of post-acquisition retained reserves of Krakow	830
((W2) 3,320 × 25%)	
	1,070

7   *Exchange differences arising during the year*

	SOCI $'000
On translation of net assets of Krakow:	
Closing NA at CR (W2)	4,280
Opening NA @ OR [(15,408 – 9,000 + 3,744) / 4.0]	(2,538)
	1,742
Less: retained profit as translated ((W3) 2,400 – 3,744 / 3.90)	(1,440)
	302
On goodwill (W4)	14.7
	316.7

30 Objective test questions: Consolidated statements of cash flow

30.1 **D**

	$m
B/f	410
Depreciation	(115)
Revaluation	80
Purchases (β)	305
C/f	680

30.2 **B**

	$'000
Balance b/f	1,860
Revaluation	100
Disposal	(240)
Depreciation	(280)
	1,440
Additions (β)	1,440
Balance c/f	2,880

30.3 **C**   The only cash inflow from TP is the dividend received by the shareholders. TP paid a dividend of $100,000 after NS had acquired its shares, therefore NS received 30% of this dividend: $30,000.

31 AH Group

AH GROUP CONSOLIDATED STATEMENT OF CASH FLOWS FOR THE YEAR ENDED 30 JUNE 20X5

	$'000	$'000
Cash flows from operating activities		
Profit before taxation	19,450	
Adjustment for		
Depreciation	7,950	
Profit on disposal of property	(1,250)	
Interest expense	1,400	
	27,550	
Decrease in trade receivables (W2)	470	
Increase in inventories (W2)	(3,100)	
Decrease in trade payables (W2)	(1,420)	
Cash generated from operations	23,500	
Interest paid (W4)	(1,480)	
Income taxes paid (W5)	(5,850)	
Net cash from operating activities		16,170
Cash flows from investing activities		
Acquisition of subsidiary, net of cash acquired (2,000 – 50)	(1,950)	
Purchase of property, plant and equipment (W1)	(11,300)	
Proceeds from sale of property	2,250	
Net cash used in investing activities		(11,000)
Cash flows from financing activities		
Repayment of interest-bearing borrowings	(1,000)	
Dividends paid (6,000 + (W3) 200)	(6,200)	
Net cash used in financing activities		(7,200)
Net decrease in cash and cash equivalents		(2,030)
Cash and cash equivalents at beginning of period		3,900
Cash and cash equivalents at end of period		1,870

Note. Dividends paid could also be shown under financing activities; dividends paid to non-controlling interest could also be shown under either operating activities or under financing activities.

Workings

1   *Property, plant and equipment*

	$'000
B/f	44,050
Depreciation	(7,950)
Disposal	(1,000)
Acquisition of subsidiary	4,200
	39,300
Additions (balancing figure)	11,300
C/f	50,600

PROPERTY, PLANT AND EQUIPMENT

	$'000		$'000
Opening balance	44,050	Depreciation	7,950
Acquisition of subsidiary	4,200	Disposal	1,000
Additions (bal fig)	11,300	Closing balance	50,600
	59,550		59,550

2   *Inventories, trade receivables and trade payables*

	Inventories $'000	Trade receivables $'000	Trade payables $'000
B/f	28,750	26,300	32,810
Acquisition of subsidiary	1,650	1,300	1,950
	30,400	27,600	34,760
Increase/(decrease)(balancing figure)	3,100	(470)	(1,420)
C/f	33,500	27,130	33,340

3   *Non-controlling interest*

	$'000
B/f	1,920
SPLOCI	655
Acquisition of subsidiary (5,000 × 25%)	1,250
	3,825
Dividends paid (balancing figure)	(200)
C/f	3,625

NON-CONTROLLING INTEREST

	$'000		$'000
Cash paid (bal fig)	200	Opening balance	1,920
		On acquisition (5,000 × 25%)	1,250
Closing balance	3,625	P/L	655
	3,825		3,825

4   *Interest payable*

	$'000
B/f	1,440
SPLOCI	1,400
	2,840
Interest paid (balancing figure)	(1,480)
C/f	1,360

INTEREST PAYABLE

	$'000		$'000
Cash paid (bal fig)	1,480	Opening balance	1,440
Closing balance	1,360	SPLOCI	1,400
	2,840		2,840

5   *Income taxes paid*

	$'000
B/f	5,450
SPLOCI	6,250
Acquisition of subsidiary	250
	11,950
Tax paid (balancing figure)	(5,850)
C/f	6,100

INCOME TAXES PAYABLE

	$'000		$'000
Cash paid (bal fig)	5,850	Opening balance	5,450
		Acquisition of subsidiary	250
Closing balance	6,100	P/L	6,250
	11,950		11,950

32 Objective test questions: Related parties

32.1 **C** Providers of finance are not considered to be related parties simply by virtue of the normal dealings with the entity. Suppliers are also not related parties simply by virtue of the resulting economic dependence. Laura McRae, however, is a close family member of a person having control over Linney – she is therefore a related party.

32.2 **A** IAS 24 requires the financial statements to disclose the nature and information about the transactions and outstanding balances, including commitments and bad and doubtful debts. Junior employees are not key management personnel and, therefore, are not related parties. IAS 19 requires details of the pension scheme to be disclosed.

32.3 **A** No disclosure is required of intragroup related party transactions in the consolidated financial statements, since they are eliminated.

32.4 **B** Statement 1 is incorrect – all material related party transactions must be disclosed regardless of whether they are at market value.

Statement 3 is incorrect – two associates are not related as joint significant influence is not considered to be a close enough relationship. An associate and a joint venture are related because the power over a joint venture (joint control) is stronger than that over an associate (significant influence).

33 Objective test questions: Earnings per share

33.1 **A**

Earnings on dilution:	$'000
Basic	1,850
Add back interest (2,000 × 6% × 70%)	84
	1,934

Shares on dilution:	'000
Existing	10,000
Conversion (2m × 4/5)	1,600
	11,600

Basic EPS = 1,850 / 10,000 = 18.5c

Diluted EPS = 1,934 / 11,600 = 16.7c

33.2 **A** TERP

$$5 \times 1.8 = \quad 9.0$$
$$1 \times 1.5 = \quad \underline{1.5}$$
$$\underline{10.5} / 6 = \quad \$1.75$$

Shares:

	'000
5,000 × 5/12 × 1.8 / 1.75	2,143
6,000 × 7/12	3,500
	5,643

EPS = 7,600 / 5,643 = $1.35

33.3 **D**

	Shares '000
B/f (7,500 / 0.5)	15,000
Full market price issue (4,000 × 9/12)	3,000
Bonus issue (18,000 / 3)	6,000
	24,000

EPS = 12 / 24 = 50c

33.4 **D**

	Shares '000
B/f	4,000
Bonus issue	1,000
	5,000

EPS = 3.6 / 5 = 72c

EPS 20X7 = 70c × 4,000 / 5,000 = 56c

34 Pilum

(a)   Earnings per share

	$
Profit for the period	1,403,000
Less: Preference dividends	(276,000)
Earnings	1,127,000
Earnings per share =	1,127,000
	4,120,000
	27.4c

(b)   The first step is to calculate the theoretical ex-rights price. Consider the holder of five shares.

	$
Before rights issue (5 shares × $1.78)	8.90
Rights issue (1 share × $1.20)	1.20
After rights issue (6 shares)	10.10

The theoretical ex-rights price is therefore $10.10 / 6 = $1.68.

The number of shares in issue before the rights issue must be multiplied by the fraction:

$$\frac{\text{Fair value immediately before exercise of rights}}{\text{Theoretical ex-rights price}} = \frac{\$1.78}{\$1.68}$$

Number of shares in issue during the year

Date	Narrative	Shares	Time	Bonus fraction	Total
1.1.X4	B/f	4,120,000 ×	9/12 ×	1.78 / 1.68	3,273,929
1.10.X4	Rights issue (1 for 5)	824,000			
		4,944,000 ×	3/12 ×		1,236,000
					4,509,929

$$\text{EPS} = \frac{\$1,127,000}{4,509,929}$$

= 25.0c

(c) The maximum number of shares into which the loan stock could be converted is on the 31 December 20X5 terms of 90 $1 ordinary shares for every $100 of loan stock (90 / 100 × 1,500,000 = 1,350,000 shares). The calculation of diluted EPS should be based on the assumption that such a conversion actually took place on 1 January 20X4. Shares in issue during the year would then have numbered:

	$
Basic number of shares	4,120,000
Maximum number of shares on conversion (90 / 100 × 1,500,000)	1,350,000
Diluted number of shares	5,470,000

And revised earnings would be as follows:

	$	$
Earnings from (a) above		1,127,000
Interest saved by conversion (1,320,975 × 8%)	105,678	
Less: attributable tax (105,678 × 30%)	(31,703)	
		73,975
		1,200,975
∴ Diluted EPS =		1,200,975
		5,470,000
=		22.0c

Tutorial note.

Proof of liability component given in question:

	$
Principal (1,500,000 × 0.681 [5 year 8% DF])	1,021,500
Interest (1,500,000 × 5% × 3.993 [5 year 8% AF])	299,475
	1,320,975

35 Objective test questions: Ethics in financial reporting

35.1 **B** The directors' proposed course of action would not comply with the CIMA *Code of Ethics'* principle of professional competence. Providing for $75,000 does not comply with IAS 37, which requires the most likely outcome to be provided for when there is a single outcome. Here, this would be $150,000.

35.2 **D** The CIMA fundamental principles state that a professional accountant should not disclose any information acquired as a result of professional or business relationships to third parties without proper and specific authority, unless there is a legal or professional right or duty to disclose. The CIMA *Code of Ethics* contains no requirement to disclose information when requested by the police or the tax authorities. In certain circumstances, a professional accountant may need to disclose information to third parties without obtaining consent (for example, whistleblowing).

35.3 **B** John faces a self-review threat, as determining the appropriate accounting treatment of the business combination would require him to rely upon the work he had carried out himself previously.

35.4 **B** IAS 7 does permit dividends paid to be either treated as an 'operating' or 'financing' cash flow which makes Statement 1 incorrect. However, IAS 8 only allows a change in accounting policy which results in information that is more relevant to the economic decision-making needs of users and more reliable, rather than simply for the personal gain of the directors.

The bonus based on the predetermined operating cash flow target represents a self-interest threat because if the directors reclassify the dividends from 'operating' to 'financing', the operating cash flow will be higher and the directors more likely to earn their bonus.

Statement 4 is incorrect because, while the directors have the option of contacting the CIMA Ethics Helpline, there is no obligation to do so and, in this situation (given that the proposed treatment complies with IAS 7) appears a bit extreme.

36 Objective test questions: Analysis of financial performance and position

36.1 **D** The low asset turnover suggests a capital-intensive industry. This rules out the estate agency or architectural practice. Supermarkets can also be capital-intensive but tend to operate on low profit margins.

36.2 **A**

	$'000
Profit before interest and tax	230
	%
Capital employed (3,500 + 1,000)	4,500
	= 5.1%

36.3 **C** This will reduce working capital and means that it will take longer to build up working capital needed for production. The other options will all speed up the operating cycle.

37 DM

(a) *Report to investor*

Date: October 20X5

This report has been prepared at your request based upon the financial statements of DM for the last two years to 31 December 20X4. A number of ratios have been calculated and these, together with some supermarket sector comparatives, are included in the appendix to this report.

Profitability – revenue

During 20X4 DM has opened six new stores which is an expansion rate of 17% – although this has led to an increase in revenue of only 3%. It has also led to a fall in annual sales per store although the **annual store sales** for DM are still considerably higher than the sector average. However this may simply be due to the fact that DM has larger stores than the average. The reduction in annual sales per store may also be due to the fact that not all of the new stores were fully operational for the entire year.

Profitability – gross profit margin

Gross profit margin has remained the same for the last two years and is marginally **higher than the industry average**. In contrast the operating profit margin has increased 18% over the two-year period, although we have no sector comparative to compare this to. However, we are told that the directors have reviewed the useful lives of the non-current assets and in most cases have increased them. This, in turn, will reduce the annual depreciation charge and, therefore, increase operating profit even though there has been no real improvement in operating performance.

Profitability – net profit margin

Net profit margin for DM has increased from 2.9% to 3.7% and is now approaching the sector average. As the interest cost and tax expense have largely remained constant between the two years then this increase in net profit margin is due to the increased operating margin, which in turn may be due to the change in depreciation charges.

Asset utilisation – asset turnover

The overall non-current asset turnover has **increased slightly over last year** but is still lower than the sector average. This increase could be due to the new stores, although the non-current asset figure has remained almost the same as last year – which is surprising, due to the opening of the

new stores. However, it is possible that most of the capital expenditure on the new stores was actually incurred last year, before the stores were brought into operation.

Asset utilisation – current ratio

The **current ratio is low** in both years, as would be expected in a supermarket, but has improved. There is also a distinct increase in the amount of cash being held. The inventory turnover period has not changed, although there has been a slight increase in the payables payment period which will have a positive effect on cash flow. Finally, the level of gearing has remained fairly constant and would not appear to be a problem.

Conclusion

DM has been **expanding** in the last two years and has appeared to **maintain and indeed improve its profitability** during this period. Its gross profit margin compares well with the sector average, as do sales per store, although the net profit margin has not kept pace with the sector average. It is possible, however, that the increasing operating profit margin and, therefore, net profit margin have been **manipulated** by the directors by the **increase in useful lives of the non-current assets** and consequent reduction in depreciation charges, This may have been done in order to encourage a high offer in any takeover bid that might be made. The directors would, of course, benefit personally from the sale of their individual stakes in the company at a high price, but from the evidence we have it is not possible to state conclusively that this is the case. Further information would be required.

APPENDIX – RATIOS

	20X4	20X3	Sector
Gross profit margin	78/1,255 × 100 = 6.2%	75/1,220 × 100 = 6.1%	5.9%
Operating profit margin	57/1,255 × 100 = 4.5%	46/1,220 × 100 = 3.8%	
Net profit margin	33/1,255 × 100 = 2.6%	23/1,220 × 100 = 1.9%	3.9%
Annual sales per store	1,255/42 = $29.9m	1,220/38 = $32.1m	$27.6m
Non-current asset turnover	1,255/680 = 1.85	1,220/675 = 1.81	1.93
Current ratio	105/317 = 0.33	71/309 = 0.23	
Inventory turnover	47/1,177 × 365 = 14.6 days	46/1,145 × 365 = 14.7 days	
Payables payment period	297/1,177 × 365 = 92 days	273/1,145 × 365 = 87 days	

(b)   Limitations

Sector comparatives can provide useful information in ratio analysis but, as with all comparisons, there are both general and specific drawbacks. These include the following.

(i)   The sector figures are an **average** figure for the sector and therefore can be easily **affected by** just a **few abnormal** results or figures.

(ii)   The companies included in the sector figures may be of **different sizes**, which may affect their sector results.

(iii)   The companies included in the sector figures may have **different year ends**, which may affect the statement of financial position figures used in a variety of ratios – particularly in the retail business.

(iv)   As with all comparisons the different companies in the sector may have **different accounting policies**, which may mean that their results and resulting ratios are not strictly comparable.

(v)   There are a number of **different ways of calculating various key ratios**; if different companies in the sector calculate them in these different ways they will not be comparable.

INDEX

Note. **Key Terms** and their page references are given in **bold**.

Notes

Review Form – Paper F2 Advanced Financial Reporting (11/18)

Please help us to ensure that the CIMA learning materials we produce remain as accurate and user-friendly as possible. We cannot promise to answer every submission we receive, but we do promise that it will be read and taken into account when we update this Study Text.

Name: _____   Address: _____
_____
_____

How have you used this Study Text?
(Tick one box only)

☐ Home study (book only)

☐ On a course: college _____

☐ With 'correspondence' package

☐ Other _____

Why did you decide to purchase this Study Text? *(Tick one box only)*

☐ Have used BPP Texts in the past

☐ Recommendation by friend/colleague

☐ Recommendation by a lecturer at college

☐ Saw information on BPP website

☐ Saw advertising

☐ Other _____

During the past six months do you recall seeing/receiving any of the following?
(Tick as many boxes as are relevant)

☐ Our advertisement in *Financial Management*

☐ Our advertisement in *Pass*

☐ Our advertisement in *PQ*

☐ Our brochure with a letter through the post

☐ Our website www.bpp.com

Which (if any) aspects of our advertising do you find useful?
(Tick as many boxes as are relevant)

☐ Prices and publication dates of new editions

☐ Information on Text content

☐ Facility to order books off-the-page

☐ None of the above

Which BPP products have you used?

Text	☑	Passcard	☐
Kit	☐	i-Pass	☐

Your ratings, comments and suggestions would be appreciated on the following areas.

	Very useful	Useful	Not useful
Introductory section	☐	☐	☐
Chapter introductions	☐	☐	☐
Key terms	☐	☐	☐
Quality of explanations	☐	☐	☐
Case studies and other examples	☐	☐	☐
Exam skills and alerts	☐	☐	☐
Questions and answers in each chapter	☐	☐	☐
Chapter overview and summary diagrams	☐	☐	☐
Quick quizzes	☐	☐	☐
Question Bank	☐	☐	☐
Answer Bank	☐	☐	☐
Index	☐	☐	☐

Overall opinion of this Study Text	Excellent ☐	Good ☐	Adequate ☐	Poor ☐

Do you intend to continue using BPP products?   Yes ☐   No ☐

On the reverse of this page is space for you to write your comments about our Study Text. We welcome your feedback.

The BPP Learning Media author team can be e-mailed at: learningmedia@bpp.com

TELL US WHAT YOU THINK

Please note any further comments and suggestions/errors below. For example, was the text accurate, readable, concise, user-friendly and comprehensive?